Shakespeare: Text and Performance

SHAKESPEARE:
TEXTS AND
CONTEXTS

Edited by Kiernan Ryan

D0549348

in association with

The Open University

This book forms part of an Open University course: AA306, *Shakespeare: Text and Performance*. Details of this and other Open University courses can be obtained from the Student Registration and Enquiry Service, The Open University, PO Box 197, Milton Keynes MK7 6BJ, United Kingdom: tel. +44 (0)845 300 60 90, e-mail general-enquiries@open.ac.uk

Alternatively, you may visit the Open University website at http://www.open.ac.uk where you can learn more about the wide range of courses and packs offered at all levels by the Open University.

To purchase this publication or other components of Open University courses, contact Open University Worldwide Ltd, The Berrill Building, Walton Hall, Milton Keynes MK7 6AA, United Kingdom: tel. +44 (0)1908 858785; fax +44 (0)1908 858787; e-mail ouwenq@open.ac.uk; website http://www.ouw.co.uk

The Open University
Walton Hall, Milton Keynes
MK7 6AA

First published in the United Kingdom in 2000 by
PALGRAVE MACMILLAN in association with The Open University

PALGRAVE MACMILLAN
Houndmills, Basingstoke, Hampshire RG21 6XS and
175 Fifth Avenue, New York, N.Y. 10010
Companies and representatives throughout the world

PALGRAVE MACMILLAN is the global academic imprint of the Palgrave Macmillan division of St. Martin's Press, LLC and of Palgrave Macmillan Ltd. Macmillan® is a registered trademark in the United States, United Kingdom and other countries. Palgrave is a registered trademark in the European Union and other countries.

A catalogue record for this book is available from the British Library

ISBN 0-333-91316-7 (hardback) – ISBN 0-333-91317-5 (paperback)

First published in the United States of America in 2000 by PALGRAVE MACMILLAN

ISBN 0-312-23035-4 (cloth) – ISBN 0-312-23036-2 (paperback)

Library of Congress Cataloging-in-Publication Data

Shakespeare : texts and contexts / edited by Kiernan Ryan.
p.cm.
Includes bibliographical references and index.
ISBN 0-312-23035-4 (cloth) – ISBN 0-312-23036-2 (pbk.)
1. Shakespeare, William, 1564-1616 – Criticism and interpretation. 2. Shakespeare, William, 1564-1616 – Problems, exercises, etc. I. Ryan, Kiernan, 1950-
PR2976 . S3386 1999
822.3'3–dc21   99-052644
                                                              CIP

Copyright © 2000 The Open University

All rights reserved. No part of this publication may be reproduced, stored in a retrieval system, transmitted or utilized in any form or by any means, electronic, mechanical, photocopying, recording or otherwise, without written permission from the publisher or a licence from the Copyright Licensing Agency Ltd. Details of such licences (for reprographic reproduction) may be obtained from the Copyright Licensing Agency Ltd, Saffron House, 6–10 Kirby Street, London EC1N 8TS; website http://www.cla.co.uk.

Any person who does any unauthorised act in relation to this publication may be liable to criminal prosecution and civil claims for damages.

The author has asserted his rights to be identified as the author of this work in accordance with the Copyright, Designs and Patents Act 1988.

This book is printed on paper suitable for recycling and made from fully managed and sustained forest sources.

Edited, designed and typeset by The Open University

Printed in Europe by the Alden Group, Oxfordshire

1.4

Contents

Preface

Shakespeare: Texts and Contexts is the first book of a three-volume series designed for the third-level Open University course *Shakespeare: Text and Performance*. The focus of this first book is both on the texts of a selection of Shakespeare's plays and on the many contexts in which they have been produced, from their first performances to contemporary reproductions. In *Shakespeare: Texts and Contexts*, we introduce nine of Shakespeare's plays: *A Midsummer Night's Dream*, *Richard II*, *Macbeth*, *Antony and Cleopatra*, *Hamlet*, *Twelfth Night*, *Measure for Measure*, *King Lear* and *The Tempest*. This selection is designed to include examples of the four main dramatic genres in which Shakespeare wrote – comedy, history, tragedy and romance – and to span the whole course of his professional career as a playwright. In addition to the nine chapters on the plays, there are two short intervals, one describing the original theatrical contexts of the plays, and the other discussing the different textual versions of the plays available to us.

Shakespeare: Texts and Contexts is best read in conjunction with the other two books for the course. The second book, *Shakespeare 1609: 'Cymbeline' and the 'Sonnets'*, looks at two texts on the margins of the established canon of Shakespeare's greatest plays. As such, it throws that canon into clear relief, and provides important points of contrast and comparison with the nine plays studied in the first book. The third book, *A Shakespeare Reader: Sources and Criticism*, also supplements *Shakespeare: Texts and Contexts*. It contains the chief dramatic and narrative sources used by Shakespeare for the nine plays, as well as a substantial collection of key Shakespeare criticism from the last 70 years.

Shakespeare: Text and Performance updates and expands the Open University's 1983 *Shakespeare* course. There are, however, significant continuities with the earlier course. The commitment of Open University teachers like Arnold Kettle, Graham Martin and Brian Stone to close reading, historical contextualization and a lively question-and-answer style of teaching is sustained throughout this course. In addition to building upon these foundations, the course emphasizes two further aspects of Shakespeare studies. In the first place, it pays detailed attention to Shakespeare in performance, on stage and on film. The question of how we are to understand the relationship between the written text and the dramatic performance is posed at all stages of the course. Secondly, the new theoretical approaches to the study of Shakespeare of the last 30 years are thoroughly integrated into the analyses of the plays. The impact of feminist thought, cultural materialism, new historicism, post-colonialism and queer theory on the study of Shakespeare in recent times has precipitated a remarkable transformation in Shakespeare studies, and each chapter gives attention to these provocative theoretical and critical interventions.

Designed both for Open University students studying *Shakespeare: Text and Performance* and the general reader seeking an accessible route into contemporary Shakespeare studies, these three course books are intended to be read together with *The Norton Shakespeare* (ed. S. Greenblatt, W. Cohen, J.E. Howard and K.E. Maus, W.W. Norton, New York and London, 1997). Quotations from Shakespeare's works in the first two books are taken from this edition and the introductions, commentary and supplementary primary material are referred to extensively. Selections of sources and criticism reproduced in the second volume and the Reader consciously avoid repeating material contained in *The Norton Shakespeare*.

Open University courses undergo many stages of drafting and review, and thanks are accordingly due to a number of people for their invaluable contributions to the final product: Lizbeth Goodman and Stephen Regan, who chaired the course through most of its development; Robert Doubleday and Roberta Wood, who were the course managers for the duration; Julie Bennett and Gill Marshall, who were the course editors; Caroline Husher, who was the graphic designer; Robert Gibson, who was the compositor; Tony Coulson, who was the picture researcher; and Pat Phelps, who was the course secretary. Finally, Kiernan Ryan, the external adviser and editor, and Michael Scott, the course assessor, gave sage guidance at crucial moments in the evolution of the course.

David Johnson
Course Chair

Chapter 1

A MIDSUMMER NIGHT'S DREAM

Penny Rixon

Aims

The aims of this introductory chapter are twofold: to help you understand one of Shakespeare's most popular plays, and to open up some of the fundamental issues involved in Shakespeare studies. By the end of this chapter you should have a thorough knowledge of the characters, settings, themes and ideas in the play, and thus be able to contribute with confidence to discussion of its meaning. You should also be clear about why the play is classified as a comedy. More generally, you should have a firmer grasp of the fact that Shakespeare's plays were written for performance, and that any discussion of their meaning needs to consider the range of choices available to performers. Finally, you should have some understanding of the way that social and political concerns of Shakespeare's world are embedded in the play, while recognizing that subsequent interpretations, whether in academic writing or stage and film performance, will be shaped by the concerns of the community that constructs them.

Reading and understanding the play

Presumably as a result of the notion that children will like anything with fairies and a few laughs in it, generations of schoolchildren have been introduced to Shakespeare through *A Midsummer Night's Dream*. There *is* plenty in it to appeal to young people, but the rest of this chapter will attempt to persuade you not to underestimate this most sophisticated and multi-layered of comedies. Indeed, in recent years the play has become one of the prime sites of controversy in the wider debate about the nature, meaning and status of Shakespeare's drama.

You could explore many themes in *A Midsummer Night's Dream*, but the main reason for making it the first of the plays to be studied in this book is the way that it draws attention to the experience of theatre itself. It is not the only one of Shakespeare's plays with a play-within-the-play, but it goes even further than *Hamlet* in its dissection of the processes of theatre, containing scenes that show the director assigning roles and rehearsing the cast as well as the end result, which in this case is a performance at court. In fact, many of the concerns of scholars working in modern performance studies – for instance, the idea of theatre as a sign system and the role of the audience in creating meaning – are actually addressed in the *Dream*.

First, however, it is important to become familiar with the play as a whole, and the next section encourages close reading of the text. Exercises to guide your reading are provided, but these are not meant to privilege one kind of critical response over another. One thing to establish at the outset is that no approach to a play can be free of bias, and you are at liberty to disagree with anything in this chapter, or in any of the others for that matter. The interpretation of the play offered here is only one response to *A Midsummer Night's Dream*, one which may seem alien to someone from a different generation, culture or social background, but it is hoped that, by the end of this chapter, you will have acquired a sound enough grasp of the evidence, textual and non-verbal, to make your own contribution to the debate. A whole volume on this play alone would be needed for an exhaustive commentary, so the goal here is first to cover points that often provoke questions from students, and secondly to cover those that introduce issues to be discussed at length in the second half of the chapter: what this play implies about the nature and status of the theatre in Shakespeare's world, how it handles human relationships, and exactly what kind of comedy it is. In addition, there will be some discussion of the way it reflects cultural concerns of Shakespeare's own society.

To get the most out of this chapter you should first read through the whole of Act 1. At this stage, it doesn't matter if you don't understand every word of the text. If you feel obliged to consult notes and glossaries every time you are not sure of a word, you will have a very boring time, so look up only what you need to make sense of what is going on, and concentrate on the following questions:

What are these characters doing?

What ideas are embodied in their language?

How do you respond to what is going on?

From the very beginning, try to keep the idea of performance in mind: when a character says something, think about whether the language implies that a gesture or action goes with it, and try to imagine the physical bodies speaking those words or *not speaking* at all. It's easy to forget when we're reading that characters are on stage even when silent and may be making a significant non-verbal contribution to the scene. At this point it's not important to know how Shakespeare's actors may have performed, although later in the course you will learn more about the original performers and the resources at their disposal.

What are these characters doing?

Pared down to essentials, a summary of the action might read as follows: there is an opening conversation between a man, clearly a ruler, and a rival queen whom he has conquered in battle. Their discussion of their imminent marriage is interrupted by another man, a subject of the first, who demands justice, explaining that his daughter is, contrary to the law, insisting on making her own choice of marriage partner and consequently rejecting his candidate. The ruler tells the daughter that if she continues her disobedience, the law will allow her only a choice between death and a nunnery, and she is then left alone with her preferred suitor to consider what to do. The couple decide to escape into the forest, where Athenian law is invalid, and confide their plan to another character, a girl who is in vain pursuit of the first girl's other suitor. Left alone, this young woman tells us that she intends to reveal the escape plan to the man that she adores in the hope of gaining his gratitude and enjoying his company while he pursues the fugitives. As she leaves, some humble working men enter and begin planning an entertainment to honour the ruler's marriage celebrations. Parts are allocated and a date set for rehearsal, with the forest as the venue.

What ideas are embodied in their language?

Of course, there is a lot more to Act 1 than this brief narrative conveys. Take the first seventeen lines: they supply the necessary information that Theseus and Hippolyta are preparing for their wedding, but the language is also subtly alerting us to key ideas, even if we are not entirely conscious of them. For instance, the repeated mention of the moon introduces one of the most important motifs of the play. The moon had a particularly rich set of associations for a sixteenth-century audience, not least because of the way Elizabeth I's propaganda machine had exploited the link between the Virgin Queen and the chaste moon goddess of classical mythology, Diana. In addition, the 'silver bow' simile introduces a recurring motif linked with the notion of Cupid's agency in provoking love and also hints at Hippolyta's former identity as Queen of the Amazons, a race of female warriors noted for their ferocious skill in archery.

The contrast between Theseus's perception of the waiting period as interminable and Hippolyta's belief that the wedding will be here in no time can lead us down two different paths. If we believe that the Amazon is entering the marriage reluctantly, we may think her speech an expression of regret that so little time as an independent being is left to her. On the other hand, the exchange suggests that perception may be unreliable, a theme that will assume great importance in the play as a whole. In fact, the notion is picked up again in Helena's speech at the end of Scene 1, where she seems to be implying that our emotions can make something appear to be what it is not: 'Things base and vile, holding no quantity, / Love can transpose to form and dignity' (1. 1. 232–3).

The simile in lines 5–6 touches on a darker side of human relationships: the comparison is between the delaying moon and the wished-for death of a stepmother who has been keeping the heir from enjoying a decent income, reminding us that relationships breed hatred as well as love. It may even have offered any political dissidents in Shakespeare's audience a secret laugh at the expense of the old Queen, who would not name her successor and then die with dignity, but who insisted on presiding over a society that was visibly stagnating.

The fact that the play is a comedy doesn't mean that it ignores pain, suffering and evil: in the first act, for example, we have the repeated references to the harsh penalties facing Hermia and an acknowledgement of Helena's suffering as a result of Demetrius's treachery. These explicit concerns are reinforced by a recurring strain of language that links love with pain. For example:

> Hippolyta, I wooed thee with my sword,
> And won thy love doing thee injuries.

(1. 1. 16–17)

> And by that fire which burned the Carthage queen
> When the false Trojan under sail was seen.

(1. 1. 173–4)

Bottom and company refer to a play well known to contemporary audiences as being about a pair of lovers doomed to die because of parental opposition to their relationship. The most dramatic instance is in Lysander's speech, which paints a bleak picture of human beings adrift in a cruel universe, able at best to experience only an illusion of happiness:

> Or if there were a sympathy in choice,
> War, death, or sickness did lay siege to it,
> Making it momentany as a sound,
> Swift as a shadow, short as any dream,
> Brief as the lightning in the collied night,
> That, in a spleen, unfolds both heaven and earth,
> And, ere a man hath power to say 'Behold!',
> The jaws of darkness do devour it up.
> So quick bright things come to confusion.

(1. 1. 141–9)

Of course, in performance you can adopt strategies which play down the seriousness, but just looking at the language of this first scene might raise doubts about whether the play is a comedy at all.

The language of the second scene sounds very different. For one thing, there is a change of medium: whereas the courtiers used both blank verse and rhyming couplets, the workmen speak in prose. In part, this change follows the convention of giving poetry to characters high in the social scale and prose to lesser mortals, but it's as well not to rely too much on such crude generalizations, because one of Shakespeare's great strengths is the versatility with which he handles both verse and prose. It is important to realize also that Bottom's prose is no closer to the way people spoke in real life than Theseus's poetry. The change merely signals that a different response is called for. The men may appear to speak in a much more literal way than their 'betters', but their language is artfully exploited for comic purposes. For example, Bottom's attempts to use an impressively wide vocabulary ironically express the truth when he gets the words wrong, as in 'there we may rehearse most *obscenely*' (1. 2. 87–8, emphasis added), when he probably means something like 'seemly', while Quince's joke about French crowns a few lines earlier suggests an earthier alternative to the elevated notions of love proclaimed in Scene 1. The joke is actually lost on most modern audiences, because it relies on a point which Shakespeare's contemporaries would have picked up instantly: that hair loss is a symptom either of syphilis itself or of the treatment for it. You probably wouldn't know that unless you had looked up the relevant editorial note, which brings us to the third question.

How do you respond to what is going on?

Obviously there's likely to be a wide range of answers here, but it's interesting to think about how far we are affected by the main event in Scene 1. Were you deeply moved by the cruelty Hermia seems about to suffer? Might a sixteenth-century spectator have responded differently? Of course, for many modern audiences the idea of a father having the power 'to leave the figure or disfigure it' is abhorrent, if not incredible, whereas in Shakespeare's time the father's power over the family was seen, by the dominant class at least, as one of the main props of social order. In this case, however, the father is going well beyond what most sixteenth-century thinkers would sanction, and the kind of legalistic language used by some of the participants suggests that we are meant to see Athens as unreasonably rigorous, particularly since Hermia is not trying to form a connection with someone socially or morally undesirable. In Shakespeare's society, among the best-selling products of the newly dominant print culture were books advising people how to conduct human relationships, and these contemporary conduct books generally insisted that, important though parental approval was, no parent should ever pressure a child into marrying someone he or she couldn't love.

What is more, performance considerations are important here because of Hippolyta. She says nothing after the first few lines, so she is a very good example of a character who may be overlooked by a reader but cannot be overlooked by a theatre company, which has to decide how she will react to what goes on. In performance her role can make a great deal of difference to the audience's response to the scene. While remembering that no dramatic character has any existence outside the fabric of the play, we should note that Hippolyta's silence has led many directors and performers to give her a more positive role in the scene then her language suggests. For example, a director who wants to generate indignation at the kind of treatment suffered by Hermia can ask Hippolyta to register steadily growing fury and use body language to suggest that she is not going to let Theseus enforce the law without a fight. In two fairly recent productions (Adrian Noble, 1994 and Jonathan Miller, 1996) Stella Gonet and Angela Down made one feel that Theseus was in for a distinctly uncomfortable time once out of the public eye, and thus prepared the audience for his decision to override the law in Act 4; while Clare Benedict (English Shakespeare Company (ESC), 1997), looked so desolate as she left the stage that one felt that harder men than Theseus would have capitulated. Similarly, there is potential variation in our response to Egeus. Even if we feel that what he is doing is monstrous, we will probably be less involved if he is portrayed as a ridiculous old buffer who has lost his temper and is unlikely to get his own way in the long run than if he is cold, rational, and evidently someone with a lot of influence.

Another factor that may be affecting your response is your knowledge that this play belongs to the genre of comedy. We'll be exploring in more detail later what that word encompasses, but at present it's as well to note that, in the same way as you suspend your compassion when Tom batters Jerry in cartoons, you may be disengaging yourself from an emotional response to the seriousness of events in Scene 1 because subconsciously you expect that all the obstacles will somehow be removed by the end of the play. Not everyone will be able to do this, however, and some may find this first scene uncomfortable.

Bearing in mind the points made above, the next step is to read Act 2. As before, you will need to make sure that you understand who does what to whom – some people find it helpful to write a brief summary – but the focus of the discussion will be on the following questions:

> To what extent does Shakespeare establish the fairies as a different species from the human beings in the play?

> How would you present the fairies (using costume, movement, lighting and any other means you can think of), if you were staging the play for a modern audience?

> How do you respond to the further developments in the lovers' story?

To what extent does Shakespeare establish the fairies as a different species from the human beings in the play?

In one way, the fairies are all too human. Their capacity for envy, spite and destructive pettiness is apparent in the quarrel over the changeling child, and although Titania spells out the dire consequences of that quarrel for human beings, neither she nor Oberon is prepared to compromise. Indeed, seeing that he can't get the boy by fair means, Oberon turns immediately to the foulest, devising a plot that will torment and degrade his consort:

> Be it ounce, or cat, or bear,
> Pard, or boar with bristled hair,
> In thy eye that shall appear
> When thou wak'st, it is thy dear.
> Wake when some vile thing is near.

> (2. 2. 36–40)

Puck's favourite leisure activity is humiliating people, and there is a hint that his fun may go beyond harmless practical jokes in 'Mislead night wanderers, laughing at their harm' (2. 1. 39). At the same time, he does recognize the authority of the Fairy King, who is also capable of unsolicited acts of kindness: witnessing the misery of an individual human, a complete stranger, he determines to use his power to make her happy. The words that spring to mind to describe the fairies' actions are 'capricious', 'unpredictable', and therefore, given their superhuman powers, 'dangerous' as well. Titania's long speech describing the devastation wrought by 'our dissension' graphically underlines the extent of their capacity for damage, particularly when you remember that in a predominantly agricultural society, unseasonable weather meant that people starved to death. In fact, people *had* been starving in the mid-1590s as a result of poor harvests caused by bad weather, and there was widespread unrest in the country as a result. Some critics think that cynics in the audience might have seen a parallel here between Titania and an English monarch too preoccupied with 'self affairs' to care about her hungry subjects.

How would you present the fairies (using costume, movement, lighting and any other means you can think of), if you were staging the play for a modern audience?

Directors in the latter part of this century have tended to feel that the malign element is not well served by costuming the fairies in gauze wings and tutus, although that was the fashion in Victorian times, and that kind of approach persisted for quite a long time in amateur productions. Though few have gone as far in the other direction as George Devine (1954) in presenting the fairies as nightmarish visions with talons and reptilian faces, there has been a strong tradition in the last 50 years of using costume and body language to stress that they are an alien race.

Moreover, the text, if you attend to it carefully, does emphasize their difference from human beings. One of the characteristics repeatedly stressed is their diminutive size: in this scene, the Fairy who accosts Puck implies this point in his/her first speech with its list of miniaturized tasks, and talks of elves creeping into acorn cups to hide; while Oberon describes a snake's skin as 'Weed wide enough to wrap a fairy in' (2. 1. 256). Other non-human characteristics are the Elizabethan equivalent of supersonic speed – 'I do wander everywhere / Swifter than the moonës sphere' (6–7) – and the ability to make oneself invisible at will.

So how would you represent all this on stage, where you don't have access to the kinds of cinematic special effects that would allow you to take Shakespeare at his word and present credible fairies that *could* hide in an acorn cup? If you had problems answering this question, you are not alone: in the play's production history the fairies have traditionally given the most trouble. We don't know how Shakespeare's own company dealt with them, but the later seventeenth century began a tradition of taking his references to size as literally as is possible, and thus casting children in most of the fairy parts, a fashion which persisted for some 300 years, but has mercifully now been abandoned.

If size is no problem, what about speed and agility? Would you cast athletes who look as though they could beat the 100 metre sprint record, if not quite put a girdle round the earth in 40 minutes? Or an acrobat like Robert Lepage's Puck, Angela Laurier (1992), who could contort her body in ways that seemed almost inhuman? Are you going to make the fairies fly? Nineteenth- and earlier twentieth-century productions regularly used flying apparatus, but modern productions tend to avoid this kind of machinery, although Peter Brook employed gantries, trapezes and stilts very successfully to give the fairies an extra dimension in which to move (Figure 1).

And what about representing someone becoming invisible, as Oberon does at line 186 of Act 2, Scene 1? Shakespeare's actor may have donned a special robe as a visual signal when speaking this line, while productions of the early twentieth century experimented with various kinds of torches, but more recent productions have tended simply to rely on the words to stimulate the audience's imagination. If you haven't had much experience of theatrical production, it will take a while for you to become familiar with this approach to Shakespeare. Maybe these problems didn't trouble you because you have seen a production that found effective ways of solving them, or because you take for granted the fact that the theatre works a magic of its own, which has nothing to do with literal reality. I'll take up the latter point in more detail in my discussion of Act 3.

We are still a long way from exhausting the decisions that need to be made about the fairies. There is plenty to say about casting, because in the play's performance history theatrical practice has varied considerably, not least with regard to the number of roles involved. Earlier periods had hordes of fairies in Titania's train, but economic pressures mean that modern theatres must make do with the bare minimum, or even fewer if cuts are made in the text. Gender is another variable. In the nineteenth century, the Fairy was normally a woman and her first speech was sung, but by 1970 ideas had changed so much that Brook preferred to eliminate the character, distributing the lines among Moth, Mustardseed, Cobweb and Peaseblossom, who were played by three men and one woman. Miller (1996) gave the speech to Peaseblossom, a brisk manservant with a strong northern accent, who delivered his lines in the manner of a put-upon employee recounting a tiresome day at work, while the ESC (1997) split the lines among a nightmarish group of predatory males on stilts. Puck was also an adult male in this production, as he was for Miller, Noble (1994) and Tara Arts (1997), but in the nineteenth century the role was almost always played by a female, often a child, and adult women were cast by Kenneth Branagh (1990) and Lepage (1992). Oberon too was a 'principal boy' role in the Victorian period, when elaborate musical arrangements were given to the character, but the role now seems to be an exclusively male one. So how about casting a man as Titania? (If your instinct is to reject this suggestion as ridiculous, you might want to think carefully about how you would support an argument against it.)

Figure 1 *Oberon (Alan Howard) puts Titania (Sara Kestelman) to sleep with his wand whilst Puck (John Kane) looks on in the Royal Shakespeare Company production of* A Midsummer Night's Dream *directed by Peter Brook, 1970. Photo: Joe Cocks Studio Collection, Shakespeare Centre Library.*

One complicating factor, at least since Frank Dunlop's 1967 production, has been the question of whether to double Hippolyta with Titania and/or Theseus with Oberon. Brook's adoption of this device established a new orthodoxy, one no doubt welcomed by theatre management because it is cheaper and by actors because the doubled roles are more fulfilling. So whereas a pre-Dunlop director would be expected to justify the decision to double, I suspect the reverse is now true. Clearly, the decision is an important one, and we will come back to its implications later.

However the fairies are represented, they are beginning to have a devastating effect on some of the human beings who have wandered into their domain, which brings me to the final question about this act.

How do you respond to the further developments in the lovers' story?

Perhaps you thought that Helena's betrayal of her bosom friend's escape plot was getting its just reward when Demetrius spurned her. Alternatively, you may have excused treacheries motivated by desperation and felt sympathy for the misery she expresses in 2. 2. 94–105. Again, there is a range of possibilities in performance, but I think Shakespeare has made it quite difficult for a director who wants to wring real emotion out of this scene. Helena may be suffering, but the way she expresses herself in 2. 2. 94–105 gives ample scope to the actor who wants to play her as ridiculous: for example, Doon Mackichan (Miller, 1996) got a huge laugh by inspecting herself in the mirrored set, turning with a flounce to the audience and delivering 'No, no; I am as ugly as a bear' with a kind of petulant self-pity. Considered objectively, Lysander's behaviour is astoundingly cruel, but we are not encouraged to consider it objectively. The preposterousness of his change is emphasized by the way he shares a rhyming couplet with Helena:

HELENA   Lysander, if you live, good sir, awake.

LYSANDER [*awaking*] And run through fire I will for thy sweet sake.

(2. 2. 108–9)

And his language in the ensuing speeches is so extreme as to keep reminding us that he is under a magic spell. Moreover, his claims to be now exercising reason are so patently ridiculous that it is difficult to resist laughing at him, although the line 'Of all be hated, but the most of me' (2. 2. 148) can strike a darker note, as can Hermia's terror as she wakes from the nightmare.

The crucial point is that, although this scene deals with potentially tragic material – the misery of unrequited love, betrayal and the death of love – unless the director works very hard, we are not going to feel deeply. When you study *Hamlet*, you are likely to react very differently to the central character's rejection of Ophelia.

Now let's move on to Act 3. This time discussion will focus on the following questions:

What kind of assumptions do Bottom and his fellows make about the experience of theatre, and how do you respond to their ideas?

To what extent does a darker note intrude into this middle act?

Do you think that the comic spirit of the play is threatened by anything that happens?

It is worth noting here that the workmen, briefly introduced in Act 1, Scene 2 as artisans and comic players, are identified as 'clowns' in the stage directions to Act 3, Scene 1. Robin refers to them as 'rude mechanicals' (3. 2. 9), which explains why the term 'mechanicals' continues to be used as a collective term for the workmen.

What kind of assumptions do Bottom and his fellows make about the experience of theatre, and how do you respond to their ideas?

As far as this question is concerned, Bottom is clearly aware of the dangers of putting on a show for those in power, and before rehearsal begins he wants some points clarified. The first one – the problem of violence on stage – pinpoints a topic that is still of great concern today, although we probably don't share the mechanicals' masculine perspective. Bottom fears that the very appearance of an unsheathed sword on stage, let alone the enacting of suicide, will terrify the ladies, while Snout and Starveling, returning to the problem raised in the earlier rehearsal about the effects of the lion roaring, now doubt whether they ought to include the creature at all. On one level, the fun proceeds from our knowledge that these actors are never going to be remotely frightening. On a deeper level, the scene opens up the crucial question of the difference between real life and artistic representation, asking us whether witnessing a suicide on stage is the same as seeing a man kill himself in real life. The next problems, raised by the fledgling director this time, are first, how to represent the moon shining, and then how to deal with the fact that some scenes require a wall, when walls – even prop walls – are not portable. The assumptions underlying this part of the discussion are less clear-cut, but I think the workmen are implying that if something is important to the plot, it must be literally represented on the stage, otherwise the audience will not believe in what's going on.

As any company must, they devise solutions to their problems. Starveling first suggests that they 'leave the killing out', a joke that would have had an added resonance for the educated members of the original audience, who knew that humanists had criticized the popular theatre for representing violence on stage instead of having it related by a messenger, as the Greeks did. Bottom's suggestion will let them have their cake and eat it, however: he will adapt the convention of the Prologue to explain to the audience that what they are watching is make-believe, so no-one really gets hurt; and just in case that doesn't work, Snug must avoid wearing an illusionistic costume, and interrupt his mauling with a gentle speech reminding them that he is really a human being. As far as the lighting is concerned, for a moment it looks as though they will opt for a kind of realism – 'the moon may shine in at the casement' (3. 1. 49–50) – but that solution is rejected in favour of the starkly non-realist idea of turning the moon into a character. Quince's brainwave gives Bottom the solution to the scene-change problem also, and Wall is born.

So what we have here, although the mechanicals don't recognize it as such, is a debate about different notions of theatrical representation. At one point, it is assumed that there is no boundary between reality and representation; at another, that reality isn't convincing enough in a theatre, so a sign system must be devised in order to communicate the key ideas to the audience. It's as well to remember that in Shakespeare's non-realist theatre, there was no scenery to speak of and no artificial lighting was used, so for his contemporaries the humour lies in the fact that these poor amateurs can't see that simply imagining a wall or moonlight – or a character becoming invisible – presents no problem, as long as the language itself offers adequate cues. For modern audiences, used to sophisticated lights that can simulate moonlight and walls that can sprout from the stage or glide from the wings, but also familiar with studio theatre and low-budget fringe productions, the effect of the joke is different: we probably focus more on the mechanicals' absurd over-confidence in their powers as actors. In both cases, laughter surely proceeds from the audience's sense of superiority to these poor bunglers: *we* are much too sophisticated to blur the line between the theatrical world and the real one, and *we* don't require realistic scenery or lighting as long as the production spells out the rules of the game it wants us to play.

But is the laugh perhaps on us? As we watch these inadequate actors planning a potential flop, how many of us remember that Quince, Bottom and Co. are, on a different level, accomplished actors compelling our participation in a make-believe world? When an actor enters, disguised not as a lion but as an ass, yet still asserting that he is Bottom the weaver, how many of us preserve the distinction between the real world and the illusory one? Even when Shakespeare has Puck remind us of what he is in real life – 'I'll be an auditor – / An actor, too, perhaps, if I see cause' (3. 1. 67–8) – we still believe in him as the goblin rather than the performer playing that goblin. Shakespeare is opening up complex questions about the nature of theatrical experience here, and perhaps one of the themes that is beginning to emerge is that real magic for late-sixteenth-century Londoners is what takes place in a theatre. After all, they (and we) are quite prepared to believe a normal-sized actor when s/he suddenly whisks us into a miniature world where a bee's honey sac makes a decent meal:

> The honeybags steal from the humble-bees,
> And for night tapers crop their waxen thighs
> And light them at the fiery glow-worms' eyes
> To have my love to bed, and to arise;
> And pluck the wings from painted butterflies
> To fan the moonbeams from his sleeping eyes.

> (3. 1. 150–5)

It is almost as though Shakespeare is saying that the real magic is the fact that he can make the audience believe in anything, even as he shows them exactly how he is doing it (Figure 2).

To what extent does a darker note intrude into this middle act?

The fairies' magic *can* have a sinister tinge, although once again it's as well to remember that it all depends on how Act 3 is staged. The workmen's terror as Puck swoops among them can be funny, but if the production uses sound and special effects to bring to life Puck's descent into brutishness – 'Like horse, hound, hog, bear, fire, at every turn' (3. 1. 99) – a more troubling effect is likely. Similarly, if Bottom remains stoutly unmoved by Titania, the result is less disturbing than if, as some directors have chosen, he shows real fear. The Queen *can* be played as malevolent, particularly when she says, 'Out of this wood do not desire to go' (134), or as so infatuated as to be ridiculous. One of her comments shifts, though only for a moment, into a different, and much darker, key. As she carries Bottom off to her bower, she says:

> The moon, methinks, looks with a wat'ry eye,
> And when she weeps, weeps every little flower,
> Lamenting some enforcèd chastity.

> (3. 1. 179–81)

Figure 2 *Jonathan Miller's production of* A Midsummer Night's Dream, *1996, Almeida Theatre, London.*
Photo: Ivan Kyncl.

Even after many years of engagement with this play, I still find this comment puzzling, firstly because of its ambiguity. 'Enforced' could mean 'imposed', just as in the threat made to Hermia in Act 1, but it could also mean the opposite, so that the Moon goddess is seen as weeping for a violation of her sacred principle. And I wonder why this glimpse of a universe of pain for women should come at this point, when the only female character on stage is very much in control. It is certainly possible to play the lines for laughs, as though they apply to the soon-to-be ravished Bottom, but the aching beauty of the verse resists complete surrender to gross comedy.

Do you think that the comic spirit of the play is threatened by anything that happens?

Performance is once again the deciding factor here. It is in the lovers' scene that I find the greatest potential menace. In 3. 2, Hermia faces the fact that the man who vowed 'end life when I end loyalty' (2. 2. 69) now loathes her; the lifelong friendship of two women is apparently shattered; and the rivalry of the two young men looks set to erupt in violence that may end in the death of either of them. Moreover, the scene seems to cast doubt on the durability of any kind of affection, since it appears that, under stress, apparently civilized men and women revert to the law of the jungle. In fact, the nineteenth century, which tended to play the lovers in a romantic rather than comic mode, found this part of the play both unfunny and uncomfortable, although the objections were largely based on gendered considerations: the women's abandonment of all trace of decorum seemed to violate contemporary notions of propriety, so the quarrel scene was usually heavily cut. The tendency since Brook has been to accentuate the comic element with fast action, choreographed fighting between the women and much ridiculous posturing on the part of the men, so that we are laughing too much to dwell on the serious implications. Moreover, if costumes are not of the period when weapons were routinely carried, lethal violence seems less likely. Still, vicious things are said in the heat of the moment: is it really possible that the lovers can 'wend' back to Athens 'With league whose date till death shall never end' (3. 2. 374)?

Now to Act 4, which provides a transition from the dream-world of the wood back to the 'real' world of Athens. The focus this time is on the following question:

What kind of relationship between dreams and reality is implied in this part of the play?

This is quite a difficult question, which goes to the heart of this play, but once again the possibility of different choices in performance means that there is more than one valid answer to the question. For example, if Theseus and Hippolyta have been doubled with Oberon and Titania, their entrance at 4. 1. 99, 3–4 will have a completely different meaning from a production in which two sets of artists have played the roles. It is no coincidence that the fashion for doubling coincided with an interest in applying insights from the discipline of psychology to the play, although more recent interpretations have extended its application to new areas. In the 1970s, though, the dream was seen as allowing the Duke and his consort to work through a conflict in their relationship that leads him to reassess Egeus's conduct. Thus, after claiming in Act 1 that not even the ruler could set aside the law, Theseus peremptorily declares, 'Egeus, I will overbear your will' in 4. 1. 176. If the roles are not doubled, a different relationship between dream and reality applies: Theseus and Hippolyta are not implicated in the crazy events of the night, and the former's change of heart may be simply a pragmatic response to Demetrius's renunciation of Hermia.

In the case of the lovers, the savagery of the night is indeed dispelled and the spirit of reconciliation reigns, although Theseus's incredulity has a wider application for the audience than the character intends, when he asks:

> How comes this gentle concord in the world,
> That hatred is so far from jealousy
> To sleep by hate, and fear no enmity?

> (4. 1. 140–2)

Oberon's most merciful action has been to obliterate the memory of the night's events, so that former relationships are as they were before, except, of course, in the case of Demetrius, who now finds that:

> ... my love to Hermia,
> Melted as the snow, seems to me now
> As the remembrance of an idle gaud
> Which in my childhood I did dote upon.

> (4. 1. 162–5)

Claiming that his pursuit of Hermia was an aberration, he has now 'come to [his] natural Taste' (173). Perhaps he has, but it is worth recalling that his love for Hermia, unlike Lysander's, actually originated in the world of Athens, the world that, according to Theseus, is governed by reason, judgement and the rule of law. It is worth recalling too the language Helena used when talking of his defection:

> For ere Demetrius looked on Hermia's eyne
> He hailed down oaths that he was only mine,
> And when this hail some heat from Hermia felt,
> So he dissolved, and showers of oaths did melt.

> (1. 1. 242–5)

The imagery emphasizes the transience and unreliability of love, and the images of health and nature that he applies to his new feeling for Helena ring slightly hollow when we remember that his present love for her is the result of being under a magic spell woven in the 'dream'. If you are going to argue that Lysander was merely deluded when he fell for Helena, being a victim of the love-juice applied by Puck, then you have to admit that Demetrius's love for his wife-to-be is founded on a delusion, as is the newly restored harmony among the quartet. And this clearly makes Helena's line, 'I have found Demetrius like a jewel, / Mine own and not mine own' (4. 1. 188–9), double-edged. It seems that, in this scene, Shakespeare is deliberately blurring the boundaries between the conscious world and that of the dream, and the language of the lovers when they are left alone reinforces this effect:

> DEMETRIUS   These things seem small and indistinguishable,
> Like far-off mountains turnèd into clouds.
>
> HERMIA   Methinks I see these things with parted eye,
> When everything seems double.

> (4. 1. 184–7)

Perhaps one answer to the question of why harmony has been re-established among the humans is the fact that the Fairy King and Queen have at last recognized their responsibilities to the cosmic order and are now 'new in amity' (84). Yet their reconciliation too is founded on a delusion. Oberon makes it quite clear that, although he felt sorry for Titania when he saw her degradation, he made sure that he got the changeling child, the cause of their earlier quarrel, before he released her. Titania, like the lovers, has no memory of the night before, and she is therefore at the mercy of whatever story he concocts in answer to her request for an explanation of what has transpired:

> Tell me how it came this night
> That I sleeping here was found
> With these mortals on the ground.

> (4. 1. 97–9)

What I want to stress at this stage is that there is no simple answer to the question of how dream relates to reality in Act 4, and perhaps Bottom's soliloquy brings this out most clearly. As he wakes, he has plainly gone back to the point at which Puck put the ass's head on him (Figure 3), but when he comes to full consciousness he locates the events of the night firmly in the world of dream and vision, which is not

Figure 3 *Pete Postlethwaite (Bottom) and Nicholas Woodeson (Puck) in the Royal Shakespeare Company production of* A Midsummer Night's Dream *directed by Bill Alexander, 1986. Photo: Ivan Kyncl.*

communicable by an ordinary man like him. He believes that the only way to comprehend the vision is to transform his experience into art; he 'will get Peter Quince to write a ballad of this dream' (4. 1. 207–8). Yet in the end he finds it impossible ('Not a word of me' (4. 2. 29)) and no ballad of the dream is written – except, of course, for the one on the stage before us, penned by Shakespeare himself.

All that remains is to read the last act of the play and reflect on the following questions:

> How do you respond to the opening conversation between Theseus and Hippolyta (5. 1. 1–27)?
>
> How far do you identify with Theseus and the lovers in their response to *Pyramus and Thisbe*?
>
> Why does Shakespeare let the fairies have the last word?

How do you respond to the opening conversation between Theseus and Hippolyta (5. 1. 1–27)?

To begin with the opening exchange between Theseus and Hippolyta: even if Theseus has been played as a relatively sympathetic figure up to this point, it is surely very difficult to endorse his repudiation of anything that can't be apprehended through his particular brand of reason. He is no systematic philosopher, but 'reason' for him seems to be based on what can be proved by the evidence of his own senses, whereas lunatics, lovers and poets all share a distorted perception. The comparison offers yet another comment on the relationship between perception and reality. The other important theme it connects with is the relationship between reason and love. Neither, it seems to me, can claim the victory at this point in the action. The lovers and Titania have demonstrated how giving way to emotion can lead human beings into some pretty ludicrous situations, but the 'rational' law of Athens, which will condemn a girl to death or sterility at a whim of her male relative, is intolerable to anyone with any sense of justice.

What is more, when we consider Theseus's attack on the life of the imagination, it is possible to argue that the joke rebounds on him. Both as a character in the play, given life by the combined efforts of playwright, production team, actor and audience, and as a well-known personage from 'antique Fables', considered respectable even by humanist intellectuals like Sir Philip Sidney, he owes his very existence to the power of the imagination. The joke is even more apt if the actor playing Theseus has just participated in the forest scenes as Oberon. More significantly, when he implies in his closing couplet that all imagination can do is offer empty delusions – 'How easy is a bush supposed a bear!' (5. 1. 22) – we, as an audience, are in a position to contradict him. We have seen that whatever went on in that wood is not 'airy nothing' (5. 1. 16). Far from distorting reality, the power of imagination may have *revealed* the reality beneath deceptive appearances, or caused us at the very least to realize that there may be more than one way of looking at a situation. Theseus's standing as an authority figure is, I think, somewhat diminished by this exchange, particularly since Bottom's reaction to this dream was so much more sensitive. It is interesting that Hippolyta's rational reply to her husband, in which she points out that the objective evidence suggests that something very unusual has taken place, gets no answer. Perhaps, in a performance, Theseus could be shown as taking advantage of the lovers' appearance to ignore her, because his male authority cannot admit that a woman is more intelligent than he is.

How far do you identify with Theseus and the lovers in their response to *Pyramus and Thisbe*?

This question raises quite complex issues. However mediocre the production, there are usually some laughs to be had from it, but that doesn't mean that we necessarily identify with the onstage audience of courtiers; indeed, many people today feel uncomfortable at their behaviour. The question to ask is whether this kind of reaction derives solely from modern democratic notions, or whether the feeling is provoked by something in the text, so that at least some members of Shakespeare's audience might have shared this reaction.

First, it must be admitted that, by the standards of Shakespeare's own drama, poor Quince's effort is pretty dreadful. It would be hard not to notice how lame the verse is, especially in comparison with the technical skill displayed in the framing play. Shakespeare's rhyming couplets never have a redundant syllable, but Quince's writing is packed with bits of meaningless padding to make up the correct number of feet in a line or to achieve a rhyme: 'if you would know', 'at the which, let no man wonder', 'the truth is so', 'Thy stones with lime and hair knit up in thee', and so on (5. 1. 128, 133, 161, 189). He can't even manage a rhyme at some points: by no stretch of pronunciation can 'sinister' rhyme with 'whisper', for example. A complete ignorance of literary decorum ensures that some of the most moving moments are sabotaged by unwitting bawdiness or bathos, as in: 'My cherry lips have often kissed thy stones' (188), where 'stones' is contemporary slang for testicles; or: 'I kiss the wall's hole, not your lips at all' (198); or: 'O dainty duck, O dear!' (270). When Bottom and company add their own contributions from the School of Coarse Acting – and I suspect that the kind of 'business' used now probably doesn't differ much from what went on in Shakespeare's time – the resulting effort is dire enough to deserve a shower of rotten fruit at any period in history.

On the other hand, it's worth noting that they are offering the play as a gift, not asking people to pay to see it, and, when Theseus commissions the performance, he claims to be doing so in a spirit of generosity, taking account of the intentions of the donors rather than their competence: 'Love, therefore, and tongue-tied simplicity / In least speak most, to my capacity' (104–5).

He understands how intimidating his position can be, and in the phrase 'Noble respect' (92) he implies knowledge of the duty of courtesy that a prince such as he owes to those who offer tribute to him. Yet when the Prologue, in the person of Quince, mangles his opening speech – and in performance the murdered punctuation is often shown to be the result of severe stage fright – the Duke leads the jeering: 'This fellow doth not stand upon points' (118). Thereafter, the courtiers seem to forget their manners and use the actors as butts for their own displays of wit and repartee, with only Hippolyta showing a modicum of sensitivity. That some of the workmen are discomfited by this reception is implicit in Moon's exasperated improvisation, when he has abandoned his lines after repeated rude interruptions:

> All that I have to say is to tell you that the lantern is the moon, I the
> man i'th' moon, this thorn bush my thorn bush, and this dog my dog.

> (5. 1. 247–9)

Miller (1996) made the point even more clearly by having Theseus appropriate the lantern and pass it to the courtiers, who all remained oblivious of how upset Starveling was at being deprived of his most important prop. The courtiers' display of boorishness reaches its climax in Theseus's 'Marry, if he that writ it had played Pyramus and hanged himself in Thisbe's garter it would have been a fine tragedy' (5. 1. 342–4), where he offers his friends a chance to snigger at the uncomprehending yokels while pretending to compliment them.

Why does Shakespeare let the fairies have the last word?

One reason is to complete our detachment from Theseus: he has just ridiculed belief in them, but the speeches of Puck and Oberon suggest that only they stand between him and the kind of ill fortune to which all mortals are subject. Theseus's last speech implies a cosy world of order and luxury with himself in control, but this belief is challenged immediately by the driving rhythm and sinister content of Puck's first soliloquy, where lion and wolf seek their prey, and those excluded from the cosy palace drag out their lives in labour, misery and fear:

> Now the wasted brands do glow
> Whilst the screech-owl, screeching loud,
> Puts the wretch that lies in woe
> In remembrance of a shroud.

> (5. 2. 5–8)

He reminds the audience that, whatever Theseus thinks about spirits, there is a malevolent, threatening world outside the palace, and harmony and peace in human relationships are always fragile:

> Now it is the time of night
> That the graves, all gaping wide,
> Every one lets forth his sprite
> In the churchway paths to glide.

(5. 2. 9–12)

Moreover, this character, who gets the *very* last word in the play, further undermines Theseus's authority as a cultural arbiter at the same time as he delicately brings to a climax the play's concern with the nature of the theatrical experience. 'If we shadows have offended' (Epilogue, 1), begins Puck's closing speech to the audience. On one level he is calling himself a shadow because he is spirit, not flesh, but on another he is ironically quoting Theseus's earlier description of actors: 'The best in this kind are but shadows, and the worst are no worse if imagination amend them' (5. 1. 208–9). If the audience shares Theseus's perspective and thinks that even the best theatre is a waste of time, Puck seems to console them with the thought that they have lost no more than if they had slept for a couple of hours. But the use of this comparison, which is highly charged for an audience that has just witnessed how much dreams can reveal of a level of experience beneath the veneer of social life, suggests a whole new understanding of what the theatre can achieve – something that Theseus's reductive dismissal entirely ignores. The remainder of Puck's speech probes the nature of the relationship between actors and audience, suggesting that neither party has exclusive control over the performance or its reception. Perhaps the full impact of the epilogue is lost to us, because it exploits the bond between the player and the regular playgoers of sixteenth-century London, who saw him as something else last week and will see him 'make amends ere long' (Epilogue, 12) in another role, yet will still believe on some level in the character he chooses to create, however many incarnations he adopts.

To sum up: I think the fairies get the last word because they represent the world of imagination, both as spirits and as performing artists, and if Shakespeare's audience felt as exhilarated as I have done at the end of some of the greatest productions of this wonderful play, they would have needed no further convincing that theatre offers something rich and strange. The double nature of the language in the epilogue acts as a kind of transition from the performance to the reality outside the theatre, and 'Give me your hands' (Epilogue, 15), with its delicate play on the notion of applause and the handshake between friends, offers us the opportunity to celebrate the collective nature of the experience we have just undergone. That point conveniently acts as a transition here too, leading into a discussion of some of the general issues raised by this play.

Analysing the play

Since the *Dream* is possibly your introduction to Shakespearean comedy, it seems sensible to begin by looking at the notion of comedy itself and its implications for the way we respond to the play. Defining the nature of comedy is not as easy a task as it may sound, because most of the definitions people offer are subject to so many exceptions. For example, the 'common-sense' option is to say 'Something that makes you laugh', but most theorists working in this field reject the notion that laughter is an inescapable component of comedy. Even if you think that these theorists have missed the point, you have to acknowledge that what makes *you* laugh may well not be funny to other people in your own community, let alone to others in a different culture or historical period. Working through the play reveals how much of Shakespeare's wordplay is unintelligible and thus completely unfunny even to an English-speaking audience these days. What is more, laughter can often be an instinctive response to something that is not comedy in any sense of the word, so common sense isn't much help in this case. Some people might claim that comedy deals with the lighter side of life, but again a quick survey of *A Midsummer Night's Dream* exposes the shortcomings of that answer, reminding us that its language underlines the facts of premature death, hunger, war, betrayal, rape, unrequited love and many more of the shocks, natural and unnatural, that flesh is heir to. More promising is the argument that certain kinds of convention are characteristic of comedy: features such as mistaken identity and the use of disguise; particular kinds of physical action, such as gross difficulties with material objects, eccentric mannerisms and slapstick fighting; or the comic exploitation of language, with characters misusing or misunderstanding words. These devices *are* common ingredients of comedy, indeed some of them go back to its origins, and they are all found in the *Dream*; but most of them appear also in a play which is unequivocally designated a tragedy, as you will see when you read *King Lear*. Furthermore, it simply isn't possible to sustain the argument that they are so essential to all kinds of comedy that they can be regarded as tests of whether something belongs to the genre or not. Claims that a happy ending or one or more marriages are constant features of comedy are vulnerable to similar objections. What this exercise reveals is that trying to define comedy is rather like trying to find a watertight definition of 'game': we probably all recognize an example when we come across it, but framing a formula that includes every possible instance is another matter altogether.

It may be more fruitful to ask what Shakespeare and his contemporaries understood by comedy. Sir Philip Sidney, whose *A Defence of Poetry* (1595) is probably the most influential manifesto of élite culture in the period, puts the humanist position:

> But I speak to this purpose, that all the end of the comical part
> be not upon such scornful matters as stirreth laughter only,
> but, mix with it that delightful teaching which is the end of poesy.

> (Quoted in Kimbrough, 1969, p.151)

The type of comedy Sidney has in mind is that created by Shakespeare's great contemporary, Ben Jonson, who claims in the Prologue to *Every Man in His Humour* (1598) that the proper concern of the comic dramatist is

> ... deeds, and language, such as men do use:
> And persons, such as Comedy would choose,
> When she would show an Image of the times,
> And sport with human follies, not with crimes.

> (Jonson, 1986 edn, p.21)

Jonson's comedies are full of characters who exemplify contemporary vices and affectations in extreme forms, and this kind of comedy is still very common on stage and screen, often tending to centre on politics or the media these days. Jonson (and

Sidney) believed that, as people laugh at characters displaying extreme forms of undesirable behaviour, they are learning to recognize their own folly. Today a more likely rationalization might be that this kind of satirical comedy helps to correct social abuses by exposing the perpetrators to ridicule.

A Midsummer Night's Dream does not fit within this tradition, though. It contains some characters from myth, others from fairyland, and a setting that is more never-never-land than ancient Greece. The action of the play does not draw its main impetus from contemporary concerns, although in a broader sense there is a deep involvement with the social and cultural undercurrents of the period. Indeed, it is perfectly clear from Sidney's exasperation with popular comic drama that it is doing something very different from the kind of comedy prescribed by Aristotle. In language as strong as that of the most dyspeptic modern theatre critic, he rages at the wholesale adulteration of genre:

> But besides these gross absurdities, how all their plays be
> neither right tragedies, nor right comedies, mingling kings and
> clowns, not because the matter so carrieth it, but thrust in the
> clown by head and shoulders, to play a part in majestical matters,
> with neither decency nor discretion.

> (Quoted in Kimbrough, 1969, p.150)

Sidney accuses the comedians of dealing in 'scurrility, unworthy of any chaste ears' (Duncan-Jones and Dorsten, 1973, p.115). He is completely missing the point, but it's as well to remember that humanism is the prestige cultural influence in this period, and to argue that Shakespeare's greatness lay in developing a kind of comedy that drew as much on popular tradition as on learned sources would have met as much bafflement from someone like Sidney as if you had suggested that he post his latest treatise on the Internet.

Yet it is popular culture that supplies the dominant comic impulse of the *Dream*, and in particular the phenomenon of carnival, which has emerged as an exciting focus of study in more recent literary criticism. Most people nowadays probably associate carnival with the period around Shrove Tuesday, the day of self-indulgence before the period of abstinence known as Lent, but research has shown that in early modern Europe it was an integral part of the pattern of the whole year, manifesting itself in a series of festivities, of which St Valentine's Day, May Day, Midsummer's Day, Christmas and Twelfth Night were the principal occasions. The carnival spirit is subversive in the fullest sense of the word, temporarily turning the world upside down, giving servants authority over master and mistress, and children authority over schoolteachers: in short, inverting hierarchy and thus dethroning deference and respect for rank. In carnival, the urges of the body dominate and people are allowed to stuff themselves, get drunk and, although this form of licence is more controversial, indulge freely in sex. So carnival mocks refinement and restraint, implying that, since life is for the most part harsh and full of privations, you should grab what you can when you can and forget about the consequences. And in its preoccupation with the body's needs it carries a reminder that we are all equal: whether we play the role of king, courtly lover or peasant in our normal lives, we are all the same when the costumes come off, all subject to the demands and indignities of the flesh.

Carnival was an integral part of medieval Catholic culture. By Shakespeare's time England was officially Protestant, and it has been argued that, as carnival rituals became less important in the new culture, the carnival spirit migrated into the commercial theatre, and its presence there is thought by some to be one reason why certain groups were so violently opposed to the new art form. In fact, historians are deeply divided over the extent to which carnival was a long-term force for subversion. Some argue that the temporary suspension of hierarchy functioned as a safety valve in the community, actually strengthening the power of established authority, but others claim that the spirit of carnival gnawed away at hierarchy and privilege, contributing to genuine social change. What I would like to do now is to use this notion of the carnival spirit as a way of exploring *A Midsummer Night's Dream*.

The very title invites the attempt, because it locates the play in one of the most important festivals of the year, and there are several references to others. Lysander, for example, refers to a place 'Where I did meet thee once with Helena / To do observance to a morn of May' (1. 1. 166–7), and Theseus, stumbling across the sleeping lovers, assumes that they 'rose up early to observe / The rite of May ' (4. 1. 129–30). When we explore the relationship between Athens and the wood from the perspective of the relationship between everyday life and carnival, some interesting insights emerge.

Athens at the beginning of the play is the world of regulation and discipline, a society that takes observance of a rigidly patriarchal law to an unacceptable extreme. The father owns his child, and a recurring strain of language implies that all human relationships have become materialistic transactions:

> As she is mine, I may dispose of her,
> Which shall be either to this gentleman
> Or to her death, according to our law
> Immediately provided in that case.

> (1. 1. 42–5)

> Lysander, yield
> Thy crazèd title to my certain right.

> (1. 1. 91–2)

> And what is mine my love shall render him,
> And she is mine, and all my right of her
> I do estate unto Demetrius.

> (1. 1. 96–8)

As is usual in patriarchal society, the institution of marriage privileges the male, as Hermia makes clear when she talks about 'his lordship whose unwishèd yoke / My soul consents not to give sovereignty' (81–2). Theseus's own situation is even more telling. For all his attempts at gallantry, he has reduced the symbol of matriarchy, the warrior Queen of the Amazons, to a conquered vassal, whose inferior status is sealed and confirmed by her marriage to him. She has no voice in the state, which is perhaps why Shakespeare gives her no words in the scene where the Duke administers justice. It is clear that the whole ideology of Athens suppresses the voices of women and children – in fact, all those whom the social structure has rendered powerless. Hermia, for example, fears that even the mild degree of assertiveness she needs to employ to state her case may leave her vulnerable to accusations of impropriety:

> I do entreat your grace to pardon me.
> I know not by what power I am made bold,
> Nor how it may concern my modesty
> In such a presence here to plead my thoughts.

(1. 1. 58–61)

Moreover, her behaviour at the beginning of her forest adventure reveals that in Athens women's sexuality is strictly controlled, as is normal in patriarchal cultures. She has been so strongly conditioned to value her reputation for chastity that she cannot allow her chosen husband and protector anywhere near her on the night before she expects to marry him:

> But, gentle friend, for love and courtesy,
> Lie further off, in human modesty.
> Such separation as may well be said
> Becomes a virtuous bachelor and a maid.

(2. 2. 62–5)

The double standard of sexual morality is implicit in the way that Demetrius's treachery to Helena is clearly of minor importance to the Duke, taking second place to 'self-affairs' (1. 1. 113); whereas even to be suspected of an indiscretion may be fatal to a woman's reputation.

This is an extreme version of patriarchal society, but it has certain similarities to Shakespeare's England, where the whole weight of the establishment was behind a wife's subordination to her husband, the father's authority over his child, and control of women's sexuality. In fact, obedience is a key issue that has much wider ramifications than in modern society, because in the hierarchical model of society beloved of the Tudor establishment, the patriarchal family structure underpins the political one. Thus in one sense it is entirely predictable that Theseus should tell Hermia 'To you your father should be as a god' (1. 1. 47). Like Queen Elizabeth I, the Duke has a vested interest in upholding the authority of fathers, since he is the 'father' of his subjects.

In some respects, the world of fairyland also has striking similarities to that of Athens, just as carnival and ordinary life co-exist within the same social framework. Both Athens and fairyland have social hierarchies headed by ruling figures, and in both the principle of deference to a sovereign is recognized. As we have seen, these similarities can be emphasized in performance. Not quite so obvious, perhaps, are similarities in the way the action unfolds in both environments: there is a clash of wills over possession of a child, and a husband/ruler wins a fight with his wife/consort. But the differences are even more interesting.

As far as the parent–child relationship is concerned, in contrast to Egeus, who sees his child as a commodity, Titania has freely adopted the changeling boy out of love for his dead mother and 'Crowns him with flowers, and makes him all her joy' (2. 1. 27); she gives him up only when deluded by a powerful magic spell. In Oberon's world, circumstantial factors are ignored when it comes to love between the sexes; when the Fairy King sees a girl languishing for love, he feels it only right that she should have the man she longs for. Desire is justification enough for union, and no other consideration is relevant. Fairyland differs from Athens also in the fact that it is not a patriarchal society. Titania is an independent monarch with her own court, which is parallel, not subservient, to her husband's, and Oberon makes his demand as to an equal who is being rather tiresome, not to someone who ought to obey him. There is no attempt to present Titania's resistance in terms of contemporary beliefs about a wife's subordination, and the reason Titania gives for withholding the boy suggests that, in her world, it is acceptable to honour a commitment to another woman above that to a husband:

> But she, being mortal, of that boy did die,
> And for her sake do I rear up her boy;
> And for her sake I will not part with him.

> (2. 1. 135–7)

Oberon's anger seems to proceed more from thwarted will and jealousy than from a sense that his authority has been violated. When he gets his way, the language does not imply that he is justifiably putting a shrewish wife in her place.

Even more interestingly, the fairy world seems to impose no restraints on women's sexual behaviour. Whereas in Athens and sixteenth-century London, women are very definitely 'not made to woo' (2. 1. 242), as Helena complains, Titania's 'courtship' of Bottom is aggressive and peremptory in the text, let alone in the way it has been realized by some directors, who have exploited the sexual element in it; Trevor Griffiths, drawing on extracts from Brook's promptbook from 1970, notes that at 'The summer still doth tend upon my state; / And I do love thee' (3. 1. 137–8), Titania 'leapt upon Bottom with her legs around his waist', and at the end of the scene there was 'a triumphal parodic wedding procession with paper plates and streamers being thrown as Bottom was chaired off with an erect phallus created by an actor's arm between his legs' (Griffiths, 1996, p.151). Oberon has himself created this situation, and, on seeing Titania wrapped around her beastly lover, there is no trace of the conventional outrage of a cuckolded husband – 'Her dotage now I do begin to pity' (4. 1. 44) – as he congratulates himself on having obtained the changeling boy. In fact, a kind of open marriage seems to prevail in fairyland, since both Oberon and Titania have both enjoyed a long history of irregular liaisons, and the conventional double standard of sexual morality seems not to apply:

OBERON   How canst thou thus for shame, Titania,
Glance at my credit with Hippolyta,
Knowing I know thy love to Theseus?
Didst thou not lead him through the glimmering night
From Perigouna whom he ravishèd,
And make him with fair Aegles break his faith,
With Ariadne and Antiopa?

> (2. 1. 74–80)

Fairyland seems to be a culture of sexual liberation by the standards of the day; or it might be more accurate to describe it as a world where the spirit of carnival reigns. I haven't mentioned Puck yet, but it is important to note that this character powerfully represents the concept of play and fun for its own sake.

Once in that carnival world, the humans cast off the restraints of normal life. Helena has hardly been in the wood ten minutes before her maidenly modesty begins to evaporate. Having said that all she wanted was 'To have his sight thither and back again' (1. 1. 251), she then mounts an assault on Demetrius as blatant as Titania's on Bottom, although with considerably less dignity:

> I am your spaniel, and, Demetrius,
> The more you beat me I will fawn on you.
> Use me but as your spaniel: spurn me, strike me,
> Neglect me, lose me; only give me leave,
> Unworthy as I am, to follow you.

> (2. 1. 203–7)

Spaniels, while symbols of fidelity, are still beasts, and the use of the metaphor is perhaps as significant as the ass's head for Bottom, injecting a note of eroticism as evident in the sixteenth century as in the twentieth. Demetrius, slower to succumb to the sway of the forest, reminds Helena of the conventions of the world they belong to. For a woman, such conduct is to 'impeach your modesty too much' (214): in other words, Helena is asking for someone to deprive her forcibly of 'the rich worth of [her] virginity' (219). Men are protectors only so long as women play by Athenian rules. Helena herself recognizes that her conduct unnaturally reverses the gender roles: 'Apollo flies, and Daphne holds the chase' (231).

Logic would seem to dictate that the young women abandon their chastity as part of the experience in the wood, but in fact Helena's ardent plea is as far as sexual liberation goes for the courtly lovers. That may, however, have more to do with Elizabethan uneasiness about female sexuality than with dramatic logic. Shakespeare and his fellow dramatists frequently use the comic device of a *pretended* irregular liaison, but in all the extant comic drama produced during Shakespeare's lifetime, very few females commit actual fornication and adultery without some kind of punishment, and in only a handful of plays is the attitude one of comic acceptance. Titania is an exception, but then she is not a human being. (You may wish to consider Cleopatra in this context when you come to Chapter 4.)

There were no taboos on stage violence in Shakespeare's theatre, however, so perhaps the escalating conflict between the four can be read as emblematic of the shedding of sexual as well as social inhibitions. It is worth bearing in mind that May Day and St Valentine's celebrations, both of which are mentioned in the play, had specifically sexual connotations, and the girl who loses her virginity in one of these sylvan rituals is virtually proverbial. In this play, on the surface of things they only lose their tempers, but the sexual implications are clear. (Perhaps that is one reason why the Victorians were uneasy with the quarrel scenes.)

So Helena, having been propositioned by the spellbound Lysander in 2. 2, initially reacts with a restrained reminder of the male duty of gallantry towards a woman of his class – 'I thought you lord of more true gentleness' (2. 2. 138). But, the next time we see her, she has abandoned politeness and is roundly accusing him of chronic philandering:

> Weigh oath with oath, and you will nothing weigh.
> Your vows to her and me put in two scales
> Will even weigh, and both as light as tales.

> (3. 2. 131–3)

Hermia is conscious of the fact that frustration with Demetrius is already driving her 'past the bounds / Of maiden's patience' (65–6). When all four are brought together, the courtly façade is rapidly stripped away and animal passions reign, with the delicate maidens revealing the humanity beneath their courtly breeding – 'She was a vixen when she went to school' (325) – and trying to scratch each other's eyes out. Women, traditionally the calming influence on male aggression, have to be physically kept apart by the men; and the men abandon their accustomed courtesy to women, as Lysander hurls insults at the girl he swore to love forever. The world turned upside down indeed. Not to mention the fact that a queen pays homage to a humble working man and takes him for her lover. Bottom's sojourn in fairyland is the carnival experience *par excellence*: freedom from the daily grind of work and menial tasks, as much as he can eat, and unrestricted sex with the Fairy Queen.

It is important to understand that the carnivalesque structure doesn't necessarily imply any judgement about which is better, the values of carnival or those of everyday life, with all its restraints and regulations. They are complementary facets of human experience, operating cyclically, just as the moon alternates with the sun. Furthermore, as was stressed earlier, the carnival spirit is a levelling force, subtly undermining claims to élite status, whether based on birth, morality or education, and asserting the validity of the demands of the body against more rarefied notions of the superiority of the spiritual. And, perhaps most important of all, the carnival spirit pokes fun at those who take life, and themselves, too seriously. From the carnival perspective, human life is simply too lacking in dignity to generate deep feeling, and characters who insist on pretending the contrary deserve to be laughed at.

Viewed from this perspective, the relationship between Athens and the forest world could be seen as commenting ironically on the elaborate fictions that human beings construct to dignify their lives: epic stories like that of Theseus, or the Battle of the Centaurs; elevated notions of eternal love, where death is preferable to the loss of the beloved; laws that claim to guarantee justice for all. But what goes on in the forest suggests that it is the dream world that may come closer to reality and the real motives of most human beings. What is more, the play's concern with the nature of theatrical experience is interwoven with the carnivalesque structure, creating a remarkably sophisticated texture for those able to apprehend it, and offering the possibility of a truly subversive reading.

Before we consider the play's preoccupation with its own theatricality in more detail, you may find it helpful to reread the following scenes:

Act 1, Scene 2, in which the mechanicals cast their play.

Act 3, Scene 1, where their rehearsal is interrupted by Puck.

Act 4, Scene 1, 196–211, when Bottom wakes up.

Act 4, Scene 2, where Bottom returns to his workmates.

Act 5, Scene 1, in which *Pyramus and Thisbe* is performed.

The first thing to say about this spotlighting of the theatre itself is that *A Midsummer Night's Dream* is not unusual in this respect, as you will see when you come to *Hamlet* and *The Tempest*. Even in plays without an inset play, Shakespeare will frequently challenge the audience with a direct reference to the nature of the experience in which they are participating.

You may want to look out for such moments in *Antony and Cleopatra* and *Twelfth Night*. Nor is Shakespeare alone; much of the drama produced by his contemporaries shares this self-consciousness. For example, Francis Beaumont's *The Knight of the Burning Pestle* (*c*.1607) is built around a device by which members of the audience intervene in the performance and demand changes in the script, because they feel that the play is satirizing their class.

The next thing to bear in mind in these days of Bardolatry and Lord Lloyd Webber is that Shakespeare's society had no such regard for dramatists and performers. The players, even a well-established group like Shakespeare's company, had a distinctly precarious status, and powerful groups of people not only denied that the theatre had any value, but also targeted it as a potent source of harm. And the popular theatre, although clearly valued by members of the court and intelligentsia, was found wanting by the standards of élite culture. Once again, *A Defence of Poetry* offers the most eloquent evidence, and in the extract below the author indulges in sarcasm at the players' expense:

> Now you shall have three Ladies walke to gather flowers, and then we must beleeve the stage to be a garden. By and by we heare newes of shipwrack in the same place, then we are too blame if we accept it not for a Rock. Upon the back of that, comes out a hidious monster with fire and smoke, and then the miserable beholders are bound to take it for a Cave: while in the meane time two Armies flie in, represented with foure swords & bucklers, and then what hard hart wil not receive it for a pitched field.

> (1989 edn, p.148)

If this sounds familiar, it's probably because it's exactly the kind of attitude we saw dramatized in the earnest discussion at Quince's first rehearsal of *Pyramus and Thisbe*, and later in the scoffing of the audience at the performance:

STARVELING [*as Moonshine*]	This lantern doth the hornèd moon present.
DEMETRIUS	He should have worn the horns on his head.
THESEUS	He is no crescent, and his horns are invisible within the circumference.
STARVELING [*as Moonshine*]	This lantern doth the hornèd moon present. Myself the man i'th' moon do seem to be.
THESEUS	This is the greatest error of all the rest – the man should be put into the lantern. How is it else the man i'th' moon?

(5. 1. 231–9)

This is not to argue that Shakespeare is explicitly echoing Sidney, but to suggest that one of the play's aims is to send up the kind of literalism espoused by humanist intellectuals who worshipped Aristotle. This literalism is fundamentally at odds with what Shakespeare does. Reference was made earlier to the notion of letting the audience know the rules of the game and sticking to them, which is surely a basic requirement of all theatre; nothing, however, says that these rules have to be circumscribed by what is possible in real life. If you go to see *La Traviata* or *Les Misérables*, you don't jeer at the death scene, because in real life consumption robs you of the breath to say goodbye, let alone tackle a demanding piece of singing; instead, you subconsciously adjust to the conventions that govern nineteenth-century opera or the modern musical. Similarly, Shakespeare's audience was conditioned to expect that the language would tell them whether the scene takes place in the darkness of night or bright moonlight; whether they are in the Forest of Arden or before the walls of a besieged city; whether a ship is being wrecked or an entire regiment on the march; and they did not demand that the company create a naturalistic simulation of any of these. Although Shakespeare did not join the debate about theatre in his prologues or by writing treatises, it is possible that one of the reasons for the *Dream*'s preoccupation with matters theatrical is to ridicule rigid theories that misunderstand how the popular theatre works.

Indeed the play goes even further by exposing the fictions and pretences at the heart of social relationships in a similar way to carnival; in other words, it reveals the way that those in power construct a performance to legitimize their position and mask the realities of social organization. We saw earlier that the night offers only a 'fruitless vision' (3. 2. 372) for most of the characters, but Puck's epilogue hints at the way that an afternoon in the theatre can offer new perspectives on life for the audience, if they, unlike the snobbish and stupid courtiers, will open their minds to what the theatre has to give. Here the play's repeated allusions to the way that our eyes may mislead us become involved in more subversive meanings.

For example, we might recognize that Egeus's determination to make his daughter obey him is as wilful and irrational as Oberon's determination to have the changeling boy, yet in Athens the law, supposedly based on reason, supports his right until something – maybe Hippolyta's anger, maybe just a whim – makes Theseus set it aside in this one case. We might perceive that in a state of nature men and women begin as equals, and the only way for one gender to dominate the other is to use trickery and deceit; in a state of civilization, patriarchal law achieves the same end. We might see that marriage could be such an oppressive institution that the only way to tolerate it is to live, like Demetrius, in cloud-cuckoo land. We might observe that characters from the dominant class of Athens, let loose in an environment where individual appetites reign and where normal social restraints are absent, degenerate into breaking sacred oaths, cheating on friends and lovers, screaming abuse at each other, and fighting with tooth and claw like wild beasts. Then they wake up, go home, and resume their appointed roles in society as guardians of the humbler souls in their charge. There they pretend to value the contributions of the ordinary people, but secretly snigger and despise the products of popular culture. However, the audience at Shakespeare's theatre, watching the great ones audit *Pyramus and Thisbe*, would have seen through this hypocritical performance and learned the truth. And, even more ironically, it is the mechanicals' performance that makes *us* laugh, even if that wasn't their intention, not the laboured witticisms of the rude courtiers.

What is more, the great story of tragic love, as played by the mechanicals, collapses in exactly the same kind of bathos as the grandiose passions of the courtly lovers did in the wood. The ridiculous antics of Pyramus and Thisbe reinforce the frame play's exposure of the elevated sentiments of idealized love, the kind of rhetoric in vogue at court in the late sixteenth century. 'And then end life when I end loyalty' (2. 2. 69), says Lysander to Hermia, followed by 'And run through fire I will for thy sweet sake' (109) to Helena not long afterwards. Demetrius 'Made love to Nedar's daughter, Helena, / And won her soul' (1. 1. 107–8); but that was before he noticed the sexual attractions of Hermia. The two women had a friendship so intense that it was 'As if our hands, our sides, voices, and minds / Had been incorporate' (3. 2. 208–9), but sexual jealousy tore that 'ancient love asunder' (216) in five minutes.

The spirit of carnival recognizes that sexual desire is at the heart of all this posturing. Puck says it all:

> And the country proverb known,
> That 'every man should take his own',
> In your waking shall be shown.
> Jack shall have Jill,
> Naught shall go ill,
> the man shall have his mare again, and all shall be well.

> (3. 3. 42–7)

Of course, we might see none of this subversive material; just as in Hans Holbein's portrait of *The Ambassadors* (see Figure 14), where you have to be in a certain position to see that the apparent blob on the canvas is actually a human skull, so also in *A Midsummer Night's Dream*, what you see depends on where you stand. I don't want to claim that this play is a savage satire on the society in which it was produced, but I do think that, far from being a piece of escapist froth, it explores important cultural issues, although in a relatively genial way.

Epilogue

By now some readers may be uneasy or plain furious at what I have been suggesting, so to finish I would like to pinpoint some of the issues which, in my experience, lead to debate in any group studying Shakespeare.

The first one is the question of who 'owns' the meaning of Shakespeare's work. I've never taught a class yet who didn't say at some point, 'But surely Shakespeare didn't mean all this?' – referring to the kind of interpretations this chapter has explored. I certainly don't imagine Shakespeare consciously throwing in a dash of subversive laughter here and a dig at the dominant ideology there, but I think the question itself is a red herring. For a start, the process of artistic creation is often a mystery to the artist him/herself, and secondly, even if it weren't, present-day literary criticism and performance practice both reject the notion that the artist's intention is the prime determinant of the meaning of the work.

The question seems particularly acute when we are dealing with Shakespeare, because so many people feel so passionately about his works, and people raised in Britain often seem to believe that they have some sort of proprietary right to the meaning of his texts. And, as you will see when you study the history plays, there are still vested interests involved in peddling the line that Shakespeare consistently supported the principle of order in the state, 'family values' and established political authority. So it is not surprising that a radically new interpretation of a play like the *Dream*, whether by a director or a literary critic, often elicits angry cries of 'That's not Shakespeare!' There may well be instances when that statement is valid, but it's a good idea to examine one's conscience rigorously when making such a claim to ensure that it's not a way of legitimizing one's own prejudices. I don't think

Figure 4 *Programme cover for the Tara Arts production of* A Midsummer Night's Dream *directed by Jatinder Verma, 1997, Lyric Theatre, Hammersmith. Photo: Hugo Glendinning.*

that anyone has the right to dictate the meaning of *A Midsummer Night's Dream*, and one of the strengths of the play is that every time you think that no one can possibly find anything new in it, someone does. Miller (1996) finally broke away from the Brook tradition and found comedy in Act 1 that has eluded many earlier productions, while the latest revelation at the time of writing is that it is possible to play Puck as a nightmarish goblin suffering from psychotic tendencies and an obsession with Sellotape (ESC, 1997). That is the darkest production I have seen, and I'm not sure that it was entirely successful, but I wouldn't want to protest that it's 'not Shakespeare'.

It is not, however, and never can be, what people in the late sixteenth century experienced at a performance, which brings me to the second question: to what extent is the meaning of the play circumscribed by the cultural conditions that obtained when it was created? This chapter has drawn on both sixteenth-century history and modern performance practice, and some readers may feel that my apparent willingness to give them equal status is highly suspect.

Clearly, it enriches our experience of *A Midsummer Night's Dream* to know how sixteenth-century spectators would have understood references to the moon, or how they regarded fairies. Yet that doesn't mean that a production which is inspired, among other things, by the director's perception of a similarity between the antics of Puck and those of the young Krishna (Jatinder Verma for Tara Arts, 1997) is out of order simply because it draws on areas of experience unknown to Shakespeare and his contemporaries (Figure 4). What is more, even if the Globe were a completely accurate reconstruction of Shakespeare's theatre, and even if we were able to mount a performance there which was identical in every detail to Shakespeare's own practice, we would still be a world away from the experience of the original audiences, because our whole way of experiencing the world is different from theirs. And, as has repeatedly been stressed, the audience has a powerful role in the creation of meaning. We all bring different things to a play, and that fact has serious implications for the creation of meaning: I am suggesting, in effect, that your personal experience, whoever and wherever you are, may extend the possibilities of interpreting this play. This was not an acceptable claim to make 20 years ago, and it is still something that many people find unconvincing. In the end, each of you must find your own position on these matters, but I hope that, if I have done nothing else, I have made those of you who dismissed *A Midsummer Night's Dream* as a trivial play realize that it might be something more.

References

Duncan-Jones, K. and Dorsten, J. Van (eds) (1973) *Miscellaneous Prose of Sir Philip Sidney*, Oxford: Clarendon Press.

Kimbrough, R. (ed.) (1969) *Sir Philip Sidney: Selected Prose and Poetry*, San Francisco: Rinehart Press.

Jonson, B. (1986) *Every Man in His Humour*, 1598, London: Methuen/Royal Shakespeare Company.

Griffiths, T.R. (1996) *Shakespeare in Production: A Midsummer Night's Dream*, Cambridge: Cambridge University Press.

Sidney, P. (1989) *A Defence of Poetry*, 1595, Oxford: Oxford University Press.

SHAKESPEARE'S THEATRE

Helen Hackett

Aims

This interval invites you to imagine the experience of an Elizabethan performance of *A Midsummer Night's Dream*. It asks you to consider a number of questions. Where would you go to see the play? What kind of 'playing space' was the play originally designed for? How did this affect the kind of drama that Shakespeare wrote? How did his playing spaces shape his conceptualization of the world? At the end of the interval you should be able to answer these questions with confidence.

Shakespeare's playing spaces

The journey to the playhouse

Let's suppose that you've travelled back in time to 1595, the probable year of *A Midsummer Night's Dream's* first performance. Now you have to make another journey, out of the City of London, where most playgoers lived, to its suburbs, beyond the City walls. You may think that you're heading for the Globe, the playhouse now most well known as Shakespeare's dramatic home; but in fact the Globe was not built until 1599. Instead you're heading for the Theatre, the most likely location for the first performance of the *Dream* (Gurr, 1992, p.239).

The new Globe reconstruction has drawn attention to the site of that playhouse on Bankside, in a disreputable entertainment district that also contained brothels and a bear-baiting pit. However, the playhouses occupied a variety of locations, as you can see from the 1572 map of London (Figure 5), labelled with the approximate site of every playhouse built between 1567 and 1629.

The Theatre and the two other earliest Elizabethan playhouses, the Curtain and the Red Lion, were on the northeastern edge of London. What this location and Bankside had in common was that they were outside the walls of the City of London, an enclave with its own jurisdiction. The governing City Fathers were mostly merchants – the City was, then as now, a commercial centre – Puritan in outlook, valuing hard work and duty. The earliest Elizabethan dramatic productions, in inn-yards within the City, were suppressed as incitements to idleness and decadence. Even their survival beyond the City walls led Puritans like

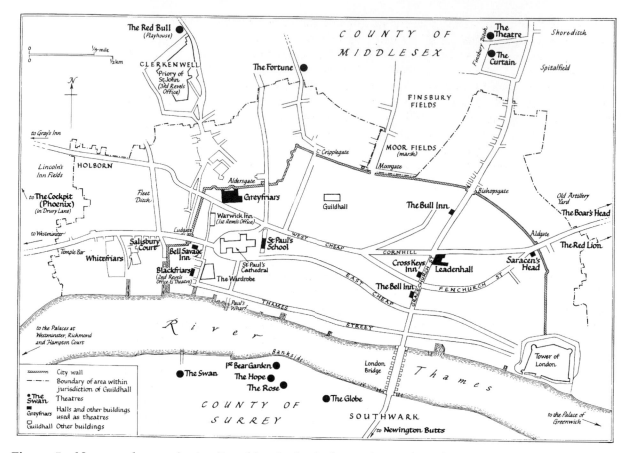

Figure 5 *Names and approximate sites of London's playhouses imposed on the Braun and Hogenberg map of 1572. From Peter Thomson,* Shakespeare's Professional Career, *Cambridge University Press, 1992, pp.76–7. Reproduced by permission of Cambridge University Press.*

John Northbrooke in 1577 to call for the demolition of the new purpose-built suburban playhouses, since

> Satan hath not a more speedie way and fitter schoole to work and teach his desire, to bring men and women into his snare of concupiscence and filthie lustes of wicked whoredome, than those places and playes, and theaters are.

(Quoted in Howard, 1994, p.25)

The court, centred in Westminster to the west of the City, was more favourable to the players, who were regularly summoned by the queen to contribute to festive occasions, or invited to entertain at the private houses of nobles or gentlemen. Within *A Midsummer Night's Dream* the performance of *Pyramus and Thisbe* after Theseus and Hippolyta's wedding is an amateur example of such a performance, while *Hamlet* also depicts the one-off employment of a playing company by a court. Some scholars have speculated that *A Midsummer Night's Dream* might have been commissioned for an aristocratic wedding at which Elizabeth I was present, although this is disputed (Wells, 1967, pp. 12–14; Holland, 1995, pp.111–12).

You might also have seen an early production of *A Midsummer Night's Dream* outside London altogether. The City was frequently hit by outbreaks of plague, and the playhouses, as places where, as a City proclamation put it, people were 'close pestered together', presented an obvious clanger of the spread of infection. The worst plague outbreaks enforced the closure of the playhouses in 1581–2, 1592–3, 1603–4, 1608–9, 1609–10, and several later seasons (Gurr, 1992, p.78). At such times the players went on tour; in 1592–3, for instance, one company performed at Leicester, then at court for Christmas, then at York, Rye, Ludlow, Shrewsbury, Coventry, Bath and Ipswich, probably in inn-yards (ibid., p.38). Titania may be calling up fresh memories of this recent time of affliction when she speaks of how:

> ... the moon, the governess of floods,
> Pale in her anger washes all the air,
> That rheumatic diseases do abound.

(2. 1. 103–5)

Elizabethan playing, then, took place in various kinds of marginal spaces, which reflected its uncertain social status: in provincial inn-yards; on temporary stages at court; and, primarily, in purpose-built playhouses which served a largely citizen audience, yet were mostly outside the City, almost in the fields, as Figure 5 shows. These marginal spaces had much in common with the wood outside Athens, where the central acts of *A Midsummer Night's Dream* take place: a location beyond authorized boundaries, where game-playing and role-playing are freely possible, with all their attendant excitements and risks. Keeping hold of this idea of the Elizabethan playhouse as a space outside and beyond, where 'shaping fantasies' (5. 1. 5) are generated, let's continue our journey to the Theatre, the playing space for which *A Midsummer Night's Dream* was probably written.

Entering the theatre

It is almost 2 pm, the hour when the performance will begin. As you approach the playhouse, you see a building that is either round or polygonal, like the present-day 20-sided Globe reconstruction at Bankside. It has a timber frame filled in with plaster, and a thatched or perhaps tiled roof.

All the evidence about the Elizabethan playhouses – written, pictorial and archaeological – shows that there was considerable variety in their designs and capacities, just as there are differences among the theatres in modern London. Even so, the Theatre was probably very like the Globe: both had an 'amphitheatre' design, with the audience surrounding three sides of the stage, reflecting the origins of Elizabethan drama in inn-yard performances. Indeed, the Theatre was the 'parent' of the Globe: the Globe was built when the Theatre's owners, to evade a legal dispute, secretly dismantled the older playhouse and had its frame timbers transported across the river and re-erected.

You can get some idea of the outside view of an amphitheatre playhouse from the view of London in Figure 6 and the detail of Wenceslas Hollar's engraving of the 'Long View' of London (1647) on page 3287 of *The Norton Shakespeare*. However, there are two problems with these representations. Claes Jan Visscher's depiction of an apparently octagonal Globe (Figure 6) seems to have been based on hearsay, since he never visited London, yet it has inspired many subsequent images of the

Figure 6 *Detail from engraving of London*, Londinium Florentissima Britanniae Urbs, *1616 by Claes Jan Visscher. Photo: Guildhall Library, Department of Prints, London.*

playhouse. Hollar's version is more reliable, but shows the Globe in its second incarnation: the playhouse burned down in 1613, when a cannon fired as part of a performance of Shakespeare's *Henry VIII* ignited the thatch, and was then rebuilt. Analysis of some wall-angles uncovered by an archaeological dig has revealed that the original Globe was neither octagonal nor circular, but 20-sided. A more extensive dig of the Globe's neighbour, the Rose playhouse, in 1989, found it to be fourteen-sided, tulip-shaped, and much smaller (Figure 7).

As you enter the playhouse, you have a choice of standing in the yard or entering one of the three tiered galleries (Figure 8). William Lambarde recorded in the 1590s that audiences at playhouses and bear-pits alike 'first pay one pennie at the gate, another at the entrie of the Scaffolde, and the thirde for a quiet standing' (Gurr, 1992, p.122). The scaffold was the gallery; and a 'standing' was simply a viewing-place, whether standing or sitting. The weekly income of an industrious craftsman, such as a mason or carpenter, was about six shillings; apprentices earned much less, but often had free board and lodging. Playhouse prices were affordable for most working people (ibid., p.12).

Figure 7 *The foundations of the Rose playhouse, uncovered in 1989. The sets of round concrete pillars belong not to the Rose but to a recently demolished modern office block. Photo: Copyright Andrew Fulgoni/Fulgoni Photography/MoL.*

It's worth reflecting that you might easily have spent your penny not on a play but on a bear-baiting, situated nearby and costing exactly the same. This may tell us something about the bloodthirstiness of Elizabethan audiences (Hawkes, 1996), and indicates the status of their theatre-going as a less highbrow pursuit than it is today. Even so, Elizabethan playhouses offered opportunities to flaunt class superiority: for sixpence you could sit in the 'lords' rooms', in the galleries nearest to the stage, or even directly above it. Here you might not get the best view – the actors would often have their backs to you, and action towards the back of the stage would be hard to see – but the rest of the audience would get a good view of you.

Let's suppose that you have chosen to stand in the pit. Directly in front of you is the stage, extending from one side of the building into the middle of the yard. It might be 40 feet across, a large space that takes entering actors some seconds to cross.

Figure 8 *Wide view of stage and interior galleries of Shakespeare's Globe, Bankside, during a performance of Julius Caesar, 1999. Photo: John Tramper reproduced by permission of the New Globe.*

Shakespeare's scripts have points where one group of characters continues speaking as another group enters, filling an otherwise awkward gap as they take their positions: in the *Dream,* for instance, look at 2. 1. 57–8 and 3. 2. 38–43. Behind the stage you can see the 'tiring-house', where the players change into their costumes, or *attire* themselves. The mechanicals reproduce this arrangement in the wood outside Athens: This green plot shall be our stage, this hawthorn brake our tiring-house' (3. 1. 3–4). As well as being a dressing-room, the tiring-house is the backdrop for the action, and has two or more doors where actors make their entrances. These are used at the beginning of Act 2, Scene 1 of the *Dream:* 'Enter a FAIRY at one door and ROBIN GOODFELLOW *[a puck] at another';* and at *2. 1. 57, 1–2: 'Enter* [OBERON] *King of Fairies at one door, with his train, and* [TITANIA] *Queen at another, with hers'.* The entry of the two trains from different doors both provides an impressive spectacle and graphically represents the hostile opposition of the two monarchs.

The tiring-house also had a central alcove, the 'discovery-space', which could be uncurtained to reveal a shop, tomb, study or closet. It was used mainly for static tableaux, but also for concealment: Polonius behind the arras in *Hamlet* probably lurked in the discovery-space behind its curtains (Gurr, 1992, pp.4, 149, 151). Perhaps it was used in *A Midsummer Night's Dream* as Titania's bower, solving the problem that she has to be asleep on stage, yet unnoticed by the other characters, from 2. 2. 30 to 3. 1. 114.

Along the top of the tiring-house is a gallery which, as well as providing lords' rooms, might also be used for parts of the action; in the 1594–5 season you might have seen it used for the balcony scene in *Romeo and Juliet*. Extending out above this is the 'heavens', a canopy over the stage, supported by two pillars, which provides some shelter from the weather and enables things or people to be lowered towards the stage. As you continue to look upwards, you see the 'hut' above the heavens from where the machinery for descents and other special effects can be operated. Next to this is a platform, level with the roof of the playhouse, on which a trumpeter stands ready to announce the beginning of the performance; and next to this again is a flagpole, with a flag ready to be raised to announce that a play is in progress.

You may feel quite dazzled by the colourful and elaborate decoration of these structures. Both hostile Puritan preachers and admiring foreign travellers described the decor of the playhouses as sumptuous and gorgeous. In 1611 Thomas Coryat derided the playhouses of Venice as 'very beggarly and base in comparison of our stately play-houses in England' (Mulryne and Shewring, 1997, p.21). The woodwork was carved and painted, sometimes to simulate marble; the underside of the heavens was painted with celestial spheres and symbols; and the tiring-house facade was covered with ornate tapestries. The designers of the Globe reconstruction have been painstaking in seeking to recreate such decor and to incorporate Elizabethan symbolism.

Under your feet in the yard, there is a bed of hazelnut shells, by-products of soap production which were used for road surfacing; a layer of them was found in the yard at the Rose during the archaeological dig. Above your head is the sky, and, of course, the English weather.

At a performance of *The Winter's Tale* during the reconstructed Globe's opening season, I found that the play's lines about bad weather were given new vividness by torrential rain, and the actors were quick to emphasize such lines for rueful laughs. Perhaps Titania's long speech about unseasonally bad weather had similar resonance on an open-air stage (2. 1. 88–114). Nevertheless, the surviving records of 75 years of playhouse productions, from the reign of Elizabeth to the Interregnum,[1] include not one reference to bad weather as a deterrent (Gurr, 1987, p.36). Of course, the galleries and the stage were sheltered anyway

If you want refreshment, you can hail one of the vendors in the yard, who offer bottled ale, apples and nuts and will ply their trade among the crowd throughout the performance (ibid., pp.36–7). You have found a good 'standing'; the trumpet sounds, the flag goes up, and the play begins. There is no dropping of the house-lights to announce the division of 'real life' from the play, and, as the actors begin to appear on the stage, they are lit by the same natural daylight as you are. This, combined with the thrust of the stage into the midst of the audience, makes the fictional figures on stage very much sharers of the same space and same world as you, their spectator. It is time to 'Awake the pert and nimble spirit of mirth' (1. 1. 13).

Who are the actors?

One of the first details of the 1595 performance of the *Dream* that might strike you as Hippolyta enters for the first scene, is that she is played by a boy, as were all female parts on the Elizabethan stage. On the other hand, you might not notice this at all; you might simply see a woman convincingly played. Some of Shakespeare's scripts.

---

[1] The period between the monarchies of Charles I and Charles II, when there was a Commonwealth (1649–59)

draw attention to the boy behind the female role. Critics like Lisa Jardine (1983) have suggested that boy/girl roles offered homoerotic attractions to male spectators. In many other cases, though, the ambiguous gender of the woman played by a boy is passed over in complete silence and does not seem to be an issue. In the *Dream*, many of the attitudes struck by the female characters rely overtly on their womanliness, such as Hermia's defiance of her father's conventional treatment of her as his property on the marriage market (1. 1); the warmth of the past female friendships between Hermia and Helena (3. 2.199–219) and between Titania and her pregnant Indian votaress (2. 1. 122–37); and, perhaps above all, Titania's sensuality in her scenes with Bottom, saying as she embraces him, 'the female ivy so / Enrings the barky fingers of the elm' (4. 1. 40–1). In all these cases, we must assume that the boy actors' skill left no doubt about the femaleness of their roles. Flute is not such a professional; when assigned the part of Thisbe, he protests, 'Nay, faith, let not me play a woman. I have a beard coming' (1. 2. 39–40).

Besides the boy players who took female roles in the mainly adult acting companies, there were also some companies made up entirely of boys. These originated in the choir schools at St Paul's and the Chapel Royal, and were popular in the 1580s and again around 1600. Their competition with the adult players is referred to in *Hamlet* (c.1600). The Elizabethan dramatists John Lyly, Ben Jonson, George Chapman, John Marston, Francis Beaumont, John Fletcher, Thomas Middleton and Thomas Dekker wrote plays for them, demonstrating how able they must have been and how seriously they were taken.

The boy playing Hippolyta had a challenging task, as he almost certainly appeared also as Titania, just as the actor playing Theseus probably also played Oberon. This doubling of roles has become conventional following Peter Brook's revolutionary production of 1970, and for modern audiences it has Freudian resonances, as the Fairy King and Queen act out the repressed emotional turbulence between the Duke of Athens and the Amazon queen, who is his captive bride. However, it probably also reflects Elizabethan practice as dictated by the simple expedient of the number of players in the company. Each company had only eight to twelve chief players, plus hired men for smaller parts (see below). The same practical consideration makes it probable that Titania's fairies were played by the same actors as the mechanicals (Holland, 1995, p.24), even though in later centuries they have often been represented as ballerinas (Hackett, 1997, plates 3–5).

The leading members of the 1595 cast would be well known to regular playgoers. Bottom was probably played by Will Kemp, a 'star' for whom many of Shakespeare's earlier 'clown' roles were written. Such clowns tended to get laughs by extemporizations and visual humour. Richard Tarlton, Kemp's predecessor, was reputed to have audiences in stitches merely by sticking his head through the tiring-house tapestries and pulling faces (Gurr, 1992, p.88). Hamlet seems to express the playwright's impatience with such improvisation:

> ... let those that play your clowns speak no more than is set down for them; for there be of them that will themselves laugh to set on some quantity of barren spectators to laugh too.

(3. 2. 34–7)

After Kemp left Shakespeare's company in 1599, their leading comedian was Robert Armin, a gifted singer for whom Shakespeare wrote the more sophisticated parts of Feste in *Twelfth Night* and the Fool in *King Lear*. Meanwhile tragedians, such as

Edward Alleyn and Richard Burbage, came more into vogue. Alleyn delighted popular audiences at the Red Bull and the Fortune with 'stalking and roaring' performances (Gurr, 1992, p.113), as satirized through Bottom's enthusiasm to play a tyrant, 'a part to tear a cat in':

> The raging rocks
> And shivering shocks
> Shall break the locks
> Of prison gates.

> (1. 2. 22–7)

Such bombastic and gory rhetoric was imitated from the Latin author Seneca by playwrights of the early 1590s such as Christopher Marlowe and Thomas Kyd, and by Shakespeare in his early tragedy *Titus Andronicus* (c.1590). However, Shakespeare's later tragic roles, including Hamlet, Lear and Othello, were created for Burbage, who was renowned for his ability to 'personate' character and to 'paint' emotions in lifelike colours (Gurr, 1992, pp.113–4). It appears that Shakespeare's company led the way in seeking a more naturalistic style of representation; and it's worth remembering that roles written by Shakespeare were partly shaped by the capabilities of the colleagues available to play them.

Each actor was given a 'cue-script' to learn, containing only his own speeches with the last few words of each preceding speech. These are the 'parts' that Quince hands out to be learned at 1. 2. 80–2. Flute is confused by the cue-script: he misses his cue to start speaking, then ploughs on through his whole text, cues and all, without allowing Bottom/Pyramus to reply (3. 1. 80–4).

Who is the audience?

The fellow playgoers who surround you at the Theatre in 1595 are a mixed bunch. According to the poet John Davies, at a typical 1590s amphitheatre playhouse

> A thousand townsmen, gentlemen, and whores,
> Porters and serving men together throng.

> (Quoted in Gurr, 1992, p.217)

Many of the people you can see are citizens: that is, members of City guilds who are employers rather than employees, a group extending from wealthy merchants to more humble artisans. Numbers of their craftsmen-employees and apprentices are also present. Less numerous, but possibly more conspicuous, are members of the gentry – those able to live without manual labour and entitled to family coats-of-arms. Shakespeare, no gentleman by birth, bought himself into this class in 1596 by purchasing a coat-of-arms for his father. You may well see younger gentlemen behaving ostentatiously, many of them students at the Inns of Court, the centre of legal training, which also provided a kind of finishing school for sons of the wealthy. You may also rub shoulders with foreign tourists; the playhouses were already an attraction on the London tourist trail, and visitors have left us some of the most detailed descriptions of them.

Women are there as well as men. A Venetian visitor to the Fortune in 1617 was impressed that 'These theatres are frequented by a number of respectable and handsome ladies, who come freely and seat themselves among the men without the slightest hesitation' (ibid., p.217). Gentlewomen were escorted by their pages, and citizens' wives by their husbands or their apprentices; respectable women did not go to the theatre alone. They wanted to distinguish themselves from prostitutes, and to protect themselves from cutpurses and ruffians, all of whom were regular fixtures of the playhouse crowd. However, despite the anxious toning down of their play by Peter Quince's company (1. 2. 61–72; 3. 1. 8–20), there is no evidence that the presence of ladies provoked any dilution of the bloodthirsty spectacles of the Elizabethan and Jacobean stage.

As you stand in the yard, your fellow 'groundlings' are hard to ignore. Dekker in 1609 called them 'garlic-mouthed stinkards', while Marston in 1600 described being 'pasted / To the barmy Jacket of a Beer-brewer' in the playhouse throng (Gurr, 1987, p.19). They react to the performance by clapping, shouting, hissing, and even throwing tiles or fruit onto the stage. In about 1600 Michael Drayton described sitting in the 'thronged Theater' at the Rose, listening to the 'Showts and Claps at ev'ry little pawse, / When the proud Round on ev'ry side hath rung' (ibid., pp.45–6). So while the natural lighting and apron stage served to engage the actors with the audience, the absence of a modern hushed reverence towards the stage made the audience both distracted and distracting.

A consciousness of fellow audience-members and their responses is made use of in two ways in *A Midsummer Night's Dream*. At several points we stand alongside Oberon and Robin to watch the antics of the four lovers: Robin asks his master, 'Shall we their fond pageant see?' (3. 2. 114), and the two fairies become an on-stage audience. Later, another on-stage audience, the aristocrats watching *Pyramus and Thisbe* in Act 5, show off their own sophisticated wit at the players' expense. As we have seen in Chapter 1, poor Starveling becomes so exasperated by their interventions that he abandons his long-winded, versified script:

> All that I have to say is to tell you that the lantern is the moon, I the
> man i'th' moon, this thorn bush my thorn bush, and this dog my dog.

(5. 1. 247–9)

The courtiers may be reproducing the behaviour of young gallants, for whom playgoing was an opportunity to flaunt their own wit: in 1601 Marston described the kind of 'juicles husk' who would come to a play only to rubbish it, interjecting 'that's not so good, / Mew, blirt, ha, ha, light Chaffy stuff (Gurr, 1987, p.47). Shakespeare carefully balances our sympathies between the mechanicals, who suffer from the cruel jibes of the nobles and yet are no good at acting, and the nobles, who are right to identify deficiencies in the performance but become annoyingly uncharitable and self-congratulatory.

The comic rusticity of the mechanicals flatters the urban sensibility of Shakespeare's audience. Many citizen-playgoers, though, would have been migrants from the countryside, participating in the rapid growth of the metropolis in the period (Manley, 1995, p.126). The *Dream* invites them to look back to the country nostalgically, as a place of childish folklore, as in the description of Robin Goodfellow's tricks (2. 1. 32–57).

Props and costumes

Although *A Midsummer Night's Dream* opens in Theseus's palace, the props used to represent this were probably minimal. A contemporary sketch of the Swan playhouse (*The Norton Shakespeare*, p.3292) shows only a bench on stage with the three actors, and it has been estimated that 80 per cent of all Shakespeare's scenes written for the Globe could have been performed on a completely bare stage (Gurr, 1992, p.191). Even so, an inventory of props compiled in 1598 by Philip Henslowe, manager of the Rose playhouse, is fairly extensive, beginning with 'i rocke, i cage, i tombe, i Hell mought [mouth]' (ibid., p.187). One important prop was the chair of state, a raised throne placed in the centre of the stage for the many scenes of the Elizabethan and Jacobean theatre presided over by monarchs and judges, making graphic stagings of power possible. In the opening scene of *Richard II*, the king may have occupied the chair of state to hear the conflicting claims of two noblemen, and questions as to how adequately he fills the seat of power begin to be implied.

It seems that, when a script demanded material representation of a particular setting or object, this would be produced, but in other cases much of the work of representation would be done by language. In *A Midsummer Night's Dream* there is one obvious place where a material prop is needed: *'Enter ...* BOTTOM *with the ass-head'* (3. 1. 90, 1), an early stage direction which seems to refer to a specific company prop. Elsewhere, when Titania and then the Athenian lovers lie down in the wood to rest, they may have used 'moslsle banckes' like those in Henslowe's inventory (ibid.). However, before Titania sleeps, both her bank and the wood around it have been vividly created in the imagination by the *poetry* of the play: by Oberon's lyrical description of the 'bank where the wild thyme blows' (2. 1. 249–56), and in the fairies' songs evoking the 'spotted snakes' and 'thorny hedgehogs' of the woodland (2. 2. 9–10). If a real mossy bank was used, it was an almost inconsequential supplement to these depictions in language. Similarly, at 2. 1. 186, Oberon announces 'I am invisible'; Henslowe's inventory recorded 'a robe for to go invisibell' (Foakes and Rickert, 1961, p.325), but even if Shakespeare's company also owned one, the verbal announcement is both a necessary explanation and sufficient in itself to engage our imaginations. As Theseus puts it, it is 'the poet's pen' which 'gives to airy nothing / A local habitation and a name' (5. 1. 16–17). Even a limited reading of Shakespeare tells us that his plays must have engaged with his audiences as much through language as through spectacle.

However, even if props were relatively sparse, spectacle was present in other forms. There were special effects, including the extensive use of fireworks and smoke (Gurr, 1992, p.186). An actor like Bottom, who had to stab himself, or be stabbed, probably concealed in his armpit a sponge or bladder containing vinegar or calves' or sheep's blood. In George Peele's *The Battle of Alcazar* (c.1589), where three characters must be executed and disembowelled on stage, the play text carries the note '3 violls of blood & a sheeps gather' (a bladder containing a liver, heart and lungs (Gurr, 1992, p.182)). Sound effects included cannons, peals of bells and military drums, and the simulation of horses' hooves, bird-song and thunder (ibid., pp.184, 186).

Another form of spectacle was sumptuous costumes, which were valuable assets of the playing companies. Henslowe's 1598 inventory includes 'A scarlett cloke Layd downe with silver Lace and silver buttens', 'A crimosin Robe strypt with gould fac[ed] with ermin' (Gurr, 1992, pp. 193–200), and many more such lavish garments. Their opulence is partly explained by the report of Thomas Platter, a German traveller, in 1599, that:

> it is the English usage for eminent lords or knights at their decease to bequeath and leave almost the best of their clothes to their serving men, which it is unseemly for the latter to wear, so that they offer them then for sale for a small sum to the actors.

(Ibid.)

The colour of a costume was often symbolic, as with Hamlet's black and Malvolio's yellow stockings (ibid.), and Bottom's concern to play Pyramus in the right colour of beard (1. 2. 76–8).

It is unlikely, however, that Bottom, either as himself or as Pyramus, wore exact period dress appropriate to the ancient Greek setting. A sketch by Henry Peacham of an early staging of *Titus Andronicus (The Norton Shakespeare*, p.3291) shows the main character in something like a toga, but the other men are dressed as Elizabethan soldiers. Reference to the 'Athenian garments' of the lovers in the *Dream* (3. 2. 350) may indicate a similarly token effort at historical representation.

'Come, now a roundel and a fairy song'

A further kind of spectacle was the popularity of processions, like the one at 4.1. 99, 3–4, where the blowing of horns announces the entry of Theseus with Hippolyta 'and all his train' from the hunt. The horns both signify that the ducal party has been hunting and provide a heraldic announcement of its stately entrance. Trumpets were often used like this to mark ceremonial or military action.

Music and dancing were extremely important in staging. Music was often associated with magic, evoking wonder and the presence of supernatural forces. The chief activities of the fairies in the *Dream* are 'moonlight revels' of singing and dancing (2. 1. 141), while Titania and Oberon invoke still music to lull Bottom and the lovers into a deep sleep (4. 1. 80,1). At the end of the play, when the fairies sing and dance to bless the bridal house, the harmony of music and the patterning of dance symbolize the new, happy order formed by the conjugal unions (5. 2. 21–52).

The standard musical instruments at the amphitheatre playhouses were drums, trumpets, fiddles and flutes, played from within the tiring-house. Later, around 1607–9, the influence of the hall playhouses (see below) led to greater use of music, not just to accompany the action, but also before the performance and between the acts. The amphitheatres began to convert the space above the stage into a music room, and to employ more string and woodwind players (Gurr, 1992, p. 148).

The play was often followed by a clown's jig: a knockabout dance accompanied by a farcical or topical narrative ballad. Kemp was famous for his jigs; hence, as Bottom, he imagined singing the ballad of 'Bottom's Dream' 'in the latter end of a play' (4. 1. 208–10), and offered a comic rustic dance called a 'bergamask' at the end of *Pyramus and Thisbe* (5. 1. 345). However, after 1600, jigs receded from Globe performances and persisted only at less fashionable playhouses.

The business side of playing

By law, each playing company had to be authorized by a noble or royal patron. In the early 1580s, for instance, the leading companies were the Earl of Leicester's Men, Sussex's, Warwick's, Essex's and Oxford's. Nevertheless, the players were independent commercial organizations, not the salaried or exclusive employees of such patrons, who would pay them only for particular commissioned performances. Flute's expectation that Bottom would have won a pension from the Duke for his performance of Pyramus would have been exceptional (4. 2. 18–22).

Shakespeare began his career with Pembroke's Men, for whom he wrote his early histories and *The Taming of the Shrew*. From 1594, however, two companies became dominant, the Admiral's Men and the Lord Chamberlain's Men; from 1598 they held a legally confirmed monopoly of the London stage, shared from 1602 by a third company, Worcester's Men. Shakespeare joined the Lord Chamberlain's Men, whose patron was the court official empowered to oversee plays and all connected business, and who were therefore in effect the official playing company of the court. In 1603 this was made even plainer, when James I granted a Royal Patent to make them the King's Men.

Each company usually had an impresario-landlord or 'housekeeper', who owned the playhouse and its props and playbooks. Henslowe was housekeeper of the Admiral's Men at the Rose, while that of the Chamberlain's Men was James Burbage, father of the actor Richard. The playhouse owner conventionally took half of the gallery takings, and predictably there were sometimes legal disputes between housekeepers and companies over their relative shares in costs and profits.

The eight to twelve chief players of each company were 'sharers' in both profits and expenses, such as props, costumes, rent and the wages of hired men. Some of these hired men, paid weekly, filled supporting roles; others were stage-managers, wardrobe keepers, and musicians. By 1596 the Chamberlain's Men had eight sharers, including Shakespeare, Richard Burbage, Will Kemp and John Heminges, an actor who was later one of the editors of the First Folio (the earliest collected edition of Shakespeare's plays, published in 1623).

After James Burbage's death in 1597 the Chamberlain's Men took a radical step in financing their new playhouse, the Globe, two years later. The company's sharers, including Shakespeare, formed a consortium that contributed to the costs of the construction and thereby became entitled to a cut of the housekeeper takings: in effect, they became their own landlords. This proved to be one of Shakespeare's most profitable investments, and put the company on a more stable and secure footing (Gurr, 1992, chapter 2).

The playwright on the production line

The playhouses operated a repertory system, whereby a different play was performed every day. The records of the Admiral's Men for the 1594–5 season show that they performed six days a week, offering a total of 38 plays, of which 21 were new; a new play would be introduced roughly once a fortnight (ibid., pp.103–4). Later, when a stock of plays had been accumulated, the demand for new ones was less intense. Even so, the pressure on writers to produce quickly and prolifically was evidently considerable. There was much collaboration: a consortium of up to five writers might be assembled to write a single play, or one writer might be drafted in to make additions to a play by another. One playwright, Thomas Heywood, claimed to have been involved in the authorship of 220 plays (ibid., p.19).

The writer was customarily allowed one day's profit from each play. Some writers, like Ben Jonson, were freelances moving between companies; but Shakespeare was resident playwright with the Chamberlain's Men from 1594 until his death, probably on some kind of long-term contract. In this again he seems to have exercised his business acumen, which is also evident in the fact that, when he joined the Chamberlain's Men, he appears to have taken his earlier scripts with him. This was against contemporary convention, which treated play-texts as the property of the company not the author (ibid., pp.18–22).

Censorship

The Crown regulated the playhouses through the Revels Office. Not only did the Master of the Revels have charge of bringing plays to court, but from 1581 every performed play had to be licensed by him, for a fee. This gave him the power of censorship, especially of 'matters of religion or of the governaunce of the estate of the common weale', as specified in a 1559 royal ordinance. The omission of the deposition scene from early Quartos[2] of Shakespeare's *Richard II* reveals the hand of the censor, and some texts of other plays survive with manuscript censor's cuts (ibid., pp.72–9).

The hazards of incurring official displeasure are illustrated by the case of John Stubbs, author of a 1579 pamphlet criticizing the queen's plan to marry the French Duke of Anjou: both he and the pamphlet's distributor were sentenced to have their right hands cut off. Jonson was imprisoned in 1597 for a seditious play, and again in 1605 for his contribution to *Eastward Ho!,* written with Chapman and Marston for a boys' company, which satirized James I and his Scottish followers. Yet comment on potentially sensitive topical matters could and did take place on the stage, in encoded forms which Annabel Patterson has described as 'functional ambiguity' (1984, p.18). Dramatic fiction enables the expression of political comments in forms implicit enough to evade the censor's prohibition, yet recognizable to the audience. For instance, when *A Midsummer Night's Dream* was first performed, Elizabeth I had recently been celebrated by Edmund Spenser as England's *'Faerie Queene'*. In showing the subjugation of the Fairy Queen by her husband as a happy and rightful ending, the play may reflect the view that rule by an unmarried and autonomous woman was an aberration from the natural order (Montrose, 1986).

Hall playhouses

There remains another kind of playing space for which Shakespeare and his contemporaries wrote. The boy companies had used indoor hall playhouses within the City walls, and in 1608 the King's Men acquired one of these, the Blackfriars playhouse. Despite being within the City, it was exempt from City jurisdiction because it was inside an ancient monastic precinct. The King's Men now alternated between the Globe in the summer and the Blackfriars in the winter; and other companies followed their lead with the opening of the Whitefriars (1608), the Cockpit (1616), and Salisbury Court (1629).

The halls were called 'private' playhouses, partly to place them beyond the supervision of the Master of the Revels, and partly to attract a more socially aspiring clientele. They had much smaller capacities than the amphitheatres – 600 at the Blackfriars compared with at least 3000 at the Globe – and they charged much higher prices.

The Blackfriars playhouse was a rectangular building, with the stage probably across one of the shorter sides. Sixpence gained admission to the two or three tiers of timber galleries, which formed a curved or polygonal array around three sides of

---

[2] See Interval 2 for details of the text versions of Shakespeare's plays.

the stage. The pit contained benches, where a seat cost an extra shilling, initiating the modern practice of charging more, not less, for a viewing-point immediately in front of the stage. Up to ten gallants could pay a total of two shillings to enter through the tiring-house at the back of the stage and sit on a stool on stage. There were also boxes at the side or back of the stage, available for half-a-crown. These and the on-stage stools made the acting space rather small.

We have good evidence of what a hall playhouse looked like in Figure 9, a set of designs by Inigo Jones, possibly intended for the Cockpit. These are the basis for the Inigo Jones Theatre at the Bankside Globe reconstruction site, enabling the company to emulate Shakespeare's by moving indoors for winter performances. Figure 10 also appears to show a performance at a hall playhouse, although scholars have debated its accuracy (Foakes, 1985, pp.159–61). Notice the candelabras characteristic of an indoor playhouse, and the curtains in the centre of the tiring-house wall that may conceal a discovery-space.

The hall playhouses introduced divisions between acts, since pauses were needed to trim the candles. The amphitheatres had presented the action continuously over two to three hours, but they now adopted act-divisions (Gurr, 1987, p.33). Playing by candlelight, though, seems to have made little other difference to staging. Like the amphitheatres, the halls began performances at 2 pm, so daylight through the windows combined with the candlelight must have created quite a well-lit space. Night scenes were indicated, just as at the amphitheatres, not by artificial lighting variations but by props and through language, like the insistent verbal reminders throughout the middle acts of *A Midsummer Night's Dream* that we are in a forest lit by the moon and stars (for example, 2. 1. 60; 3. 1. 179; 3. 2. 61, 178, 189). The mechanicals face the problem of bringing moonlight into a chamber, but their literal-minded solutions – opening a casement to let in the real moon, and casting Starveling as the Man in the Moon – are presented as patently absurd (3. 1. 41–53).

The hall playhouses used more music, both as a kind of overture and to mark act-divisions. The Blackfriars musicians were renowned and gave concert perform-ances; in 1602 a consort of lutes, mandolins, bandores (a guitar-like instrument), violins and flutes played for an hour before the play to entertain the visiting Duke of Stettin-Pomerania (Gurr, 1992, p.148).

The stage as world, the world as stage

The reviser of John Stow's *Annales* commented on the building of the Salisbury Court playhouse that:

> this is the seaventeenth Stage, or common Play-house, which hath beene new made within the space of three-score yeeres within London and the Suburbs ... I neither knew, heard, nor read, of any such Theaters, set Stages, or Play-houses, as have been purposely built within mans memory.

> (Ibid., p.121)

He is describing the sudden explosion of a new cultural medium, comparable to the growth of television or the rapid current development of various forms of computerized 'hyper-reality'. It is striking how rapidly Shakespeare and his contemporaries grasped its potential, and with how much sophistication. The

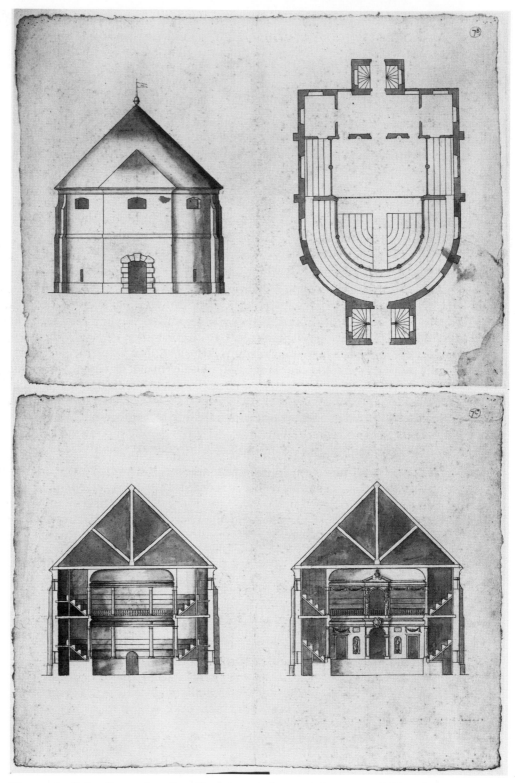

Figure 9 *Inigo Jones, drawings for a conversion to a theatre, probably relating to the Cockpit in Drury Lane (or the Phoenix). Worcester College, Oxford, Sheets 7B and 7C. Reproduced by permission of the Provost and Fellows of Worcester College, Oxford*

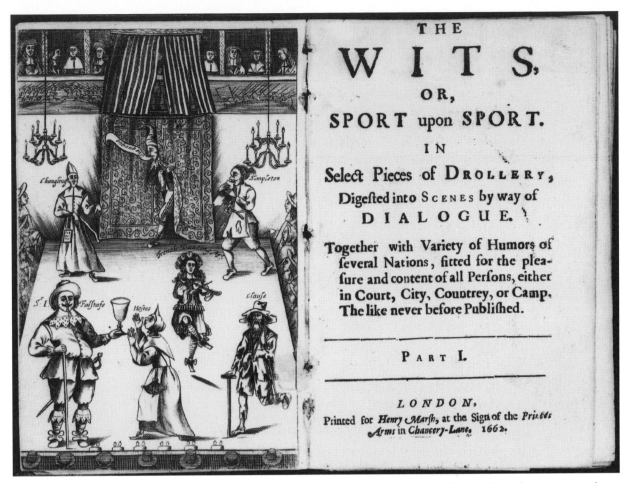

Figure 10 *Engraved frontispiece and title page of* The Wits, or, Sport upon Sport, in select pieces of drollery, digested into scenes by way of dialogue: together with variety of humours of several nations, fitted for the pleasure and content of all persons, either in court, city, countrey, or camp: the like never before published, *Henry Marsh, London, 1662. Reproduced from the original in the Henry E. Huntington Library and Art Gallery, San Marino, California by permission.*

Elizabethan amphitheatre playhouse could give body to fairies and to ancient heroes like Theseus; and while it might not have been able to simulate moonlight or a palace or a wood, collaboration between the writer, the players and the audience could give them a virtual reality. In this sense the playhouse came to be seen as a capsule, which could contain the whole world; and the world could be newly understood through its translation into the medium of the playhouse.

When Theseus speaks about imagination, he intends to mock:

> The poet's eye, in a fine frenzy rolling,
> Doth glance from heaven to earth, from earth to heaven,
> And as imagination bodies forth
> The forms of things unknown, the poet's pen
> Turns them to shapes, and gives to airy nothing
> A local habitation and a name.

(5. 1. 12–17)

His words, however, produce the opposite effect: a celebration of the power of the poet, and the stage for which he writes, to create a new heaven and a new earth. Different senses of this magical and complex relationship between the stage and the world recur throughout Shakespeare's works.

We can see, then, that an understanding of the playing spaces for which Shakespeare wrote gives us more than just a closer knowledge of the material details of original performances. Beyond this, understanding of his playing spaces is essential for us to approach an understanding of how Shakespeare conceptualized the world, through forms newly available to him, in a particular time and place.

References

Foakes, R.A. (1985) *Illustrations of the English Stage 1580–1642*, London: Scolar.

Foakes, R.A. and Rickert, R.T. (eds) (1961) *Henslowe's Diary*, Cambridge: Cambridge University Press.

Gurr, A. (1987) *Playgoing in Shakespeare's London*, Cambridge: Cambridge University Press.

Gurr, A. (1992) *The Shakespearean Stage 1574–1642*, 3rd edn, Cambridge: Cambridge University Press.

Hackett, H. (1997) *A Midsummer Night's Dream*, Writers and Their Work, Plymouth: Northcote House.

Hawkes, T. (1996) 'Harry Hunks, Superstar', in *Around the Globe*, Autumn, pp.12–13.

Holland, P. (1995) Introduction', *A Midsummer Night's Dream*, World's Classics, Oxford: Oxford University Press.

Howard, J.E. (1994) *The Stage and Social Struggle in Early Modern England*, London: Routledge.

Jardine, L. (1983) *Still Harping on Daughters: Women and Drama in the Age of Shakespeare*, Hemel Hempstead: Harvester Wheatsheaf.

Manley, L. (1995) *Literature and Culture in Early Modern London*, Cambridge: Cambridge University Press.

Montrose, L.A. (1986) '*A Midsummer Night's Dream* and the shaping fantasies of Elizabethan culture: gender, power, form', in *Rewriting the Renaissance: The Discourses of Sexual Difference in Early Modern Europe*, ed. M.W. Ferguson, M. Quilligan and N.J. Vickers, Chicago and London: University of Chicago Press, pp.65–87.

Mulryne, J.R. and Shewring, M. (eds) (1997) *Shakespeare's Globe Rebuilt*, Cambridge: Cambridge University Press.

Patterson, A. (1984) *Censorship and Interpretation: The Conditions of Writing and Reading in Early Modern England*, Madison: University of Wisconsin Press.

The Norton Shakespeare (1997) ed. S. Greenblatt, W. Cohen, J.E. Howard and K.E. Maus, New York and London: W.W. Norton.

Wells, S. (1967) 'Introduction', *A Midsummer Night's Dream*, Harmondsworth: Penguin.

RICHARD II

Chapter 2

Margaret Healy

Aims

This chapter will introduce you to a Shakespearean history play, and in particular to the play's use of history to explore some of the burning political issues of its historical moment. By the end of your study of *Richard II*, you should be in a position to discuss how the staging of majesty in this play mediated the debates about kingship in the late Elizabethan period. More generally, you should have acquired a sound grasp of the complexities of the production of theatrical meaning.

The Tragedy of King Richard the Second

On the Thursday or Friday before a major rebellion against Queen Elizabeth I's government on Sunday 8 February 1601, a number of the conspirators sought out representatives of the Lord Chamberlain's Men:

> On Thursday or Friday sevennight, Sir Chas. Percy, Sir Josceline Percy, Lord Monteagle, and several others spoke to some of the players to play the deposing and killing of King Richard II, and promised to give them 40s. more than their ordinary, to do so. [The Lord Chamberlain's Men] had determined to play some other play, holding that of King Richard as being so old and so long out of use that they should have a small company at it, but at this request they were content to play it.

> (State Papers Domestic, Elizabeth I 1598–1601, vol.CCLXXVIII, art.85)

As these trial documents reveal, they proceeded to offer the players substantially more money than they would normally earn to perform an 'old' play on the day before their planned insurrection. That play was almost certainly Shakespeare's *Richard II*. The conspiracy to overthrow Elizabeth's regime failed miserably, however, and a member of the theatrical company, the actor Augustine Phillips, shortly found himself in the dock being cross-questioned about the troupe's seditious activities: the staging of *Richard II* on the eve of a rebellion. Sixty years later, Charles II's government banned the play – it was deemed too politically dangerous.

What was so inflammatory about this play? Does this anecdotal history suggest that the Shakespearean stage sought to do rather more than simply satisfy its audience's appetite for entertainment? Did it have an active political remit, too? These are the fascinating questions we are setting out to address in this chapter. An exploration of how *Richard II* might have been perceived and understood at the original moment of its production – the late 1590s – will be our focus. Before looking at the play in detail, some preliminary consideration of Shakespeare's use of medieval history, and of what type of play this is, will help to set the scene.

What type of play is Richard II?

'comedie': 'a stage play handled merrily'
'tragedie': 'a solemne play, describing cruell murders and sorrowes'

(Cawdrey, 1613 edn, unpaginated)

As Interval 1 has highlighted, however artistically accomplished Shakespeare's plays are, they were designed in the first instance as commercial ventures. This inevitably meant that, in order to draw in the crowds and become box-office successes, the dramatist's wares had to appeal to the varied tastes of a broad spectrum of theatregoers. Building on what we know about the relative popularity of types of play in this period, and on the very simple but extremely useful definitions above, it is fair to assume that, whilst the merriness and sweetness of romantic comedy made it the biggest box-office earner, tragedies satisfied the more acerbic and bloodthirsty cravings of some Elizabethan palates. But, as we have begun to see with A *Midsummer Night's Dream*, Shakespeare's plays can seldom be slotted neatly into one of these categories: they usually combine the merry with the solemn, and are often rich confections of two or more genres. Predominantly a tragic history with comic elements, *Richard II* is just such a mixed or 'hybrid' form: it made sound commercial sense, of course, to appeal to a range of tastes simultaneously. The play was probably first performed around the same time as A *Midsummer Night's Dream*, 1595–6, by the Lord Chamberlain's Men. Like the *Dream* – but very much more so – part of its success can be attributed to its exploitation of matters of topical interest in the 1590s. Indeed, *Richard II*'s engagement with the burning issues of the day probably lies behind the high demand for the text of the play, which was published as *The Tragedy of King Richard the Second* in Quarto format in 1597, and twice again in 1598 with Shakespeare's name on the title page (an unusual occurrence). No previous Shakespearean play text had proved so popular.

Richard II, in common with Shakespeare's *Henry IV* Parts 1 and 2, *Henry V* and *Henry VI* Parts 1, 2 and 3, deals with events that led up to the bloody feuds, known as the Wars of the Roses, fought between the houses of Lancaster and York from the 1450s to 1485. These 'houses' were really large extended families, together with their retainers and followers. Henry IV (Bolingbroke), Henry V and Henry VI were Lancastrians. Edward IV's accession in 1461 marked the triumph of the Yorkists in the first period of the Wars. Histories were popular reading in the sixteenth century, and consequently a wealth of history books provided ready sources for dramatists like Shakespeare to piece together the basic plot of late medieval history. Some were called chronicles, such as Raphael Holinshed's *Chronicles of England, Scotlande, and Irelande* (1577), Edward Hall's *The Union of the Two Noble and Illustre Famelies of Lancastre & Yorke* (1548) and Jean Froissart's chronicle (*The Chronicle of Froissart*), translated from the French by Sir John Bouchier, Lord Berners, in 1523–5. Others, like Samuel Daniel's *The Civile Warres* (1595) and William Baldwin's *A Myrroure for Magistrates* (1559), took the form of long poems. However, Shakespeare did not just follow his sources slavishly; as we will see in our study of the opening scenes of *Richard II*, he sometimes made up episodes that cannot be found in any of the history books.

According to all the above histories, Richard's overthrow by his cousin Henry Bolingbroke, and his subsequent murder, initiated a trail of unrest, culminating in 30 years of the carnage and anarchy of civil war. This drew to a close when the first Tudor monarch, the Lancastrian Henry VII, defeated Richard III at the Battle of Bosworth Field, ascended the throne, and united the warring houses by marrying Elizabeth of York. Elizabeth I was Henry VII's granddaughter, and it has been a view popularly held in the twentieth century that Shakespeare's history plays uphold and reinforce the orthodoxies of Elizabeth's government. Influential twentieth-century Shakespearean critics, such as John Dover Wilson (1939) and E.M.W. Tillyard (1944), have supported the idea that the history plays are essentially 'hymns to Tudor Order', celebrations of 'the saviour of England' – the House of Tudor – which brought order and stability to the English nation (Dover Wilson, 1939, p.40). Indeed, it has become part of the mythology of our culture that the reign of Elizabeth I was a model of peace and contentment, and that this stable context gave rise to a rich harvest of English writing, notably Shakespeare's plays. This is most likely to be the view you are familiar with, and we will hear more of it later, but you may already be beginning to feel that this interpretation sits uneasily with the controversy surrounding *Richard II* in 1601 outlined above.

Shakespearean scholars are divided about the meaning and political implications of *Richard II*: about whether it flatters or undermines Elizabeth's regime. In the highly politicized world of late-twentieth-century Bardology, an increasing number of critics have pitted themselves against what they have described as the 'conserva-tive' Tillyardian line. Far from underpinning the ideology of Elizabeth I's regime, they argue, Shakespeare's drama was more questioning and radical than has previously been recognized. By the end of this study of *Richard II* in its original historical context, you will be in a position to decide for yourself which interpretation seems more sound, or, indeed, to reject both of them as unconvincing.

Advocates of these opposing views agree that Shakespeare used the histories of medieval monarchs to explore issues relating to ideology and government in his own day. One reason why Renaissance playwrights commonly did this might be – back to the box office again – that playgoers were interested in history and in contemporary controversies, and history plays satisfied both tastes simultaneously. Another related reason is that sensitive contemporary political issues could be touched on in the guise of the past. All plays had to be scrutinized and licensed by the Master of the Revels and it would have been highly dangerous to comment directly and critically on the government of the day. In fact, *Richard II* relentlessly explores the meaning of *just* kingship. This was potentially a highly contentious subject, given that the monarch in this period was at the centre of the English political system, and the most powerful person in the country.

Kid-glove treatment of the topic was required, and to some extent the traditional function of histories, particularly those that detailed the falls of illustrious men, served to license considerations of the thorny issue of vice among the powerful. As the following quotation from Sir Philip Sidney's *A Defence of Poetry* (1595) explains, histories and historians were expected to serve an edifying function in Shakespeare's day: 'The historian ... authorizing himself ... upon other histories, whose greatest authorities are built upon the notable foundation of hearsay ... denieth ... that any man for teaching of virtue, and virtuous actions is comparable to him' (Duncan-Jones, 1989, p.220). Sidney's rather sceptical discussion of histories (he suggests that plagiarism was rife, and reduces history to 'hearsay') implies that the aim of sixteenth-century history was not so much the objective representation of the facts of the past, as the provision of persuasive models and precepts for the ethical and political instruction of rulers. Baldwin's engaging poetical history advertised its instructive function on its title page: 'A Myrroure for Magistrates, wherin may be seen by example of other, with howe grevous plages vices are punished: and howe frayle and unstable worldly prosperitie is founde, even of those, whom fortune seemeth most highly to favour.' Tragedies, too, could serve as warnings to erring rulers to mend their ways: 'High and excellent Tragedy … that openeth the greatest wounds, and showeth forth the ulcers that are covered with tissue: that maketh kings fear to be tyrants' (Duncan-Jones, 1989, p.230). If we think back to Chapter 1 on the *Dream* and Ben Jonson's definition of comedy as preoccupied with 'human follies', it is fair to assume that 'crimes' were the moral fulcrum of tragedy. One humanist playwright of this period, Fulke Greville, even announced, rather provocatively, that his tragedies were concerned to 'trace out the high ways of ambitious governors' (Greville, 1938 edn, p.221).

We might conclude from these cumulative reflections on history and tragedy that playgoers in Shakespeare's day went to a tragical history like *Richard II* expecting to see, not a pale reflection of times past, but a more stimulating vision, one pertinent to the conduct of government in their own times. However, if they did not expect a mirror image of the past, reflecting things exactly as they were, neither did they expect to be confronted with a transparent vision in which characters and their deeds were more or less what they seemed all the time. Sixteenth-century playgoers were much more attuned to listening and watching for duplicity than we are. In fact, as we shall see throughout this study of Shakespeare, Elizabethan theatre demanded vigilant spectators, constantly on the look out for hypocrisy and eager to sift out the 'seemers' from more honest types. We will now investigate this more closely in relation to the opening scenes of *Richard II*.

The theatre of power

As you read the opening scene, do not allow yourself to be held up by the play's unfamiliar language and densely rhetorical style, which we will consider in more detail later. Concentrate instead on the broader brushstrokes of meaning. Ask yourself the following questions. **What is happening? Who is accusing whom of what? Is there anything to suggest that one knight is more guilty than the other? What sort of monarch does Richard II seem in this scene?**

The play opens on an extremely formal, ceremonial note: the king is presiding in state at Windsor Castle over a bitter quarrel between two rival feudal lords (one the king's cousin), who are accusing each other of 'treason'. It is a very static scene, the bulk of it being taken up by long-winded, hot-blooded and boastful speeches in which the knights protest their innocence, preen their chivalric feathers and malign their enemies. Mowbray's speeches are more defensive and incriminating than Bolingbroke's. He finds it necessary to answer specific charges and explain that he has not squandered the money he has been given to pay the king's soldiers, nor murdered the Duke of Gloucester (the king's uncle). He does admit, however, to having made an attempt on the life of John of Gaunt (Bolingbroke's father and uncle of the king) in the past and subsequently to have been pardoned. King Richard seems in control throughout. Indeed, he appears the picture of ideal majesty – one 'not born to sue, but to command' (1. 1. 196). He is respectful of his elder-statesman uncle (158), but exhibits a superior stance of mockery and impatience towards the two boastful, sparring knights (see 18–19, 152–7, 200–1). He seems anxious to be an impartial arbitrator – as he tells the assembled court – and to bring about peace.

Now read Scene 2. (There is no equivalent of this episode in the history chronicles or poems: it is Shakespeare's invention.) Does this scene shed a different light on the opening one?

This brief scene serves to undercut any initial impression of Richard as an ideal monarch. Far from upholding the law, Richard is revealed by his elderly kinsmen's pained and impassioned speeches to be an agent of bloody murder: he has 'caused' his uncle Gloucester's death. (This is a fact that the history chronicles confirm.) This suggests that Richard's self-presentation as an unbiased, kingly peace-maker in the first scene was a sham. He is, in fact, implicated in Mowbray's crimes. His pat rhyming couplets in the first scene, for example – 'Forget, forgive, conclude, and be agreed; / Our doctors say this is no time to bleed' (1. 1. 156–7), alluding to the practice of medicinal blood-letting – take on a rather different hue in the light of the second scene. Detached mockery becomes heartless and inappropriate flippancy given the serious nature of the charge in which he is implicated and the degree of pain Gloucester's death has caused his aged relatives. Bolingbroke's action in challenging Mowbray and upholding the law gains credit in the light of this scene.

Now turn to Scene 3. Why does the king stop the fight? Why does he reduce the term of Bolingbroke's banishment?

Students of this play often find the events in this scene and the way they are put together rather perplexing. Why, for example, does Richard suddenly call a halt to the tournament, having allowed all the preliminary pomp and ceremony to go ahead? One answer might be that this provides a wonderful opportunity for the king to demonstrate, in public, the exercise of his supreme monarchical authority and his laudable, altruistic concern to prevent bloodshed. (In fact, Richard's sudden intervention is exactly what is recorded in the history chronicles: the playwright is following his sources closely here.) In terms of stagecraft, the tournament episode offers a superb occasion for colourful spectacle.

The king's reduction of the term of Bolingbroke's banishment, ostensibly because of Gaunt's 'sad aspect', seems, however, to be a complete Shakespearean invention. (The history chronicles, particularly Froissart's, describe Richard's act of clemency as a politic stratagem designed to 'please the people' who, by this stage in Richard's reign, are dissatisfied with their monarch and favour Bolingbroke.) As the next scene of the play will reveal, and as the last one suggested, Richard could not give a fig for his uncle, and he is envious and wary of his cousin Bolingbroke for being beloved of the people. Thus, although the king publicly declares that he is motivated by a desire to prevent civil strife, he is actually eager to save his own skin.

Shakespeare has constructed these opening scenes of *Richard II* to expose the gap between Richard's public 'shows' of just kingship and the fact that he is a two-faced actor–king. All is not what it seems, and the spectator's task is to discern the reality beneath the 'shows' in this theatre of power.

The meaning of kingship

Now read the play through at least once. You might wish to listen to an audio production as you do so. Take nothing at face value: remember that persuasive rhetoric, like the 'shows' of government, can be very misleading (and also very entertaining, as Shakespeare clearly understood). Our focus is on the political meanings of this play and in order better to grasp these, you need to consider, as you read, the following fundamental question. **What arguments are voiced in the play for and against the overthrow of Richard and his replacement by Bolingbroke?**

You may well be surprised at how few arguments are adduced in favour of retaining Richard on the throne in the face of the crimes he is alleged to have committed. The same argument is trotted out time and again by both his supporters and his critics, and clung to tenaciously by Richard himself. Gaunt is the first to rehearse it, at 1. 2. 37–41, in answer to the Duchess of Gloucester, who is calling for him (her brother-in-law) to avenge her husband's murder. What the elderly statesman is saying, in effect, is that although his nephew is responsible for the Duke of Gloucester's murder, he is paralysed to act because Richard is 'anointed', God's representative on earth, and as such his actions are not subject to earthly law – the king is answerable only to God.

Later in the play Richard describes his invulnerability in similar terms:

> Not all the water in the rough rude sea
> Can wash the balm from an anointed king.
> ... for heaven still guards the right.

(3. 2. 50–1, 58)

He seems truly to believe that he has special status conferred by his birth – the divine right of kings – and is untouchable because he is protected by God. The Bishop of Carlisle restates the same belief several times, but most forcefully and at length – and to his cost, for he is arrested for capital treason as a result – in the scene in which Richard's royal authority is transferred to Bolingbroke (often termed the deposition scene):

> What subject can give sentence on his king?
> And who sits here that is not Richard's subject?
> ... And shall the figure of God's majesty,
> His captain, steward, deputy elect,
> Anointed, crownèd, planted many years,
> Be judged by subject and inferior breath,
> And he himself not present?

(4. 1. 112–13, 116–20)

This was a view widely held in Tudor England and one that the increasingly centralized and power-hungry governments of Elizabeth I, James I and Charles I sought to promulgate. It is not difficult to imagine why. The Church, whose head was the monarch rather than the Pope by this post-Reformation stage,[1] was a prime vehicle for relaying this myth. It is illuminating to compare the above speeches with a passage from *An Homilie Against Disobedience and Wilfull Rebellion* (1571), one of the Homilies or tracts that were required by law to be read out every Sunday in all English churches:

---

[1] The term 'Reformation' refers to the movements for liberal reform which took place in the western church in the sixteenth century and which had wide-ranging political, social and economic effects.

By these two places of the holy Scriptures, it is most evident that Kings, Queenes, and other Princes ... are ordeined of GOD, are to bee obeyed and honoured of their subjects: that such subjects, as are disobedient or rebellious against their Princes, disobey GOD, and procure their own damnation.

(Quoted in Gurr, 1984, appendix)

An Homilie repeats this warning several times and goes on to proclaim that 'rebellion is worse than the worst government of the worst prince' and that those who contravene the monarch's will inevitably provoke God 'the more to plague them'. Furthermore, just as in Shakespeare's play, *An Homilie* threatens that God's plagues (pestilence, war and famine) will descend on the population should the anointed monarch be crossed by rebellion. As Richard warns the Earl of Northumberland:

God omnipotent,
Is mustering in his clouds on our behalf
Armies of pestilence.

(3. 3. 84–6)

The Bishop of Carlisle likewise prophesies that 'Disorder, horror, fear and mutiny / Shall here inhabit' (4. 1. 133–4) if Richard is deposed. This prophecy seems to be becoming true at the close of *Richard II* and – as Elizabethan theatregoers would almost certainly have understood – eventually bore horrific fruit in the shape of Northumberland's rebellion[2] and culminated in the Wars of the Roses. Indeed, some of those present in the original audiences would undoubtedly have seen Shakespeare's *Henry VI* Parts 1, 2 and 3 and *Richard III*, which were staged before *Richard II*, but which depict these later chaotic phases of English history.

Here, then, is fuel for a traditional reading of Shakespeare's version of history as underpinning Tudor orthodoxy. These Shakespearean speeches preach the divine right of kings and reinforce the Tudor homilies' warnings that God will punish rebellion against a monarch. Surely this confirms our playwright as a propagandist for Elizabeth I's government?

Yet there remains the not inconsiderable problem of Richard's 'crimes' and their disastrous effect on 'this sceptred isle' (2. 1. 40). The play seems to tell us (and show us) a great deal about Richard's ineptitude as a monarch, as do most of the historical accounts. Holinshed's *Chronicles*, a major source for this play's 'facts' of Richard's reign, alleges, for example, that he was prodigal, ambitious and lustful. Baldwin's *Myrroure* painted an even harder-hitting picture of an unjust monarch:

I am a kyng that ruled all by lust,
That forced not of vertue, ryght, or lawe,
But alway put false Flatterers most in trust.

(1960 edn, p.113, lines 31–3)

---

[2] The historical Northumberland did eventually rebel against King Henry IV. After fleeing to France, he again revived the rebellion and invaded England. According to Holinshed, he died in unsuccessful combat.

As an extant medieval poem called *Richard the Redeless* (counsel-less) (*c*.1399) testifies, even within Richard's own lifetime (it was probably written a few months after his deposition), his unjust, lascivious and spendthrift exploits were notorious (see Barr, 1993). This poem – which claims to be a cautionary 'mirror' for future princes – represents Bolingbroke's successes as divinely engineered: Richard had been 'rightfully' deposed, because he wilfully disregarded the rights of his subjects. However, there were a few anti-Lancastrian histories (mostly French chronicles) that coloured Richard's life in far more favourable shades, delineating a portrait of a long-suffering monarch, Christ-like in his patience and divinity. Shakespeare's history alludes to, and indeed manages to fuse, elements of both these 'types' of Richard II (remember his evocations of Christ, Judas and Pilate in the deposition scene). Yet Richard's very belief in himself as superhuman, above the law and protected by divinity, makes him appear rather naïve and foolish at times, and even seems to constitute the source of his downfall. He learns that he is 'flesh and blood' rather too late in the day to save himself and his country from bloodshed and ruin. Perhaps the text ensures that what audiences actually see and hear of the 'anointed' king modifies their responses to the very idea of divine right.

Let us now pursue Richard's misdemeanours further by looking closely at the famous deathbed speech of Gaunt, which highlights many of the king's abuses (2. 1. 31–68). **What is Gaunt saying, and why is he saying it like this?**

The gist of Gaunt's charge is that this anointed monarch has managed to ruin an ideal place ('This other Eden, demi-paradise', 'This blessèd plot, this earth, this realm, this England'), which had hitherto been well defended against such ruin ('This fortress built by Nature for herself / Against infection and the hand of war') and brimming with princely heirs ('this teeming womb of royal kings'), through 'his rash fierce blaze of riot', his 'eager feeding' and 'Light vanity'. Richard is prone to excesses, riotous behaviour and vain frivolity. He and his queen have also failed so far to produce an heir, a point sharpened by Queen Isabel's speeches in 2. 2, which are pregnant with the pathos of 'nothing'. Gaunt prophesies that Richard's uncontrolled appetites will destroy him and his country, which is already shamefully decayed as a result of the king's fiscal abuses and willingness to trade land and property rights for his own profit or political advantage. As the Duke of York confides to Gaunt (2. 1. 17–28), and as Gaunt subsequently confirms to Richard's face, Richard's deafness to wise counsel, coupled with his susceptibility to flattery, has fuelled his dereliction of his sacred duty. In short, 'God's deputy' has brought corruption to the garden of Eden.

By this stage in the action, Gaunt has established himself as one of the play's prime exponents of Richard's 'anointed' status. Gaunt is clearly not a rebel, but an upholder of the orthodox view of monarchy and, as a man about to expire (as he reminds us), he stands to gain or lose nothing from his impassioned outburst. The 'sceptred isle' speech is intensely patriotic and carefully crafted to manipulate the audience's emotions and thoughts. Look at the density of majestic and heroic images and allusions in lines 40–58, for example, and the repetition of 'this', and the stress placed upon it, in consecutive lines of the blank verse. The elaborate metaphors and the rhetorical patterning ('this ... this ... this') seem to build up to a crescendo, keeping us hanging on for the main verb ('Is now leased out' (59)) which – finally, after 20 lines – sends the whole speech plummeting down. All 'this' – England's greatness and splendour – is 'now' a thing of the past. It has been devoured by its monarch's vanity, imaged graphically here, through the bird-of-prey metaphor, as an 'insatiate cormorant' (38).

The bird most usually associated with monarchs in the Renaissance[3] was the pelican, often depicted selflessly tearing her own flesh from her breast to feed her young on her blood. Shakespeare's choice of the cormorant image powerfully conveys that Richard's behaviour was, in Gaunt's experience at least, a horrific inversion of the norm, a point that is reinforced by his subsequent deployment of the pelican image in 2. 1. 127. Thus, the impact of what the old statesman is saying is magnified by the way he says it; although his outburst appears to be driven by emotion and spontaneous thought, the speech is highly rhetorical and artificial. Many people find Gaunt's speech deeply moving in its appeal to English nationalism and sentiment. Indeed, an actor would have to work extremely hard, against the grain of the text, to produce an insincere Gaunt from this, although I can imagine a director attempting to undermine Gaunt's credibility by playing him as a demented old fool raging at youth from his deathbed.

Richard is, however, perhaps the most authoritative 'historian' of his own sins. In 1. 4, the dramatist opens a window onto the king's inner self and less scripted behaviour by allowing the audience to observe him off the formal stage, confiding in, and conniving with, his parasitical, courtly chums. Richard's public performance of just majesty in the previous scene is completely undercut by this one. We witness him remorselessly confirming his poor husbandry and greed:

> And for our coffers with too great a court
> And liberal largess are grown somewhat light,
> We are enforced to farm our royal realm,
>
> (1. 4. 42–4)

and we hear him reveal his spite, hypocrisy and penchant for blasphemy:

> Now put it, God, in his physician's mind
> To help him to his grave immediately. ...
> Pray God we may make haste and come too late!
>
> (1. 4. 58–9, 63)

Time and again, Richard's sins, excesses and negligence are confirmed by other voices, both élite and base. Think of the words and maxims of the gardener, for example, about the 'wasteful King' and 'this disordered spring' (3. 4. 56, 49). **Turn to the text and scrutinize the servant's words in 3. 4. 41–8. What is the gardener's man saying, and how is he saying it?**

Why should we do our job and keep this garden in order ('Keep law and form and due proportion'), the servant asks, when the garden of England ('our sea-wallèd garden') is being allowed to go to rack and ruin? By implication, the most important husbandman in the land (the king) is failing to set a good example, a point rendered explicit by the gardener's subsequent lines. The servant's comparison of the current state of England to an untilled, unkempt garden overrun by caterpillars gives vivid and pointed expression to his meaning. His own garden is, by contrast, a 'model' of good management ('firm estate').

---

[3] The period of social, political and intellectual developments that occurred in European civilization following the Middle Ages, along with a revival of interest in classical learning.

Things are clearly topsy-turvy in the world of the play: the rulers, not the servants, should be providing models. Sixteenth-century spectators would have been quick to pick up the weed and caterpillar images, and might well have applied them to their own times: Elizabeth's court in the 1590s was said to be plagued by idle parasites like the Members of Parliament Bushy, Green and Bagot – the 'caterpillars' of the commonwealth. The perceptive servant's words certainly highlight the knock-on effect of an unjust monarch: if the ruler is rotten everyone suffers, and only the timeservers thrive. Many among the original audiences would undoubtedly have sympathized and identified with this view from below of ineffectual government, voiced by a commoner (like themselves, perhaps).

In 2. 1, the noblemen Northumberland, Willoughby and Ross provide us with a similarly critical view from the higher ranks of society:

NORTHUMBERLAND   The King is not himself, but basely led
                 By flatterers.

(242–3)

ROSS   The commons hath he pilled with grievous taxes,
                 And quite lost their hearts.

(247–8)

WILLOUGHBY   And daily new exactions are devised,
                 As blanks, benevolences, and I wot not what.

(250–1)

NORTHUMBERLAND   More hath he spent in peace than they in wars.

(256)

WILLOUGHBY   The King's grown bankrupt like a broken man.

(258)

NORTHUMBERLAND   Reproach and dissolution hangeth over him.

(259)

ROSS   He hath not money for these Irish wars,
                 His burdenous taxations notwithstanding,
                 But by robbing of the banished Duke.

(260–2)

There seems to be nothing – murder, robbery, extortion, corruption, blasphemy – to which God's 'anointed' will not stoop, but the people most qualified to halt England's downward slide – Richard's princely uncles and the country's elder statesmen – have failed to take action, apparently paralysed by the king's 'divine right' to do as he pleases.

The playwright's characterization of York (2. 2. 109–15) as a dithering and inept politician – tugged this way and that by his divided loyalties and indecision – functions superbly in this play both to challenge the king's unlawful seizing of 'Hereford's rights' (202)[4] and to highlight Bolingbroke's trespass in bearing arms

---

[4] Henry Bolingbroke was Duke of Hereford.

against his sovereign, whom he is bound by 'oath' to obey. 'Hereford's rights' would have included both the special privileges granted to those of royal blood and rights of property, including money and land. The main thrust of this speech is that York does not know what to do, because he is in a dilemma that he cannot resolve and his conscience is torn. In fact, it is York's dilemma that lies at the heart of this play: whose 'right' is more right, the wronged subject's or the corrupt king's? In the end, York determines to 'remain as neuter' (2. 3. 158), to do nothing except fall back on God and let him settle the quarrel, which Bolingbroke eventually wins.

Northumberland is of distinctly firmer mettle, and it is his resolve to see his type of justice carried out and to back Bolingbroke's 'rights' that largely secures Richard's overthrow. He acts as a sort of vocal foil to the Bishop of Carlisle in the deposition scene and throughout the play. Carlisle stands for divine right and royal absolutism, whilst Northumberland upholds the rights of the Commons (the public) and the law of the land. Thus, it is Northumberland who has the bishop peremptorily charged with treason after his speech that asks, 'What subject can give sentence on his king?' (4. 1. 112), and it is he who demands of the king:

> ... that you read
> These accusations and these grievous crimes
> Committed by your person and your followers
> Against the state and profit of this land.

> (4. 1. 213–15)

But is Richard 'worthily deposed', as Northumberland desires 'the souls of men' (their consciences) to believe (216–17)?

The dividing line in the debate that runs through *Richard II*, and is thrown into relief by these two characters, is whether one should or should not believe in anointed kingship – the divine, hereditary and absolute right of a monarch to rule, come what may. Modern spectators like ourselves are unlikely to believe in it, but if we put ourselves in the shoes of sixteenth-century theatregoers, we can imagine the unease aroused by Northumberland's words and by the spectacle of an anointed monarch being overthrown, and then murdered. If we think about it a little further, some among the play's original audiences would have lived to see a real-life 'anointed' king, Charles I, tried for his 'excesses' and crimes against the people, deposed and subsequently decapitated on the stage of a scaffold in 1649. The spectators at that bloody event would undoubtedly have been searching their consciences in a similar, but inevitably more pressing, way than Shakespeare's play demanded of its viewers, in an effort to determine whether true justice had been enacted, as the Parliamentarians alleged. In fact, the confrontation between two theories of kingship – one based on inherited right and the other on office – which is most fully developed in *Richard II* through the roles of the two kings and their spokesmen, Carlisle and Northumberland, was destined to remain centre stage in political discussions right through to the dispute between Royalists and Cromwellians in the later stages of the English Civil War.[5] As Sir John Strangeways, a Royalist Member of Parliament imprisoned in the Tower of London, put it in 1647: 'We maintayne that the king is king by inhaerent birth-right; they say his kingly power is an office upon trust' (Russell, 1990, p.131).

---

[5] The wars between Parliamentarians and Royalists lasted from 1642 to 1651. After the execution of Charles I in 1649, the Parliamentarians, led by Oliver Cromwell, fought and overcame the supporters of Charles II, and a Commonwealth was established when the monarch fled abroad.

With hindsight, we can see that Shakespeare's *Richard II* is shot through with flashes of the most heated political argument of his day: what could and should one do with a monarch deemed unjust, unlawful and ineffectual? In order better to understand these debates, and the location of *Richard II* within them, it is helpful to turn the pages of the most popular books of political discussion in the sixteenth century: advice books or 'mirrors' for princes.

Political 'mirrors' and Richard II

Political 'mirrors' were much admired by humanist scholars, because they derived from ancient Greek and Roman models, and humanists wrote such texts in abundance. Undoubtedly the most famous in northern Europe, the one that triggered controversies over kingship in England and was fingered by well-to-do schoolboys up and down the land, was Erasmus of Rotterdam's *The Education of a Christian Prince* (1516). The pedagogue Laurence Humphrey pronounced this to be obligatory reading for the children of noblemen, and the statesman and scholar Sir Thomas Elyot developed his advice book – *The Book Named the Governor* (1531), which was the most popular English 'mirror' – from Erasmus's model. It is important to remember that texts do not exist in hermetically sealed isolation from one another or from the culture that produced them; rather, they are 'porous' structures, which communicate with other texts and with the 'complex network of institutions, practices, and beliefs that constitute the culture as a whole' (Greenblatt, 1982, p.6). Echoes of both Erasmus's and Elyot's volumes of instruction for young governors can be found in Shakespeare's history plays, most notably *Richard II*. This, in its turn, as a tragical history of an illustrious man, constituted an illuminating 'mirror' for those in power. These texts might thus be said to coexist in an intertextual 'network'. No wonder the imagery of mirror and perspective is used so extensively in *Richard II*: it seems to draw attention wittily to the serious role of the 'mirror' for rulers, and to the play's allusions to other textual 'mirrors'.

What were these allusions? Let us look briefly at the main political thrust and stylistic techniques of Erasmus's advice book. Erasmus wrote *The Education of a Christian Prince* in 1516, shortly before he became tutor to the future King Charles V of France. As he confided in a letter to his English friend, the statesman and scholar Sir Thomas More, he was deeply disillusioned and dismayed by the behaviour of Europe's princes, who seemed to be generally prone to folly, bordering for the most part on tyranny, which was responsible for the costly wars currently tearing Christendom apart (Erasmus, 1968 edn, p.27). Erasmus's unparalleled stature as a philosopher and educator of future monarchs gave him the authority to challenge the status quo, and even to upbraid and condemn Europe's most reprehensible princes. *The Education of a Christian Prince* remorselessly dissects the meaning of kingship, employing analogies from medicine, gardening and the theatre (as Shakespeare's *Richard II* does), to illustrate its argument and drive its message home. It argues that Europe's princes have become 'plagues to the world' (ibid., p.157), milking their subjects for taxes in order to satisfy their excessive appetites. It repeatedly laments that the behaviour of some princes has deteriorated to such a degree that the ideas of 'good man' and 'prince' seem to have become 'the very antithesis of one another' (ibid., p.189). Heavily imbued with the philosophy of Plato's *Republic*,[6] Erasmus's treatise insists that only those of the highest moral

---

[6] *The Republic* explores in dialogue form the concept of justice and its fulfilment in society, in which rules are allocated to men in one of three classes corresponding to rationality, appetite and spirit.

integrity, with their bodily passions under the control of reason, who put the interests of their subjects and the state before their own pleasures, are fit to govern. Others are 'sham' princes – actors decked out in symbolic regalia – and they should resign (ibid., p.152). Erasmus challenges his princely protégés as they scrutinize themselves in his uncompromising mirror: 'If these conditions are not to your liking, why do you desire the burden of ruling? Or if you inherited this authority, why do you not yield it to another?' (ibid., p.182). He warns that those who fail to do so and who go on to make a 'farce' of 'the laws of Christ', vaunting their power 'under the glory of Christ as a pretext', will be severely punished by God: 'There is but one death for all – beggars and kings alike. But the judgement after death is not the same for all. None are dealt with more severely than the powerful' (ibid., p.154). (These are among the very things upon which Shakespeare's Richard II anxiously ruminates in his prison cell (5. 5. 1–42).) Erasmus had no time for ineffectual and greedy princes, who, like Richard II and later Tudor and Stuart monarchs, shored up their crumbling power bases with claims to divinity, threats of divine retribution, symbolic ornaments and lavish spectacle:

> If a necklace, a scepter, royal purple robes, a train of attendants are all that make a king, what is it that distinguishes a real king from the actor? It is the spirit befitting a prince ... The crown, the scepter, the royal robes ... are all marks or symbols of good qualities in a good prince; in a bad one, they are accusations of vice.
>
> (Ibid., p.152)

Elyot's English 'mirror' was rather more guarded in its approach, avoiding the sticky and dangerous topic of tyrannical monarchs (the Tudors did not hesitate to decapitate their critics). Even Elyot's treatise, though, warns its governor that the 'weighty or heavy cloak' of authority will 'shortly be taken of him that did put it thee, if thou use it negligently', maintaining that rulers were first and foremost men, with no more of 'the dew of heaven, or the brightness of the sun, than any other person' (1962 edn, p.165). This, you may recall, is the crucial lesson Richard II learns a little too late, and his 'cares' – the burden of authority – are indeed taken from him. He is effectively coerced into yielding his authority to another. Nevertheless, I would argue, Shakespeare's play leaves us wondering whether Richard really did have some 'dew of heaven' about him: 'plagues' of unrest did follow his deposition, after all.

The political thrust of these early-sixteenth-century 'mirrors', which emphasized the accountability of kingship, was developed by later humanist theorists, most notably George Buchanan, one-time tutor to James VI of Scotland (later James I of England). It was Buchanan's radical political philosophy that was so influential among Puritans in the period leading up to and during the English Civil War. Buchanan's treatise, entitled *De Jure Regni Apud Scotos* (*The Powers of the Crown in Scotland*, 1579), argues in true republican style that 'authority resides with those persons in whom the people, or the majority of the people, have vested it' (1949 edn, p.133), and since 'the whole people is the source of the law' (ibid., p.130), the public might 'hold the ruler accountable' (ibid., p.131). Like Erasmus, Buchanan stressed the dual nature of kingship: 'the ruler is not a king only, but is as well, a man ... He is, in fact, an animal' (ibid., p.56). Taking things a step further in the direction of regicide, he proceeded to justify the deposition of 'beastly' rulers, even advocating 'vengeance on an arrogant and worthless tyrant' (ibid., p.122). Buchanan's treatise was banned as subversive in England, but it still seems to have achieved considerable circulation. We know, for example, that Ben Jonson possessed a copy; its ideas were probably fairly common currency in the 1590s. Can echoes of these ideas be heard in *Richard II*? The voice of Northumberland surely resonates with Buchanan's, and is pitched against that of Carlisle – the voice of the English Church and of Tudor political orthodoxy. Indeed, the voices of Tudor orthodoxy and heterodoxy seem to clash throughout *Richard II*, continuously competing for space and authority.

Is Richard 'worthily deposed'?

Let us now move on to consider the crucial issue of whether Richard is 'worthily deposed', as Northumberland wishes the 'souls of men' to believe (4. 1. 216–17). If we could respond to this with certainty, on the basis of the textual evidence alone, we would also know the answer to the question that has preoccupied so many critics of the play this century: on which side of the political fence did Shakespeare sit? Did he support divine right and royal power at whatever cost, or did he countenance the idea of deposition in certain circumstances? The trouble is, the text defies such clear-cut approaches: its author's own perspective on deposition is carefully obscured from view. The script is crafted with extraordinary skill to manipulate its readers' minds and emotions this way and that, for and against Richard's and Bolingbroke's conflicting claims to the title of king. Episodes such as Gaunt's deathbed scene (2. 1) and the one prior to that (1. 4), in which Richard exposes his worst qualities in company with Green, Bagot and the Duke of Aumerle (his cousin), alienate spectators from Richard. But other theatrical strategies, such as the portrayal of Queen Isabel's unwavering devotion to her husband and Richard's moving soliloquy prior to his murder, tend to sway the audience in the opposite direction. Furthermore, the stately rhetoric of the court scenes is repeatedly undercut by cynical reflections and soliloquies, which continually destabilize the meaning of the play. (Look again, for example, at Richard's words in 1. 3. 123–37, and then at his lines in the subsequent scene, 1. 4. 19–35.) Sometimes, too, God seems to be on Bolingbroke's side – Richard's Welsh supporters disperse because of unpropitious portents from heaven – and at others on Richard's: as we have noted, 'plagues', of sorts, did follow in the wake of his dethroning, as history confirms.

The play prompts the audience to consider (in the manner of Erasmus's political 'mirror') whether kingship resides in an anointed body and a hereditary name supported by the outer trappings of majesty (the crown and sceptre), or in an ordinary man's body, a man who commands the support of the Commons to perform an office burdened with care. It poses these important questions but it does not resolve them, for ultimately it refuses to endorse completely any of its competing voices. Even the two kings seem rather less than certain, at times, which of them is the legitimate monarch. Thus, in an angry outburst, Richard exclaims: 'God save the King, although I be not he. / And yet Amen, if heaven do think him me' (4. 1. 165–6). A little later, he confesses that he knows 'not now what name' to call himself and questions 'if' his word is 'sterling yet in England' (249, 254). His riddling words force the audience to confront their own bewilderment and misgivings about this issue. *Richard II* is, in this sense, an 'open' text. Readers can only consult their own consciences for answers, since the playwright does not provide any.

Why should Shakespeare's play have been so evasive? It obviously made sense for the writer to camouflage his own viewpoint, both to escape censorship and to avoid incurring the wrath of Elizabeth I's government, but it was also a clever artistic strategy. For it is surely more pleasurable and satisfying to grapple with ideas and uncertainties for oneself than to be told directly what to think.

By now you may well be disagreeing with me strongly about the meaning of this play. It is very likely that you have reached a decision about whether Richard is 'worthily deposed', and I have been suggesting that no such decision can be reached on the basis of the text of the play. If you have seen *Richard II* staged, you have probably witnessed one of the two monarchs – the anointed or the Commons' choice – being promoted over the other: one view of monarchy being affirmed and the other undermined. Whilst the meaning of drama ultimately resides in the production and in the individual spectator's responses to it, the meaning of a script on a page resides in the words, their arrangement on the page, and in the readers' imaginings. In the case of this text, which is considered to be unusually close to Shakespeare's manuscript, the words, and the events constructed out of them, are inconclusive. Given this, your response to my question will have been shaped (and quite appropriately so) by things extraneous to the text: by your imagination, your values and beliefs, and possibly, too, by your memory.

The meaning of the deposition scene

In order to test this point, let us scrutinize more closely the important issue of dramatic meaning. Reread the most dramatically spectacular episode of the play – the Parliament scene – from 4. 1. 98 to the end of Act 4. **Does anything in the text of the play – the words on the page in front of you – confirm whether or not Richard is 'worthily deposed'?**

This episode, as it appears on the page, is carefully poised to preclude any easy pronouncements about whether Richard is 'worthily deposed'. The audience knows that the king has committed 'crimes', but according to orthodox Tudor political thought even tyrannical behaviour on the part of a monarch did not sanction rebellion against God's anointed. The claims of the two kings and the voices of their supporters seem to be equally balanced against one another, and both monarchs are 'traitors' implicated in sins against God: Richard because he has 'unkinged' (210) his own anointed body and Bolingbroke because he has usurped the authority of God's deputy. The well and water imagery works to reinforce this sense of equipoise – as one king rises, the other king falls. The skilfully weighted lines interspersed throughout the Parliament scene (for example, 'On this side my hand, on that side thine' and 'Your cares set up do not pluck my cares down' (173, 185)) add to this sense of symmetry and equally matched 'rights'. Indeed, from its inception with York's opening words (98–101), the unkinging episode raises serious questions about whether Richard has been deposed at all, or whether he has in fact 'yielded' and willingly 'resigned' his sceptre to his royal cousin.

It is as if this unworthy monarch, steeped in his Erasmus (who was obligatory reading for noblemen and royalty in Shakespeare's day), has actually decided to heed that 'mirror's' advice, and hence to 'yield' his authority to another, better man. This amounts to shrewd and extremely witty dramaturgy: by planting the seeds of sixteenth-century debate about kingship in the fertile soil of medieval history, the play brings vividly to life for its Elizabethan audience the most contentious political issues of the Renaissance. As this scene confirms, Richard is rather partial to looking at himself in mirrors, and he does appear to 'undo' (4. 1. 193) himself in a very stagey, spectacular manner, which resonates with passages from *The Education of a Christian Prince*. But, as Richard's words contrive to suggest, there are problems about Erasmus's advice: can an anointed monarch ever really unking himself? Whilst God's deputy might 'undeck the pompous body of a king' (240) – divest himself of the external props of majesty, the crown and the sceptre – he cannot, perhaps, 'wash away [the] balm' (197) or the 'substance' of kingship, which 'lies all within' (285), with its cares and sorrows. This episode raises the knotty issues surrounding kingship and deposition, but it does not resolve them. Directors of this play can, however, impose their own resolutions, and very frequently they do.

A director wanting to create a version of this scene that would encourage audiences to imagine that divine right was inviolable, and that Richard was unworthily deposed, would inevitably begin with the casting and portrayal of the characters of the two kings. An 'anointed' Richard would need to attain a lofty, tragic stature in this scene, one that conveyed his special God-given credentials for the role, as well as his profound, martyr-like suffering under the destructive influence of the watching 'Pilates' and 'Judases'. Under the direction of David Giles (BBC, 1979), Derek Jacobi portrayed a masterful Richard of this type (Figure 11). His voice was sonorous and conveyed authority, befitting a monarch and a gifted rhetorician–poet, yet it quivered with emotion at crucial points and projected a Christ-like humility too. Jacobi's monarch oozed nobility and sincerity, and he appeared to cry real tears brought on by emotional pain that seemed to arise from deep within his soul. His tortured facial expressions and bodily gestures further worked to suggest a Richard who was undergoing spiritual renewal, growing through his suffering, reaching a new understanding of his old self and his tragic mistakes. His angry outbursts appeared to be directed as much against himself – his previous follies and crimes – as against his adversaries. Jacobi's Richard was attired quite simply – no visible excesses now. When he called for the mirror to peruse his new self, his was definitely not a flattering glass (mirrors could symbolize narcissistic self-love in the Renaissance), but rather a glass of self-awareness (mirrors could symbolize this too), enabling him to reach an enhanced understanding of deeper, inner truths. The entire episode conveyed the self-questioning and soul-searching of a man carried away with emotion and largely oblivious to onlookers: introspection ('turning his eyes upon himself') as opposed to exhibitionism.

By contrast, Bolingbroke (Jon Finch) in this production fitted the label of 'conveyer' (one who steals) attached to him by Richard (4. 1. 307). His demeanour suggested haughtiness. He was clad in an elaborate black velvet costume decorated with gold and silver thread, and he proclaimed 'In God's name I'll ascend the regal throne' (104) rather too self-righteously at York's invitation. He physically ascended to sit above Richard throughout most of the scene on a bulky throne on a raised dais, appearing to lord it over the overthrown monarch. He showed no mercy towards his suffering cousin and exhibited no sense of regret about his own actions, although a certain embarrassment was suggested by his inability to look his cousin in the face. He also appeared to flinch, as I recall, when the camera zoomed in on him after Richard's speech, which pronounces him 'not greatly good' (253). When Jacobi/Richard branded Bolingbroke's henchmen 'Pilates' and passionately screamed, 'water cannot wash away your sin' (230, 232) and 'Conveyers are you all, / That rise thus nimbly by a true king's fall' (307–8), close-up shots of York writhing with shame could only have served to convince viewers that they were watching a truly noble monarch, who had been bullied into renouncing his rightful title and authority. David Warner's production of *Richard II* in 1962 at Stratford-upon-Avon went even farther than this in shaping a vision of an 'anointed' monarch, ultimately creating a martyr out of Richard. His king appeared to undergo

Figure 11   *Derek Jacobi as Richard II in the BBC production directed by David Giles, 1979. Photo: BBC.*

a spiritual transformation, gradually evolving from a monarch of vanity and guile to become a tall, white-robed, Christ-like figure.

A director who desired to persuade spectators that the king was worthily deposed might fashion his 'unjust' Richard as petty, malicious and full of self-pity: as an immature personality prone to temper-tantrums, tears and histrionics, and incapable of spiritual growth. This king would be a witty juggler with words, a mocking and insincere riddler, whose games with language would be displayed in their most consummate form in the mirror scene. His would definitely be a flattering glass, dashed upon the ground in a petulant fit of rage. In his 'Say that again' speech (4. 1. 283–94) to Bolingbroke (whose words have just implied that Richard's display of sorrow is mere show), his tone would be disdainful and recalcitrant, and he would appear to be attempting merely to score points in a kind of witty one-upmanship. This may sound rather implausible, but Michael Pennington, directed by Michael Bogdanov (ESC, 1989), styled just such a Richard out of the role, and his performance was compelling and not without humour (Figure 12). The spiteful pronouncements of this egocentric king of excess splashed spittle in his opponents' faces, and he was seen to grin at inappropriate moments. Arrogance was his hallmark, and his fussy, expensive clothing conveyed his preoccupation with fashion and ostentation. Historically, this was, after all, a monarch who loved costly finery and who is credited with having introduced the handkerchief to England. Pennington's Richard, absorbed in externals, clung tenaciously onto his crown and sceptre – the props of majesty – while vocally proffering them to Bolingbroke, clearly his despised and envied cousin.

In pronounced contrast to the first part of the twentieth century, the latter half has seen several unsentimental, unsympathetic depictions of Richard. Michael Redgrave's portrayal of the outgoing king (Stratford, 1951) made him redolent of cruelty and envy, whilst Ian Richardson (Stratford, 1973) depicted him as dangerous, unpredictable and cunning. At the American Shakespeare Festival in 1962, where he was portrayed as an unsavoury gangster lacking the shrewdness and strength essential to the success of his enterprise, Richard definitely reached an all-time low.

Michael Cronin's Bolingbroke, playing opposite Michael Pennington in the ESC's 1989 production, was not much more likeable than his cousin. Strangely, actors hardly ever make something likeable out of Bolingbroke. Indeed, ruthless and unpleasant Bolingbrokes have dominated the stage history of the play in the twentieth century. However, under the direction of Deborah Warner (The Cottesloe, Royal National Theatre, 1995), David Threlfall reversed this trend by fashioning a masterful and seemingly just usurper out of the role – one who might well have helped to convince audiences that Fiona Shaw's boyish, immature Richard was 'worthily deposed' (Figure 13). Threlfall's Bolingbroke appeared noble, sincere and wise, as well as disturbed by the usurpation that duty to his country had compelled him to undertake. He nevertheless seemed calm, in control and determined, but not proud or self-motivated: a man fit for 'office'. This Bolingbroke was, notably and refreshingly, as accomplished a versifier as his cousin. In fact, Bolingbroke's speeches outside this scene do suggest this attribute, which directors usually play down (see, for example, 1. 3. 138–41 and 254–66).

Figure 12 *Michael Pennington as Richard II in the English Shakespeare Company production directed by Michael Bogdanov, 1989. Photo: Laurence Burns.*

The fact is that the Shakespearean text of this scene – the words on the page – supports both the pro-Lancastrian and the anti-Lancastrian interpretation of the famous 'deposition' episode. As well as paying careful attention to the balance of voices and structures in *Richard II*, Shakespeare had an extraordinary ability to write into the play ambiguities and paradoxes, which ultimately allow contradictory interpretations. Consider, for example, Bolingbroke's words, 'So we shall proceed without suspicion' (4. 1. 147–8). The tone of the actor's voice, where he places stresses, his demeanour and gestures are crucial to the import and impact of the line: to whether the audience is ultimately persuaded that he is sincere and just or an ambitious, self-serving politician.

Figure 13   *Fiona Shaw as Richard II and David Threlfall as Bolingbroke in the Royal National Theatre production directed by Deborah Warner, 1995. Photo: by courtesy of Neil Libbert.*

Mirrors, perspectives and theatrical meaning

It is the mirror episode, however, that contains the prime examples of the play at its most equivocal and enigmatic. As anyone who has lingered among the Renaissance paintings in the National Gallery or the Portrait Gallery in London will be aware, our educated ancestors were extremely fond of symbols and riddles, which often leave modern spectators feeling ignorant and frustrated. Just as twentieth-century viewers of the paintings who are not specialists in the period need to turn to the descriptions alongside the paintings to make any sense of them, so modern readers of *Richard II* must rely on the glossary to unravel the symbolism associated with mirrors in the Renaissance.

For example, the painting *The Ambassadors* by Hans Holbein (Figure 14), which was mentioned in Chapter 1, shows two richly costumed men gazing out at the viewer. They are leaning on a tall bench, which is littered with curious objects including books, globes of the world, and arithmetical and musical instruments. In order to discern the distorted, shadowy object between their feet – which the painting invites us to do – the viewer must move around, observing the painting from different angles, until at last, when viewed 'awry', that is, from an oblique position, a skull suddenly comes into focus. What does it all mean? Educated Elizabethans would undoubtedly have discovered a religious lesson in the 'awry' perspective. The death's head or *memento mori*[7] would remind them that in their pursuit of worldly ambition (the achievements of which are symbolized by the objects on the bench), and like the two worthy ambassadors, they must not lose sight of more enduring, but less immediately discernible, spiritual goals and truths. In the sixteenth century, striving to see from different angles (as Holbein's painting demands, and *Richard II* continuously badgers its spectators to do) had well-established religious associations. Similarly, 'glasses' or mirrors were by their very nature associated with multiple and complex perspectives, because they can distort the truth (like a fairground mirror) or they can present a true likeness.

Now look again at the beginning of an earlier scene, 2. 2, which is preoccupied with perspectives, and try to make sense of the perplexing conversation between the queen and Bushy. What is the gist of their exchange?

In this scene, Queen Isabel is expressing shadowy anxieties and forebodings about the future. Bushy uses imagery associated with perspectives to try to nullify her misgivings (14–24): he suggests that looking 'awry' has brought these troubled thoughts into focus; if she had gazed head on ('rightly') through her 'blinding tears', she would have discerned 'nothing but confusion' – 'as it is'. Almost immediately, however, Bushy's 'centric' view is undermined: the queen's intuitive, crooked gaze, which Bushy has sought to belittle, bears fruit, in the shape of Green's announcement. Isabel's premonition of 'nothing', which has caused her to tremble with fear, *is* something, namely Bolingbroke. Her fears turn out to be justified: perceiving things 'awry' does seem to be associated with seeing more truly in this play.

Elizabethan spectators of *Richard II* would have been well aware that they were being presented with a puzzle – a struggle for the meaning of true kingship, which necessitated looking from all angles and grappling with shadows beneath the surface of the play. Throughout the deposition scene, for example, the central

---

[7] Latin for 'reminder of death'.

Figure 14 *Hans Holbein the Younger,* The Ambassadors, *1553, oil on oak, 207 x 209.5 cm, National Gallery, London. Reproduced by permission of the Trustees of the National Gallery.*

problem the audience must reflect on is this: is the Richard they are watching really sorrowful and repentant and capable of spiritual renewal (and therefore perhaps unworthily deposed), or is his grief insincere and insubstantial – a mere show – like his empty words and his claims to divinity? Similarly, they must decide whether Bolingbroke is honest or a hypocrite. Does he depose Richard for 'just' reasons, with the interest of the Commons to the fore, or is he an ambitious, self-seeking contender for the throne – an 'unjust' usurper?

As we have seen, the characterization of the two lead roles in *Richard II* will shape the audience's responses. How the actor playing Richard uses his voice, his expressions and gestures, how he is dressed and where he is positioned on the stage in relation to Bolingbroke are crucial, and the same goes for Bolingbroke. But other dramatic structures are important, too, and some of these reside in the text of the play itself.

Can you think, for example, of any episodes earlier in the play that would conflict with the portrayal of Richard in the deposition scene as anointed and Christ-like in his suffering?

Act 1, Scene 4 is an obvious problem: Richard's speeches here confirm that he is a selfish hypocrite, and – importantly – a monarch who takes God's name in vain. Then there is Gaunt's moving deathbed scene (2. 1), in which he seems to have the measure of his disastrous princely nephew. These two episodes, but particularly 1. 4, seem to militate against a view of Richard as a martyr.

Directors determined to purvey a view of the play as underpinning Tudor orthodoxy, however, can and do find ways round such disturbing obstacles to a coherent vision. Gaunt can be portrayed as a foolish old man raging at the young while dying, and whole speeches that incriminate Richard and alienate the audience from him can be cut from 1. 4 and elsewhere. Directors and actors often work hard against both the grain of the Shakespearean text and the descriptions of Henry IV in sixteenth-century histories to fashion a dislikeable, ambitious and prosaic Bolingbroke out of the role. This inevitably increases Richard's stature and strengthens his claim to be the 'true' king.

So far, we have seen that the script and the reader's and/or director's beliefs and imagination, together with memories of past performances and their realization on the stage, all play a part in determining what a play means. However, we have as yet uncovered nothing that reveals why *Richard II* appears to have meant something subversive around 1601 and incurred the wrath of Elizabeth I. It did not, after all, depict a *Tudor* monarch behaving badly – or did it? Let us pursue this further by focusing on the meaning of *Richard II* in the closing years of Elizabeth I's reign.

Why was Richard II *considered subversive in 1601?*

> The idea of the developments of the closing years of Elizabeth's reign as providing an appropriate background of national confidence, strength and unity to [the] stupendous cultural achievements no longer finds much favour with historians, most of whom now see this as a time of economic crisis, dislocation and hardship, financial bankruptcy, political disintegration, declining political morality and burgeoning corruption: an age in which things turned terribly sour.

> (Ashton, 1984, p.180)

Far from being a haven of peace and contentment in the 1590s, England – that 'other Eden, demi-paradise' (2. 1. 42) – must have seemed to many Elizabethans to have been growing to resemble the gardener's man's account in *Richard II* of an untended garden with 'knots disordered', 'Swarming with caterpillars' and choked with weeds (3. 4. 44–8). Things had, as Robert Ashton comments, 'turned terribly sour'. The queen's godson, Sir John Harington, described the last decade of Elizabeth's reign as a time when 'malcontents' abounded in city and country, complaining that 'a few favorites gett all, that the nobilitie is depressed, the Clergy pilled and contemned, forraine invasions expected, the treasure at home exhausted, the coyne in Ireland imbased, the gold of England transported, exactions doubled and trebled' (Albright, 1927, p.694). Harington laid particular emphasis on the problem of the Irish expenses,[8] unguardedly lamenting the stratagems the queen found herself embroiled in, such as borrowing 'coyne of hir poore subjectes in England without

---

[8] A major rebellion had broken out in Ulster in 1595, and in 1599 Elizabeth sent a large army to deal with it. This was a costly enterprise.

purpose ever to pay it agayne' (ibid., p.691). Sources close to Elizabeth had also complained as early as the mid-1570s about her 'letting of the realme to farme', and, as an extortionate 'landlorde', alienating the hearts of her subjects (ibid., pp.710–11). In fact, the charges against Elizabeth had grown unsettlingly close to those used to oust her royal forebear, Richard II, from the throne.

Papers that survive from this period reveal that Elizabeth Tudor was being likened in some circles to her troublesome ancestor. This was potentially disastrous for the queen, because Richard II, according to the Tudor chronicles, was the epitome of tyrannical majesty. As Holinshed's *Chronicles* records: 'He ... beganne to rule by will more than by reason, threatning deathe to eche that obeyed not his inordinate desires' (1577, p.1098). Elizabeth's nearest kinsman, Henry Carey, saw fit to apply the analogy when the Earl of Leicester's power was at its height and he felt neglected and passed over by his monarch: he complained, 'I was never one of Richard II's men' (Albright, 1927, p.691). Alluding to Richard II had clearly become an indirect way of casting aspersions on the queen.

In the light of such comments, we should perhaps wonder whether it was not without a certain amount of trepidation that Shakespeare staged a play about Richard II in the 1590s, particularly a play that assailed Richard with the same accusations as those being levelled against Elizabeth in the latter years of her reign. These emphasized the monarch's failure to produce an heir (a very touchy subject for the childless queen) and likened England to a disordered garden. The latter might well have been a coded way – for those in the know – of criticizing Elizabeth's government, since the queen was particularly fond of portraits that depicted her standing in front of well-ordered knot gardens (for example, a portrait of Elizabeth I, *c*.1585, attributed to Marcus Gheeraerts and now in Wellbeck Abbey), symbolic of the peaceful, harmonious world of Tudor England under her rule.

Any criticisms of the queen's administration had to be made in indirect and camouflaged ways. In fact, they demanded that the reader of a text or spectator of a play search among the oblique, shadowy perspectives for truths. Elizabeth's government and the English Church, of which she was the head, sought through various forms of propaganda, such as the Sunday Homilies, royal pronouncements and symbolic portraits of the queen, to disseminate the belief that the Tudors were God's deputies and under his divine protection, and that they had brought order and harmony to the nation. We might call this the 'centric', or orthodox, viewpoint. The reality of what Tudor subjects felt and experienced probably differed considerably from this, especially at the turn of the seventeenth century. There is evidence of growing dissatisfaction with the Tudors' increasingly absolutist styles of government in the course of the sixteenth century. Furthermore, like Richard II, Henry VIII and Elizabeth I suffered the 'guilt of kindred blood' (think of the murdered Duke of Gloucester and the decapitated queens Anne Boleyn and Mary Queen of Scots), and like him they found mechanisms for extorting money unlawfully from their subjects, and for draining the state's coffers. Their administrations, like that of Richard, verged on tyranny.

In the mid-1590s, when the play was first staged, the analogy between Richard II and Elizabeth I appears to have been covert enough and insufficiently understood by the public at large to prevent the play being proscribed. Notably and importantly, though, all the Quartos of *Richard II* published in Elizabeth's lifetime omitted the deposition scene, suggesting that the most controversial episode had been censored.

By 1601, however, something else had given the story of Richard and Bolingbroke a particularly seditious slant: it had become entangled in the Earl of Essex's own propaganda exercise, which was intended to pave the way for a major coup against Elizabeth I's government. Capitalizing on the ageing queen's unpopularity and her failure to name a successor – which was raising anxieties about a Spanish, Roman Catholic invasion – this ambitious nobleman, who had a strong popular and élite following, had been fashioning himself as the flower of the gentry of England and a hero of the Protestant, anti-Spanish cause. Furthermore, as a descendant of Thomas of Woodstock (the murdered Duke of Gloucester), he had a solid blood-claim to the English throne and, in fact, shared the noble lineage of Bolingbroke. It would appear that, some years before his attempt to oust Elizabeth from the throne, Essex had been shaping himself as a just usurper in the Bolingbroke mould, an upholder of the people's rights and of the law, while supporting characterizations of his monarch as a fickle Richard II type.

Essex's followers, among them the historian Sir John Hayward, were obviously keen to help disseminate these myths, and the latter assisted by writing a book entitled *The Life and Raigne of King Henrie the Fourth*, which was published in 1599. It proved immensely popular, selling 600 copies within the first three weeks, but its appearance caused its author to be peremptorily incarcerated in the Tower of London. Like Shakespeare's *Richard II*, this history was an equivocal and contradictory tale of the two kings, but, according to the queen's lawyers, its dedicatory epistle to Essex rendered the history 'treasonable'. Written in a particularly tortuous style of Latin (undoubtedly to evade the censors), the epistle was lavish in its praise of Essex and predicted a glorious future for him, explicitly drawing parallels between him and Bolingbroke and shockingly describing the usurper as 'our beloved Henry' (1642 edn, sig. A3r). Further incriminating the text in the events it foreshadowed, the preface to the reader went on to assert how 'Histories' (such as, by implication, the one to follow) provided precepts and 'lively patterns, both for private directions and for affayres of state' (ibid.). In essence, Bolingbroke the deposer is made to prefigure Essex in this work, which represents the usurper as a chivalric, popular hero, and as the people's choice to replace 'dissolute and uncontrouled' Richard (ibid., pp.117 and 130).

Hayward's history had, therefore, served to render any history of Richard and Bolingbroke in the period around 1600 highly suspect: the Richard–Elizabeth parallel was now widely understood, especially by the authorities. When Essex's supporters asked Shakespeare's company to perform *Richard II* on the eve of their rebellion against the government, they were effectively implicating the Lord Chamberlain's Men in their insurrection. This is why, at the trial of Essex and his fellow conspirators some months later, a representative of the players found himself in the dock being cross-questioned by her majesty's lawyers. Essex's attempted coup had proved a disastrous failure, and he and many of his fellows were condemned to death. In the event, none of Shakespeare's company was severely punished. For the time being, though, history plays of the existing type ground to a halt, and no English history could be published without special authority from the Privy Council.

During the English Civil War, the history of Richard II (along with that of Edward II) was again called into play, this time by Charles I's deposers. The following is an extract from a pamphlet, *The People Informed of their Oppressors* (1648), produced by the Parliamentary propagandists:

> Upon the deposing of these two kings [Richard II and Edward II], I shall make this observation, that it pleased God to place in their Thrones (as a sure signe of his approbation) two such Princes, as were not else in all Europe to be found; Edward the third, and Henry the fourth, the latter of which (besides the great advantage that His reign brought to the kingdom in general) was the happy Father of Henry the fifth, the most pious and most glorious King, that ever swayed the English Scepter. That kings may be deposed, is cleer by the forementioned precedent, ... precedents are law.

> (Anon., 1648, p.8)

The happy outcome of Richard's deposition – construed as the eventual enthronement of Henry V, 'The most pious and most glorious king, that ever swayed the English Scepter' – was used to justify the deposition and beheading of Charles I. God had smiled on England after Richard's deposition, and he might do so again. There are many polemical pamphlets of this kind from the 1640s that use the history of Richard to make the same point – that God was on the side of the just deposer. It is small wonder that, after the Restoration of the monarchy, Charles II proclaimed Shakespeare's *Richard II* subversive and banned its staging. The play was again censored when there were attempts to revive it in the politically turbulent 1680s, which culminated in the deposition of James II and which sounded the death knell of royal absolutism. The circumstances surrounding the play, and its stage history – its performance on the eve of a rebellion against a monarch – appear to have given its meaning a powerful subversive charge.

Playing majesty: mock kings and lords of misrule

However, there is yet more to theatrical meaning than this: acting styles and generic expectations (expectations based on the kind of art being presented) profoundly influence an audience's understanding of a play. Let us consider the latter point first by addressing the following questions. How formal and serious a play is *Richard II*? Where is the comedy alluded to at the start of this chapter?

Richard II has been repeatedly described in the twentieth century as one of the most stately and formal of Shakespeare's plays. Many critics and theatrical directors have decided that the play contains almost no comedy, and there are certainly no comical subplots involving 'low-life' characters, which we find in many of Shakespeare's tragedies. Yet there is comedy if we look for the form of popular humour that our Elizabethan forebears enjoyed – festive comedy of the carnival type. The trouble is that this source of laughter has largely disappeared from our culture and consequently it is difficult for modern readers both to locate carnival forms, and to understand them, without help. Fortunately, the scholarship undertaken by cultural historians in the last 20 years or so has served to alert us to the presence of this rich source of folk humour in English Renaissance drama. **Can you detect any signs of the carnival spirit and laughter that were discussed in relation to *A Midsummer Night's Dream*?**

The festive spirit of laughter is most apparent in this play in the scene that portrays the York family engaging in a farcical parody of kneeling and begging pardon from the new king (5. 3). Bolingbroke's theatrically self-conscious lines highlight the intentional comedy of this interlude: 'Our scene is altered from a serious thing, / And now changed to "The Beggar and the King"' (77–8). It is as if the playwright is determined to make the audience recognize and laugh at this burlesque of lordship, this sending up of the rituals associated with nobility and majesty. The same effect – of making greatness and its codes appear ridiculous – is achieved by the gage-throwing scene (4. 1), in which one by one the petty feudal lords add their gauntlets of 'valour' to a veritable heap piling up on the stage floor. The ludicrousness of the spectacle is underpinned by the language: 'There is my gage, Aumerle, in gage to thine' (33).

With its mock kings and lords of misrule, its mock tournament (described by Mowbray as 'This feast of battle with mine adversary' (1. 3. 92)), its crowning and uncrowning, and its cyclical depiction of fortune – as one king rises the other king falls ('From Richard's night, to Bolingbroke's fair day' (3. 2. 214)) – *Richard II* is riddled with the forms and language, and infused with the mocking spirit, of carnival (Bristol, 1985). Elected mock kings or lords of misrule led the celebrations during holiday festivals, replacing the usual authority figures but often wearing similar clothes. They paraded about with the symbols of their status – in the case of festivals at court, the crown and sceptre – and parodied the behaviour and rituals of majesty. These periodic festivals throughout the calendar year were times to let off steam and play games (such as jousting on hobby horses); they were topsy-turvy times, when, for example, a court fool could become a king and vice versa. But they had a more serious side too: each time true kings, queens, lords and ladies were dethroned, or even underwent a mock killing, as sometimes happened, they were reminded of the limitations of their human authority and their relation to Christ. It seems that the connecting of fools with kings, and kings with the fall of fortune, was a culturally recognized, ritualistic way of warning rulers of the need for humility and justice, for keeping power in perspective (Billington, 1991). We know that some monarchs were less than happy about mock-king games. The young James VI of Scotland, for example, had to witness his tutor George Buchanan parodying his haughty kingly behaviour for fifteen days. Buchanan said he was seeking to provide James with a graphic lesson about the foolish use he was making of his sovereignty.

In this light it becomes easier to see Richard II in Shakespeare's play as a mock king of excess (as lean old Lenten Gaunt takes pains to tell us when he says his grief 'hath kept a tedious fast, / And who abstains from meat that is not gaunt?' (2. 1. 75–6)), presiding over his 'caterpillar' lords of misrule, and over a kingdom characterized by inversions of the law, and disorder. What was the effect of this carnival context, and why did the playwright deliberately draw attention, early on in the play, to its presence, through Gaunt's punning on his name and invocation of its idiom? First, it undoubtedly functioned to increase the entertainment value of the play, lightening the mood and introducing merriment. Secondly, and importantly, the deployment of traditional festive forms gave the playwright greater licence to explore his highly sensitive major theme: effective rule and its opposite. We know that the mock-king convention was deliberately used between 1588 and 1601 as a means of evading restrictions on the staging of controversial matter. Yet undoubtedly such stage representations of élite and royal behaviour had a cumulative consequence of which Elizabethan and Jacobean playwrights may or may not have been aware: namely, that by making the rituals and trappings of greatness familiar, and by subjecting them to scorn and laughter, the mystique of majesty was gnawed away and undermined (Orgel, 1981). The 'shows' of kingship were exposed as just that, and majesty was revealed as made, not born, paving the way for the deposition and killing of an actual 'anointed' monarch half a century later.

Metadrama and words, words, words

This leads us into a consideration of the closely related issue of acting styles in the performance of *Richard II*, and the play's unrelenting rhetoric and highly stylized verse.

Consider, for example, the Duchess of Gloucester's final speech in the second scene of Act 1, especially such lines as: 'Grief boundeth where it falls, / Not with the empty hollowness, but weight' (58–9), and 'empty lodgings and unfurnished walls, / Unpeopled offices, untrodden stones' (68–9). The proliferation of negated words ('*un*furnished', '*un*peopled') in the Duchess's lines powerfully conveys her sense of loss, emptiness and sorrow. Here, as throughout this play, words are deployed in startlingly novel and thought-provoking ways. *Richard II* weighs, measures and tastes words (1. 2. 58–9; 1. 3. 207; 2. 3. 6); it gives substance and shape to abstract concepts like 'grief' and 'care', but it also cancels and empties words linked to concrete things, denying them substance (as in 1. 2). In a clever reversal of this strategy, Richard populates his lonely prison cell with the verbal signs of his thoughts (5. 5. 1–41).

Nevertheless, the unflaggingly ornate and gorgeous poetry of *Richard II* can be experienced as alienating. These are the reflections on this topic of a famous actor, and former Richard II, Sir John Gielgud:

> Everyone speaks in images, parentheses, and elaborate similes, whether gardeners, exquisites ... the continually artificial style tends to become somewhat indigestible on the stage, and stands between the audience and their desire to get on more intimate terms with the characters and situations.

(1984 edn, p.142)

Acting the part of Richard II in 1929, Gielgud had tried to follow the late-nineteenth- and early-twentieth-century trend of dramatic representation, aiming at realism, and a style of acting that would allow an in-depth exploration of Richard's tragic 'personality'. But, as he discovered, trying to create a wholly naturalistic piece of theatre out of a Shakespeare play is fraught with difficulties. Richard II's overwrought, 'artificial' style of speech constitutes a particular obstacle to realism. Gielgud argued, too, that the gage-throwing scene ran the 'dangerous risk of seeming ridiculous', and recommended that future directors make 'discreet cuts' to avoid 'bathos', omitting this scene and the one depicting the York family 'Interlude' (ibid., p.143). Generations of directors have followed his advice and cut the mocking scenes, leaving audiences under the illusion that this is an unremittingly serious play. However, Shakespeare never intended his audience to be on 'intimate terms' with his characters. The latter is a very modern expectation and one that, as twentieth-century readers and spectators, most of us are likely to share. Immersed in the ancient European tradition of emblematic theatre, Renaissance dramatists were interested in exploring wider public issues such as religion, government and morality, and characters tended to be vehicles for ideas – complex types rather than complex personalities.

The profound exploration of the politics of kingship achieved by *Richard II* demanded the critical distancing achieved by 'metadramatic' techniques. Metadrama is a theatrical style that continuously reflects upon its own artifice, upon the play as a play and upon the business of acting (as in *A Midsummer Night's Dream*). Such techniques shuttle the audience between states of absorption and detachment, conviction and scepticism, creating the illusion of life and then piercing through the veil of that illusion to reveal the constructed nature of roles, both on the stage and in the real world. Thus, at crucial points in *Richard II* – often in scenes heavy with pathos – the audience is stimulated to recognize majesty as a rehearsed production. For example, in 3. 3, gazing up at the tragic sight of the defeated sun-king on the battlements, York muses, 'Yet looks he like a king' (67), thereby encouraging the audience to scrutinize Richard and ask what a king should look like. He then proceeds with 'Alack, alack for woe / That any harm should stain so fair a show!' (69–70). **In the light of the above discussion, how do you imagine Richard in this episode?**

The effect of this scene will depend entirely on its direction and on how the king is portrayed. I envisage him decked out like a 'pageant' prince, desperately wielding his crown and sceptre in an effort to convince himself and others that he is still fit for the role of king.

This play seems to deploy all its resources to badger its spectators into scrutinizing meaning from unconventional perspectives and to alert them to the fact that 'shows' and words in the theatre of power are apt to be misconstrued and to mislead ('Mistake me not, my lord, 'tis not my meaning' (2. 3. 74)).

Critical meaning in history

It is now time to close the circle, and to end where we began in this chapter, by reflecting briefly on the dominant critical perspective on *Richard II* in the earlier part of the twentieth century, and its wider implications for the study of Shakespeare. I have in mind the highly conservative view of Shakespeare's histories expounded by John Dover Wilson in a lecture delivered before the German Shakespeare Society in 1939 (just before Germany invaded Poland in World War II) and developed by E.M.W. Tillyard in *Shakespeare's History Plays* in 1944. The latter volume, which was extraordinarily influential for several decades, stated authoritatively that in Shakespeare's time 'orthodox doctrines of rebellion and of the monarchy [were] ... shared by every section of the community' (1959 edn, p.64). Dover Wilson's lecture had argued, similarly, that 'all' Elizabethans were terrified of disorder, so that 'the historical and political thought ... of Shakespeare and his contemporaries was determined by their fears of chaos and their gratitude to the royal house [the Tudors] which had saved England from it' (1939, p.42). According to Dover Wilson, Bolingbroke could only have been perceived as an 'utterly illegal ... usurper' threatening England's peace (ibid., p.50). For him, Shakespeare's play was 'a mirror' (ibid., p.49) reflecting universally held beliefs in divine right and royal absolutism. Dover Wilson concluded his lecture with the pointed observation 'that these plays should be of particular interest to German students at this moment of ... history' (ibid., p.51).

In the light of your study of *Richard II*, can you detect flaws in Tillyard's and Dover Wilson's assumptions?

There are two very basic and major flaws. First, the reading of history underpinning their criticism is erroneous and misleading: the history surrounding the unrest of the 1590s, the Essex rebellion, and the Elizabeth I–Richard II analogy, was well documented early in the twentieth century. Secondly, it is only by blocking out large parts of the script and ignoring the heterodox voices that reverberate throughout the play that such a view is sustainable. In short, these critics have respected neither history nor the substance of the text. Furthermore, to suggest that *Richard II* presents a 'mirror image' of reality is simplistic in the extreme.

Look again at the extract from the concluding sentence of Dover Wilson's lecture quoted above. Does it offer any way of accounting for his prejudiced reading of the play?

I think it does: his criticism is clearly strongly shaped by the stresses of his own historical moment and his subsequent anxiety about disorder. A fear of chaos as Europe teeters on the brink of war pervades Dover Wilson's lecture, in which Bolingbroke begins to resemble that troublesome usurper of power in the late 1930s, Adolf Hitler.

Can we draw any conclusions from this to improve our study of Shakespeare? Because everyone brings the weighty baggage of background and beliefs to their reading of a text, literary criticism is inevitably subjective. However, the worst excesses of biased interpretation can and should be guarded against by grounding one's analysis firmly in the evidence of the work (the whole of the work as opposed to selected parts of it), and by keeping a keen eye on the historical and cultural circumstances that gave birth to the text.

This does not mean, however, that a theatre director's vision should follow the same rules and seek to preserve Shakespeare in the formalin of scholarship. Whilst scholarship should be respectful of the text, and of history, many would consider it foolish to strap theatre into a straitjacket that denied directors and actors the licence to cut, adjust and recreate in order to make meaningful, satisfying theatre out of scripts that are now 400 years old. In order to survive, theatre must be vital and vibrant. As the Shakespearean actor Ian Richardson succinctly put it: 'If you enter into a choir-boy-filled cathedral atmosphere with Shakespeare, you are going to strangle him out of existence' (Loney, 1990, p.34). On the other hand, theatregoers often have strong opinions about 'authenticity' in the staging of Shakespeare: what is your view?

Finally, do you think Shakespeare's *Richard II* is a conservative, radical or politically neutral play?

As this study of *Richard II* has sought to show, the production of theatrical meaning is multifaceted and complex. The text of the play, its realization on the stage, the circumstances surrounding a particular performance, and the values, beliefs and experiences that individual spectators bring to bear on a production, all shape a play's import and effect. Hence the meanings of a play are highly unstable. However, if we restrict ourselves to thinking about the words on the page, it is possible to conclude that, because *Richard II* voices both sides of the kingship debate and endorses neither directly, it is essentially neutral: that is, it refuses to stack the cards in favour of either the 'divine right' or the 'office upon trust' view of kingship. Nevertheless, it must be conceded that a play about an inept, childless, tyrannical monarch whose defects and crimes were remarkably close to those of the reigning monarch (according to Elizabeth's critics) in the late 1590s, smacks neither of conservatism nor of political neutrality. Staging such a play in the closing years of Elizabeth's reign was fraught with danger, as the players found to their cost when they performed it on the eve of the Essex rebellion. Indeed, my own inclination to read the play 'awry' persuades me that Shakespeare's drama was more questioning, and had more politically destabilizing consequences, than many critics in the twentieth century have been willing to concede. *Richard II* does, after all, seem to promote views of kingship that were certainly at odds with the orthodox Tudor line in the late 1590s. Furthermore, mocking monarchy on the public stage undoubtedly helped to undermine the authority and power of majesty, paving the way for the deposition and execution of a real monarch on the public stage of a scaffold 50 years on in the English Civil War.

References

Albright, E.M. (1927) 'Shakespeare's *Richard II* and the Essex conspiracy', *PMLA*, vol.XLII, pp.686–720.

Anonymous (1648) *The People Informed of their Oppressors*, London.

Ashton, R. (1984) *Reformation and Revolution 1558–1660*, London: Granada.

Baldwin, W. (1960) *A Myrroure for Magistrates*, 1559, in *The Mirror for Magistrates*, ed. L.B. Campbell, New York: Barnes & Noble.

Barr, H. (ed.) (1993) 'Richard the Redeless', in *The Piers Plowman Tradition*, London: Everyman, pp.101–33.

Billington, S. (1991) *Mock Kings in Medieval and Renaissance Drama*, Oxford: Clarendon Press.

Bristol, M. (1985) *Carnival and Theatre: Plebeian Culture and the Structure of Authority in Renaissance England*, London and New York: Methuen.

Buchanan, G. (1949) *De Jure Regni Apud Scotos*, 1579, trans. C.F. Arrowood, in *The Powers of the Crown in Scotland*, Austin: University of Texas Press.

Cawdrey, R. (1613) *A Table Alphabeticall of Hard Usuall English Words*, 1604, London.

Duncan-Jones, K. (ed.) (1989) *Sir Philip Sidney: A Critical Edition of The Major Works*, Oxford: Oxford University Press.

Elyot, T. (1962) *The Book Named the Governor*, 1531, ed. S.E. Lehmberg, London: Dent.

Erasmus, D. (1968) *The Education of a Christian Prince*, 1516, trans. L.K. Born, New York: W.W. Norton.

Gielgud, J. (1984) 'Stage directions', 1963, in *'Richard II': Critical Essays*, ed. J.T. Newlin, New York and London: Garland, pp.139–44.

Greenblatt, S. (ed.) (1982) *The Power of Forms in the English Renaissance*, Oklahoma: Pilgrim Books.

Greville, F. (1938) 'Life of Sydney', in *The Poems and Dramas of Fulke Greville*, vol.II, ed. G. Bullough, Edinburgh: Oliver & Boyd.

Gurr, A. (ed.) (1984) *King Richard II*, Cambridge: Cambridge University Press.

Hayward, J. (1642) *The Life and Raigne of King Henrie the Fourth*, 1599, in *Cotton and Hayward Histories of Henry III and IV*, London.

Holinshed, R. (1577) *The Laste Volume of the Chronicles of England, Scotlande, and Irelande*, London.

Loney, G. (ed.) (1990) *Staging Shakespeare: Seminars on Production Problems*, New York and London: Garland.

Orgel, S. (1981) 'Making greatness familiar', in *Pageantry in Shakespearean Theater*, ed. D.M. Bergeron, Athens, GA: University of Georgia Press, pp.19–25.

Russell, C. (1990) *The Causes of the English Civil War*, Oxford: Oxford University Press.

State Papers Domestic, Elizabeth I 1598–1601, London.

Tillyard, E.M.W. (1959) *Shakespeare's History Plays*, London: Chatto & Windus (first published 1944).

Wilson, J.D. (1939) 'The political background of Shakespeare's *Richard II* and *Henry IV*', *Shakespeare Jahrbuch*, vol.75.

MACBETH

Chapter 3

Stephen Regan

Aims

This chapter will introduce you to Shakespearean tragedy. After briefly surveying some of the prominent theories of tragedy from classical civilization to the present, the chapter will turn to an extended discussion of *Macbeth* and consider this play's relationship to the volatile politics of its time. By the end of the chapter, you should be better able to understand *Macbeth* in terms of seventeenth-century ideas about witchcraft, gender and sovereignty, and to appreciate the possibilities of meaning that emerge when the play is performed on the modern stage and screen.

An introduction to tragedy

Tragedy is one of the oldest forms of drama, dating back to the ancient Greek writers of the fifth century BCE. From the surviving plays of Aeschylus, Sophocles and Euripides, modern critics have been able to construct a set of theories about the nature and function of tragedy in classical culture, and about its characteristic structures and dramatic devices. Much of our current knowledge about the role and significance of classical tragedy, however, comes from Aristotle's *Poetics*,[1] one of the seminal texts of western literary criticism. Aristotle's ideas about tragedy have been hugely influential and persistent, although some commentators have too hastily assumed that Aristotle was designing a grand, all-encompassing theory of tragedy that would hold good for all ages, rather than describing the plays of his near-contemporaries. It would be unwise to look for a direct correlation between ancient Greek tragedy and the much later tragedies of Shakespeare, but Aristotle's thoughts about the fate of the tragic hero, the structure or plotting of tragedy and its complex emotional effect can nevertheless provide a useful starting-point for discussion of a play like *Macbeth*. (If you have not already done so, you should read the complete play now in order to appreciate the discussion that follows.)

Aristotle noted that tragic drama induced in its spectators a set of conflicting feelings, including both pity and terror, which were ultimately reconciled by *catharsis* (a purging or release of these emotions). The dramatic representation of tragic incidents could leave an audience feeling relieved, or even uplifted, rather than dismayed or depressed. According to Aristotle, the tragic effect is maximized when the hero or protagonist is neither pre-eminently just and virtuous nor entirely given to vice and depravity, but a person of an intermediate kind. In terms of social

---

[1] *The Poetics* contains an analysis of the characteristics of poetry in terms of the components of tragedy: plot, character, thought, diction, melody and spectacle.

rank or reputation, however, this person is generally someone of recognizable eminence and power. The ideal plot is one in which the protagonist suffers a change in fortune, from happiness to misery, as a result of some tragic flaw or error of judgement (*hamartia*). The fatal calamity often takes the form of excessive pride or *hubris* and leads to divine retribution or *nemesis*. The reversal of fortune (*peripeteia*) is accompanied or followed by moments of discovery or self-knowledge (*anagnorisis*), in which the protagonist acquires some insight or understanding through suffering and comes to see things 'as they are'.

Even with this brief summary, it should be possible to establish some similarities between classical tragedy and Shakespearean tragedy. Indeed, much modern criticism of *Macbeth* and the other tragedies has been concerned with issues such as the fatal imperfections of the tragic hero and the extent to which that person achieves some higher wisdom in the midst of adversity. At the same time, we ought to bear in mind that there is no simple or straightforward evolution of tragic drama. The English tragedy of Shakespeare's day was not based directly on Greek models, but was more obviously influenced by the plays of the Roman philosopher–poet Seneca, who had drawn on the example of Greek drama (especially the work of Euripides). It would be misleading to suggest that when Shakespeare composed *Hamlet*, *King Lear* and *Macbeth* he was working to a clear blueprint of what tragedy should be. It is better, perhaps, to think of tragedy as a changing concept or a set of assumptions that can vary in emphasis from one instance to the next, rather than as a clearly defined and consistent set of criteria. As one critic puts it, '"Tragedy" is today a concept that we deduce from the contemplation of a heap of tragedies' (Leech, 1969, p.24).

Tragedy in the early seventeenth century took its bearings not just from classical models, but also from a range of more local and immediate influences. One possible source was the Christian 'morality plays' of the fifteenth and early sixteenth centuries – plays such as *Everyman* (*c*.1500) and *Mankind* (*c*.1465) – which are essentially parables of temptation, sin and redemption. It is sometimes suggested that the tragedies written by Shakespeare and his contemporaries owe something of their ethical or didactic emphasis to the earlier morality plays. Elizabethan and Jacobean tragedy is also strongly infused with popular stories of revenge and usurpation. *Hamlet* is the most obvious example among Shakespeare's tragedies of a play preoccupied with revenge, but *King Lear* and *Macbeth* also contain significant elements of revenge (Edgar seeking revenge against his brother Edmund in *King Lear*, and Malcolm, Donalbain and Macduff all seeking revenge against Macbeth). The idea of usurpation is powerfully evident in *Macbeth*, as we will see. It might be argued, then, that Elizabethan and Jacobean tragedy has its own distinctive cultural traditions, as well as its own distinctive religious and political preoccupations.

To gain a more exact understanding of the role and function of tragedy in Shakespeare's England, we need to ask about the relationship between the writing and performance of tragic drama and the social and political conditions that prevailed at the time. *King Lear* and *Macbeth* are not just stories about exceptional individuals with tragic flaws of character, but works that emerge from, and respond to, the constitutional and ideological upheavals of the early seventeenth century. They are works written at a time of increasing scepticism about the natural and supernatural order of the universe, and about the social and political order established in close relation to that overarching, hierarchical design. In both plays, tragedy has important social origins and social repercussions; it emerges not from the failings of solitary individuals, but from the interaction of those individuals with prevailing structures of power. Tragedies were also written to be *performed*, and they took place in a theatre that, as we have already seen with *Richard II*, had an ambiguous place among the social and political institutions of the day. Many of the questions that modern critics ask about the function of tragedy have to do with its role in either legitimating or subverting the structures of authority.

It is clear, however, that writers in Elizabethan and Jacobean England raised similar questions about the function of tragedy. Sir Philip Sidney, for instance, was quite explicit about the moral and political purpose of tragedy. In *A Defence of Poetry* (1595), he referred to:

> the high and excellent Tragedy, that openeth the greatest wounds, and showeth forth the ulcers that are covered with tissue; that maketh kings fear to be tyrants, and tyrants manifest their tyrannical humours; that, with stirring the affects of admiration and commiseration, teacheth the uncertainty of this world, and upon how weak foundations gilden roofs are builded.
>
> (1989 edn, p.47)

What is Sidney saying about tragedy here?

There are several key points that are worth noting. The medical imagery suggests that tragedy has the capacity to expose corruption deep within the body politic. Tragedy also cautions kings against the abuse of power, and it reminds its audience of the transient value of material wealth. The allusion to 'the uncertainty of this world' sounds like a conventional Christian warning, but the 'gilden roofs' are a strong indication that Sidney's immediate concern is with the social and political structures of the time.

Given the popular image of Sidney as the very epitome of Elizabethan courtly society, his appraisal of tragic drama seems surprisingly radical. Sidney's was not the only voice to comment on the uses of tragedy (some of his contemporaries were more guarded about its didactic function), but it does at least raise the possibility that tragedy in Elizabethan and Jacobean England had a critical and potentially subversive role.

From the Renaissance onwards, theories of tragedy proliferated. In the nineteenth century especially, tragedy was a familiar concept in philosophical debate, and thinkers such as Arthur Schopenhauer and Friedrich Nietzsche gave prolonged and intensive consideration to the nature of tragic experience. German critics and philosophers played an important part in establishing Shakespeare's reputation. Of these, the most systematic and influential was G.W.F. Hegel (1770–1831), whose vast output included writings on literature, drama and aesthetics. Hegel elaborated a theory of tragedy based mainly on Greek drama, but one that could be applied to plays by Shakespeare, as well as to plays by his own German contemporaries. One of the central preoccupations of Hegel's theory is the extent to which tragedy can elevate its spectators and also reconcile them to the most appalling scenes of loss and destruction. Tragedy can do this, Hegel claims, by presenting us with a conflict that arises not from the collision between good and evil, but from the collision between one partial good and another. The pain we experience at the destruction of one or other or both of these different ethical powers leads to the affirmation of a more complex sense of ethical justice – what Hegel terms 'the true ethical Idea' (Paolucci, 1975, p.237) – which acknowledges the rights and wrongs of both parties. Hegel's theory is not easy to grasp, but it might help to illuminate a play like *Antony and Cleopatra* in which two sets of values – Roman and Egyptian – are weighed against each other, and the struggle between them precipitates the eventual tragedy. The problems that ensue when Hegel's theory of tragedy is applied to other plays, such as *King Lear* and *Macbeth*, were taken up by one of the most distinguished literary critics working in Britain at the turn of the nineteenth century.

A.C. Bradley (1851–1935) came into immediate contact with the ideas of Hegel when he entered Balliol College, Oxford as a student in 1869. He was made a Fellow of Balliol in 1874 and taught philosophy, but left soon afterwards, allegedly because the Master, Benjamin Jowett, disapproved of philosophy. In 1901, however, Bradley returned to Oxford as Professor of Poetry, and in 1904 he published his influential *Shakespearean Tragedy*. Some of Bradley's basic assumptions about tragedy derive from Aristotle, although they also carry the strong imprint of his Evangelical upbringing. He suggests that Shakespeare's tragic heroes are persons of 'high degree' and that these 'exceptional beings' possess some 'fatal imperfection' or commit some error (Bradley, 1967 edn, p.12). At the core of his theory, however, is a strong attachment to Hegelian ideas of conflict. Bradley modifies Hegel's proposition that tragedy emerges from the conflict of one partial good with another by distinguishing between inner conflict and outer conflict. In other words, he reconstitutes Hegel's theory of tragic conflict in terms of self-division and self-restitution, effectively shifting the focus of interest towards character. 'The centre of tragedy', he claims, lies in 'action issuing from character, or in character issuing in action' (ibid.).

Two chapters in *Shakespearean Tragedy* are dedicated to *Macbeth*. What Bradley suggests is that *Macbeth* clearly shows the hero and the heroine (Macbeth and his wife) opposed to the representatives of King Duncan, but that it would be misleading to describe the conflict in the play as being simply between these groups. If there is 'an outward conflict of persons and groups', there is also 'a conflict of forces in the hero's soul' (ibid., p.19). This is how Bradley summarizes his view of *Macbeth*: 'Treasonous ambition in Macbeth collides with loyalty and patriotism in Macduff and Malcolm: here is the outward conflict. But these powers or principles equally collide in the soul of Macbeth himself: here is the inner. And neither by itself could make the tragedy' (ibid.). Bradley also modifies Hegel's proposition that tragedy predominantly affirms an ideal of ethical justice. He suggests that the ultimate power in the world of tragedy is moral order, but insists that what moves us most deeply in tragedy is an impression of waste. Even when legitimate order is restored, we remain confronted by the inexplicable nature of tragic conflict:

> This central feeling is the impression of waste. With Shakespeare, at any rate, the pity and fear which are stirred by the tragic story seem to unite with, and even to merge in, a profound sense of sadness and mystery, which is due to this impression of waste ... We seem to have before us a type of the mystery of the whole world, the tragic fact which extends far beyond the limits of tragedy. Everywhere ... we see power, intelligence, life, and glory which astound us and seem to call for our worship. And everywhere we see them perishing, devouring one another and destroying themselves, often with dreadful pain, as though they came into being for no other end. Tragedy is the typical form of this mystery.

(Ibid., p.23)

Like Hegel, Bradley is a philosophical idealist: he upholds the idea of a moral order as a permanent and unchanging power in the universe. Like many nineteenth-century British Hegelians, however, Bradley seems to have been attracted to philosophical idealism because it served as a substitute for conventional religious belief. Although his religious upbringing is sometimes apparent in his writings, what emerges most forcefully is the profound bewilderment of late Victorian agnosticism. In a telling remark in the opening chapter of *Shakespearean Tragedy*, Bradley offers the opinion that 'Shakespeare was not attempting to justify the ways of God to men ... He was writing tragedy, and tragedy would not be tragedy if it were not a painful mystery' (ibid., p.38).

Modern tragedy

By the time *Shakespearean Tragedy* was published in 1904, Hegel's dialectical view of the basis of tragedy as the conflict between partial good and evil had already been strongly contested. In a fundamental critique of Hegel's ideas, the German political and economic theorist Karl Marx (1818–83) displaced the idealist perception with a distinctly materialist perspective. The ultimate power in Marx's scheme of things is not some abstract ethical ideal, but the general movement of history. From this perspective, the roots of tragedy are social and historical. The materialist emphasis has had a profound impact on modern theories of tragedy, especially in helping to dispel some of the earlier idealist or 'metaphysical' mystifications of tragic conflict. In *Modern Tragedy* (1966), Raymond Williams presents a view of tragedy as 'ordinary' – not the death of princes, but 'a mining disaster, a burned-out family, a broken career, a smash on the road' (pp.13–14). What Williams points to is a formal, academic separation between tragedy and 'tragedy', between the tragic experience of everyday life and an intellectual tradition. His book is a brave attempt to reconnect the divergent meanings of tragedy and to show how it manifests itself in modern culture, not least in the sphere of war and revolution. Even so, there persists in academic debate a preoccupation with tragic experience as the struggle of humanity within some unknown metaphysical order. For instance, George Steiner asserts that 'The tragic personage is broken by forces which can neither be fully understood nor overcome by rational prudence' (Drakakis, 1992, p.2). **What objections might be raised against the idealist or metaphysical view of tragedy?**

One obvious shortcoming of this theoretical position is that it seems to rob tragedy of any potential power it might possess, either as a criticism of the social order or as an agency for political change. Tragedy is conceived in terms of an endlessly recurring conflict, issuing from our flawed human nature; it teaches us that suffering and pain are an inescapable and inexplicable part of the human condition.

As Williams points out, however, there *is* an alternative perspective: 'We have to see not only that suffering is avoidable, but that it is not avoided. And not only that suffering breaks us, but that it need not break us' (1966, pp.202–3). More recently, Kiernan Ryan has subjected the conservative criticism of Bradley and his successors to a vigorous shake-up, and has proposed a more positive and optimistic reading of Shakespeare's tragedies. 'Such criticism', he argues, 'drains the tragedies of their power both to arraign the alterable causes of injustice, violence and despair, and to expand our awareness of alternative sources of human motivation waiting in the wings of past and present events' (1995 edn, p.75). In Ryan's opinion, Shakespearean tragedy is characterized by its awareness of 'alternative potentiality': the plays show how conflict issues from specific social conditions and pressures, and how the lives of human beings could evolve quite differently under other conceivable circumstances. Plays like *King Lear* and *Macbeth* have a prefigurative or 'proleptic' power, 'pointing us towards more desirable versions of human existence yet to be scripted by history' (ibid., p.76).

The materialist analysis of culture advocated by Williams has prompted a radical reconsideration of the politics of tragedy. Critics such as Catherine Belsey and Jonathan Dollimore have objected to idealist concepts of tragedy on the grounds that they mystify and obscure the real historical conditions in which the actual identities of men and women are rooted. Theories of tragedy in which destiny is governed by an unchangeable human nature have a tendency to subsume the identity of 'woman' within an essentialist idea of 'man'. In *The Subject of Tragedy* (1985), Belsey argues that, contrary to what is suggested in a good deal of literary and dramatic criticism, the plays of the early seventeenth century were sites of disputation, where ideas of identity and difference, including gender, were frequently contested. Dollimore's *Radical Tragedy* (1984) argues similarly that Elizabethan and Jacobean tragedy exercised a subversive influence in challenging gender stereotypes, exposing the workings of political power and undermining religious orthodoxy. Dollimore claims that a crisis of confidence in the institutions of Church and State, and in those holding power, is addressed in play after play. He believes that the drama of the time not only confronted and articulated that crisis, but actually helped to precipitate it.

Not all radical critics are persuaded of the subversive potential of tragedy. The renowned Brazilian theatre director Augusto Boal argues in *Theater of the Oppressed* (1979) that, in its impulse towards reconciliation and equilibrium, tragedy highlights the desirability of political order. Accordingly, he sees tragedy as 'the most perfect artistic form of coercion' (Drakakis, 1992, p.6). To some extent, of course, the question of whether tragedy is a reactionary or a radical form depends on what kind of production is envisaged and under what theatrical conditions. If the audience experiences the danger of transgression, as Boal assumes, there is also a strong likelihood that the audience experiences the attraction of transgression. It is part of the striking appeal of tragedy that, even as it strives for harmonious resolution, it cannot help but uncover the sources of conflict and contradiction. This point has been made very cogently by the cultural theorist Walter Benjamin: 'the atonement which the representative figure of the tragic hero undergoes, may bring about a restoration of Law, but it also undermines it at the same time' (Drakakis, 1992, p.7).

We have seen in the discussion of *Richard II* in Chapter 2 a plausible connection between the dramatic representation of kingship and the revolutionary upheavals of the mid-seventeenth century. Shakespearean tragedy is similarly poised between the breakdown of older forms of social organization and a new, uncertain future; in some ways, it cannot help but anticipate the political turmoil of the English Civil War (sometimes referred to as the English Revolution). If tragedy served at one level to restore and legitimize the role of the king, it also served to demystify and even degrade the sovereign image. The cultural theorist Franco Moretti argues explicitly that Elizabethan and Jacobean tragedy was one of the decisive influences in the creation of a public that for the first time in history assumed the right to bring a king to justice: 'Tragedy disentitled the absolute monarch to all ethical and rational legitimation. Having deconsecrated the king, tragedy made it possible to decapitate him' (Drakakis, 1992, p.46). With that sobering thought in mind, let us move on to *Macbeth*.

Figure 15 *Brainerd Duffield, Lurene Tuttle and Charles Lederer as the three Witches in the film* Macbeth *produced and directed by Orson Welles, 1948, Mercury Productions/Republic Pictures. Photo: Kobal Collection.*

The tragedy of Macbeth

Macbeth, like *Richard II*, is a play intensely preoccupied with regicide. Whereas the killing of the king in *Richard II* is essentially part of the play's finale, in *Macbeth* the murder of Duncan in 2. 2 initiates a violent and profound upheaval, culminating in civil war and the eventual destruction of Macbeth himself. Both plays raise uncomfortable questions about the rights and privileges of kings, about the possibilities of treason, and about what constitutes legitimate power. Even so, it is still commonly assumed that *Macbeth* was written to please James VI of Scotland, shortly after his accession as James I of England. Although there is little concrete evidence to support the conjecture, some commentators believe that *Macbeth* was one of three plays performed at Hampton Court on 7 August 1606 for James and his royal guest, Christian IV of Denmark. Whether or not this was the first performance of *Macbeth*, we can reasonably assume that Shakespeare was working on the play in 1606, that it was performed at the Globe playhouse later that year, and that its composition coincided with some critically important events in the early years of James's rule. What aspects of *Macbeth* might have *pleased* the king? We cannot adequately answer this question with reference to the text alone. A brief account of how the play meshes with its times will help us to appreciate its impact on a seventeenth-century audience, and also help us to understand its lasting significance.

The prominent issues and ideas that inform *Macbeth* were intimately connected with the intellectual and political interests of James I. The question of succession had a profound significance for this particular king, since he was the son of Mary Stuart, whose execution had been authorized by Elizabeth I. Elizabeth was a childless queen, and shortly before her death on 24 March 1603 she was obliged to name James Stuart, then James VI of Scotland, as her rightful successor. The complexities of succession and hereditary rights were clearly not lost on the Scottish king, who had already written a number of pamphlets concerned with the rights and duties of kings and their subjects. *The True Law of Free Monarchies* (1598) insists on the supreme power of the king, while *Basilikon Doron* (Greek, 'The King's Gift'), published a year later, instructs the king's son, Henry, on the distinction between good kings and tyrants. James was, himself, a principal theorist on matters of kingship.

As James I of England and James VI of Scotland, the king was able to embark upon a deep personal ambition of perfecting a union between the two countries. After his coronation in England, James had reappointed Shakespeare's theatre company, formerly the Lord Chamberlain's Men, as the King's Men, and a new play about Scotland was clearly in keeping with his intense interest in his own lineage and his hopes for the future. In 4. 1, Macbeth is shown an apparition in which eight kings and the Scottish nobleman Banquo appear, with the last king holding a 'glass' or mirror. Macbeth cries out:

> I'll see no more –
> And yet the eighth appears, who bears a glass
> Which shows me many more; and some I see
> That twofold balls, and treble sceptres carry.

(4. 1. 134–7)

This description seems designed to link James with Banquo's 'line'. Balls and sceptres frequently allude to royal authority, and here the numbers are quite specific. In Scotland two sceptres were used in the coronation ceremony, in England just one, so it seems plausible that two balls and three sceptres denote the dual kingship of England and Scotland of James and his successors. The presentation of Banquo as a brave and loyal subject and a father of kings no doubt flattered James, since he traced his ancestry back to the legendary Scotsman. *Macbeth* appears to enhance the story of Banquo, simultaneously pointing to a fruitful, unbroken unity between England and Scotland. However, Banquo seems to have been invented by Scottish chroniclers to legitimate the Stuart line of descent, and not all accounts of him are flattering. In the written sources that Shakespeare used for *Macbeth*, the mythical Banquo is presented as Macbeth's fellow rebel and assassin. This is just one instance of Shakespeare's strategic modification of his source materials.

Witches and Jesuits

The main source for *Macbeth*, as for other Shakespeare plays, was Raphael Holinshed's *Chronicles of England, Scotlande, and Irelande*, first published in 1577 and reprinted (in the edition Shakespeare used) in 1587 (see Hosley, 1968). *Macbeth* conflates two closely related events in Scottish history: the murder of King Duff (952–967) by a trustworthy noble named Donwald, and the murder of King Duncan (1034–1040) by Macbeth. Several dramatic incidents, including the encounter with the witches (Figure 15), are drawn from Holinshed's account of Macbeth, but the murderous plotting of Macbeth and Lady Macbeth in Shakespeare's play is more obviously modelled on Donwald's assassination of King Duff. Shakespeare draws a sharper contrast between Duncan and Macbeth than is found in the *Chronicles*, heightening Duncan's saintly innocence and emphasizing Macbeth's monstrous guilt. Holinshed presents Duncan as a younger and weaker ruler than in Shakespeare's play, whereas Macbeth, whose claims to the throne appear to have some justification, rules effectively for ten years after Duncan's death. We cannot, therefore, assume that *Macbeth* depicts an accurate history of Scottish political conflict in the eleventh century. There are, however, good reasons for suggesting that what the play *does* depict are conflicts and uncertainties that were palpably evident in the seventeenth-century English court.

If, in some ways, *Macbeth* can be seen to affirm the validity of the king's power, in other ways it raises issues that in 1606 were highly sensitive and politically dangerous. The setting of the play in eleventh-century Scotland effectively removed it from censorship at a time when other 'topical' plays were being banned, but *Macbeth* nevertheless engages with concerns that were immediately and powerfully relevant in Shakespeare's own day. The topic of treason, for instance, was the subject of intense debate. In 1600, just a few years before the composition of *Macbeth*, the Earl of Gowrie attempted to kill James I while the sovereign was visiting his home in Perth, Scotland. Like Duncan, James was present in 'double trust' (1. 7. 12), both as king and guest. In December 1604, the assassination attempt was dramatized in a play titled *Gowrie*, but after a few performances the play was banned and the company was cautioned for having shown the king in perilous circumstances. Of more striking and immediate relevance was the discovery on 5 November 1605 of the Gunpowder Plot, in which Catholic conspirators, hoping to restore to England 'the one and true religion', aimed to blow up Parliament and assassinate the king and his ministers. In 1606, the year in which *Macbeth* is thought to have been written and first performed, the trials and executions of Guy Fawkes and his accomplices were given spectacular publicity.

One of the alleged accomplices in the Gunpowder Plot was father Henry Garnett, the Jesuit superior in England, who notoriously exercised his right to 'equivocation' in his defence. For persecuted Catholics, equivocation was a theologically valid duplicity or ambiguity, a way of qualifying spoken assertions with unspoken reservations. When caught between conflicting loyalties to England and Rome, Catholics might say one thing while knowing another without committing a sin of deceit. As we will see, the drunken porter scene in *Macbeth* (2. 3) refers explicitly to the practice of equivocation, hinting at Father Garnett's fate, and the language of equivocation has a decisive influence on Macbeth's behaviour. It is surely remarkable that *Macbeth* was written so soon after the Gunpowder Plot threatened the life of a Scottish king. Not surprisingly, some critics see *Macbeth* as 'an audacious, even a reckless, choice of story for Shakespeare to dramatize' (Mangan, 1991, p.106), and an unlikely play with which to entertain the king. The political sensitivity of the play does not, however, rule out the possibility that it was performed at court in a way that would have flattered James by appealing to his declared interest in questions of power and succession.

One further connection between *Macbeth* and James – perhaps the most intriguing of all – can be found in the widespread interest in witchcraft at the turn of the sixteenth century. In both England and Scotland, there was a long tradition of prophets and sorcerers being held to account in government affairs, and the persecution of witches was particularly intense in the years immediately before James was crowned King of England (Figure 16). On more than one occasion, James was persuaded that he himself was the target of demonic attacks, and his deep concern with 'demonology' developed alongside his intellectual preoccupation with the theory and practice of kingship.

One of the most famous witch trials, which took place in North Berwick in 1591, involved a group of witches accused of plotting against the king's life. A nobleman implicated in the plot, Francis Stuart, Earl of Bothwell, had allegedly sought the help of witches and called for curses against the king. Bothwell, a relative of the king, had claims to the Scottish throne. James became intensely involved in the North Berwick trials, hearing some of the confessions himself, and in the years immediately following the trials he composed a treatise entitled *Demonologie* (1597). The obvious links between witchcraft and treason provided Shakespeare with compelling and topical subject-matter.

Although witchcraft was widely believed and feared in Shakespeare's time, there were many diverse and conflicting opinions about its power and influence. In *The Discovery of Witchcraft* (1584), Reginald Scot offered a rational enquiry into witchcraft, and concluded that many witches were either innocent victims or cunning impostors. Although James banned Scot's book in 1603, he eventually came to share some of its scepticism. Views about how witches practised their rites and how they might be recognized also varied considerably. Shakespeare's witches, as we will see, are composite 'types', based on both English and Scottish records, but two prominent sources are worth mentioning here. Holinshed's *Chronicles* (Hosley, 1968) refers to 'the weird sisters', employing 'weird' not in the conventional sense of

Figure 16 James I of England, *engraving by Simon van de Passe, frontispiece of*
The Workes ... of James I, *1616, from Bodleian Library, University of Oxford,*
E.14.Th.Seld.

'strange' but pertaining to fate or destiny. Shakespeare's witches are referred to as
the 'weird Sisters' (1. 3. 30)[2] and the 'weird Women' (3. 1. 2). As well as drawing on
Holinshed, Shakespeare makes use of certain details from James's visit to Oxford in

---

[2] *The Norton Shakespeare* (p.2567) notes that the Folio uses 'weyward', which is derived from the Old
English word 'wyrd' meaning 'fate'.

1605, when Dr Matthew Gwinn, a Fellow of St John's College, welcomed him with a show of three sibyls. These woodland creatures (probably boys in costume) greeted James by acknowledging the prophecies concerning Banquo's line of descent and then, in turn, hailed him as King of Scotland, King of England and King of Ireland.

Undoubtedly, *Macbeth* draws on numerous sources concerned with witchcraft, and on a variety of popular views of magic and prophecy. The weird sisters powerfully exploit the fears and suspicions that were widespread in the early seventeenth century. How should we, as modern readers, regard the witches in *Macbeth*, and how might the witches be represented in modern film and stage productions of the play? **Turn to the opening scene of *Macbeth*, where we first encounter the witches, and see what textual evidence there is that might be used to support a modern interpretation of their role.**

Act 1, Scene 1 is tantalizingly brief, but some significant details about the witches can be drawn from it. The three witches appear in thunder and lightning. We learn little about their physical appearance at this stage, but their dialogue is revealing. The speech of the witches is highly stylized or ritualized. They speak in turn – each witch speaks three times – and then join to deliver a choric conclusion. Their lines are noticeably short or 'clipped' compared with the usual ten-syllable verse lines of other characters in *Macbeth*, and the use of a pronounced rhythm and rhyming couplets adds to the ritualistic effect of the opening scene. Their conversation deals with time and place: they agree to meet Macbeth on the heath after the commotion of battle is over. Then each witch responds to a summons from a demon companion or 'familiar'. (Graymalkin is thought to be a cat; Paddock is a toad; and 'Anon' simply means 'soon'.)

The alliterative choric couplet is highly significant, since it initiates the language of paradox and ambiguity so strongly characteristic of *Macbeth*. The 'fog and filthy air' (11) hint at obscured vision and the torpid atmosphere that engulfs much of the action in the play. 'Fair' implies things that are pleasant and beautiful, but also things that are just, while 'foul' hints at both dirt and malice (10). The collapse of any firm distinction between these terms anticipates the moral ambiguities of the play.

Further knowledge about the witches can be gained from 1. 3. Again, the witches enter in thunder. This time we see them questioning each other about where they have been, and in the process they reveal their penchant for curses and charms. The First Witch curses a sailor's wife, who has refused to share a meal of chestnuts. The woman's husband is master of the *Tiger*, quite possibly the ship of that name which left the Isle of Wight on 5 December 1604 and returned from a tempestuous voyage after 567 days at sea. The numbers in 'sennights nine times nine' (21) conceivably refer to the duration of the voyage. The First Witch promises to sail in a sieve, transform herself into a deformed rat and stir up the winds (all activities commonly associated with witches at the time *Macbeth* was written). Although the witches can make the sailor's life a misery, their power is not absolute: 'Though his barque cannot be lost, / Yet it shall be tempest-tossed' (23–4). 'The weird sisters' close their counsel by perfecting a charm (33–5), once again invoking the magical number three, which was associated with the three Fates or Destinies in classical mythology.

The encounter with Banquo and Macbeth in this scene provides the first occasion when the witches are observed by other characters in the play. **What do we learn about the witches from Banquo and Macbeth?**

Banquo describes the appearance and clothing of the witches as 'withered' and 'wild' (38), noting how each places a 'choppy' ('chapped' or 'cracked') finger on her 'skinny' lips (42–3). In some respects what Banquo describes is a familiar image of the domestic or village witch. At the same time, his description is disconcerting: it hints at something unnatural or supernatural in the air. The witches 'look not like th'inhabitants o'th' earth / And yet are on't' (39–40). Their physical appearance unsettles conventional assumptions about gender:

> You should be women,
> And yet your beards forbid me to interpret
> That you are so.

(1. 3. 43–5)

A curious stage direction tells us that the witches 'vanish', once again hinting at mysterious flight. Banquo compares the witches to 'bubbles' (77) and asks, 'Whither are they vanished?' (78), to which Macbeth replies: 'Into the air, and what seemed corporal / Melted as breath into the wind' (79–80).

As we will see later, the presentation of the witches raises crucial questions for the performance of *Macbeth*. Are we to suppose that an audience must see what Banquo sees? Should the witches be portrayed as actual women or as supernatural beings?

Let us now try to summarize our views of the weird sisters and, as we do so, reflect on how they might be played on stage. We have seen that the witches are associated with disorder in nature, including stormy weather; they are accompanied by 'familiars' or demon followers; they can transform themselves into animals; they have a fondness for charms and curses; they invert accepted moral values; they have the physical features of old women and yet look *not* like the inhabitants of the earth. If the appearances of the witches are ambiguous, so too is the strange prophetic language that they speak. Macbeth twice bids the witches to speak (45, 76) and calls them 'imperfect speakers' (68) – not because they are inarticulate, but because their speech is incomplete and offers only brief glimpses of what might be to come.

Part of the difficulty of imagining Shakespeare's witches in performance is that they conform with historical records, which suggests that they should be portrayed naturalistically, and yet they possess an enigmatic, other-worldly aura that calls for a style or method of representation beyond the strictly naturalistic. Modern productions of *Macbeth* sometimes founder by being pulled too strongly in one direction or another, with the witches either indulging in crude physical comedy or vanishing into the ether without leaving much of an impression. Critical commentary, too, has veered between the witches as indubitable historical personages and the witches as ghostly symbolic forces or psychological projections. Are the witches the implacably malevolent fates who dictate the 'life to come', or are they merely the strange interlocutors in a narrative of violent and reckless self-destruction?

In this particular reading of the play, let us try to keep our options open for a while and see what alternative interpretations of the witches emerge. Rather than seeing the witches as palpably evil, we might try to imagine them as the embodiment of all the anxieties, hostilities and fears that so-called civilized society habitually represses. Seen from this perspective, the witches become a designated group within a particular social and political order; they signify all that is deviant and perverse according to the prejudices of a ruling élite. Their unnatural appearances and practices serve to legitimate what is considered 'normal', natural and acceptable. If the witches embody the repressed elements of an enlightened society, acting as scapegoats for an ugly set of prejudices, they are also capable of threatening that society by exposing it for the sham it is. What is fair is seen to inhere in what is foul and vice versa, until any neat distinction between the terms dissolves and disappears. We are led to question whether Macbeth and his bloody companions are any more civilized than the witch who goes about killing swine. Is one of the reasons Banquo is startled by the appearance of the witches that their indeterminate gender undermines the assertion of manliness on which a political and military order has been established? The cultural theorist Terry Eagleton finds 'positive value' in the witches' subversion of social hierarchy, and is inclined to see the weird sisters as 'the heroines of the piece':

> They are poets, prophetesses and devotees of female cult, radical separatists who scorn male power and lay bare the hollow sound and fury at its heart. Their words and bodies mock rigorous boundaries and make sport of fixed positions, unhinging received meanings as they dance, dissolve and re-materialize. But official society can only ever imagine its radical 'other' as chaos rather than creativity, and is thus bound to define the sisters as evil.

(1986, pp.2–3)

The roots of tragedy

We have spent a good deal of time in the company of the witches, not just because they continue to give *Macbeth* a compelling fascination for audiences around the world, but because our view of the witches is likely to have a decisive effect on how we approach the rest of the play. At this point, it would be a good idea to look briefly over the remaining scenes in Act 1, noting any interesting structural patterns or relationships between scenes. **How would you describe the pace and momentum of the first few scenes in *Macbeth*?**

As a general observation, it is worth pointing out that the action in the play is swift and intense, but the speed and energy carry in their tow a clutch of brooding dilemmas and complexities which begin to surface as early as 1. 3. Some readers and spectators, not surprisingly, see Macbeth caught up in a vortex of evil, hurtling ineluctably towards his destruction.

Some very influential critics have endorsed this view of the play. G. Wilson Knight, for instance, in his celebrated study of Shakespearean tragedy, *The Wheel of Fire* (1930), suggests that '*Macbeth* is the apocalypse of evil', as well as Shakespeare's 'most profound and mature vision of evil' (1949 edn, pp.140, 158). The problem with this kind of analysis is that evil is conceived in a vaguely philosophical or metaphysical way, without much regard for social and historical detail, so that the origins and causes of tragic conflict are ultimately evaded. Wilson Knight concedes that 'the ultimate evil remains a mystery' and suggests unhelpfully that 'it comes from without' (ibid., pp.157–8). Bradley likewise insists upon 'the *incalculability* of evil' in *Macbeth* (1967 edn, p.386, emphasis added). As we have already seen in the preliminary discussion of tragedy, this insistence on reading Shakespeare's plays as universal conflicts of good and evil has the effect of flattening them out into moral allegories and only serves to diminish, rather than elaborate, their tragic substance and appeal. Without entirely dispelling the mystique of evil in *Macbeth*, we will try in the rest of this chapter to determine to what extent the roots of tragedy are social.

Looking at the overall shape of Act 1, you might have noticed how the two scenes involving the witches (1 and 3) alternate with two scenes involving Duncan and his attendants (2 and 4). This pattern seems to be carried through to the end of Act 1, with Lady Macbeth 'standing in' for the witches. (Although Lady Macbeth appears in all three of the closing scenes (5, 6 and 7), Scene 6 is principally concerned with the arrival of Duncan and Banquo at Macbeth's castle in Inverness.) This arrangement of scenes establishes a strange affinity between the witches and Lady Macbeth. Scenes 1, 3, 5 and 7 might be regarded as scenes of female temptation, whereas the other scenes are more obviously concerned with public displays of male power and chivalry among the king and his attendants. Before asking what kind of affinity exists between the witches and Lady Macbeth, let us look briefly at the social and political circumstances in which Macbeth comes to power. **What impression of the Scottish kingdom are we given in the early scenes of Act 1?**

Duncan's first words in the play – 'What bloody man is that?' (1. 2. 1) – are a vivid indication of the violent and uncertain state of the nation. (The man to whom he refers is the Sergeant or Captain, who is bleeding as a result of having fought to prevent the king's son, Malcolm, being taken prisoner.) The emphasis throughout 1. 2 is on acts of military prowess in stemming the tide of rebellion. *Macbeth* is sometimes seen, in a rather facile way, as a play about the conflict between order and disorder, but the early scenes of the play raise important questions about the kind of order that exists *before* Macbeth seizes the crown. Duncan's opening words suggest that he is an observer rather than a participant in Scotland's battles. His dependence on 'brave Macbeth' (16), while perhaps indicating a pragmatic exercise of power and self-protection, points to a serious vulnerability in his kingdom.

Speaking things strange

One of the most obvious means by which our attention is drawn to the social instability in *Macbeth* is through the parallel instability of its language. **Look carefully at the Captain's report of the battle, and note any potential ambiguities or uncertainties in the speech.**

> Doubtful it stood,
> As two spent swimmers that do cling together
> And choke their art. The merciless Macdonald –
> Worthy to be a rebel, for to that
> The multiplying villainies of nature
> Do swarm upon him – from the Western Isles
> Of kerns and galloglasses is supplied,
> And fortune on his damnèd quarry smiling
> Showed like a rebel's whore. But all's too weak,
> For brave Macbeth – well he deserves that name! –
> Disdaining fortune, with his brandished steel
> Which smoked with bloody execution,
> Like valour's minion
> Carved out his passage till he faced the slave,
> Which ne'er shook hands nor bade farewell to him

> Till he unseamed him from the nave to th' chops,
> And fixed his head upon our battlements.

(1. 2. 7–23)

Allowing for the unfamiliarity of seventeenth-century English, the Captain's speech seems unusually convoluted. Even if we suppose the speech to be a naturalistic account of a wounded man lapsing into incoherence, there are lingering difficulties. The opening simile comparing the two sides in the battle to 'two spent swimmers that do cling together / And choke their art' is in keeping with the elaborate decorum that characterizes much of the language in *Macbeth*. (We will see many examples of this: 'So well thy words become thee as thy wounds: / They smack of honour both' (43–4), Duncan later tells the Captain.) The difficulties of interpretation that arise from a densely figurative idiom are compounded by the disjointed syntax of the speech (note the number of dashes). Towards the end of the speech, the comma after 'slave' creates a moment of confusion. Does the word 'Which' refer to Macbeth or his opponent ('the slave')? The anonymous pronoun 'him' also creates uncertainties. Just as we establish that Macbeth has 'unseamed' his opponent 'from the nave to th' chops' and 'fixed his head' upon the battlements, we are given an odd anticipation of Macbeth's own decapitation later in the play. The Captain describes Macdonald as 'Worthy to be a rebel', a curious appraisal that throws some doubt on Duncan's first mention of Macbeth as 'worthy gentleman' (24).

When the Thane of Ross appears, Lenox comments that his hasty look 'seems to speak things strange' (47). Ross, like the Captain, has an obvious liking for figurative embellishment in his speech, and he describes Macbeth as 'Bellona's bridegroom' (54), imagining his victory over the Thane of Cawdor as a wedding with the Roman goddess of war. Duncan denounces the Thane of Cawdor as a traitor and bestows the title on Macbeth. Later, in 1. 3, when Ross greets Macbeth with the new title, he does indeed 'speak things strange':

> The King hath happily received, Macbeth,
> The news of thy success, and when he reads
> Thy personal venture in the rebels' sight
> His wonders and his praises do contend
> Which should be thine or his; silenced with that,
> In viewing o'er the rest o'th' self-same day
> He finds thee in the stout Norwegian ranks,
> Nothing afeard of what thyself didst make,
> Strange images of death. As thick as hail
> Came post with post, and every one did bear
> Thy praises in his kingdom's great defence,
> And poured them down before him.

(1. 3. 87–98)

The syntactical twists and turns of Ross's speech seem in excess of his attempt to describe the confusion that lingers in the aftermath of the battle, and they lead to puzzling ambiguities. Ross reports that Duncan has heard of Macbeth's 'personal venture in the rebels' sight' and 'finds thee in the stout Norwegian ranks', both statements being open to misconstruction. It is difficult to determine what Ross means when he says of Duncan that 'His wonders and his praises do contend / Which should be thine or his'. He seems to imply that there is a conflict in Duncan's mind and that this leaves him dumbfounded, but, not surprisingly, editors of *Macbeth* have found these lines difficult to gloss. Editors have also disagreed extensively about the simile, 'As thick as hail / Came post with post'. The implication is that one messenger (on post-horse) has quickly followed another with compliments for Macbeth, but the association of the compliments with a shower of hailstones is not an entirely promising one. Some editions of *Macbeth* contain the lines, 'As thick as Tale / Can post with post', suggesting 'as rapidly as witnesses with reports of your feats can ride post-horses post-haste' (Andrews, 1993, p.16). The lines 'Nothing afeard of what thyself didst make, / Strange images of death' seems relatively straightforward as a description of Macbeth's fearless response to those he killed in battle. Nevertheless, the lines foreshadow the strange images of death that *do* induce a terrified response in Macbeth after the murder of Duncan. When Ross finally announces Macbeth's new title, he presents it as 'an earnest of a greater honour' (102) (a pledge of even better to come), ironically reiterating the prophecy of the witches.

In a play ostensibly concerned with 'decorum', a high incidence of linguistic slippages and disjunctive statements points to a widespread social and political crisis. It is not just the witches or the drunken porter who speak with double meanings; the entire play seems to be pervaded by a sense of 'doubleness' and doubt. The Captain tells with amazement of how Macbeth and Banquo were 'As cannons overcharged with double cracks, / So they doubly redoubled strokes upon the foe' (1. 2. 37). For the witches in 4. 1, 'double, double' is appropriately rhymed with 'toil and trouble' (10). The first words spoken by Macbeth in 1. 3 – 'So foul and fair a day I have not seen' (36) – are an echo or double of the witches' double discourse in the opening scene of the play: 'Fair is foul, and foul is fair'. Everywhere, a visual and verbal distortion seems to confound the senses, and things are not what they seem.

The instabilities of language that provide an indication of instabilities in the social order also reveal a deep crisis of identity at the personal or psychological level. The impending tragedy of Macbeth is registered most intensely in the occasional asides and soliloquies, which denote a mood and attitude of rapt self-attention but also increasing self-division. Pondering the truth that 'I am Thane of Cawdor' (1. 3. 132), Macbeth is propelled from 'present fears' (136) to 'horrible imaginings' (137):

> My thought, whose murder yet is but fantastical,
> Shakes so my single state of man that function
> Is smothered in surmise, and nothing is
> But what is not.
>
> (1. 3. 138–41)

It is here – in the profound disturbance of identity, in the radical split between consciousness and material existence – that tragedy can be seen to stir. By the end of the next scene (1. 4), Macbeth's murderous thoughts have gathered momentum and some dark deed seems imminent.

Issues of kingship

Before proceeding, let us ask what claims Macbeth might have to the throne of Scotland. A first reading of the play might suggest that Macbeth has no legitimate claim to the Scottish throne and that his usurpation of Duncan's role is based entirely on a ruthless exercise of power. However, the issue of kingship in *Macbeth* is by no means simple or straightforward. Duncan addresses Macbeth as 'valiant cousin, worthy gentleman' (1. 2. 24). 'Cousin' was a familiar term of address for any nobleman, but according to historical sources Duncan and Macbeth were, in fact, blood relations. Close family ties were not, however, the only legitimate means of succession. Although *Macbeth* is set in eleventh-century Scotland (strictly speaking, a pre-feudal age), the social and political organization it depicts is essentially feudal: there is an established system of thanes or lords with their own fiefdoms or spheres of power, and great emphasis is laid on personal obligations, conduct, loyalty and honour. Within this feudal system it was common enough for a king to be elected. Although such a king held authority among his peers, he was in other ways their equal. An audience watching *Macbeth* in 1606 would have been accustomed to a much more refined and elaborate idea of kingship, strongly informed by claims to absolute power and divine right. In a subtle way, *Macbeth* draws on conflicting ideas of royal power; it raises uncomfortable questions about succession, about the personal qualities of kings and about what constitutes effective rule.

Act 1, Scene 4 is a key scene for understanding some of these uncertain issues of kingship. Duncan's response to the execution of the treasonous Thane of Cawdor suggests a thoughtful and trusting king:

> There's no art
> To find the mind's construction in the face.
> He was a gentleman on whom I built
> An absolute trust.

> (1. 4. 11–14)

Coming immediately before his expression of gratitude to Macbeth, these lines are loaded with dramatic irony, but they also, perhaps, throw doubt on Duncan's judgement. The irony is doubled in Macbeth's declaration of his service and loyalty to the king, and of his dutiful intention of 'doing everything / Safe toward your love and honour' (26–7). What look like excessive compliments bestowed on Macbeth by Duncan can be understood within the context of feudal obligations and contracts, but there are moments when Duncan seems unconsciously to promote Macbeth's ambition. 'More is thy due than more than all can pay' (21), he tells Macbeth, and he later confides to Banquo, 'It is a peerless kinsman' (58), implying that Macbeth is without equal. The critical moment in 1. 4 is when Duncan establishes his estate on Malcolm, his eldest son, naming him Prince of Cumberland. This public naming confirms that succession in the Scottish monarchy did not necessarily depend on hereditary rights or 'primogeniture'. Macbeth's surprise and disappointment (powerfully depicted in Roman Polanski's 1971 film version of the play) are evident in his departing aside, with its taut rhyming couplets, its vivid imagery and its forthright diction:

> The Prince of Cumberland – that is a step
> On which I must fall down or else o'erleap,
> For in my way it lies. Stars, hide your fires,
> Let not light see my black and deep desires;
> The eye wink at the hand; yet let that be
> Which the eye fears, when it is done, to see.

> (1. 4. 48–53)

Macbeth's determination to fulfil his 'deep desires' leads us to one of the most profound concerns in the play: the issue of legitimacy. What constitutes legitimate power? Under what circumstances might rebellion be considered legitimate? How do we distinguish between legitimate and illegitimate violence? As we will see, the play's preoccupation with power and violence inevitably raises questions about gender and sexuality.

Deep desires: gender and power

One of the most remarkable aspects of *Macbeth* is its unflinching depiction of how 'deep desires', which might otherwise be a source of human affection and solidarity, are brutally degraded and perverted. The highly charged sexual energy that exists between Macbeth and Lady Macbeth is channelled into a tragically wasteful and self-consuming lust for power. Writing to his wife about the prophecy of the witches, Macbeth tells of how he 'burned in desire to question them further'(1. 5. 3–4), but the letter also shows how that fiery yearning is single-mindedly directed at future 'greatness'. In the same letter, Macbeth addresses his wife as 'my dearest partner of greatness' (9–10) and bids her rejoice in the knowledge of 'what greatness is promised thee' (11). Lady Macbeth, in turn, addresses her husband as 'great Glamis' (20) and recognizes the essential nature of his ambition: 'Thou wouldst be great' (16). A shared desire for social advancement is couched in a deeply erotic vocabulary. There is a strongly physical, as well as verbal, expression in Lady Macbeth's promise to 'chastise with the valour of my tongue / All that impedes thee from the golden round' (25–6). Still more revealing, in her first speech in the play, is her intimate awareness of a previously unacknowledged sensitivity in Macbeth's constitution:

> Yet do I fear thy nature.
> It is too full o'th' milk of human kindness
> To catch the nearest way.

> (1. 5. 14–16)

How should we interpret this image of 'human kindness', and in what way does it qualify or contradict the earlier testimonies to Macbeth's 'nature' in Act 1? For modern readers, 'human kindness' suggests unselfish, generous behaviour, but in its earlier usage the phrase has connotations of human *kind* or *kin* (as in kinsman or kinship). Milk signifies nourishment and natural 'goodness', perhaps anticipating later images of child-rearing. As Ryan points out, the phrase suggests 'a tender, nurturing attention to others, sustained by a sense of shared identity with one's fellow human beings, and by a sense of the obligations attendant on this feeling of community with one's kind' (1995 edn, p.96). What Lady Macbeth's speech alludes to is her husband's essential humanity, his shared sense of human endeavour and purpose. This recognition of Macbeth's 'kindness' sits oddly alongside the prevailing image of 'Bellona's bridegroom', ruthlessly dispatching his enemies. We have already intimated that one of the symptoms of an unstable social order is an unstable sense of selfhood or identity, and in *Macbeth* this manifests itself most obviously in shifting definitions of manhood and manliness. One of the functions of Lady Macbeth, in subtle collusion with the witches, is to unsettle conventional 'norms' of gender by throwing into confusion the very question of what it means to be a man. **Look again at the opening of 1. 5, and note the ways in which Lady Macbeth might be equated with the witches.**

First of all, it seems significant that, when we first encounter Lady Macbeth, she is reading the letter in which Macbeth recounts how 'the weird sisters' greeted him. Her own thoughts of impending greatness flow from her reflections on what the witches have revealed. She seems intent on collaborating with 'fate and metaphysical aid' (27), and her summoning of Macbeth – 'Hie thee hither / That I may pour my spirits in thine ear' (23–4) – smacks of 'supernatural soliciting' (1. 3. 129–30). Lady Macbeth's first appearance in the play has interesting parallels with the first appearance of the witches. Both Lady Macbeth and the witches are initially set apart from the world of male authority and presented as if in their own domains. Both hail Macbeth on his entrance, and both place temptation in his way. Both transgress conventional ideas of femininity. The puzzled response of Banquo to the witches:

> You should be women,
> And yet your beards forbid me to interpret
> That you are so
>
> (1. 3. 43–5)

suggests that they have refused to conform to an implied norm of feminine decorum and appearance. Lady Macbeth seems intent on casting out the bodily, biological traces of her sex:

> Come, you spirits
> That tend on mortal thoughts, unsex me here,
> And fill me from the crown to the toe, top-full
> Of direst cruelty. Make thick my blood,
> Stop up th'access and passage to remorse,
> That no compunctious visitings of nature
> Shake my fell purpose, nor keep peace between
> Th'effect and it. Come to my woman's breasts,
> And take my milk for gall, you murd'ring ministers,
> Wherever in your sightless substances
> You wait on nature's mischief. Come, thick night,
> And pall thee in the dunnest smoke of hell,
> That my keen knife see not the wound it makes,
> Nor heaven peep through the blanket of the dark
> To cry 'Hold, hold!'
>
> (1. 5. 38–52)

This speech is a powerful negation of the qualities and attributes customarily ascribed to women and associated with fertility and nurturing. It seems futile to question whether Lady Macbeth is literally or metaphorically invoking 'the spirits'; her affinity with the witches is clearly pronounced, especially in the incantatory repetition of 'Come, you spirits ... Come to my woman's breasts ... Come, thick night'. Whatever supernatural effects the witches and Lady Macbeth conjure up, their 'perverted' femininity serves to bring conventional gender roles and boundaries into question.

In 1. 6, Lady Macbeth plays hostess to Duncan and Banquo. To the king she is both 'honoured hostess' (10) and 'Fair and noble hostess' (24). But, in the light of what is to come, these appellations have no more substance than the sweet and nimble air that seems to surround Macbeth's castle. Banquo's pleased recognition of the 'temple-haunting martlet' (4) that nests on the walls of the castle ironically anticipates Lady Macbeth's intense rejection of nature's gentle ways. This brief scene of about 30 lines serves as an ironic preface to the preparations for murder that follow, but it is also a powerful reminder of the radical split between signs and meanings in *Macbeth*, which we will return to later. Duncan's acknowledgement of Macbeth's 'great love, sharp as his spur' (23) resounds throughout the rest of the play. Lady Macbeth's declaration of service – 'In every point twice done, and then done double' (15) – is echoed in the opening words of Macbeth's soliloquy at the start of 1. 7 ('If it were done').

Macbeth's soliloquy

Strictly speaking, there are two kinds of solo speech attributed to Macbeth. There are relatively brief *asides*, when Macbeth turns away from other characters on the stage and seems to address the audience in confidence (see the end of 1. 4, for example). There are also *soliloquies* (from the Latin: *solus*, 'alone' and *loqui*, 'to speak'), when Macbeth is more obviously isolated and intent on 'speaking his mind' in private.

The opening of 1. 7 heightens this sense of isolation by having Macbeth deliver a soliloquy as the banquet for Duncan gets under way in the background. **Look at this soliloquy now. How does the language of the speech seek to persuade us of Macbeth's tormented consciousness?**

> If it were done when 'tis done, then 'twere well
> It were done quickly. If th'assassination
> Could trammel up the consequence, and catch
> With his surcease, success: that but this blow
> Might be the be-all and the end-all, here,
> But here upon this bank and shoal of time,
> We'd jump the life to come. But in these cases
> We still have judgement here, that we but teach
> Bloody instructions which, being taught, return
> To plague th'inventor. This even-handed justice
> Commends th'ingredience of our poisoned chalice
> To our own lips. He's here in double trust:
> First, as I am his kinsman and his subject,
> Strong both against the deed; then, as his host,
> Who should against his murderer shut the door,
> Not bear the knife myself. Besides, this Duncan
> Hath borne his faculties so meek, hath been
> So clear in his great office, that his virtues
> Will plead like angels, trumpet-tongued against
> The deep damnation of his taking-off,
> And pity, like a naked new-born babe,

Striding the blast, or heaven's cherubin, horsed
Upon the sightless couriers of the air,
Shall blow the horrid deed in every eye
That tears shall drown the wind. I have no spur
To prick the sides of my intent, but only
Vaulting ambition which o'erleaps itself
And falls on th'other.

(1. 7. 1–28)

This long, complicated speech seems to enact the mental chaos and ethical confusion that grip Macbeth at this critical moment in the play. The language works to persuade us of an actual speaking voice and seems to grant us privileged access to the innermost depths of a deeply disturbed consciousness. The twists and turns in the sentence structure, the sudden proliferation of metaphors from fishing, riding and jumping, the dense theological, legal and ethical vocabulary, all contribute to an impression of intellectual and emotional instability. From the outset, a sense of confusion and uncertainty is apparent in the soliloquy. Although Macbeth, like Lady Macbeth, is concerned with getting things 'done' and doing them thoroughly, the overall impression is one of immobility. The conditional tense of the opening lines, reinforced by the close proximity of 'If', 'when' and 'then', suggests evasion. Macbeth speaks evasively of Duncan's murder as 'it', and then resorts to the euphemistic 'assassination'. The vocabulary in the opening lines of the speech is simple and yet the syntax tends towards obfuscation.

As we read this speech, we should remember that we are reading poetry and that many of its rhetorical effects derive from its poetic devices, including its densely patterned imagery. The speech is written in blank verse – unrhymed lines of roughly ten syllables each – which strives to emulate the pace and rhythm of human speech.

It is not easy to paraphrase the first dozen lines of the soliloquy ('If it were done ... To our own lips'). Macbeth's initial concern is to get the murder over with, but in a way that will limit or eradicate its possible repercussions. The fishing image suggests a need to 'trammel up the consequence', that is, to catch it in a net to prevent it spreading. The immediate juxtaposition and word-play of 'surcease, success' are also indicative of this need for effective containment. The repetition of the word 'here' is curious. The first 'here' seems to mark the end of a sentence, suggesting Macbeth's desire to end the repercussions of Duncan's death *here* (upon earth), but the momentum of the speech propels us forward and the second 'here' induces reflections on risking 'the life to come'. The fishing imagery is neatly continued in 'this bank and shoal of time', suggesting that earthly existence is a shallow stretch of water compared with the eternity of the sea. Some editions of *Macbeth* print 'bank and school of time', referring to a judge's bench or 'bank' and anticipating the stress on judgement and teaching that follows. However we read these lines, we are pulled away from considerations of the afterlife towards a meditation on natural justice and a realization that any abuse of justice is likely to rebound on the perpetrator. The poisoned chalice is a particularly apt image in view of the proceeding banquet, which ought to signify communal loyalties.

The soliloquy shifts towards considerations of feudal obligations and ties of kinship: 'He's here in double trust ... The deep damnation of his taking-off' (12–20). The structure of the soliloquy at this point suggests a careful, rationalizing approach ('First, as I am his kinsman ... then, as his host'), but the speech cannot hold back the overwhelming force of Christian retribution, and the imagery of angels and trumpets summons thoughts of Judgement Day and 'deep damnation'. The idea that Duncan's virtues will 'plead like angels' carries connotations of both begging for pity and pleading in court. What begins as pragmatic expediency ends in urgent metaphysical speculation, with the awesome crescendo of the closing lines: 'And pity, like a naked new-born babe ... And falls on th'other' (21–8).

The elevated rhetoric of these lines is combined with a startling series of images and verbal echoes. Pity is emblematized in the archetypal image of the 'naked new-born babe', both recalling Duncan, who was 'clear in his great office' (spotless, innocent) and anticipating Lady Macbeth's violent response to the idea of the innocent child later in 1. 7. The image also looks forward to the revelation that Macduff 'was from his mother's womb / Untimely ripped' (5. 10. 15–16). 'Striding' suggests either 'standing over' or 'riding over', and 'blast' suggests both a gust of wind and a trumpet blast. The verb 'blow' echoes the violent noun in line 4. The 'sightless couriers of the air' asks us to imagine invisible (or blind?) horses, ridden by a host of angels. Pity will summon universal sorrow: the idea that 'tears shall drown the wind' refers to eyes watering in a strong breeze, but perhaps also to the wind dying down in a shower. The spur ironically recalls Duncan's homage to Macbeth's 'great love, sharp as his spur' (1. 6. 23), and carries through the earlier references to rising and jumping. The closing image suggests two possible readings: a rider leaping over a fence, only to fall on the other side, and a rider trying to 'vault' into the saddle and ending up on the other side of the horse. In addition, the lines perhaps allude to the 'vaulting ambition' and 'fall' of Lucifer.

The many puzzling ambiguities and complexities in Macbeth's soliloquy are entirely in keeping with the idea of an insecure, unstable identity, and also with the idea of an unstable order in which legal, ethical and theological discourses clamour for recognition. As the incomplete line at the end of the soliloquy suggests, the speech is interrupted by the entrance of Lady Macbeth. Even so, Macbeth seems to have decided against the killing of the king, and he tells his wife, 'We will proceed no further in this business' (1. 7. 31). **What is it, then, that undermines this apparent decision and leads Macbeth to the eventual murder?**

Part of the explanation can be found in the speech by Lady Macbeth that immediately follows. As we have already seen, the vocabulary of political power and the vocabulary of sexual intimacy become enmeshed in an all-encompassing 'desire'. Lady Macbeth chastizes her husband for his inhibitions:

> From this time
> Such I account thy love. Art thou afeard
> To be the same in thine own act and valour
> As thou art in desire?

> (1. 7. 38–41)

Macbeth's response is to assert his manhood –

> Prithee, peace.
> I dare do all that may become a man;
> Who dares do more is none

> (1. 7. 45–7)

– but Lady Macbeth's swift reply further undermines it:

> What beast was't then
> That made you break this enterprise to me?
> When you durst do it, then you were a man;
> And to be more than what you were, you would
> Be so much more the man

(1. 7. 47–51)

and Macbeth is stirred to action. As David Norbrook has pointed out (1987, p.101), the frequent stress on 'doing' has sexual overtones, as does Lady Macbeth's provocative question, 'What cannot you and I perform upon / Th'unguarded Duncan?' (69–70).

What Lady Macbeth extols is an idea of manliness that excludes compassion and nurturing. In this she is following the dictates of a society that offers praise and rewards for violence. Her negation of her own mothering instincts defies conventional gender boundaries and suggests that women desirous of social advancement must become as men:

> I have given suck, and know
> How tender 'tis to love the babe that milks me.
> I would, while it was smiling in my face,
> Have plucked my nipple from his boneless gums
> And dashed the brains out, had I so sworn
> As you have done to this.

(1. 7. 54–9)

Macbeth's response confirms the supremacy of 'males' in the social hierarchy:

> Bring forth men-children only
> For thy undaunted mettle should compose
> Nothing but males.

(1. 7. 72–4)

By the end of Act 1, Macbeth is sufficiently motivated to do the deed. His tragedy is prompted not by some vague, metaphysical evil, but by a violent and unassuageable appetite for power, in which his very identity as a man is put to the test. Macbeth's willingness to listen to the witches provides one possible motive for his downfall, and the challenge to his manhood is enough to goad him into murder.

Equivocation: the play of signs and meanings

The fluctuation between different conceptions of manhood is just one instance of a fundamental instability of signs and meanings in *Macbeth*. Throughout the play, words and images are continually redefined and misinterpreted. This crisis of meaning extends beyond the level of verbal confusion to the point where the evidence of the senses can no longer be trusted. Visual perception, in particular, becomes fraught with uncertainty. We have already seen how Duncan misplaces his trust in appearances and how, after the execution of the Thane of Cawdor, he has reason to wonder, 'There's no art / To find the mind's construction in the face' (1. 4. 11–12). Two scenes later we find him rhapsodizing on the setting of his own impending doom:

> This castle hath a pleasant seat. The air
> Nimbly and sweetly recommends itself
> Unto our gentle senses.

(1. 6. 1–3)

In the minds of Macbeth and Lady Macbeth, a more severe dissociation of signs and meanings takes place. Even before the murder of the king, Macbeth is given to hallucination:

> Is this a dagger which I see before me,
> The handle toward my hand? Come, let me clutch thee.
> I have thee not, and yet I see thee still.
> Art thou not, fatal vision, sensible
> To feeling as to sight? Or art thou but
> A dagger of the mind, a false creation
> Proceeding from the heat-oppressèd brain?
> I see thee yet, in form as palpable
> As this which now I draw.
> Thou marshall'st me the way that I was going,
> And such an instrument I was to use.
> Mine eyes are made the fools o'th' other senses,
> Or else worth all the rest. I see thee still,
> And on thy blade and dudgeon gouts of blood,
> Which was not so before. There's no such thing.
> It is the bloody business which informs
> Thus to mine eyes.

(2. 2. 33–49)

On occasions such as this, the senses seem to conspire against each other. The repetition of 'I see before me ... I see thee still ... I see thee yet ... I see thee still' insists on the primacy of visual sensation, and yet Macbeth concedes, 'There's no such thing'. The apparition of the dagger provides a further indication, following the soliloquy in 1. 7, that Macbeth, while desiring the death of the king, cannot permit himself to be fully conscious of the deed. Immediately following the murder, Macbeth's senses seem repulsed by his bodily actions, and the disjointed nature of his being is vividly rendered in the image of self-molestation and the hypnotic vision of a sea of blood:

> What hands are here! Ha, they pluck out mine eyes.
> Will all great Neptune's ocean wash this blood
> Clean from my hand? No, this my hand will rather
> The multitudinous seas incarnadine,
> Making the green one red.

(2. 2. 57–61)

Macbeth's words at the end of 2. 2 are a powerful summation of his own psychic dislocation and a reminder of how frequently the action of the play is precipitated by imperfect knowledge: 'To know my deed 'twere best not know myself' (71).

The events of Act 2 are swift and intense. The central incident – the killing of the king – is compressed into four short scenes of just over 300 lines. Act 2 opens in darkness with the uneasiness of Banquo and his son Fleance, and it closes in the early light of morning with Macduff, Ross and an Old Man reflecting on the murder and its consequences. The murder is carried out in 2. 2, but its revelation is preceded by the comic banter of the drunken Porter. The opening of 2. 3 might, as some critics believe, function as comic relief, providing a brief respite from the shock of Duncan's murder, but perhaps it carries an additional significance. **Read the first 40 lines of the scene again, and think about their relevance to some of the issues we have discussed so far.**

On stage, the Porter's delay in opening the door to Macbeth's castle provides a convenient interval for Macbeth to wash his hands and change his clothes before greeting his visitors. It is clear, however, that the punning, riddling speech of the Porter alludes to issues that recur throughout the play. The word 'equivocate', for instance, recalls the involvement of Father Henry Garnett in the Gunpowder Plot and raises the topical issue of treason. Equivocation also aptly suggests the persistent and pervasive uncertainties of meaning in *Macbeth*. The Porter's speech is full of sexual innuendoes and bawdy puns, and these fasten our attention, once again, on the play's preoccupation with manhood. The suggestion that 'drink may be said to be an equivocator with lechery: it makes him, and it mars him' (28–30) cleverly deflates the earlier celebration of virility.

Macduff is not short of a few puns of his own, and his retort that 'drink gave thee the lie last night' (34) implies that drink cheated the Porter of his senses, made him lie down and also caused him to urinate (a pun on the Elizabethan 'lye' for urine). The Porter replies in kind, suggesting that the drink 'lies' in his throat, despite his efforts to urinate ('took up my legs sometime' (37)) and vomit ('made a shift to cast him' (37)). Lying in the throat also alludes to someone being killed in the act of lying (thus ensuring their eternal damnation), and it sets up the idea of the Porter wrestling with drink (which takes him by the throat and tries to overthrow him). The idea of vomiting or 'casting out' anticipates the purging of the state that Macbeth's crime necessitates.

The drunken Porter's antics have their origins in the English medieval miracle plays, which celebrated Christian redemption. In the popular depiction of 'the harrowing of hell', Christ passes through the gates of hell to conquer Satan and death. The Porter, a parody of Saint Peter, imagines himself as 'porter of hell-gate' (1), welcoming the eternally damned. Although he quickly abandons the role ('this place is too cold for hell. I'll devil-porter it no further' (15–16)), the suggestion of Macbeth's castle as hell and Macduff as the redeemer persists. It is worth noting how much of *Macbeth* is shaped by the powerful idea of Christian redemption. Many characters, including Macbeth himself, acknowledge a Christian scheme of values and ideals. In 2. 2, Macbeth confesses how he hears two guests (possibly Donalbain and Malcolm) talking in their sleep, and how he 'could not say "Amen" / When they did say "God bless us"' (26–7). Macduff, on discovering Duncan's dead body, cries out that 'sacrilegious murder hath broke ope / The Lord's anointed temple' (2. 3. 63–4), endorsing the idea of the king as God's representative on earth. At the end of 2. 3, Banquo declares 'In the great hand of God I stand' (126), and at the end of 2. 4, the Old Man conversing with Ross and Macduff tells the two thanes: 'God's benison go with you' (41). Despite the allusions to medieval Christian drama and the extensive references to a Christian framework of belief, we should not be tempted to interpret *Macbeth* as a simple allegory of good versus evil. If we are to persist in using the word 'tragedy', we need to be attentive to the complex range of attitudes and ideas that the play embodies.

The structure and development of the tragedy

Understanding *Macbeth* as tragedy involves some appreciation of how it makes its impact as a dramatic structure on readers and spectators. How do its pace and momentum shape the emotional responses of an audience? Tragedy requires of its spectators a sustained interest and engagement in the impulses and motivations of its protagonists. Part of the fascination of *Macbeth* is that the killing of the king occurs at an early stage in the action, yet the play succeeds in holding the interest and attention of readers and spectators for another three acts. Even when Macbeth embarks on multiple killings, quickly disposing of Banquo and Lady Macduff and her children, the play seems to invite a sympathetic and considered response to Macbeth's predicament. We have seen how Duncan's murder is not simply the result of compulsive evil, but rather the consequence of 'vaulting ambition', fuelled by the attitudes and values of a particular social and political order. While Macbeth's atrocities might be expected to provoke an alienated response from readers and spectators, the poetry of the play draws attention to the ambiguities and confusions that are both a symptom of social instability and an index of psychological vulnerability.

The murder of Duncan in 2. 2 clearly fails to secure Macbeth's ambitions. What is it, then, that provokes the further killings in Acts 3 and 4, and how does the play retain its tragic potential? An answer to these questions might be found in Macbeth's soliloquy in the opening scene of Act 3. **Read these lines again and try to analyse the source of Macbeth's 'fear':**

> To be thus is nothing
> But to be safely thus. Our fears in Banquo
> Stick deep, and in his royalty of nature
> Reigns that which would be feared. 'Tis much he dares,
> And to that dauntless temper of his mind
> He hath a wisdom that doth guide his valour
> To act in safety. There is none but he
> Whose being I do fear, and under him
> My genius is rebuked as, it is said,
> Mark Antony's was by Caesar. He chid the sisters
> When first they put the name of king upon me,
> And bade them speak to him. Then, prophet-like,
> They hailed him father to a line of kings.
> Upon my head they placed a fruitless crown,
> And put a barren sceptre in my grip,
> Thence to be wrenched with an unlineal hand,
> No son of mine succeeding. If't be so,
> For Banquo's issue have I filed my mind,
> For them the gracious Duncan have I murdered,

Put rancours in the vessel of my peace
Only for them, and mine eternal jewel
Given to the common enemy of man
To make them kings, the seeds of Banquo kings.
Rather than so, come fate into the list
And champion me to th'utterance.

(3. 1. 49–73)

Fear is certainly prominent in this speech, as we can see in the notable repetition:

Our *fears* in Banquo
Stick deep, and in his royalty of nature
Reigns that which would be *feared*.

(3. 1. 50–2, emphasis added)

A few lines later, Macbeth tells us 'There is none but he / Whose being I do *fear*' (55–6, emphasis added). The speech suggests that we should take these lines in a very precise way. Banquo is depicted as brave and loyal, but what Macbeth most fears is his very 'being' – his living presence – since what destabilizes Macbeth's kingship is the line of succession foreseen by the witches. It is here that we can begin to perceive the full significance of the many images of children in *Macbeth*. Recalling the witches' prophecies, Macbeth fears that he will reign with 'a fruitless crown' and 'barren sceptre', and with 'No son of mine succeeding'. It is here, too, that we can begin to grasp the full significance of the many protestations of manhood in *Macbeth*. In addition, the spiritual consequences of his actions, which Macbeth held at bay in his soliloquy in 1. 7, now flood into his consciousness. Without offspring of his own, he has sacrificed his immortal soul ('mine eternal jewel' (69)) to make 'the seeds of Banquo kings' (71).

It is unclear whether Macbeth means to challenge or recruit the workings of 'Fate', but his sense of determination appears strained. The opening words of the soliloquy – 'To be thus is nothing' – anticipate the despairing nihilism that descends in Act 5. Macbeth's dismay at having achieved 'nothing' is echoed by Lady Macbeth at the beginning of 3. 2: 'Naught's had, all's spent' (6). The intensity of the dialogue between the new king and queen propels the action of the play into increasing darkness. The fluctuating emotions and elevated speech in 3. 2 have a rhythmic, musical grandeur typical of opera. Lady Macbeth's state of 'doubtful joy' (9) is echoed in her husband's 'restless ecstasy' (24). There is tenderness in the way they address each other as 'love' and 'chuck', but the intimacy between them is marred by increasing apprehension, restlessness and misery. Macbeth speaks of 'the affliction of these terrible dreams / That shake us nightly' (20–1). His mind is 'full of scorpions' (37). At the same time, he seems intent on the utmost destruction, disdaining both heaven and earth: 'let the frame of things disjoint, both the worlds suffer' (18). As with the preparations for the murder of Duncan, the dialogue between Macbeth and Lady Macbeth gathers pace and momentum until it issues in 'A deed of dreadful note' (45).

The murder of Banquo is heralded by some of the most stirring and evocative poetry in the entire play:

> Ere the bat hath flown
> His cloistered flight, ere to black Hecate's summons
> The shard-borne beetle with his drowsy hums
> Hath rung night's yawning peal, there shall be done
> A deed of dreadful note.

(3. 2. 41–5)

The repetition of 'Ere the bat ... ere to black Hecate', the subtle pararhymes of 'flown'/'done', 'summons'/'hums', and the decisive alliteration of 'done / A deed of dreadful note' conjure up an intoxicating rhythm. The vocabulary is powerfully and richly adjectival: 'cloistered', 'black', 'drowsy', 'yawning', 'dreadful' and 'shard-borne' (born in dung or borne on scaly wings). Macbeth's closing invocation to the night recalls Lady Macbeth's incantation, 'Come, thick night', in 1. 5. 48:

> Come, seeling night,
> Scarf up the tender eye of pitiful day,
> And with thy bloody and invisible hand
> Cancel and tear to pieces that great bond
> Which keeps me pale. Light thickens, and the crow
> Makes wing to th' rooky wood.
> Good things of day begin to droop and drowse,
> Whiles night's black agents to their preys do rouse.
> Thou marvell'st at my words; but hold thee still.
> Things bad begun make strong themselves by ill.
> So prithee go with me.

(3. 2. 47–57)

Again, the imagery and vocabulary of the poetry are richly suggestive and seem to gather and compress the multiple allusions to night and darkness that pervade the play. The reference to 'seeling night' summons up the idea of 'seeling' or sewing the eyes of a hawk to control the bird in training, and this image of blinding is immediately reinforced by the equally palpable image of 'scarfing up' (both covering and tying) the 'tender eye of pitiful day'. In a powerful act of personification, Macbeth calls on the night to 'Cancel and tear to pieces that great bond / Which keeps me pale', invoking an utter negation of his common ties with humanity, and perhaps also referring to the sixth commandment ('Thou shalt not kill'). The 'rooky wood', closely following the image of the crow in flight, is typical of the densely adjectival language in this passage. 'Thou marvell'st at my words' seems to be a cue to the audience as well as to Lady Macbeth. Once again, as Macbeth embarks on murder, the rhetorical power of the poetry encourages a fascinated interest and rapt attention among spectators.

The banquet scene (3. 4) immediately following the murder of Banquo marks a turning-point in the play. For Macbeth and Lady Macbeth, the banquet ought to be an impressive display of power and a public manifestation of their claims to royalty. Historically, the banquet represents a celebration of feudal rights and obligations.

There is, at the outset, a heavy emphasis on formal degree and social propriety. Macbeth greets his guests in accordance with this emphasis on 'position' – 'You know your own degrees' (1) – but by the end of the scene the banquet has collapsed into 'most admired disorder' (109), with Lady Macbeth bidding the guests to 'go at once' (119) and 'Stand not upon the order of your going' (118). The failure of the banquet marks the beginning of Macbeth's loss of power.

The banquet scene is important in other ways. The ghost of Banquo reinforces the impression of a rift in the play between consciousness and actuality, and it throws further doubt on the virtues of manliness. When Macbeth appears startled by the shade of Banquo, Lady Macbeth chastizes him by asking, 'Are you a man?' (57). She proceeds to mock his womanly 'fear' (60), reminding him of the 'air-drawn dagger' (61) which led him to Duncan, and when he persists in his 'fit', she further undermines his manhood: 'What, quite unmanned in folly?' (72). Macbeth's response is to insist, 'What man dare, I dare' (98). With the disappearance of the ghost, he declares 'I am a man again' (107). If the banquet scene exposes the fundamental instability of the concept of 'manliness' in *Macbeth*, it also precipitates two other critical consequences. It raises concerns about Macduff, whose absence from the feast is noted, and it leads Macbeth to further thoughts about 'the weird sisters'. At this point, there is no going back:

> ... for now I am bent to know
> By the worst means the worst. For mine own good
> All causes shall give way. I am in blood
> Stepped in so far that, should I wade no more,
> Returning were as tedious as go o'er.
> Strange things I have in head that will to hand,
> Which must be acted ere they may be scanned.

(3. 4. 133–9)

What prompts this speech is the absence of Macduff from the banquet. Among the things 'Which must be acted' is the destruction of Macduff's family. The brutal killing of Lady Macduff and her children follows swiftly, with 4. 2. presenting on stage the desperate confrontation between the murderers and their innocent victims. The slaughter of Macduff's children is one indication of how 'Stepped in' blood Macbeth is at this point in the play.

The escape of Fleance from the murderers raises further questions about the significance of children – predominantly sons – throughout the play. Lady Macbeth has 'given suck' and knows 'How tender 'tis to love the babe that milks me' (1. 7. 54–5), yet the play implies that there are no children to perpetuate Macbeth's 'line'. The simple suggestion that a child or children died in infancy has not deterred certain scholars from reflecting with great ingenuity on the question of 'How many children had Lady Macbeth?' The critical issue is succession. Without children to succeed him, Macbeth turns with enmity on the children of his rivals. It is fitting, therefore, that the ambiguous prophecies with which Macbeth is greeted when he revisits the witches (4. 1) should be spoken by the apparitions of children. A 'bloody child' (recalling the 'naked new born-babe' (21) in Macbeth's soliloquy in 1. 7) tells him to

Laugh to scorn
The power of man, for none of woman born
Shall harm Macbeth.

(4. 1. 95–7)

A child crowned, with a tree in his hand, tells him he is safe

Until
Great Birnam Wood to high Dunsinane Hill
Shall come against him.

(4. 1. 108–10)

Macbeth is unaware at this stage that Macduff was 'from his mother's womb / Untimely ripped' (5. 10. 15–16) – that is, Macduff is not strictly 'of woman born', which has a bearing on the prophecy of the 'bloody child'. Even so, Macbeth attempts to make 'assurance double sure' (4. 1. 98) that Macduff's line will not usurp his own by surprising Macduff's castle and slaughtering 'His wife, his babes, and all unfortunate souls / That trace him in his line' (168–9).

The shock of the event resounds throughout the lengthy third scene of Act 4, in which Macduff pledges his support to the downcast Malcolm and ironically asserts his manhood in defence of Scotland:

Let us rather
Hold fast the mortal sword, and like good men
Bestride our downfall birthdom. Each new morn
New widows howl, new orphans cry, new sorrows
Strike heaven on the face that it resounds
As if it felt with Scotland and yelled out
Like syllable of dolour.

(4. 3. 2–8)

When Ross arrives with the news of the murders, he first reports that Scotland 'cannot / Be called our mother, but our grave' (166–7), a reminder of how thoroughly nurture and generation have been perverted and destroyed in *Macbeth*. Macduff is momentarily provoked by Ross's revelation into a new awareness of what it is to be a man. In response to Malcolm's urging that he should 'Dispute it like a man' (221), Macduff insists that he 'must also feel it as a man' (223). This emphasis on feeling is prompted in part by thoughts of children. Although most critics interpret Macduff's statement, 'He has no children' (217), as a reference to Macbeth, it can be plausibly read (and performed) as a fitting response to Malcolm's hasty emphasis on 'great revenge' (215). Only a few lines later, however, Macduff himself cuts short any inclination to 'play the woman with mine eyes' (232) and joins Malcolm in his 'manly' (237) enterprise against Macbeth.

Doubts about manhood persist, even as the new king, Malcolm, prepares himself for the throne of Scotland. So, too, does the riddling wordplay and equivocation so strongly evident in the early scenes in the play. Malcolm's double talk and devious role-playing are a matter of caution, a way of being doubly sure of Macduff's allegiance, but his dissembling behaviour serves to undermine rather than reinforce his claim to the throne. Malcolm rehearses the 'king-becoming graces' (92) that contrast so strongly with his own declared 'voluptuousness' (62), but Macduff is happy enough that the prince should satisfy his lust: 'We have willing dames enough' (74). At one level, the scene shows us Malcolm carefully consolidating his power with England's support, but at another it reveals persistent uncertainties about what constitutes ideal kingship.

The split between signs and meanings has catastrophic consequences for Macbeth in the final act of the play, when Birnam Wood does indeed come to Dunsinane and Macduff reveals himself as one not 'of woman born'. Macbeth himself acknowledges the profound disintegration of meaning in his life, although the speech in which he does so is often regarded by critics as one of the most powerful in the entire play.

> Tomorrow, and tomorrow, and tomorrow
> Creeps in this petty pace from day to day
> To the last syllable of recorded time,
> And all our yesterdays have lighted fools
> The way to dusty death. Out, out, brief candle.
> Life's but a walking shadow, a poor player
> That struts and frets his hour upon the stage,
> And then is heard no more. It is a tale
> Told by an idiot, full of sound and fury,
> Signifying nothing.

(5. 5. 18–27)

The occasion of the speech is the announcement by Macbeth's servant Seyton of the death of Lady Macbeth. It is prompted, in part, by Macbeth's dismay that there is hardly time to mourn her going. In a speech preoccupied with life's paucity of meaning, it seems appropriate that Lady Macbeth's death should be reduced to 'a word' (17). The speech proceeds to meditate upon 'the last syllable of recorded time', implying not just the last recorded 'word' but the least part of a word. Whereas Lady Macbeth, as the founder of psychoanalysis, Sigmund Freud (1856–1939), described her, is 'an example of a person who collapses on reaching success, after striving for it with single-minded energy' (Sinfield, 1992, p.39), Macbeth evolves in a strongly contrasting way. Compared with the early soliloquies, this late speech seems remarkably percipient and rational.

It also pulls together some powerful strands of imagery from elsewhere in the play, compressing ideas of time and light in a vivid and evocative way. The entire play seems to be encapsulated in this speech. While the speech contemplates negation, its verse is measured and controlled. The repeated use of alliteration exerts a strong sense of equanimity and harmony that seems strangely at odds with the ostensible subject-matter. Similarly, whilst much of the imagery in the speech is strongly nihilistic, the biblical text it most obviously echoes is one that urges patience: 'For we are but of yesterday ... our days upon earth are a shadow' (Job 8:9). There are further biblical allusions, which appear to have been adopted from the Order for the Burial of the Dead in the Book of Common Prayer. There is not only the familiar 'earth to earth, ashes to ashes, dust to dust', but the following apt quotation: 'Man that is born of a woman hath but a short time to live, and is full of misery ... he fleeth as it were a shadow'. The closing lines of the speech echo Psalm 90, a prescribed text for the burial service: 'we bring our years to an end, as it were a tale that is told'. Whereas Macbeth had on occasion previously welcomed the passage of time – 'Time and the hour runs through the roughest day' (1. 3. 146) – now he observes time's monotonous, meaningless passing. In earlier scenes (such as 3. 4), Macbeth is the performer, possessing 'Strange things ... Which must be acted' (138–9), but now life itself is 'a poor player', pitied for the brevity of his performance.

The rhetorical sway of the poetry ensures that Macbeth remains clearly in focus, even as he turns to meet his death. The appeal of the poetry undoubtedly helps to explain why Macbeth is regarded by so many critics with sympathy and invested by others with tragic grandeur. Bradley helped to establish this critical tradition when he commented on Macbeth's appearance in the final scenes of the play: 'His ruin seems complete. Yet it is never complete. To the end he never totally loses our sympathy ... There remains something sublime in the defiance with which, even when cheated of his last hope, he faces earth and hell and heaven' (1967 edn, p.364). Are there other reasons why Macbeth 'never totally loses our sympathy'? Consider, for instance, Norbrook's thought-provoking comment: 'If the audience can sympathize with Macbeth even though he outrages the play's moral order, it may be because vestiges remain of a world view in which regicide could be a noble rather than an evil act' (1987, p.116). Norbrook's remark is an indication of how far Shakespearean scholarship has travelled since Bradley first published *Shakespearean Tragedy* in 1904. It chimes with a new historicist perspective on Shakespeare's plays in drawing attention both to the initial world-view or ideology that informs the work, and to its subsequent transmission through later generations of readers and spectators.

To read *Macbeth* historically, then, is not to consign the play to the past, but to ask how its ideas and preoccupations continue to provoke debate in our own time. We have seen how the tragedy can be located in the social confusion that attends a critical period of change and transition, and how this confusion is registered in the language of the play. The disintegration of an old feudal order coincides with the emergence of a new, self-seeking ethic, bringing with it new and unstable conceptions of political power and social organization. Although *Macbeth* is set in eleventh-century Scotland, the issues that it raises have a profound significance in the context of early seventeenth-century constitutional changes, and they extend far and wide into the history we are still living. As Ryan has argued, *Macbeth* is 'a fierce arraignment of one of the mainsprings of modern Western society. I mean the ideology and practice of individualism' (1995 edn, p.93). He sees the play as 'the tragedy of a man driven, despite the resistance of a new kind of self awakening within him, to become a savage individualist, whose defiant creed is "For mine own good / All causes shall give way" [3. 4. 134–5]' (ibid.). The challenge facing modern productions of *Macbeth* is to convey to audiences the powerful visual and verbal elements of the play, but also its tremendous historical and political significance:

> Macbeth is a splendid piece of theatrical entertainment, full of fine images,
> gothic thrills, and splendid speeches. But for our culture it is also the
> classic incarnation of the historical fact of the unleashing of the
> Renaissance Spirit – secular, individualistic, self-conscious, capitalistic,
> amoral, questing – upon the traditional Christian moral and social order.

> (Jorgens, 1977, p.148)

In the remaining parts of this chapter, we will turn our attention to some of the ways in which *Macbeth* might be performed on stage and on screen, to reveal the tragic, self-defeating nature of its hero's 'vaulting ambition'.

Text and performance

So far, we have been concentrating on critical readings of *Macbeth*, as if all the play's potential meanings were to be found between the covers of a book. We now need to extend the scope of our interpretation to include some of the many transformations of *Macbeth* that have taken place in theatrical performance, as well as in film adaptations and television productions of the play. In the first place, we need to dispel the idea of an original, pristine stage performance, authoritative and unambiguous in its interpretation of the text, from which all succeeding productions of *Macbeth* have diverged. As Alan Sinfield remarks, we must try to envisage 'diverse original audiences, activating diverse implications in the text' (1992, p.132), in order to appreciate that even in 1606 the play's meaning was a matter of debate. We must also think of the play text itself as a shifting, volatile entity, subject to excision and amendment from the very start. The reception history of *Macbeth* is not simply a matter of changing critical attitudes to the text; it embraces a rich and diverse performance history that reveals not only changing attitudes and expectations about stage design and acting styles, but also changing social values and political ideas since 1606.

Modern editions of *Macbeth* derive from a single printed text, which appeared in the First Folio of Shakespeare's work in 1623. It seems, however, that this text was the result of revisions to the play that were made after the first performance. Textual scholars have pointed to confusions and anomalies, and have suggested that Shakespeare's contemporary, Thomas Middleton, was responsible for introducing new material, probably between 1610 and 1620. For example, it is possible that there was an earlier version of *Macbeth* in which Hecate did not appear (see 4. 1). Since 1606, moreover, the text of *Macbeth* has been fleshed out in performance by a vast range of non-verbal elements – gestures, movement, costumes, setting – all of which broaden the scope of interpretation.

Theatre directors and film producers have definite choices to make about the text of *Macbeth* and how it might be realized in performance. These choices will, in turn, activate a range of possible interpretations. Before considering some of the choices made in particular productions, let us look briefly at the challenges and constraints that all productions of *Macbeth* encounter.

Which scenes in *Macbeth* are most likely to create difficulties for directors of the play, whether on stage or on screen?

When *Macbeth* is performed in daylight (as it was at the Globe playhouse in 1606), the audience has to suspend its disbelief and be persuaded that much of the action is taking place in darkness. When *Macbeth* is played indoors, the director and designer of the production do not have to rely entirely on the language of the play to simulate the condition of darkness. Even so, there are objects and occurrences in the play that require a willing suspension of disbelief among the spectators. How should the witches appear and disappear? Should the mysterious dagger be made visible to the audience, as well as to Macbeth? Should Banquo's ghost appear on stage for the banquet scene or should his place be left vacant? How should the various apparitions in 4. 1 be presented to Macbeth? What techniques of acting, staging and lighting will render Lady Macbeth's sleep-walking most effective and convincing? Is it necessary to show Birnam Wood coming to Dunsinane? Can the stage direction *'Enter MACDUFF with Macbeth's head'* (5. 11. 19, 1) simply be omitted?

These are just a few of the problems that confront all productions of *Macbeth*. Such questions require careful consideration on the part of directors and actors. The powerful presence of both Macbeth and Lady Macbeth on stage creates extraordinary problems of casting and directing, since a director must establish and maintain a particular view of the power dynamics between the two characters and also strike an appropriate balance between the title roles and the rest of the cast. John Russell Brown gives a vivid account of the enormous demands imposed on the principal actors in *Macbeth*:

> The two leading roles present performers with crisis after crisis. For example, Lady Macbeth has to command attention on her first solo appearance as she is reading a letter and then move rapidly to extreme states of excitement and resolution. Macbeth has spoken only seventeen words before he has, as Banquo says, to 'start and seem to fear / Things that do sound so fair' [1. 3. 49–50]. A few scenes later he has to see an imaginary airborne dagger and make the audience believe that, while he draws another, real dagger from its sheath. In the last act Lady Macbeth has the sleep-walking scene as the crown of her performance – an intense, isolated and almost uncharted appearance – and Macbeth veers between defiance and fear, confidence and suicidal despair.
>
> (1982, p.253)

Brown also shows how the central characters can be played in opposing ways, especially if a few lines are conveniently deleted from the text. The balance of power and initiative between Macbeth and Lady Macbeth can be subtly but decisively altered by the weight, pitch, speed and intonation of particular words. Different performances of the text can radically affect the degree of intimacy, mutability or dominance that exists between the two characters.

If the 'supernatural soliciting' of *Macbeth* places certain constraints on a production of the text, directors nevertheless have tremendous scope for innovation and experimentation. Theatre historians and critics still tend to agree that Glen Byam Shaw's 1955 production of *Macbeth* at Stratford-upon-Avon was one of the most impressive and remarkable interpretations in the twentieth century. As reviews from the time make clear, the success of Shaw's production undoubtedly had something to do with the mesmerizing performances of Laurence Olivier (Figure 17) and Vivien Leigh in the title roles. Shaw's promptbook, however, shows the extensive consideration that was given to non-verbal dimensions of the play, especially movement (Figure 18).

At key moments in Shaw's production – after the initial meeting with the witches, after Malcolm's investiture, during the banquet scenes, and even during the battle scenes – Macbeth is consistently isolated from other characters on stage. As Michael Mullin points out in *Macbeth Onstage*, this staging ensures that Macbeth is at once the centre of the action and outside it: 'In each instance Shaw moves Macbeth downstage – often down onto the forestage – and has him speak directly to the audience with the setting and the others actors posed behind him' (1976, p.255). The

Figure 17   *Laurence Olivier as Macbeth at his first entrance in the Stratford production directed by Glen Byam Shaw, 1955. Photo: Angus McBean, in the Harvard Theatre Collection, Harvard University.*

function of this 'blocking' technique is to isolate Macbeth, while at the same time bringing together those who surround him in appealing images of unity, fellowship and trust. An accentuation of the desirability of an ordered society was accompanied in Shaw's production by a strong emphasis on the restoration of peace at the end of the play. This is one particular interpretation of *Macbeth*, of course, but one especially congenial to an English theatre in the immediate post-war years.

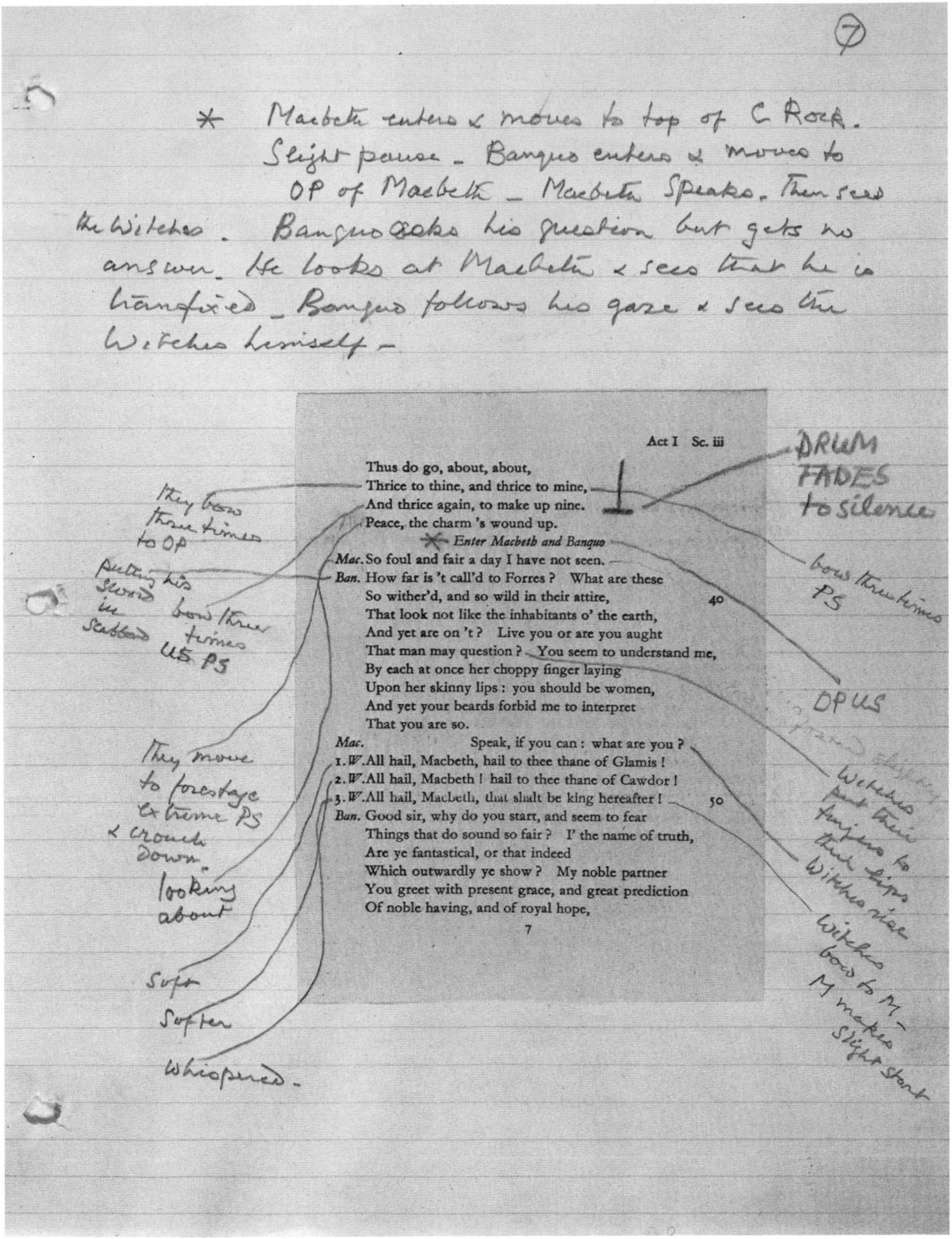

⑦

*   Macbeth enters & moves to top of C Rock.
Slight pause – Banquo enters & moves to
OP of Macbeth – Macbeth Speaks. Then sees
the Witches. Banquo asks his question but gets no
answer. He looks at Macbeth & sees that he is
transfixed – Banquo follows his gaze & sees the
Witches himself –

Act I   Sc. iii

DRUM
FADES
to silence

They bow
three times
to OP

putting his
sword
in
scabbard
bow three
times
US PS

bows three times
PS

40

OP US

Thus do go, about, about,
Thrice to thine, and thrice to mine,
And thrice again, to make up nine.
Peace, the charm 's wound up.
Enter Macbeth and Banquo
Mac. So foul and fair a day I have not seen.
Ban. How far is 't call'd to Forres ?   What are these
So wither'd, and so wild in their attire,
That look not like the inhabitants o' the earth,
And yet are on 't ?   Live you or are you aught
That man may question ?   You seem to understand me,
By each at once her choppy finger laying
Upon her skinny lips : you should be women,
And yet your beards forbid me to interpret
That you are so.
Mac.   Speak, if you can : what are you ?
1. W. All hail, Macbeth, hail to thee thane of Glamis !
2. W. All hail, Macbeth ! hail to thee thane of Cawdor !
3. W. All hail, Macbeth, that shalt be king hereafter !
Ban. Good sir, why do you start, and seem to fear
Things that do sound so fair ?   I' the name of truth,
Are ye fantastical, or that indeed
Which outwardly ye show ?   My noble partner
You greet with present grace, and great prediction
Of noble having, and of royal hope,

7

50

Witches
put their
fingers to
their lips
Witches rise

Witches
bow to M.
M. makes
Slight start

They move
to forestage
extreme PS
& crouch
down
looking
about

Softer
Softer
Whispered –

Figure 18   *Annotated text of Glen Byam Shaw's 1955 promptbook (page 43, Act 1, Scene 3). Reproduced from* Macbeth Onstage: An Annotated Facsimile of Glen Byam Shaw's 1955 Promptbook, *edited by Michael Mullin, University of Missouri Press, Columbia, 1976.*

Subsequent stage and film productions of *Macbeth* have been less sanguine about the restoration of a benevolent social order, once again suggesting that the play has the capacity to activate diverse political meanings. In assessing film versions of Shakespeare's plays alongside stage productions, we need to bear in mind not just the controlling perspective of the camera and the different perceptions it solicits, but also the cultural status of film as distinct from that of theatre. The English scholar Graham Holderness makes the point that film, like theatre, has the capacity to reinforce or subvert inherited cultural assumptions about Shakespeare, but the technological devices of film and its tenuous relationship with the cultural phenomenon of Shakespeare enhance its potential as a 'liberating' medium (1985, p.200). Holderness believes that film can provide a powerful exploration of the 'more radical possibilities of meaning' in *Macbeth*, and he writes enthusiastically about Akira Kurosawa's film *Throne of Blood* (1957), in which the action of the play is shifted from medieval Scotland to feudal Japan (Figure 19) (ibid.).

In Kurosawa's film, the text of *Macbeth* is completely abandoned, not even translated, and the framework of European Renaissance tragedy gives way to an

Figure 19 *Toshiro Mifune as Washizu in* Throne of Blood *directed by Akira Kurosawa, 1957, Toho, Japan. Photo: Ronald Grant Archive.*

oriental samurai epic. What *Throne of Blood* reveals in a powerfully concentrated way, however, is a central historical contradiction in which a language of trust, loyalty and honour conceals a vulnerable and unstable division of power. Ambition, within this feudal pattern of authority, is both fuelled and destroyed by militaristic violence. While appearing to declare its independence from *Macbeth*, *Throne of Blood* highlights and exposes the social and historical dimensions of Shakespeare's tragedy.

What kind of film production would best complement the reading of *Macbeth* proposed in this chapter? Roman Polanski's *Macbeth*, co-scripted with Kenneth Tynan and released in 1971, goes a long way towards addressing the issues of power, gender and sovereignty discussed here. Polanski's film is still unfairly criticized for its brutal and bloody depiction of events, but it seems unreasonable to complain that the violence is in excess of what is already explicit in the text. The film-maker's attitude to violence is by no means gratuitous; he has always maintained that directors have a moral duty not to conceal or diminish the nature of violence and its tragic consequences. In any case, what is most impressive in Polanski's film is not its depiction of brutal murder, but its subtle blend of naturalistic and symbolic detail, and its imaginative visual realization of verbal elements in the play. The camera is used resourcefully to produce both long, contextual shots of the social landscape and close-ups of facial expressions.

Vivid, mysterious opening shots of a remote seashore reveal the witches at dawn, burying various icons in the sand. The circle they make anticipates many of the prominent motifs that recur throughout the film: the crown, the collar used to hang the Thane of Cawdor, the coronation shield and the witches' cauldron. The icons they bury – a hangman's noose, a severed hand and a dagger – also have a wide symbolic import. The landscape itself – a tidal flat, which is flooded and then deserted by the sea – hints at the ebb and flow of fortune, but also recalls Macbeth's reference to earthly existence as 'this bank and shoal of time' (1. 7. 6). Time-lapse photography is used very effectively to hasten dawns and dusks, so that time seems out of joint and the world is bathed in shadows. The witches are played eerily but naturalistically as actual women (Figures 20 and 21). They are not old women, but women of different ages, and they dwell in underground caverns. Their ritualistic pouring of baboon's blood on the buried icons anticipates Lady Macbeth's pouring of poison into the grooms' drinks. The film abounds in connections and associations of this kind.

Polanski's *Macbeth* gives powerful realization to the dislocation of signs and meanings, and the insistent 'doubling' of words and images, in the play, often through the use of mirrors and other reflective surfaces. While washing himself after the murder of Duncan, for instance, Macbeth sees his own image reflected in a puddle and tries to dispel this with a bucket of bloody water. Macbeth's more meditative speeches, including the soliloquies, are presented in 'voice-over'. This technique heightens the contrast between Macbeth's public shows of rhetoric and his private dreams and desires. Some critics complained that the youthful Macbeth and Lady Macbeth (played by Jon Finch and Francesca Annis) lacked the emotional depth and range required for the main roles in the play, but one of the results of slightly underplaying these roles is to broaden and diversify the attention given to the social sphere that all the characters inhabit.

Figure 20 *Noelle Rimmington, Elsie Taylor and Maisie MacFarquhar as the three Witches in the opening of* Macbeth *directed by Roman Polanski, 1971, Caliban Films/Columbia Pictures, adapted for the screen by Roman Polanski and Kenneth Tynan. Photo: Kobal Collection.*

Polanski's *Macbeth* serves our purposes well in this chapter, because it accentuates the political and historical dimensions of the tragedy. In *Shakespeare on Film* (1977), Jack Jorgens argues that Macbeth's defiance of nature is linked effectively in the film with a self-gratifying individualism that modern audiences can readily understand: 'Polanski has put his finger on one of the reasons why *Macbeth* fascinates us so much. It is an extreme assertion of the individualism at the root of western social and economic systems which makes us unable to accept death' (p.169). Like his fellow countryman, the eminent Shakespeare critic Jan Kott, Polanski has a cultural perspective informed by Poland's dark and sorrowful history under Nazi occupation and successive totalitarian regimes. Some commentators have too readily assumed, however, that he regards society as irredeemable. Conservative critics who insist that 'Shakespeare's confidence in monarchy remained steadfast',

Figure 21 *Noelle Rimmington, Elsie Taylor and Maisie MacFarquhar as the three Witches in the opening of* Macbeth *directed by Roman Polanski, 1971, Caliban Films/Columbia Pictures, adapted for the screen by Roman Polanski and Kenneth Tynan. Photo: Kobal Collection.*

and who think of *Macbeth* as ending on an optimistic note, with Scotland regaining its good health, not surprisingly believe that Polanski is deeply cynical (Pearlman, 1994, p.250). It is more appropriate, perhaps, to acknowledge Polanski's refusal to settle for any easy consolation or to imbue *Macbeth* with a naïve optimism. Two striking innovations confirm the vigilance of Polanski's politics. The character of Ross is developed in the film into a cunning opportunist, who not only shifts his allegiance as the occasion demands, but also plays the mysterious third murderer who assists in the killing of Banquo. At the end of the film, he picks up Macbeth's fallen crown and passes it to Malcolm. To drive home this disturbing vision of the new dispensation, the film closes with a silent epilogue, in which the limping Donalbain encounters the witches on his way home, in a scene that ominously mirrors their fateful first encounter with Macbeth.

Conclusion

To appreciate the full political significance of *Macbeth*, we have to reach back to 1606 and try to imagine the impact of such a play at the court of James I. Whilst there is much in the play that would have appealed to a monarch with scholarly interests in kingship and witchcraft, there is also a radical questioning of what constitutes legitimate power. Far from shoring up royal absolutism, *Macbeth* conducts a troubled debate about the rights and wrongs of kings. The play is conversant with arguments that were deployed to justify the killing of an English king only a few decades later. As Polanski's *Macbeth* and other contemporary productions have shown, however, the radical potential of the play can be activated and made to comment on other oppressive political structures. Four centuries after it was written, *Macbeth* retains its appeal as a dark, provocative and deeply unsettling play.

References

Andrews, J.F. (1993) *Macbeth*, Everyman edition, London: Dent.

Belsey, C. (1985) *The Subject of Tragedy: Identity and Difference in Renaissance Drama*, London: Routledge.

Bradley, A.C. (1967) *Shakespearean Tragedy*, London: Macmillan (first published 1904).

Brown, J.R. (ed.) (1982) *Focus on Macbeth*, London: Routledge & Kegan Paul.

Dollimore, J. (1984) *Radical Tragedy: Religion, Ideology and Power in the Drama of Shakespeare and his Contemporaries*, Brighton: Harvester.

Drakakis, J. (ed.) (1992) *Shakespearean Tragedy*, London and New York: Longman.

Eagleton, T. (1986) *William Shakespeare*, Oxford: Basil Blackwell.

Holderness, G. (1985) 'Radical potentiality and institutional closure: Shakespeare in film and television', in *Political Shakespeare: New Essays in Cultural Materialism*, ed. J. Dollimore and A. Sinfield, Manchester: Manchester University Press, pp.183–201.

Hosley, R. (1968) *Shakespeare's Holinshed: An Edition of Holinshed's Chronicles*, 1587, New York: G.P. Putnam.

Jorgens, J.J. (1977) *Shakespeare on Film*, Bloomington and London: Indiana University Press.

Knight, G.W. (1949) *The Wheel of Fire*, London: Methuen (first published 1930).

Leech, C. (1969) *Tragedy*, London: Methuen.

Mangan, M. (1991) *A Preface to Shakespeare's Tragedies*, London and New York: Longman.

Moretti, F. (1992) *The Great Eclipse: Tragic Form as the Deconsecration of Sovereignty*, 1983, in *Shakespearean Tragedy*, ed. J. Drakakis, London and New York: Longman, pp.45–84.

Mullin, M. (ed.) (1976) *Macbeth Onstage: An Annotated Facsimile of Glen Byam Shaw's 1955 Promptbook*, Columbia and London: University of Missouri Press.

Norbrook, D. (1987) '*Macbeth* and the politics of historiography', in *Politics of Discourse: the Literature and History of Seventeenth-Century England*, ed. K. Sharpe and S.N. Zwicker, Berkeley: University of California Press, pp.78–116.

Paolucci, A. and Paolucci, H. (eds) (1975) *Hegel on Tragedy*, London and New York: Harper & Row.

Pearlman, E. (1994) '*Macbeth* on film: politics', in *Shakespeare and the Moving Image: The Plays on Film and Television*, ed. A. Davies and S. Wells, Cambridge: Cambridge University Press, pp.250–60.

Ryan, K. (1995) *Shakespeare*, Hemel Hempstead: Harvester Wheatsheaf (first published 1989).

Sidney, P. (1989) *A Defence of Poetry*, 1595, Oxford: Oxford University Press.

Sinfield, A. (ed.) (1992) *Macbeth: Contemporary Critical Essays*, London: Macmillan.

Williams, R. (1966) *Modern Tragedy*, London: Chatto & Windus.

Chapter 4

ANTONY AND CLEOPATRA

Arnold Kettle
edited and concluded by Cicely Palser Havely

Aims

The primary aim of this chapter is to guide your study of *Antony and Cleopatra* in such a way as to allow you to form your own opinions, based on a sound knowledge of the text. This will involve developing your skills in close and effective reading. A further aim is to demonstrate that critical opinions are historically and socially determined and that no interpretation of a text such as this can be absolute or conclusive. When you have finished this chapter, you should be able to discuss the text in some detail; be able to identify key issues highlighted by both past and more recent critical approaches; and be ready to relate this play to other texts and other critical themes that you will study elsewhere in the course.

Note: The main part of this chapter was written by the late Arnold Kettle (1916–86), the first Professor of Literature at the Open University, for a Shakespeare course that appeared in 1983. This version has been shortened and adapted for publication in the present volume.

Introduction

> On hearing about powerful love, respond, be moved
> like an aesthete. Only, fortunate as you've been,
> remember how much your imagination created for you.
> This first, and then the rest – the lesser loves –
> that you experienced and enjoyed
> in your life: the more real and tangible.
> Of loves like these you were not deprived.

(Savidis, 1992 edn, p.196)

These lines are by C.P. Cavafy, written in 1911 and translated from the Greek. Cavafy himself was, like Cleopatra, an Alexandrian Greek. I quote his twentieth-century poem because I feel it may help us to a just response to Shakespeare's seventeenth-century poem/play about people who lived in the first century BCE. We cannot, in watching or reading *Antony and Cleopatra*, pretend that we are Elizabethans or Jacobeans. Nor can we pretend that the play we are responding to is a twentieth-century play. But if we try to see both the play and ourselves as parts of history, we stand a chance of finding how best to cope with the enriching enterprise of reading it.

Antony and Cleopatra is not a 'history' or 'chronicle' play in the sense that *Richard II* is, but it is nevertheless more firmly and insistently grounded on actual historical events than, say, *King Lear* or *Hamlet* or *Macbeth*. It is historical in the sense that the events it deals with were very well known, as Shakespeare's Octavius Caesar emphasizes in the final speech of the play: 'No grave upon the earth shall clip in it / A pair so famous' (5. 2. 349–50). It is also historical in the sense of being exceptionally closely related to its main source, Plutarch's *Life of Marcus Antonius* in his *Lives of the Noble Grecians and Romans*, which had been translated from the Latin by Sir Thomas North in 1579.

One consequence of the fact that this is Roman rather than English history is that the element of national mythology or propaganda is absent. Shakespeare was therefore that much freer to present all the facts and motives and issues of his historical subject without directly offending anyone, including the authorities who controlled the theatres. There was no political reason in 1607 why Cleopatra should not be portrayed as an heroic figure, even though she is morally very shaky on issues such as honour, gluttony and sex. If her story had been seen to have *any* bearing on contemporary English politics she could only have been depicted as an example to deplore. Similarly, Antony, 'the old ruffian', forgives with 'the poor last' of 'many thousand kisses' the woman who has brought about his downfall (4. 16. 21). The values such conduct expresses could never be so compelling a force in one of the English 'histories'.

But if *Antony and Cleopatra* is not quite happily described as a 'history', it is also a 'tragedy' with a difference. This is not a play dominated by the classic Aristotelian tragic emotions of pity and terror. Even the death scenes are more surprising and impressive than pitiful and terrible. Antony's death, with the whole business of his being lifted up into the tower, is laced with a sort of grim gay humour: Cleopatra herself uses the words 'Here's sport indeed' (4. 16. 33), as though recalling those hours of angling in the Nile. As for Cleopatra's death, is there not a fundamental sense in which one wants her to die, just as she herself chooses death rather than a humiliation which would destroy all her values in living?

Am I suggesting that *Antony and Cleopatra*, despite the sense of tragic loss it embodies (Antony himself (4. 13. 29) speaks of 'the very heart of loss'), is not really a tragedy at all? Surely the structure of the play, which focuses mainly on Antony for nearly four-fifths of the action and then switches our attention almost totally to Cleopatra, implies a modification of the more usual Shakespearean tragic concentration on a single figure?

Antony and Cleopatra is an exceptionally *open* play and not only in the sense that it belongs to an open stage. It is open in the sense that the issues are laid before us by Shakespeare with an exceptionally many-sided objectivity; open in the way Shakespeare declines to offer simple moralistic judgements about the issues (such as 'should one *approve* of the Antony/Cleopatra relationship?'); and open in the sense that it is one of the least metaphysical of plays (you cannot discuss it very profitably in terms of 'good' and 'evil'). [You might return to Chapter 2 to compare the suggested 'openness' of *Richard II*.]

It is this openness which gives us a sense of breadth and objectivity, and at the same time of intimacy and a variety of possible interpretations. We often feel that we are not quite sure who, in a particular scene, is play-acting and for what purpose. It is an open play in the sense that we are often (indeed nearly all the time) left to draw our own conclusions, with Shakespeare providing us with plenty of data through the richness and wit of the language. It is an open play partly because politics is essentially a *public* activity, even though it is also, not infrequently, a highly devious one.

The main characters in *Antony and Cleopatra* are *great*, which means that they are politically powerful and what they do seldom affects them alone. Greatness or heroism is one of the recurring concerns of the play, and though there is little abstract discussion of these phenomena, there is an important sense in which we are made to think about them all the time. A twentieth-century dramatist who has some relevant things to say about heroism is Berthold Brecht. There is a famous passage in his *Life of Galileo* (1943) when Galileo recants what he knows to be the truth under the pressure of the Inquisition. His faithful co-workers are deeply distressed and one of them says, bitterly, 'Unhappy the land that has no heroes'. Galileo is silent at first and then he says 'No. Unhappy the land that is in need of heroes' (p.108). Brecht, through the method he called epic theatre, has stood our usual way of looking at things on its head in order to distance and thereby *open up* the whole question. [Brecht wrote that 'the essential point of the epic theatre is ... that it appeals less to the feelings than to the spectator's reason. Instead of sharing an experience the spectator must come to grips with things' (Willett, 1986, p.23).]

Language and dramatic impact

No play takes us more immediately into the midst of things. The two Romans, Philo and Demetrius, are caught mid-conversation, so that we, the audience, are drawn straightaway into an active, developing and highly problematic situation, which has among its elements that of a public show. [This is a device Shakespeare was to use several times in late plays such as *Cymbeline* and *The Winter's Tale*.] Philo expresses his outrage in a series of images calculated to impose the violence of his feelings – and the extremity of the situation he is discussing – on his friend Demetrius and on us. This affair of the general's has gone altogether too far. It bends, buckles, bellows, blows, bursts to overflowing. His words contrast the admired and disciplined energy of a soldier in action (thought and sinews bent and tempered in the cause of responsibility – office – and duty – devotion – to the state he serves) with the apparently disastrous obsession of this hero with 'a tawny front', 'a gypsy's lust'. (The Elizabethans thought gypsies were actually Egyptians.) The final statement

> Take but good note, and you shall see in him
> The triple pillar of the world transformed
> Into a strumpet's fool

> (1. 1. 11–13)

subsumes the rest and is at once put to the test. Philo's powerful expression of the way *his* world sees the situation is immediately followed by the entry of the lovers, also caught mid-conversation. It is as though we, the audience, are put into the position not simply of witnesses but of judge and jury, testing the Roman case against Antony and Cleopatra. They, for their part, at once counter Philo's extremity of outrage and contempt with an equally extreme claim: their love is indeed extravagant; but to them the notion of 'o'erflow[ing] the measure' (2) is not a rebuke but a self-justification. Already in this first exchange of the lovers Antony challenges the whole idea of measurement and calculation being applied to human relationships. 'There's beggary in the love that can be reckoned' (15) is much more than a snap answer to a sentimental question. Antony is expressing the anti-utilitarian view of love. He is also uttering a key word which will crop up throughout the play: 'beggary' is the opposite of 'bounty'. (See 5. 2. 8 and 42.)

The first of a stream of messengers (no play has more) arrives from Rome. The messengers in this play are more than a dramatist's technical device for overcoming the geographical distances between his spread-out characters; they are themselves human missiles fired from one world into another. But before this first messenger can get his message out, Cleopatra has provoked – with a first example of her immense talent for provocation – an extraordinarily uncompromising statement from Antony:

> Let Rome in Tiber melt, and the wide arch
> Of the ranged empire fall. Here is my space.
> Kingdoms are clay. Our dungy earth alike
> Feeds beast as man. The nobleness of life
> Is to do thus; when such a mutual pair
> And such a twain can do't – in which I bind
> On pain of punishment the world to weet –
> We stand up peerless.

> (1. 1. 35–42)

Consider how this speech uses themes and images which recur and become more meaningful as the play develops.

Rome is important both as a place and as a concept. Antony and Cleopatra take on the Roman Empire, the main political and cultural force of the Mediterranean and Middle-Eastern world. Rome is not merely a famous city, it is the centre of a huge empire, which claims to stand for order and civilization and ultimately peace (see 4. 6. 5) and is the main power factor of the world it spans. Already Antony's position in this world has been evoked by Philo's phrase 'the triple pillar of the world' (1. 1. 12) and the stakes involved have been touched on by Cleopatra's ironical words about the conquest of kingdoms (24). When Antony speaks, it is our first opportunity to test out the common Roman view of what is going on that Philo has just expressed; and what Antony says is unequivocal: 'Let Rome in Tiber melt, and the wide arch / Of the ranged empire fall' (35–6).

Already certain words which will turn out to be key words in the play as a whole, are beginning to be imposed on our imagination. 'Melt' ('Let Rome in Tiber melt') is one of them. It will reach its optimum force four acts later (in 'The crown o'th' earth doth melt' (4. 16. 65)). The 'wide arch / Of the ranged empire', which Antony, like the biblical Samson in the Philistines' temple [Judges 16] is ready to pull down upon himself, has already been prepared for by 'the triple pillar'. 'Kingdoms are clay' takes up Cleopatra's mocking phrase 'Take in that kingdom and enfranchise that' (1. 1. 24). The conquest and disposal of kingdoms is a theme that threads through the play. Recall, for instance, the short, rather surprising scene in Syria (3. 1) or Caesar's description of Antony in Alexandria proclaiming Cleopatra's children kings (3. 6), or the bargaining about kingdoms in the last act, all shadowed by Cleopatra's extraordinary vision of her lover bestriding the ocean with realms and islands dropping as plates from his pocket (5. 2. 81–93).

Antony's speech of defiant intent ('Let Rome in Tiber melt') is followed by an exchange between the lovers on a much less exalted level. We are given a taste of Cleopatra's cunning – her matchless technique for getting her own way and holding her man – and Antony's next speeches evoke little beyond the sort of hedonism and indulgence that Philo finds so shocking. Yet even the 'soft hours' (1. 1. 46) and 'pleasure' (49) are not without their tougher side. For one thing, Antony refers to the peculiar joy they have (it recurs throughout the play and is one of the things Octavius Caesar has against the lovers) of wandering through the streets and mixing with 'The qualities of people' (56). There seems to me a double process here. On the one hand, there is a kind of self-conscious, slightly suspect camaraderie involving all sorts of people, not only 'peers', which was part of the stock-in-trade of the more 'populist' Tudor monarchs. On the other hand, there is a genuine willingness to expose themselves, to bring a certain basic honesty to bear on what is happening, which the more common sort of ruling-class discretion avoids and fears. All the main characters in this play are highly conscious of acting out their roles.

In 60 lines Shakespeare has given us an intimate first glimpse of the relationship of Antony and Cleopatra and has at the same time set that situation within a framework of critical comment. He has done this partly through the *dramatic structure* of the scene (beginning and ending with the Roman soldiers' reactions) and partly through *language*, which is at the same time idiomatic (catching the tone of informal conversation) and highly wrought, building up images of public significance and considerable complexity. And the expository material of the scene – telling us where we start from – is laced with movement and contradiction. Nothing stands still, no statement or action is without its opposite to complicate and deepen the issues involved.

Act 1, Scene 2, like the first scene, opens in the midst of a conversation. Charmian has apparently overheard Alexas recommending a soothsayer to the queen and, keen to have her own fortune told, wants to know what sort of husband is in store for her. The chatter that follows (up to the entrance of Cleopatra in line 68) consists largely of bawdy banter.

Shakespeare is concerned to establish the atmosphere of the Egyptian court with its open, relaxed, often frivolous sensuality. Between the slightly pompous solemnity of the soothsayer (he has his professional standards to think about) and the irrepressible mocking tone of the young women there is an effective counterpoint. Iras's 'Go, you wild bedfellow, you cannot soothsay' (44) is just as assured, poetically, as the soothsayer's oracular pronouncements, and Enobarbus strikes his personal, down-to-earth, bluff-soldier note with marvellous effect, interrupting the rhythm as well as the tone of the talk.

Another point to note is the way Shakespeare integrates a scene like this into the play as a whole. The soothsayer will turn up again in 2. 3, reminding Antony, who has just pledged himself to Octavia, that it is in the East his pleasure lies. His prophecies, though they have less resonance than those of the witches in *Macbeth*, have a similar dramatic effect, framing or at least indicating the direction or trajectory of the story and introducing a very important concept for this play: *fortune*. It is a key word and we shall keep coming back to it. The cuckoldry which is the main subject of the women's jokes is of course deep in the play, and Charmian's ironical comment on Iras's chastity – 'E'en as the o'erflowing Nilus presageth famine' (43) – contributes to a motif of accumulating importance. Cleopatra, the serpent of the Nile, is to do that thing that ends all other deeds with the aid of the pretty worm of Nilus. The light-hearted talk of fertility in this little scene plays on one of the obsessions and paradoxes of the play: the life-giving qualities of Egypt. As Lepidus boringly reminds the company on Pompey's galley: 'Your serpent of Egypt is bred now of your mud by the operation of your sun' (2. 7. 25–6).

Cleopatra enters looking for Antony, uneasy because 'A Roman thought hath struck him' (1. 2. 73): a characteristic example of the language of the play. Is Antony just thinking about Rome or is the thought that has struck him the *sort* of thought associated with Roman (as opposed to Alexandrian) behaviour? Already in the first scene we have heard some typical 'Roman thoughts' (from Philo and Demetrius) and also Antony's defiant words about Rome. Enobarbus, in this second scene, has already hinted by his tone that there is a difference between his reactions as a Roman and those of the Egyptians. That Antony is a Roman associates him with certain values which Cleopatra (quite rightly) sees as hostile and threatening to the kind of life she and Antony have been living. The question as to whether the play is based on a Rome *versus* Egypt conflict is one which we shall have to consider and return to later in this chapter.

Cleopatra, who has been looking for Antony, changes her mind when he approaches (she is always changing her mind) and leaves him to deal with the latest messenger alone. These constant movements of characters on and off the stage are by now getting to seem a feature of the play's style, helping to express the constant tactical shifts – personal and political – that are characteristic of the play's subject-matter: shifts of power, alliances (matrimonial as well as military), place and mood. On this occasion, Shakespeare needs to have Antony face the messenger alone, for it is important that the audience should have clear access to the news of the political manoeuvres in Rome and the death of Fulvia.

In the last part of the scene (line 120 to the end) Enobarbus persists in maintaining the tone of the opening section – ironical cynicism and a quite brutal sexism – and consequently continues to speak in prose. But he is finally rebuked by 'No more light answers' (160). At this point Antony becomes every inch the Roman general, the man of action tersely assessing the situation, outlining a strategy and issuing his orders. This is no-nonsense language without the sort of philosophical aside contained in his soliloquy, and instinct with a political eloquence which contrasts totally with the language of the 'Let Rome in Tiber melt' speech of the previous scene. Now everything is Roman and well-ordered; it is the language of power. No more wandering through the streets among the city's *hoi polloi*. Instead the people have become 'slippery' (169), ungrateful, fickle. The dominant strain is of hierarchy and an established, immutable order. Antony is on the war-path. Well might Enobarbus be reduced to a monosyllabic, cowed, 'I shall do't' (180). Antony is a Roman again.

Octavius Caesar, whom we meet in Act 1, Scene 4, is at home, in every sense, in Rome. There is at once a formality, and yet a certain thinness, in the language he uses: 'It is not Caesar's natural vice to hate / Our great competitor' (2–3). The imperial 'we' and formal third person (as though he were talking about someone else) are used a little too glibly and there is a tell-tale exaggeration in the description of Antony as 'A man who is the abstract of all faults / That all men follow' (9–10).

Caesar is above all a *conventional* man, the very type of the successful Roman imperialist. The immediate contrast between him and Lepidus, who is put firmly in his place with 'You are too indulgent' (16), presents Caesar in all his essentials in this first entrance as a politician, first and last.

The Roman part of the action really gets going in 2. 2, but the short 2. 1, introducing Pompey, is important. Pompey and his two friends, already introduced as famous pirates, open up with a series of epigrams, generalized paradoxical statements, about the nature of fortune. Pompey is himself a sort of pirate, though well connected and part of the Roman establishment. His language is plain and strong:

> I shall do well.
> The people love me, and the sea is mine.
> ... Mark Antony
> In Egypt sits at dinner, and will make
> No wars without doors. Caesar gets money where
> He loses hearts. Lepidus flatters both,
> Of both is flattered; but he neither loves,
> Nor either cares for him.

> (2. 1. 8–9, 11–16)

This is political oratory of a high order, clarifying, with its wealth of comic observation, what Roman politics consists of. Pompey speaks of public matters with an insider's knowledge and confidence.

The following scene, 2. 2, is superb from its first movement, with Lepidus nobbling Enobarbus, and Enobarbus skilfully giving him his come-uppance. Then, when Lepidus tries the same line of talk on him, Antony shows that he is quite capable of looking after his own interests. The actual moment of meeting of the two major pillars of the world is, in its utter simplicity, a triumphant example of Shakespeare's dramatic art, which is also a triumph of language and, incidentally, bears out the shrewdness of Enobarbus's remarks a few moments earlier.

CAESAR   Welcome to Rome.

ANTONY   Thank you.

CAESAR   Sit.

ANTONY   Sit, sir.

CAESAR   Nay then.

> *[They sit]*

> (2. 2. 28–32, 1)

There is no stage direction in the Folio, but as the Arden edition puts it: 'surely Malone [an earlier Shakespeare editor] was right in seeing in [the scene] no more than an exchange of "After you" courtesies which Caesar, anxious to get on with business, terminates by yielding' (Ridley, 1954, p.48).

The scene operates on at least three levels: personal, political and dramatic, and it is not possible to disentangle them completely. There is the personal caginess between the two main participants, who perform a tightrope act, balancing between mutual suspicion and mutual need, an act punctuated by the ground-floor comments of the less subtle Lepidus and Enobarbus. The personal jockeying is, however, subsidiary to and directed by the political manoeuvring, which reaches its high point with the introduction of the scheme to marry Antony off to Octavia. The dramatic tension is built on our doubt as to just how far either side, but especially Antony, will actually go. At first the two adversaries seem content to score marginal points off one another. The key word is 'concern'. At what point does the one have the right to suspect or interfere with the other? Neither wishes to appear to make excessive claims for fear of undermining his own credibility, yet neither dares ignore provocations beyond a certain point. Caesar uses the line 'You praise yourself / By laying defects of judgement to me' (58–9) to press home the moral advantage he feels he has a right to as a result of the wars begun by Antony's wife and brother. Antony knows he is on weak ground here and, after getting a fulsome tribute to Fulvia off his chest, admits that all that he really has to say is that he could not help it. The way is then clear for the use of honour as a prime consideration. Enobarbus at a vital point acts as a kind of chorus (113), throwing 'Truth' into the argument and getting his knuckles rapped. What is basic to the dramatic effect is that *our* judgement should be kept open, or at least floating.

The speech of Enobarbus (196–232) is, of course, one of literature's great set-pieces of descriptive dramatic writing. It is closely based, linguistically, on North's Plutarch.

Read carefully the following passage from Plutarch describing how Antony met Cleopatra:

> Therefore when she was sent unto by divers letters, both from Antonius himself and also from his friends, she made so light of it and mocked Antonius so much that she disdained to set forward otherwise but to take her barge in the river of Cydnus, the poop whereof was of gold, the sails of purple, and the oars of silver, which kept stroke in rowing after the sound of the music of flutes, hautboys, citherns, viols, and such other instruments as they played upon in the barge. And now for the person of herself: she was laid under a pavilion of cloth-of-gold of tissue, apparalled and attired like the goddess Venus commonly drawn in picture; and hard by her, on either hand of her, pretty fair boys apparelled as painters do set forth god Cupid, with little fans in their hands, with the which they fanned wind upon her. Her ladies and gentlewomen also, the fairest of them were apparelled like the nymphs Nereides (which are the mermaids of the waters) and like the Graces, some steering the helm, others tending the tackle and ropes of the barge, out of the which there came a wonderful passing sweet savour of perfumes that perfumed the wharf's side, pestered with innumerable multitudes of people. Some of them followed the barge all alongst the river's side; others also ran out of the city to see her coming in; so that in the end there ran such multitudes of people one after another to see her that Antonius was left post-alone in the market-place in his imperial seat to give audience. And there went a rumour in the people's mouths that the goddess Venus was come to play with the god Bacchus for the general good of all Asia.

When Cleopatra landed, Antonius sent to invite her to supper to him.
But she sent him word again, he should do better rather to come and
sup with her. Antonius therefore, to show himself courteous unto her at
her arrival, was contented to obey her, and went to supper to her, where
he found such passing sumptuous fare, that no tongue can express it.

(Neill, 1994, pp.332–3)

Here you can see that Shakespeare's text (2. 2. 196–232) adds or changes surprisingly
little. Yet the changes and additions are crucially effective. Even the apparently
unimportant phrase 'I will tell you' changes the status of the long description from
objectivity to Enobarbus's own narrative, one man's impressions. The barge *becomes* a
throne and Shakespeare, by playing on the relation between burnished and burning
and on the power of water to reflect, turns Plutarch's collection of descriptive details
into a single, immensely striking and atmospheric image combining elements of
luxury and danger, clarity and mysteriousness. He combines Plutarch's pictorial
vision of the barge with the notion of the pursuit of love: 'The winds were love-sick
with them' and 'The water which they beat to follow faster, / As amorous of their
strokes' (200–3). His barge and its furnishings become *impregnated* with amorousness.
This dimension is absent from Plutarch's descriptive details.

Shakespeare opens his description of Cleopatra herself with 'It beggared all
description' (204), paralleling a phrase Plutarch uses to describe the food at the
supper. He develops this thought with two paradoxes about the 'fancy outwork
nature' (207) and the power of the fans to 'glow' the very cheeks they 'cool' (210).
With the words 'And what they undid did' (211), Shakespeare is again adding a
dimension to Plutarch's words and introducing a sense of provocation and even
contradiction into what in Plutarch is a relatively straightforward visual description
of the colourful and exotic queen. 'And what they undid did' is a good example of
the ploy Shakespeare is constantly using in the play. Recall, for instance, Antony's
words on the death of Fulvia: 'She's good being gone' (1. 2. 115), a paradox which at
first may seem to limit or obscure the situation, but which turns out to express
something deep and complex about it. The lines describing Antony, left on a more
conventional throne in the market-place, 'Whistling to th'air' (2. 2. 220–3) have a
similarly Shakespearean ring. Enobarbus often plays the philosopher and these lines
suggest that because nature abhors a vacuum, the figure of Antony left alone in the
market-place is not so much absurd – as he seems in Plutarch – as 'unnatural'.

The last four lines of the Shakespeare passage, compared with the final sentence of
the Plutarch, have a remarkable intimacy about them, for Enobarbus knows his
Antony. Enobarbus's tone of voice as he talks of his commander turns Plutarch's
description of Antony's polite (though impressed) response into an intimate
revelation of his immediate capitulation to Cleopatra's charms. What the worldly-
wise Enobarbus describes to his colleagues may not be fair to Antony, but it presents
us with a very telling version of what his friends perceive.

Although Shakespeare apparently lifted nearly all of this speech from his source, it
is even more remarkable how *different* the two passages are. For one thing, it
becomes a speech spoken by a particular person at a particular moment in the play
and therefore not necessarily an *objective* description such as an historian (like
Plutarch) aims at. Enobarbus is, we already know, a caustic and blunt figure, more
given to deflating than to glamorizing. And here he is among cronies, in front of
whom he has no reason to pose or exaggerate. That is why the punctuation of the

speech by Agrippa's comments heightens the effect and helps turn narrative into dramatic discourse. [So too does the placing or context of the speech, which pointedly follows the marriage contract with Octavia (2. 2. 131 onwards).]

Equally basic is the move from prose to blank verse, which not only compresses and heightens particular effects by laying stress on particular words, but also offers a guide to the actor. Notice the way the tenses of the verbs are changed. At the beginning Enobarbus speaks in the past tense, as Plutarch does. But as the speech goes on he moves from the past ('the barge she *sat* in') to the present tense ('A seeming mermaid *steers*'), ending with a sentence that begins in the past ('heard') and ends in the present ('goes' and 'pays'). Through the words he uses, Enobarbus is acting out the scene, drawing his listeners – and us – into it. The audience, as well as the characters on the stage, are being made to see things dramatically.

Shakespeare uses *all* his opportunities to show the central situations from many points of view. The servants in Act 2, Scene 7 have no illusions about their masters. They are acute observers and relish the situation in which Lepidus's protests of 'no more' (referring at first to his colleagues' bickerings) are at once fobbed off and justified by a continuous and liberal filling of his glass. Lepidus is a great 'reconciler', whose limitations are exposed by his ability to reconcile *himself* to almost anything.

But it is not only through the light they throw on specific aspects of their masters' characters or behaviour that these servants contribute to the play; it is also by illuminating in a general way the theme of greatness. Philo, in the opening scene, has complained that Antony, displaying himself in Alexandria: 'comes too short of that great property / Which still should go with Antony' (1. 1. 60–1) – property here meaning 'quality' or 'identity'. Antony himself has referred (without anyone feeling he is swollen-headed) to his 'greatness' (2. 2. 98) in the scene in which he and Caesar are reconciled. Now the servants are discussing very shrewdly what 'great men's fellowship' (2. 7. 10–11) involves. This discussion wends its way right through the play and constantly forces the audience to consider the problem from different angles. It is as though Shakespeare is determined to prevent us from taking the behaviour of his characters simply at their own evaluation of themselves. He is a demystifier as well as a recorder.

In the same scene Menas the pirate draws Pompey aside and proposes that he should first cut the cable of the galley and then the throats of 'These three world-sharers, these competitors' (67). Pompey's reply, rebuking Menas not for his treacherous plan but for telling him about it instead of getting on with the job, reveals the whole nature and flavour of Roman politics. It is, up to this point, the most explicit statement in the play about the relationship of the great man to those who do his work and about what the highly prized concept 'honour' means to the great ones. When Enobarbus says to Menas, pointing to the servant who carries off Lepidus, 'There's a strong fellow, Menas', Menas replies:

MENAS   Why?

ENOBARBUS   A bears the third part of the world, man; seest not?

MENAS   The third part then is drunk. Would it were all,
           That it might go on wheels.

(2. 7. 83–7)

The exchange is both funny and deep, drawing attention to the relationship between the great and the people who, sometimes literally, carry them.

What do you see as the point of the short scene that opens Act 3?

It seems to have two purposes:

1   To give a sense of the sheer panoramic size of this drama, which spans the known world.

2   To explore further the 'greatness' theme by examining the relationship of the great ones and their subordinates.

In mocking Lepidus – the weak link – in the following scene, the two 'honest soldiers' release images and thoughts which play their part in demystifying greatness as well as undermining buffoons. When Caesar, Antony and Octavia come on the scene, accompanied by an almost silent Lepidus, we inevitably begin listening to the farewells between Caesar and his sister and brother-in-law with our ears still attuned to the ironical common-sense of the two rugged soldiers, so we are not surprised to find in Act 3, Scene 6 that the conciliation has completely broken down. Octavia's return to Rome (whatever her former illusions about acting as mediator) is part of a closing of the ranks.

Caesar begins by reviewing the Egyptian situation. 'Here's the manner of't' (2) he says, and draws a picture (reminiscent in superficial ways of Enobarbus's description of the meeting at Cydnus) of Antony and Cleopatra enthroned in the market-place at Alexandria. The names of far-flung, exotic-sounding kingdoms and a roll-call of Eastern monarchs trip off his tongue.

Shakespeare does not present a list like that for nothing – nor is it there for educational purposes. It is there to impress and perhaps dazzle his audience as well as Caesar's and give greatness its historical and geographical setting.

In the part of the play that covers the battle of Actium and its immediate consequences (3. 7–3. 13), the speech-rhythms become less formal, more colloquial than ever (for example, Enobarbus's 'why, why, why?' and 'Well, is it, is it?' (3. 7. 2, 4)). Cleopatra herself has difficulty in maintaining the imperial 'we'. Even the socially inferior characters speak with great directness to their superiors ('Trust not to rotten planks' (62) and 'Let th'Egyptians / And the Phoenicians go a-ducking' (63–4)). But these powerful, rugged, colloquial sentences do not prevent the appearance of some striking poetic effects of a more complex kind. For instance, in Scene 10, Scarus, whom one best remembers for the animal images he introduces into his description of the battle – Cleopatra as a 'nag' (10) and 'like a cow in June' (14), Antony as a mallard or wild duck (19) – is given the rich summarizing phrase 'we have kissed away / Kingdoms and provinces' (7–8).

Enobarbus's problem as to whether he should abandon Antony works for the audience both as a poignant insight into his personal crisis and also as a sort of barometer, measuring the movements of that other key figure, Fortune. It is at the end of Scene 6 that he first exposes (with characteristic honesty) his inner thoughts. After his colleague Canidius has – in the matter-of-fact way of a professional mercenary who has no intention of finding himself on the losing side – revealed his plans of going over to Caesar, Enobarbus says (in soliloquy):

> I'll yet follow
> The wounded chance of Antony, though my reason
> Sits in the wind against me.

> (3. 10. 34–6)

Then in Scene 13, back in Alexandria, when Cleopatra asks him 'What shall we do, Enobarbus?' (1), he replies with dreadful economy, 'Think, and die' (2). What 'thinking' in this context means emerges in an aside:

> Mine honesty and I begin to square.
> The loyalty well held to fools does make
> Our faith mere folly; yet he that can endure
> To follow with allegiance a fall'n lord
> Does conquer him that did his master conquer,
> And earns a place i'th' story.

> (3. 13. 40–5)

There is nothing superficial about these lines (they are worth comparing with the discussion [in 3. 1] in which Ventidius follows up the same line of thought in an altogether more brutal way). Enobarbus's speech bristles with questions the play as a whole keeps raising: What is honesty? What is effective political action? Is there a point at which loyalty or fidelity to someone else involves a betrayal of one's self? What is the relation between what we call 'private' and what we call 'public'?

The situation that has made Enobarbus ready to forsake Antony's side is, significantly, not the critical moment of Antony's shame and defeat but the passage in which the lovers attempt to regroup their forces and renew the struggle. The lowest ebb of their fortunes and morale is reached with Antony's bitter, unworthy jibe 'I found you as a morsel cold upon / Dead Caesar's trencher' (117–18), and with the whipping of Thidias. That done, they seem to begin to recover their confidence. Yet this revival is undermined by the very language they use. There is Cleopatra's far-fetched image of the hailstorm (161–70), followed by a speech by Antony in which he is clearly trying to cheer himself up rather than grapple realistically with his desperate situation. His next effort, 'I will be treble-sinewed, hearted, breathed ... ' (180–7), is almost equally unconvincing until he reaches the words 'Call to me / All my sad captains' (185–6) – a marvellously evocative phrase, which really does remind us of the Antony who has been loved by the hard-boiled opportunists who are his friends.

Emrys Jones in his admirable Penguin edition of the play writes: 'Act 4, Scene 2, to Act 4, Scene 12 ... is one of dizzying instability and ultimate dissolution: Fortune is at her most treacherously inconstant, but within the individual personality there are equally volatile shifts of mood' (Jones, 1977, p.253).

The scene between Antony and Eros (Act 4, Scene 15) is a classic example of dramatic irony, in which the significance of what is going on is revealed to the audience but unclear to the main participant. *We*, but not Antony, foresee Eros's suicide. Is it simply for reasons of virtuosity and dramatic effect that Shakespeare organizes the scene this way? As so often, Shakespeare is contriving to get his effects both ways, that is, we get the full impact of Eros's selfless loyalty *and* that of Antony's suicide and, most daring of all, a wry whiff of humour – Antony himself is 'borne lightly' by his friends (4. 15. 136). This 'lightness', which is one of the striking things about the play, leaves us with a sense of wonder rather than with the more usual tragic emotions or moral lessons.

Antony is borne to Cleopatra's 'monument', from which she dare not descend. At first there is nothing of the 'lightness' just referred to in her language (she is, after all, well aware that it is her false despatch of tidings of her death that has led to Antony's end). When Charmian tries to comfort her, she replies:

> All strange and terrible events are welcome,
> But comforts we despise. Our size of sorrow,
> Proportioned to our cause, must be as great
> As that which makes it.

> (4. 16. 3–6)

It is almost as though (play-actress that she is) she is talking about her difficulty in finding language adequate for the scene that is building up.

When Antony is brought on, this quickly changes. The exchanges between them from now to Antony's death are indeed 'Proportioned to our cause' (5), for Cleopatra, in particular, is allowed an astonishing range of emotion and expression. This includes her admission of fear ('I dare not, dear, / Dear, my lord, pardon' (22–3)), her reference to Octavia, the 'sport' (33) involved in hoisting up the dying man, the phrase 'Quicken with kissing' (40), the description of Fortune as 'the false hussy' (46), and the wheedling 'Hast thou no care of me?' (62). All of these, in their many-faceted vitality, come to us against the resonance of Antony's 'I am dying, Egypt, dying' (43) and his final summary of his end: 'A Roman, by a Roman / Valiantly vanquished' (59–60).

'The *crown o'th' earth* doth melt' (4. 16. 65, emphasis added). The noblest of men has died; but just to put it that way would leave out the effect of the words 'crown' and 'melt'. Crowns and the earth do not in a normal sense 'melt', yet, as we have seen, melting is a recurring image in the play, one of those images of change (in this case disintegration) which give so deep a sense of mutability, development and loss. 'Withered' (66) is another word associated with change (we recall Enobarbus's description of Cleopatra: 'Age cannot wither her' (2. 2. 240)). What Cleopatra is expressing is her sense of loss: everything that makes life worth living, whether in making history or love, has gone. 'The odds is gone' (68) – everything out of the ordinary has come to an end. Yet the moon continues to 'visit' us. How much these last lines owe to a rhythm which suggests a continuity beyond the personal loss can be seen if you try changing the order of the words. 'And there is nothing remarkable left' has in one sense the same meaning as Shakespeare's words, but 'nothing left remarkable' (69) allows him both to get the full force of 'nothing left' and at the same time to suggest the continuing movement of the universe even after Antony's death and in this sense to 'place' the loss.

It is interesting to compare Cleopatra's words at the death of Antony with Caesar's:

> The breaking of so great a thing should make
> A greater crack. The rivèd world
> Should have shook lions into civil streets,
> And citizens to their dens. The death of Antony
> Is not a single doom; in that name lay
> A moiety of the world.

> (5. 1. 14–19)

But the language he uses, though strong, is circumspect. The image of lions and citizens changing places is clearly a figure of speech rather than a creative revelation. Yet we miss the point if we assume that the thought of fallen greatness does not move him truly, just as it has moved Antony who, dying, has spoken of himself as 'the greatest prince o'th' world ... a Roman, by a Roman / Valiantly vanquished' (4. 16. 56–60).

It is one of the great achievements of the last acts of this play that Shakespeare, whilst allowing us to be conscious of the weaknesses and limitations of *all* the characters, can nevertheless pull out every stop in his presentation of the fall of Antony and the suicide of Cleopatra. That there has been an element of hollow boastfulness as well as misjudgement in Antony's claims and actions (he even muffs his suicide) does not lessen his nobility. That Cleopatra's cowardice and deceit (her lie about her death) should contribute signally to Antony's destruction does not tarnish the heroism of her final actions.

Consider the opening lines of 5. 2:

> My desolation does begin to make
> A better life. 'Tis paltry to be Caesar.
> Not being Fortune, he's but Fortune's knave,
> A minister of her will. And it is great
> To do that thing that ends all other deeds,
> Which shackles accidents and bolts up change,
> Which sleeps, and never palates more the dung,
> The beggar's nurse, and Caesar's.

> (5. 2. 1–8)

The richness of these austere and quite unglamorous lines ranks them with the boldest and most astonishing of the play. Cleopatra is beginning a process which does not negate her less attractive features (she has not undergone a conversion) but puts them into a new perspective. There is an heroic simplicity in her words about the paltriness of Caesar and the nature of Fortune. This simplicity links with her previous words:

> No more but e'en a woman, and commanded
> By such poor passion as the maid that milks
> And does the meanest chores

> (4. 16. 74–6)

and with Charmian's later description of her as 'A lass unparalleled' (5. 2. 306). If there is an element of intrigue and play-acting in everything she does in Act 5, this certainly is not outside Shakespeare's intention (witness the audacious reference to a squeaking Cleopatra 'boying' her greatness in Caesar's triumph) but evidence, rather, of the dramatist's ability to *strengthen* the realism of his presentation by deliberately reminding us that this is a play we are watching.

The language of this fifth act is both more 'royal' and more 'democratic' than anywhere else in the play. I use the word 'democratic' in a rather special sense, because obviously it is not a word that Shakespeare, any more than his characters, would have used. But I have the conviction that a word is necessary which suggests how it is that this play can, for a modern audience, negate the hierarchical social conventions and values which lie behind and within it, and which at one level it seems to celebrate.

This applies above all to Cleopatra in Act 5. **Let us return to Cleopatra's speech (already briefly discussed), which opens the final scene. What strike you as the most noteworthy or moving features of it?**

You may well have mentioned the contrast in tone with many of her earlier speeches. It is a very sober and controlled statement, suggesting perhaps a breakthrough to a different perception of herself and the world, a new humility. It is as though the word 'desolation' (1) purges the rest of the language of exaggeration and hysteria, though certainly not of vitality. This impression is continued with 'A better life' and the word 'paltry' (2). Of all the things one might say about Caesar this is the least expected, yet the one that drives deepest home. In the image of Caesar as Fortune's knave all the great young man's pretentions are turned inside out. True greatness – it is also implied – has a simplicity and finality about it; the simplicity comes out in 'To do that thing that ends all other deeds' (5), and line 6, which speaks of *shackling* accidents and *bolting up* change, reverses an emphasis that has been so deep in the play, the emphasis on life as fluid, adventurous and – above all – changeable, like Fortune itself. Cleopatra has reached a point of comprehension that allows her to see this moment of reality unflinchingly and there comes back into the text the thought expressed in the first scene of all, 'Our dungy earth alike / Feeds beast as man' (1. 1. 37–8), only now the context is that of Caesar and the beggar. Nothing, the play seems to be saying, is more 'unnatural' than greatness.

The word 'beggar' comes into Cleopatra's language three times in the opening lines of this final scene (8, 16 and 47), adding to our sense that an extreme reversal of fortune is basic to the structure of the play. Cleopatra's first explicit reference to the possibility of her appearing in Caesar's triumph in Rome is a notable example:

> Shall they hoist me up
> And show me to the shouting varletry
> Of censuring Rome? Rather a ditch in Egypt
> Be gentle grave unto me; rather on Nilus' mud
> Lay me stark naked, and let the waterflies
> Blow me into abhorring.

> (5. 2. 54–9)

This time the words combine the spirit of the old Cleopatra and the new. This is partly because her betrayal by Proculeius, whom Antony has advised her to trust, but who has allowed himself to be used as a cover for her capture, has rekindled her indignation; but we are soon to discover, in the scene in which it is revealed that she has been cheating Caesar of half the treasure she has offered him, that the Cleopatra of Act 5 has not lost her cunning or her genius as play-actor. She is not a reformed character. Yet she is in a way the opposite of what she has been, as we realize if we recall that figure 'beggaring description' who first met Antony and compare it with the image (linked so remorselessly to nature's processes) of the woman lying stark naked on the fly-infested mud. What I find especially remarkable in this act is the way Shakespeare manages *at the same time* to give his people a uniquely powerful and emotional rhetoric and to continue to distance them in a way that leaves the audience aware of every side and trick of the situation. Even Cleopatra's references to the role she and her woman will play in Caesar's triumph (including the daring reminder that they will – as in the actual Jacobean theatre – be acted by boys) are double-edged in the sense that she herself never stops acting any more than the politicians do.

The episode (75–99) in which Cleopatra talks to Dolabella about Antony and, quite unexpectedly (for she has even less reason to trust him than Proculeius), relates to him her dream of an Emperor Antony, is extravagant to a point at which one feels it *must* be overdone, or at least the product of self-delusion. And when she asks Dolabella, 'Think you there was, or might be, such a man / As this I dreamt of?' (92–3), it is right and natural that Dolabella should reply, with great kindness, 'Gentle madam, no' (93). Yet her comeback (itself ambiguous because of the word 'but') carries us with her:

> You lie, up to the hearing of the gods.
> But if there be, or ever were one such,
> It's past the size of dreaming.

> (5. 2. 94–6)

Caesar, having magnanimously made light of Cleopatra's fraudulent inventory of valuables and delivered a summing-up full of ambiguous (not to say dishonest) phrases of mercy (175–85) withdraws, leaving the Queen of Egypt prostrate with the equally ambiguous 'My master, and my lord!' (186). But with Caesar's departure the situation is transformed by 'He words me, girls, he words me' (187), which has the double quality of being intimately colloquial and highly perceptive, not least of the part words play in the life of this play. Words, with their ability to reveal and to deceive, *are* the play. Charmian is quietly despatched to set the death plan in motion, while Iras utters a sort of lament: 'Finish, good lady. The bright day is done, / And we are for the dark' (188–9).

A brief return of Dolabella follows, confirming Caesar's real plans and Dolabella's own disinterested sympathies. When he has gone, Cleopatra describes to Iras her vision of their part in a Roman triumph, a passage of immense vividness and force, as it has to be to justify Iras's reactions to it. By the end of this exchange with Iras, Caesar's plans have become not merely intolerable but 'absurd' (222). Soon he will have become an 'ass' (298). With Charmian's return from her mission the beginnings of the ritual that will end in death are set in motion:

> Show me, my women, like a queen. Go fetch
> My best attires. I am again for Cydnus
> To meet Mark Antony.

> (5. 2. 223–5)

But before this can be done, one further vital interruption is necessary: the arrival of the Clown with the means of death. It is in the moment before he comes in, with Cleopatra alone on the stage, that Shakespeare gives her the exalted statement:

> I have nothing
> Of woman in me. Now from head to foot
> I am marble-constant.

> (5. 2. 234–6)

It is a statement that has been prepared for by its contraries, especially by the moment after Antony's death, when she has described herself as:

> No more but e'en a woman, and commanded
> By such poor passion as the maid that milks
> And does the meanest chores.

(4. 16. 74–6)

Now she, who has been so much a woman and responded so vitally to liveliness and change, can say without untruth that she accepts the opposite of all this; and she who had invoked the visiting moon in her lament over Antony can say, 'Now the fleeting moon / No planet is of mine' (5. 2. 236–7).

Genre and structure

This is an atomized play, not one that concentrates with peculiar intensity on a single situation or character. Shakespeare deliberately chose to face us with a host of highly personal, intimate situations which counteract, even as they reinforce, the public nature of so much of the play. It is a *big* story told, most of the time, in *small* scenes: a great, public, historical drama encompassing war and conquest in the Mediterranean world and yet at the same time a boudoir drama of delicacy and humour, full of subtle vignettes, witty observation, varied language and unexpected detail. The corridors of power are not of the anonymous kind.

Contrasts, thematic reprises and atmospheric effects are as important as story-line. The drama's divisions and emphases correspond broadly with a geographical division into (1) Egypt (2) Rome (3) Egypt again, though such a tripartite division does not fully correspond with significant elements in the play's construction. Episodes in Rome, for example, are interpolated in the predominantly eastern part of the play, while episodes in the East crop up in the predominantly Roman area.

It has been argued that, compared with the construction of other Shakespearean tragedies, there is insufficient concentration on the inner *problems* as opposed to the *actions* of the characters. Antony defends his Egyptian life forcefully in the first scene and then goes off to Rome without a great deal of agonizing when he hears of Fulvia's death and the changed political situation. When he has done his business with Caesar, his decision to return to Cleopatra is made with a minimum of conscientious scruple. As Dipak Nandy, commenting on the episodic nature of the play, puts it:

> The struggle between Antony and Octavius is related without dramatic
> suspense; the struggle *within* Antony between the conflicting claims of
> love and imperial duties might not exist at all, so total is the lack of any
> psychological tension.

(Kettle, 1964, p.x)

In other words, there is nothing equivalent to Macbeth's qualms about the murder of Duncan or the painful divisions revealed in Hamlet's mind, especially by the soliloquies.

But any complaint about the lack of a consistent tragic tone comes from an assumption that tragic drama necessarily operates through a process of intense concentration on the inner dilemmas of the main protagonists. It may well be that Antony is not a tragic hero in the mould of a Hamlet or a Lear and that the audience's interest is not concentrated on the inner conflicts of Cleopatra herself until the last movement of the play; but is there any reason why this should not be so?

Another aspect of the *structure* of the play is that besides being a historico-political play, it is also a love story with *two* central characters. Much of the criticism of the play's effect and construction used to come from those who were not happy about the dramatic relevance of the final act or its integration into the overall concept of the play. They worried about whether the Cleopatra of Act 5 is consistent with the Cleopatra of the earlier acts; or whether her death *resolves* dramatically the moral problem of Antony's choice between Rome and Egypt.

What lies behind such worries is the traditional case for regarding the dramatic essence of the play as the tragedy of *Antony*, hinging on the choice *he* makes between *his* duty and *his* pleasure, a fatal choice that leads to *his* downfall but is given a tragic dimension by the fact that *he* salvages, if not his Roman duty, at least *his* Roman honour, dying not as a lust-corroded coward but as 'a Roman by a Roman / Valiantly vanquished' (4. 16. 59–60).

It seems that this view of the play embodies the way most Elizabethans familiar with the story have perceived it, and most critics until recently. The trouble about it is that it leaves out, not Cleopatra altogether, but Shakespeare's Cleopatra, especially the Cleopatra who survives Antony. But in what sense does her suicide *resolve* the tragic situation Shakespeare has set up? Unless, of course, the 'moral' of the play is indeed 'Make love, not war'. Such an exalted view of the lovers' passion cancels out all the moral ambiguities with which Shakespeare invests her relationship with Antony and Rome. The Egyptian values of romantic love have emerged triumphantly over those of practical Roman politics. Such an oversimplification ignores many essential facets of the play: that the Romans on Pompey's galley behave with as much self-indulgence, though a good deal less style, than the Egyptians on Cleopatra's barge; that Antony is and remains proud to be a Roman; that Cleopatra is an accomplished politician; that greatness, with all its ambiguities, is a concept shared by the two lovers.

But perhaps the main danger of an oversimplification which equates Rome with politics and Egypt with love is that it prevents the play from saying anything very profound about either. In fact, one of the clearest ideas that arises from the play is that public and private life are linked in ways infinitely more subtle than the formula Rome *versus* Egypt can ever show. It is too simple to say that both Antony and Cleopatra put sexual pleasure before the business of government. Romantic love is exalted precisely *because* it overrides other social values and conventions which are well-established and widely respected, and therefore not without power. To King Mark, in Wagner's opera, the appalling thing about the love of Tristan and Isolde is that it destroys the values and loyalties to which – for reasons that did not at that time or ours seem ignoble – he gives a supreme importance. I have brought these other lovers into the discussion because I doubt if we shall come to grips with the significance of the love relationship of Antony and Cleopatra unless we see it as a factor in human history, rather than as something unique or metaphysical.

When Antony asserts that 'The nobleness of life / Is to do thus' (1. 1. 38–9), he is claiming that a very special human value is embodied in his liaison with the Egyptian queen, and that a world which does not recognize or incorporate such a value lacks something essential. When Cleopatra says of Antony's 'bounty' that 'There was no winter in't; an autumn 'twas, / That grew the more by reaping' (5. 2. 86–7), she is claiming that their relationship was in some essential way more 'natural' than what we usually think of as nature, and expressive of human potential and growth. It is this sense we get of a value that transcends the values of other people in the play that makes us unable to deal with Shakespeare's play in terms of easier moralistic judgements, such as 'Antony should have a stronger sense of duty'. What seems to be left out of such approaches is the value of 'bounty' or generosity of spirit, which those who admire Antony emphasize and which Cleopatra achieves in Act 5.

An open expression of romantic affection (as opposed to the half-secret, semi-illicit courtly affairs of medieval romance) represented at the time of Shakespeare an aspect of human advance. We can associate it with the new value that Renaissance, Reformation and capitalist thinking gave to individualism. Like all such historical developments, this new emphasis had negative as well as positive sides. It contributed to a conception of freedom that was, and is, by no means always to be taken at its face value. There is no reason for us, any more than Shakespeare, to idealize the love of Antony and Cleopatra. They quite often behave abominably to one another and to other people. It is significant that the great modern expression of romantic love, Wagner's *Tristan and Isolde*, should also link such love with death. But of all the false trails we should be at pains to avoid in studying *Antony and Cleopatra* the chief one is that which is embedded in the question: is this a love story or a political play? Not only is it both, but the two aspects are also mutually inseparable. Neither makes sense without the other. We can understand this better by looking in more detail at the figure of Cleopatra. Part of one's sense of the astonishing humanity of this particular play comes, surely, from the emergence of this woman – referred to in the early stages as a 'dish' (2. 6. 123) and (in the most famous and wonderful of the descriptions of her) as a feeder of male 'appetites' (2. 2. 242) – as a heroic figure who has the peculiarly *political* triumph of making great Caesar look an 'ass unpolicied' (5. 2. 298–9) (Figure 22).

Consider the basic implications here. Are we presented with the spectacle of an accomplished female ruler making particularly effective use of the traditional equipment her sexuality provides in a man's world, or does a further dimension come into play, extending and completing the scope of the tragedy?

When Cleopatra decides, after Antony's death, to face the situation in 'the high Roman fashion' and calls on her women to prepare her 'like a queen' (5. 2. 223) for a death that will commit her forever to Antony against Caesar, two apparently contradictory lines of thought and conduct thread through her words and actions. On the one hand, there is the thread of high exaltation with its key words 'royal', 'noble', 'great', 'immortal', reaching perhaps its most striking expression in the lines:

> I have nothing
> Of woman in me. Now from head to foot
> I am marble-constant. Now the fleeting moon
> No planet is of mine.

> (5. 2. 234–7)

Figure 22 *Janet Suzman as Cleopatra in the Royal Shakespeare Company production of* Antony and Cleopatra *directed by Trevor Nunn, 1972. Photo: Reg Wilson Collection, Shakespeare Centre Library.*

On the other hand, there is a quite opposite emphasis. In this thread the stress is on the womanliness as opposed to the queenliness of Cleopatra. To Iras's 'Royal Egypt, Empress!' (4. 16. 74) she replies:

> No more but e'en a woman, and commanded
> By such poor passion as the maid that milks
> And does the meanest chores.

(4. 16. 74–6)

This links, as the final act proceeds, not with her consciously insincere self-debasement (and sex-debasement) before Caesar, but with the Cleopatra who jokes with the countryman, who fears that Iras may meet dead Antony before her, to whom 'The stroke of death is as a lover's pinch / Which hurts and is desired' (5. 2. 286–7) and whose response to Charmian's 'O eastern star!' (299) is 'Dost thou not see my baby at my breast, / That sucks the nurse asleep?' (300–1).

It is the second thread to which the words 'Husband I come' (278) belong and also the scarcely coherent yet moving final words of all, which begin 'As sweet as balm, as soft as air, as gentle' (302). Without that ineffably *gentle* statement Charmian's triumphant words could not have their simple and convincing force: 'It is well done, and fitting for a princess / Descended of so many royal kings' (317–18).

Even Caesar is moved and finds it in himself to say quite simply, 'She shall be buried by her Antony' (348). The words knit together the two threads, and without any sort of idealization. The title of the play is fulfilled and Cleopatra finally emerges as a woman who is no less and no more than a human being, as capable as Antony of heroic deeds and a tragic status.

Changing critical perspectives

Cicely Palser Havely

This brief section aims to place Arnold Kettle's material between some aspects of its critical predecessors and an outline of some of the most significant critical debates about the play that have followed it. It does *not* aim to cover the whole critical literature about this play up to the end of the twentieth century. If you have time, you might like to consult the volume on *Antony and Cleopatra* in the New Casebooks series of Contemporary Critical Essays, edited by John Drakakis (1994). Several of the essays referred to below are reprinted there.

Literary critics are as much creatures of their time as the texts they study. In 1977, feminist criticism was at the height of what might be called its 'discovery' phase. With wit and anger critics such as Kate Millett (1972) began to re-read the canonical syllabus and reveal that women's repression had been endlessly recorded, re-enacted and reinforced in all the texts of the canon. Shakespeare, perhaps because of his unique status, perhaps because his sexism seemed less blatant than, say, D.H. Lawrence's, had attracted relatively little feminist attention when Linda Fitz published her breezy exposure of sexual politics in *Antony and Cleopatra* and sexual prejudice in its long line of critics:

> In Cleopatra's case, critical attitudes go beyond the usual condescension
> toward female characters or the usual willingness to give critical
> approval only to female characters who are chaste, fair, loyal and
> modest: critical attitudes towards Cleopatra seem to reveal deep
> personal fears of aggressive or manipulative women.

(Fitz, 1977, p.304)

The play, as we have seen, is full of opposites and reflections which blend into one another, but Fitz showed that the bias and preferences which masculine criticism has read into it evaporate under less partial scrutiny: 'what is praiseworthy in Antony is damnable in Cleopatra ... men may put political considerations ahead of love; women may not' (ibid.). Sexism, she was able to show, lay at the heart of many claims about the play's merit and status.

A.C. Bradley's attitude to the play now seems to epitomize Edwardian gender-prejudice. 'She destroys him' was his verdict on Cleopatra (Bradley, 1909). Yet in 1983, Kettle still felt able to cite his views, not directly on Cleopatra's respectability, but on genre. Kettle was more gender-sensitive than many critics of his generation, though he took little explicit notice of feminist criticism – still then considered by many to be 'only' about women, by women, for women. As a Marxist, he would have pounced on the class assumptions bound up with Bradley's sexism, but he apparently assumed that questions of genre are neutral, gender-free and (possibly) timeless.

You have now been introduced to the three main genres of Shakespearean drama, and later you will encounter two examples (*Measure for Measure* and *The Tempest*) which do not fit easily into the categories of history, comedy or tragedy. You may wonder whether genre is in itself a very productive topic, since it seems to elude definition, although it has clearly been considered of great significance in the past.

Kettle raises the question of the play's generic status in the first two paragraphs of his essay, and at this point you might like to return to Chapter 3 and test the various theories of tragedy which Stephen Regan introduces to see how well they might be adapted to *Antony and Cleopatra*. As a reminder, however, consider briefly the following questions:

1 Does the fact that this is a 'Roman' play make classical models of tragedy (Greek or Roman) any more appropriate?

2 Compare your responses to the ending of *Antony and Cleopatra* with those you felt at the end of *Macbeth*. Would you describe your reaction as an Aristotelian *catharsis* or a Bradleyan impression of *waste*? (These concepts were discussed in Chapter 3. Bradley in fact denied this play full tragic status, as you will see later.)

3 Is Sir Philip Sidney's notion that tragedy can 'expose corruption' illuminating?

4 Is the Hegelian notion of a conflict between 'one partial good and another' appropriate?

5 Could you write an essay on *Antony and Cleopatra* applying George Steiner's dictum that 'The tragic personage is broken by forces which can neither be fully understood nor overcome by rational prudence'?

Most audiences/readers would, I think, agree that, with its conflicts and losses, and the moving deaths of the characters we care most about, this play must be a tragedy of sorts. But its mostly male-authored critical history reveals a widespread reluctance to confer this privileged status, even though it may seem perverse to try and shoe-horn a play which confounds unity of time or place into an Aristotelian mould and then condemn it for not fitting. Bradley asserted that 'It is better for the world's sake, and not less for their own, that they should fail and die.' (But might not the same also be said of the Macbeths, if not of Hamlet and Othello?) He declares, says Fitz, 'that the play is not a true tragedy because he cannot find the tragic hero's inner struggle in Antony' (Fitz, 1977, p.314) – a point Kettle echoes above – though he might have found such a struggle if he had thought to look in Cleopatra. The editor of the New Arden edition of 1954 (M.R. Ridley) declared that this is 'not the highest kind of love' and that the play does not qualify as tragedy since it lacks the defining sense of waste, a view which ignores the play's recurrent contrast between what Antony once was and now is. Fitz showed how this widespread discomfort with the play's status was linked to a consensus that Antony was its chief protagonist and hence a general conviction that the play's structure must be flawed, since Cleopatra survives for an act of her own. The only critic she could discover who admitted that the lovers might be joint protagonists finally concluded that Antony 'comes to a miserable end' because of his infatuation with 'a thoroughly unworthy object', whose own end cannot be an authentic 'tragic fall' since she never possessed any moral status (Mills, 1964, p.35).

The issue has sometimes been sidestepped by labelling it a 'Roman' play, alongside *Julius Caesar* and *Coriolanus*, especially as it shares the same major source, Plutarch's *Lives of the Noble Grecians and Romans*. But there is too much 'Egypt' for this evasive categorization to fit. Kettle, whose egalitarian instincts rejected hierarchies of all kinds, did not dismiss attempts to consign this play to an inferior status because he rejected their intrinsic sexism, but because he clearly realized that *no* traditional forms can be easily matched to this play. He looks instead to Brecht's 'epic' theatre and to Wagnerian opera to provide not models, but illuminating analogues.

He was building on the earlier work of his own generation when he queried the oppositional readings of the play. His near contemporaries, such as G. Wilson Knight (1931), L.C. Knights (1946) and John Bayley (1981) still saw in the play's poetry a unifying transcendence, which overwhelmed humdrum questions of duty and expedience and synthesized the Rome/Egypt polarities. Kettle's Marxism was combined with a rich vein of romantic idealism, expressed in the (perhaps not altogether convincing) suggestion that 'romantic affection' represented a 'human advance' (see above). But he was also, I think, resisting the crude binarism that forms the ideological basis of so many kinds of oppression – class, racial, religious and, not least, sexual.

Antony and Cleopatra sets up oppositions, but then eludes them. It is not, as it is now widely seen to be, a play in which it is possible, let alone desirable, to take sides absolutely. But that has not always been the case. Georg Brandes, writing in 1898, characterized the imperialists' perspective thus:

> the fall of the Roman Republic results from the contact of the simple
> hardihood of the West with the luxury of the East ... when [Antony]
> perishes, a prey to the voluptuousness of the East, it seems as though
> Roman greatness expires with him.

> (Brandes, 1911, p.158)

Racism has been just as pervasive as sexism in the critical reception of the play. This contrast between the 'simple hardihood' (and implied moral superiority) of the West and the 'luxury' and 'voluptuousness' of the East is surely a classic instance of the 'Orientalism' identified by Edward Said (1978). It is only recently that critical enquiry has sought out and emphasized reflections of imperialism and colonialism in Shakespeare which had previously been ignored, not just because European expansionism was deemed to have been in its infancy in the Tudor/Jacobean era, but because it was not recognized how fundamentally colonialism had shaped European perceptions. Your work on *The Tempest* will consider in more detail how travellers' tales of 'undiscovered' regions combined with politically motivated justifications of plunder and conquest to create fictional New Worlds.

The Orient was (and still is) a fantasy-land, not a substantial geopolitical entity. It is not only in Shakespeare's play that it is represented as voluptuously feminine, a realm of luxury and indolence which contrasts with the West's long-standing self-image of strict masculine rationality: 'Cleopatra was Rome's enemy, and we in the West are Rome's heirs. The notion of Cleopatra that we have inherited identifies her as being the adversary, the Other ... an Oriental and a woman' (Hughes-Hallett, 1992).

It was no coincidence that some of the more extravagant attacks on Cleopatra belonged to an era of strident European imperialism, when young men needed to be warned that their duty was to govern their far-flung colonies and to avoid the wiles of local Cleopatras.

When *Antony and Cleopatra* was written, European colonization of the Americas and the Indies had been expanding for over a century, though British interests in such distant regions were of more recent date. *Antony and Cleopatra* is ostensibly about the expansion and consolidation of a much older empire, yet it needs to be remembered that even the Protestant rulers of Europe considered themselves to be the heirs of Rome. In this story, Augustus or Octavius Caesar played a crucial role in Christian history as the Emperor at the time of Christ's birth ('There went out a decree at the time of Caesar Augustus that all the world should be taxed' (Luke 2:1)). The stability in the Roman empire which historically followed the defeat of Antony at Actium is linked in Christian tradition with an era of 'universal peace', which coincided with the incarnation. Octavius was familiar to Shakespeare's contemporaries as one of the 'virtuous heathen' inherited from medieval tradition. As Coppélia Kahn puts it:

> In dramatizing the story [of Antony and Cleopatra] Shakespeare fell heir
> to a legacy of representation on which the Latin curriculum and the
> *studia humanitatis* [study of humanity] of the Renaissance were founded,
> a legacy organized by and centering on the mythic construction of
> Octavius Caesar as the destined victor in a prolonged power-struggle
> who instituted the *pax romana* [Roman peace] that ushered in the
> Christian era.

(Kahn, 1997, p.112)

This assimilation of Christianity's narrative of Divine Purpose to the history of Roman imperialism is nearly invisible to a modern audience, but so too is another myth of political consolidation. Like Octavius, James Stuart had unified the 'three-nooked' world of England, Wales and Scotland:

> This British Union of three in one is ... hallowed by its trinitarian
> association ... *Antony and Cleopatra* ... shows the transition from
> triumvirate to Augustan empire, and ... its Jacobean context places it
> with *King Lear* ... where the effects of division are terrifyingly recorded.

(Drakakis, 1994, p.126)

The play's relationship with history is very complex, as Kettle indicates above. But perhaps we should think also of the play's relationship with 'histories', since (as you have already learnt) Tudor and Jacobean accounts of British history do not agree with modern accounts, and sixteenth- and seventeenth-century accounts of Roman history are not at all like those in use today.

But if this Tudor/Jacobean reading of an episode in ancient history seems to suggest an endorsement of Octavius's triumph and a corresponding denigration of the lovers in complete contrast to most modern interpretations of the play, Margot Heinemann suggests that:

> for many of Shakespeare's contemporaries and patrons, this crucial
> historical turning-point had quite a different significance, and a tragic
> one, pointing not to the triumph of peace but to the corruption and
> ultimate decline of Roman civilization ... The wars of the triumvirs ...
> marked primarily the decline of the old Roman virtues or order.

(Ibid., p.174)

She concludes that 'the variety of viewpoints and judgements presented, the refusal of a single historical or ethical centre, is an especially marked feature of *Antony and Cleopatra*' (ibid., p.177) – and this is perhaps the only conclusion it is safe to reach. Certainly, the categorical moral judgements of some earlier criticism have been swept away by later preferences for relativism and ambivalence. But whilst *readings* may relish ambiguities, *productions* on the whole require a clearer point of view. The double ending of this play even seems to demand an emphatic sense of closure or of a choice affirmed. Though Vanessa Redgrave's drunken harridan eventually died with dignity at the Bankside Globe production in 1973, Octavius delivered his final line like a 'salivating necrophiliac' according to the *New Statesman* critic (17 August 1973). But such an interpretation, which suggests that there is nothing to choose between two equally degenerate forces, is rare.

Ambiguities are not, however, confined to the moral content of the play, but affect its form. Where earlier commentators saw the play's lack of conformity to traditional models of tragedy as a shortcoming, more recent critics have extolled its playful and searching subversion of generic expectations. Barbara C. Vincent has shown how the worlds of Rome and Egypt are expressed as the domains of tragedy and comedy. She points out that the Roman world endorses individuality and the pursuit of power; it self-consciously aspires to nobility and sees its workings as the operations of history, whereas Egypt is 'serenely unburdened by any historical mission' (Drakakis, 1994, p.214). (You might want to qualify that view when you consider Cleopatra's sense of herself as a ruler in her own right, who puts up a good fight for her country's independent political destiny.) Vincent's tragic/comic division parallels the gender divide in that Rome is 'unabashedly masculine' – indeed, women seem the only topic that routinely 'abashes' these Romans – while Egypt, in romantic, feminine mode, confuses identities, especially gender identities, and dissolves boundaries. However, 'neither world is content with a discrete half of the universe' (ibid., p.216). Here, Vincent takes up that reluctance to see *Antony and Cleopatra* as a series of harsh binary oppositions which we already noticed in Kettle and his immediate predecessors, but unlike them she does not resolve the play's dichotomies in a transcendent glow. Instead, she sees these opposites in a constant play of mutual exploration. Hence the nature and limitations of tragedy and comedy, masculinity and femininity, are illuminated by their proximity:

> If seen as part of the action of the play, the contest of genres explains
> the conflict of interpretations which the play has generated. Does
> Cleopatra unman and destroy Antony, ironically weakening and
> dividing him until he suffers the torment of defeat by a lesser man? Or
> does she help him achieve his quest for identity, completing the Roman
> warrior in a greater, more magnanimous hero, and raising him out of
> the dying world of history – the fortunate Caesar's dominion – into the
> sublime comic realm of legends, demi-gods, amid ever-reviving
> theatrical heroes? Since each genre is all-encompassing, each can supply
> a credible interpretation of almost any aspect of Antony's story. One
> man's 'dotage' is another man's (or woman's) 'nobleness of life'.

(Ibid., p.217)

You have seen that, although Shakespearean comedy is frequently enhanced by an acknowledgement of the proximity of tragedy, incursions of comedy into tragedy provoke different kinds of unease. This play's Rome seems particularly wary of comic invasions. When Antony is at his most self-consciously Roman, he cannot take a joke. Yet Rome has its own brand of comedy, a 'manly' humour embodied in Enobarbus's robust appraisal of Cleopatra as 'a wonderful piece of work' (1. 2. 139–40) and not entirely absent from his account of Cydnus, with Antony 'barbered ten times o'er' (2. 2. 230). Even Octavius can manage to joke in this vein occasionally: 'If Cleopatra heard you, your reproof / Were well deserved of rashness' (2. 2. 127–8). It is a measure of Antony's displacement that, whilst too formal to be consistently at ease in Egypt, he cannot see the funny side in Rome. Although he eventually pays the price, Enobarbus can function in both worlds.

Antony cannot. He betrays Cleopatra in Rome not because his passion for her is not genuine (at least, it has been doubted far less than hers for him) but because, unlike Enobarbus, he literally cannot account for her in the Roman world. He can talk about crocodiles and pyramids and other tourist attractions, but not about Cleopatra herself.

In some recent interpretations of the play, Octavius has been cast as if he represented a clipped, imperial Englishman; but in many ways it is Antony – or Antony in Rome – who conforms even more to that stereotype. Much has been said about the inconstancy of Cleopatra's character; much less about the vacillations of Antony. In Rome, he is not what he was in Egypt – and in neither is he the man he once was in Roman memories. Indeed, the slanderous readings of Cleopatra that Fitz recorded have all diverted attention from Antony's shortcomings. We hear about his legendary past, about his Jovian generosity, his dolphin-like delights, but like Dolabella we might be more sceptical. The man who in the first scene declares that 'The nobleness of life is to do thus' (1. 1. 38–9) rebukes *himself* in the next for the 'dotage' (1. 2. 106) he is accused of in the play's opening phrase. We are, I would suggest, no more able to judge the reliability or depth of his passion than Cleopatra's, yet the question is never asked of him. No wonder that recent critics have come to doubt the 'transcendence' of this high-profile political love-scandal: it could never survive the exposure of the double-standard. As long as no-one questioned Antony's inconstancy and treachery, or wondered whether personal betrayal might be transferred to political judgements, the absence of any unambiguous core in the relationship could be represented as a transcendent mystery. In the 1930s, G. Wilson Knight (1931) and J. Middleton Murry (1936) had placed an almost religious value on the play's evocations of love, just as its chief protagonists do. But the play as a whole does not seem to confirm this. Murry even ascribed to the 'royalty' of the lovers a lofty spiritual significance, and it is strange to find traces of this attitude lingering in the interpretation of a Marxist like Kettle. But the cultural materialists, who are in some respects his successors, are made of tougher stuff. Jonathan Dollimore sees power struggles where a more idealistic or perhaps more self-deluding generation read 'love': 'It is a simple yet important truth, one which the essentialist rhetoric is never quite allowed to efface: to kiss away kingdoms is also to kiss away the lives of thousands' (Drakakis, 1994, p.258).

Far from being a traditional Roman or Renaissance hero, Dollimore's Antony is a man of contradictions, who trades his political power for sexual freedom, but expresses his sexuality in terms of the very power he has lost: 'a fantasy transfer of power from the public to the private sphere, from the battlefield to the bed' (ibid., p.259). To some extent his reading reiterates conventional male anxieties about a sound man seduced: his Antony is infatuated, masochistic and self-destructive.

No reading of the play is ever likely to produce a Cleopatra who is an idealized, straightforward modern woman, to whom no responsibility for the catastrophe can be attributed. Even if we construe a Shakespeare of remarkably independent thought, he was still a man of his time. But perhaps more important, he was, as has been repeatedly pointed out, a man of the theatre, and in that crucible of social experiment you have already seen the charges sparked by commoners playing kings and boys acting women's roles. You have also already seen how in *Macbeth* the practicalities of gender impersonation spill over into sustained exploration of the nature of masculinity and femininity. Cross-dressing, often thought to be exclus-ively a convention of comedy, infiltrates the tragedies too and supplies one of the many ambivalences in this play. Indeed, you might want to consider whether the alleged manliness of Cleopatra and the purported emasculation of Antony do not contribute to that identification of Egypt with the comic spirit that Vincent suggested. Certainly her reading casts light on an aspect of Antony which other critics have shown to be at odds with his heroic status: 'no matter what Antony actually says or does, he and his fellow Romans are disposed to construe her presence as an influence, and her influence as, simply, emasculating domination' (Kahn, 1997, p.118).

Simply because she is her country's ruler, Cleopatra usurps a male role. As her country's spokeswoman, she defies the idealized silence of the stereotype. Whether this puts the character in a position of dominance and relegates her lover to subservience and emasculation, or opens the play to an exchange of sexualities which is part of the couple's mutuality, is for you to decide. It may be slightly absurd to attempt to discover an Antony of the late twentieth century, getting in touch with his feminine side, but it is Antony's quarrel with the pragmatism and aggression of Rome which surely makes his death a lamentable waste. Muddled and divided though he may be, Antony embodies qualities that the Roman world is poorer without.

Perhaps the most surprising omission from Kettle's account of the play is much reference to it as a text for *performance*. Despite his love of the theatre, especially opera, he had some sympathy for L.C. Knights's opinion that 'the only profitable approach to Shakespeare is a consideration of his plays as "dramatic poems"' (1946, p.4). He points out the self-conscious 'theatricality' of the play but does not develop this theme, partly because performance studies were in their infancy in the early 1980s, and in many editions the only references to the theatre would be a frequently dreary catalogue of productions. Nowadays, as you have seen in earlier chapters, texts are scrutinized for their references to the medium in which they are realized, and the clues such references provide to meaning and interpretation. Here there is only room to introduce a theme which you may return to later, and I suggest you begin by looking at the twin death scenes of Antony (4. 16) and Cleopatra (5. 2. 208–356) (Figure 23).

Cleopatra's death is obviously staged; it has even been rehearsed: 'She hath pursued conclusions infinite / Of easy ways to die' (5. 2. 345–6). It is her alternative to the staging she fears in Rome: 'The quick comedians / Extemporally will stage us' (5. 2. 212–13) – but that exposure is itself a kind of travesty of the equally public performance she willingly gave when she hopped 'forty paces through the public street' (2. 2. 235). She is not just an actor in her own drama, but its producer too. When Fulvia dies, she gives Antony his stage-directions:

> ... prithee turn aside and weep for her,
> Then bid adieu to me, and say the tears
> Belong to Egypt. Good now, play one scene
> Of excellent dissembling, and let it look
> Like perfect honour.

> (1. 3. 76–80)

But Antony cannot follow her instructions. Indeed, although he is as inconstant, various and fragmented a character as his lover, he is much less comfortable as an actor of his different roles. He cannot even play the Roman very well, as his botched death shows. He too prefers a death of his own choosing to being 'windowed in

Figure 23 *Vanessa Redgrave as Cleopatra in the Riverside Studio Theatre production* of Antony and Cleopatra *directed by Vanessa Redgrave, 1995. Photo: Neil Libbert.*

great Rome' (4. 15. 72), but cannot stage-manage it: Eros outwits him, and his own attempt is clumsy. Cleopatra then quite literally upstages him. Although on one level it is fear that prevents her leaving her monument, the hauling up of Antony to join her is a spectacular *coup de théâtre*, which demonstrates not her timidity but her flair, her willpower, her strength and ingenuity. That she hardly lets him speak his dying words also suggests a greater command of the histrionic moment. Indeed, considered from this perspective, it is Cleopatra who is the star, Antony the waning has-been. Her most intimate moments are a photo-opportunity. The transactions of political power and sexuality played out in a glare of publicity constitute a familiar scenario in the last days of the twentieth century.

References

Bayley, J. (1981) *Shakespeare and Tragedy*, London: Routledge & Kegan Paul.

Bradley, A.C. (1909) *Oxford Lectures on Poetry*, London: Macmillan.

Brandes, G. (1911) *William Shakespeare: A Critical Study*, 1898, trans. W. Archer and D. White, London: Heinemann.

Brecht, B. (1963) *The Life of Galileo*, 1943, trans. D.I. Vesey, London: Eyre Methuen.

Drakakis, J. (ed.) (1994) *Antony and Cleopatra: Contemporary Critical Essays*, London: Macmillan.

Fitz, L. (later, Woodbridge) (1977) 'Egyptian queens and male reviewers', *Shakespeare Quarterly*, vol.28, Summer, pp.297–316.

Hughes-Hallett, L. (1992) *Cleopatra: Histories, Dreams and Distortions*, London: Vintage Books.

Jones, E. (1977) *Shakespeare: Antony and Cleopatra*, Harmondsworth: Penguin.

Kahn, C. (1997) *Roman Shakespeare: Warriors, Wounds and Women*, London: Routledge.

Kettle, A. (ed.) (1964) *Shakespeare in a Changing World*, London: Lawrence & Wishart.

Knight, G.W. (1931) *The Imperial Theme*, London: Methuen.

Knights, L.C. (1946) *Explorations*, London: Chatto & Windus.

Middleton Murray, J. (1936) *Shakespeare*, London: Cape.

Millett, K. (1972) *Sexual Politics*, London, Abacus.

Mills, L.J. (1964) *The Tragedies of Shakespeare's 'Antony and Cleopatra'*, Bloomington: Indiana University Press.

Neill, M. (1994) *Anthony and Cleopatra*, World's Classics, Oxford: Oxford University Press.

Ridley, M.R. (ed.) (1954) *Antony and Cleopatra*, New Arden Shakespeare, London: Methuen.

Said, E.W. (1978) *Orientalism*, London: Routledge & Kegan Paul.

Savidis, G. (ed.) (1992) *C.P. Cavafy: Collected Poems*, trans. E. Keeley and P. Sherrard, Princeton: Princeton University Press (first published Hogarth Press, London, 1975).

Willett, J. (1986) *Brecht on Theatre*, London: Methuen.

EDITING SHAKESPEARE'S PLAYS

Ann Thompson and Neil Taylor

Aims

This interval will identify and distinguish between the primary documents – the Folios and the Quartos – that contain the works of Shakespeare. It will help you to gain a sense of how the editing and subsequent re-editing of these texts have affected the meaning of Shakespeare's works.

Shakespeare's texts

Is there such a thing as a Shakespeare text? If we mean by this a single, unchallengeable, authoritative document that we could consult in a library somewhere, the answer has to be no.

We need to recognize that the *written* text is a problematic entity. Shakespeare was a professional writer operating in a predominantly oral culture. Literacy was the privilege of a few, and the fixity we associate with written texts was challenged by the conditions under which plays were composed and performed.

Shakespeare may well have had an unusual degree of personal security and stability in his working conditions – he was, after all, an actor, a shareholder and the resident playwright in a prestigious company[1] – but we have to imagine him producing manuscripts of plays under severe pressure as he tried to meet the practical, professional demands of the company. London acting companies were vulnerable on two fronts: legally, because actors were classified as the equivalent of vagrants, and because all playscripts were subject to official censorship; economically, because they were competing for audiences within a limited population, and because the frequent eruptions of the plague led to prolonged closures of the theatres in the summer months.

Plays did not have long runs – just a few performances – so there would be a constant demand for new plays. We know that when playwrights were commissioned by companies to write plays, they sometimes handed them over as finished manuscripts, but sometimes they submitted them in instalments, act by act. On receipt, the play would usually be copied out again at least once by a scribe, and in the process it might well be altered, either accidentally or deliberately. Then someone wrote out each actor's part separately. Finally, these parts were committed

---

[1] See Interval 1 for details of the acting companies as businesses.

to memory. What happened to the scripts in rehearsal and performance we can only imagine, but we have Hamlet's speech to the Players (*Hamlet*, 3. 2) as evidence that at least some actors annoyed playwrights by departing from their scripts.

Once handed over, the play became the property of the acting company rather than the writer, and it was usually only officially printed once the company believed it could make no more money out of it. Whilst some playwrights were keen to oversee the printing of their plays in the printing house, Shakespeare was probably not one of them. Printers made mistakes, and proof-reading was something done on the job while printing was taking place. Books would therefore come out in a number of different states – some pages in one copy corrected and others not, different pages in another copy corrected and others not.

All of this means that the idea of 'the text' of a Shakespeare play has to be a fluid one. Everything suggests process more than product, the generation of multiple texts rather than a single, final version.

Printed texts

In 1623, seven years after Shakespeare's death, there appeared a large-format collected edition of almost all his plays: this volume is referred to by scholars as the 'First Folio' (F1). However, about half of Shakespeare's plays had already appeared in print during his lifetime, published singly in pocket-size paperbacks known as 'Quartos'. The terms 'Folio' and 'Quarto' simply describe the size of the books' pages. The sheets of paper used by printers were each folded in half once to create a book with pages of Folio size. These folded sheets were then sewn together and bound to make up a book. A smaller format book could be made by folding the paper in half a second time, so that the original sheets were now in *quarters*, creating a book with pages of Quarto size.

Many of the Shakespeare Quartos seem to have been unauthorized, and some of them are abbreviated and garbled to the extent that scholars have supposed they were put together from memory by actors or 'reporters', who wanted to exploit the success of a play by selling a text to a publisher. Some of them, on the other hand, seem to have been printed from good manuscripts deriving from Shakespeare himself or from an authentic playhouse transcription.

A modern editor faced with a play that exists in more than one early printed text usually has to make a decision about which text to print – we say 'usually' because, for example, two recent editions of Shakespeare's complete works, the Oxford edition (1986) and the Norton edition (1997), offer their readers more than one text of *King Lear*. In choosing which text to print, an editor is obliged to develop an explanation or theory of the differences between the surviving versions. The differences may be due to carelessness in copying or printing; cutting or rewriting for performance purposes; or authorial revision.

King Lear offers many examples of all such differences. In the first place, we have evidence that the printers of the Quarto edition of 1608 themselves corrected 167 errors as they went along. Subsequently, further errors were picked up in the Folio. An example is line 103 of the opening scene in the Quarto, which reads 'The mystresse of *Heccat*, and the might'. The F1 editors altered this to 'The miseries of *Heccat* and the night'. Most modern editors believe that both texts are wrong about the second word and change it to 'mysteries' – a correction found in the Second Folio (F2) of 1632. They usually accept F1's alteration of 'might' to 'night'.

King Lear also seems to many modern scholars to demonstrate rewriting for theatrical production and authorial cuts. However, the assumption that Shakespeare revised and rewrote his plays is a relatively recent one; editors in the past tended to assume that Shakespeare wrote only one 'final' or 'definitive' version of each play and that their job was to recover it and present it to their readers. This led to the practice known as the 'conflation' of texts, whereby editors would add to one text passages found only in another and choose variant readings according to their judgement of which text was superior. In the case of *Hamlet*, editors since Nicholas Rowe (1674–1718) have usually included all the passages found only in the Second Quarto (Q2) *and* all the passages found only in F1. This has resulted in the longest possible version of the play, a version which may never have existed in Shakespeare's time and which may contain repetitions and apparent contradictions that the author never intended.

For some plays – *A Midsummer Night's Dream* and *Richard II*, for example – the differences between the surviving early texts are relatively unimportant. For others – notably *Henry IV* Part 2, *Hamlet*, *Troilus and Cressida*, *Othello* and *King Lear* – the differences are numerous and significant, to the extent that these plays can be said to exist in more than one 'authentic' form: perhaps a Shakespearean original and a Shakespearean revision. In an ideal world, an editor might wish to present two texts of each of these plays (three in the case of *Hamlet*), but publishers and readers might not be receptive to such a practice. It has become, however, an obligation to indicate as far as possible the extent to which an edited text is constructed from more than one source. Modern editions of Shakespeare are beginning to make use of a number of different typographical conventions to draw the attention of readers to variant wordings. For example, in the 1997 Arden edition of *King Lear*, superscript 'F's and 'Q's are used to mark words found only in the Folio or only in the Quarto text of the play (see Figure 24).

In the case of *King Lear*, the 1608 Quarto has around 300 lines that are not in the Folio, but the Folio has 100 lines that are not in the Quarto. There are something like 850 verbal variants between the two texts and several speeches are assigned to different speakers. The military action of Acts 4 and 5 is handled differently and there are substantial changes in characterization. Some recent scholars and editors have maintained that the Folio text represents Shakespeare's revised version. Critical and evaluative judgements are involved in so far as those who believe in the revision theory tend to argue that the omissions and additions make the Folio a *better* version of the play than the Quarto, that they are not accidental or random changes but the results of a thoughtful process performed by the author after the play had been first staged. They have argued, for example, that Shakespeare himself must have decided to cut the 'mock trial' episode where the mad Lear attempts to arraign his two elder daughters, which appears in 3. 6 in the Quarto. They have suggested that he deliberately made the play bleaker in the Folio by omitting the lines at the end of 3. 7 in which the servants express their compassion for their blind master. (When Peter Brook cut these lines in his 1962 production for the Royal Shakespeare Company, most reviewers and audiences seem to have received it as a wanton desecration of the text rather than an implementation of a cut already present in the Folio.) Conversely, other scholars have argued that such changes do not improve the play and hence cannot have been made by the author, but represent cuts made in the theatre by someone else.

5.3.304	*King Lear*

LEAR

And my poor fool is hanged. No, no, ᶠnoᶠ life!

Why should a dog, a horse, a rat have life   305

And thou no breath at all? ᵠOᵠ thou'lt come no more,

Never, never, never, ᶠnever, never.ᶠ

[*to Edgar?*] Pray you undo this button. Thank you, sir.

    ᵠO, o, o, o.ᵠ

ᶠDo you see this? Look on her: look, her lips,

Look there, look there!   *He dies.*ᶠ

---

absorption with Cordelia, or trance-like condition he seems to have fallen into at 290; actors have rocked Cordelia, mumbled over her, or even moved aimlessly about the stage (see Rosenberg, 317), but always out of touch, until this moment, when Lear speaks in mid-sentence, as if bringing to consciousness a continuing train of thought.

304 **fool** a term of endearment, referring to Cordelia, who has been hanged; but also recalling Lear's other favourite, the Fool, not heard of since he left the stage at the end of 3.6. The double reference, making us suppose the Fool dead too, gives a special poignancy to these six short words, which penetrate to the very heart of loss. Many have speculated that the parts of Cordelia and the Fool were doubled, since they never appear on stage together (see, for example, Booth, 32–3 and 129), but there is strong evidence that Robert Armin, a mature adult actor, played the Fool, while Cordelia would have been played by a boy; see Wiles, 144–5, 155, and Introduction, pp. 50–1.

307 **Never . . . never** perhaps the most extraordinary blank verse line in English poetry; the relentlessness of *no*, repeated five times in the preceding lines, is now matched by the repetition of *never*, making what follows the more startling. The line also recalls the

repetition of *nothing* in the opening scene; see Introduction, p. 78.

308 **Pray . . . button** Lear is usually taken as referring to a button on his own robes or doublet, echoing *come, unbutton here* at 3.4.107, and as having a last attack of the *mother* (see 2.2.246). It could also conceivably be a button on Cordelia's costume (some women wore bodices that buttoned at the front, a style of dress favoured by Queen Anne), or an imaginary button. We do not know how Cordelia was dressed in this scene; it is possible that she was in male attire, if she had been fighting with her army. To whom is Lear speaking? Oxf, following the suggestion of Warren, 'Kent', 71, adds the SD '*To Kent*', but it is Edgar who is close to Lear, notices that he faints and tries to revive him, and Edgar whose role is enlarged in the final scene, so it is likely that he responds here; see 249 and n. It is also possible to have an attendant help Lear, if a director wishes to maximize the sense of Lear's new-found humility and make the most of a king addressing a menial as 'sir'.

309–10 ***Do . . . there!** These lines, added in F, made it possible for Bradley, 291, to argue that Lear dies in joy, believing Cordelia to be breathing and alive. If Lear does think so, he is deluded, or perhaps delirious, and

---

305 have] *Q2, F; of Q*   306 thou'lt] *F; thou wilt Q*   308 SD] *this edn; to Kent / Oxf*   sir.] *F; sir, O,o,o,o. Q; O,o,o,o,o. Q2*   309 look, her lips] *Johnson;* Looke her lips *F;* looke on her lips *F2*

Figure 24 *Page 390 of the Arden Shakespeare* King Lear *edited by R.A. Foakes (third series), Thomas Nelson & Sons Ltd, Walton-on-Thames, 1997. Reproduced by permission of the publishers.*

The case of *Hamlet* is made even more complicated by the existence of three early texts: the First Quarto (Q1, 1603), the Second Quarto (Q2, 1604/5) and the Folio of 1623. Q1 at around 2200 lines is only about half the length of the other texts and has usually been ignored by editors, who dismiss it as a 'bad' reported text. Even so, it has occasionally been consulted for its stage directions on the grounds that whoever compiled it must have seen or been involved in an early performance. It has different names for some of the characters, the order of events is somewhat changed, and there is one short scene that does not appear in either of the other texts. Q1 has been performed with reasonable frequency in recent years and it has influenced the staging of the longer texts in so far as directors have sometimes chosen to follow its lead in placing the 'To be or not to be' speech in 2. 2 rather than in 3. 1.

Q2 at around 3800 lines is the longest text of the play and is thought by scholars to have been printed from Shakespeare's manuscript. It has 230 lines that are not in the Folio, while the Folio (which seems to derive from a theatrical transcript) has 80 lines that are not in Q2. Again there are hundreds of verbal variants. As in the case of *King Lear*, several recent editors have argued that the Folio text represents Shakespeare's revision of the play, believing that he made the cuts as well as the additions. The editor of the 1987 Oxford edition of *Hamlet* prints the passages that are found only in Q2 in an appendix, while the editor of the 1985 New Cambridge edition prints them in square brackets. Both argue that the cuts improve the play. In *The Norton Shakespeare*, the Q2 passages are given in italic type. As with *King Lear*, some significant passages are involved, most notably Hamlet's last soliloquy (4. 4. 9.22–9.56), which does not appear at all in the Folio, and a number of shorter passages in 1. 1, 3. 4 and 5. 2. We shall be discussing some of the differences as we work through the play in the next chapter.

There is no absolute proof that the Folio texts of *King Lear* and *Hamlet* represent authorial revisions. Nor is there absolute proof that Q1 of *Hamlet* is a reported text of the play deriving from something like one of the longer texts. Scholars used to argue that it was Shakespeare's 'first sketch', preceding the more sophisticated versions. We do not have to claim that one text is in every respect better than another: we may find that we prefer one passage in Q1 and another passage in the Folio. Even if we could prove that a particular reading is a Shakespearean revision, we might decide that his first thoughts were superior. We do have to acknowledge, however, that these plays (and others) survive in texts that are different from each other in ways that require our attention. As editors, we have to decide which words to print, justify our decisions, and alert our readers as far as possible to other choices we might have made. We hope to demonstrate, as we consider *Hamlet* in Chapter 5, that the differences between the texts, whilst sometimes a source of frustration, can be a source of fascination and fruitful speculation. You may find it interesting to compare the versions of the 'To be or not to be' soliloquy in Q1 and the Folio, shown in Figures 25 and 26.

The Tragedy of Hamlet

And so by continuance, and weakenesse of the braine
Into this frensie, which now possesseth him:
And if this be not true, take this from this.

    King Thinke you t'is so?

    Cor. How? so my Lord, I would very faine know
That thing that I haue saide t'is so, positiuely,
And it hath fallen out otherwise.
Nay, if circumstances leade me on,
Ile finde it out, if it were hid
As deepe as the centre of the earth.

    King. how should wee trie this same?

    Cor. Mary my good lord thus,
The Princes walke is here in the galery,
There let *Ofelia*, walke vntill hee comes:
Your selfe and I will stand close in the study,
There shall you heare the effect of all his hart,
And if it proue any otherwise then loue,
Then let my censure faile an other time.

    King. see where hee comes poring vppon a booke.

Enter Hamlet.

    Cor. Madame, will it please your grace
To leaue vs here?

    Que. With all my hart.   *exit.*

    Cor. And here *Ofelia*, reade you on this booke,
And walke aloofe, the King shal be vnseene.

    Ham. To be, or not to be, I there's the point,
To Die, to sleepe, is that all? I all:
No, to sleepe, to dreame, I mary there it goes,
For in that dreame of death, when wee awake,
And borne before an euerlasting Iudge,
From whence no passenger euer retur'nd,
The vndiscouered country, at whose sight
The happy smile, and the accursed damn'd.
But for this, the ioyfull hope of this,
Whol'd beare the scornes and flattery of the world,
Scorned by the right rich, the rich curssed of the poore?

The

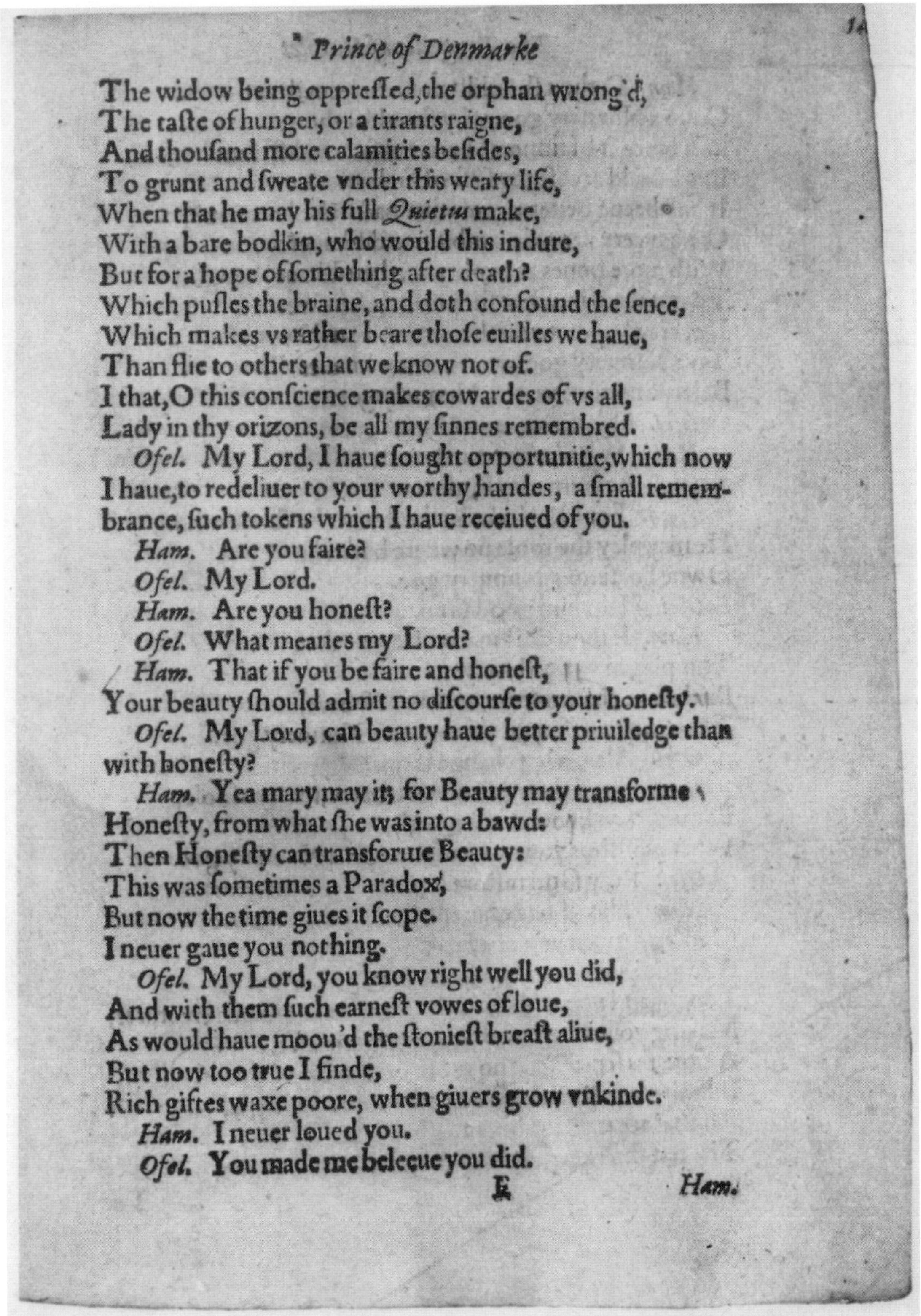

The widow being oppreſſed, the orphan wrong'd,
The taſte of hunger, or a tirants raigne,
And thouſand more calamities beſides,
To grunt and ſweate vnder this weary life,
When that he may his full *Quietus* make,
With a bare bodkin, who would this indure,
But for a hope of ſomething after death?
Which puſles the braine, and doth confound the ſence,
Which makes vs rather beare thoſe euilles we haue,
Than flie to others that we know not of.
I that, O this conſcience makes cowardes of vs all,
Lady in thy orizons, be all my ſinnes remembred.

   Ofel. My Lord, I haue ſought opportunitie, which now
I haue, to redeliuer to your worthy handes, a ſmall remem-
brance, ſuch tokens which I haue receiued of you.

   Ham. Are you faire?

   Ofel. My Lord.

   Ham. Are you honeſt?

   Ofel. What meanes my Lord?

   Ham. That if you be faire and honeſt,
Your beauty ſhould admit no diſcourſe to your honeſty.

   Ofel. My Lord, can beauty haue better priuiledge than
with honeſty?

   Ham. Yea mary may it; for Beauty may transforme
Honeſty, from what ſhe was into a bawd:
Then Honeſty can transforme Beauty:
This was ſometimes a Paradox,
But now the time giues it ſcope.
I neuer gaue you nothing.

   Ofel. My Lord, you know right well you did,
And with them ſuch earneſt vowes of loue,
As would haue moou'd the ſtonieſt breaſt aliue,
But now too true I finde,
Rich giftes waxe poore, when giuers grow vnkinde.

   Ham. I neuer loued you.

   Ofel. You made me beleeue you did.

              E   *Ham.*

Figure 25 *Pages from* The Tragicall Historie of Hamlet, Prince of Denmark *[First Quarto],*
1603. British Library c.34.k.1.

The Tragedie of Hamlet.   265

With turbulent and dangerous Lunacy.

Rosin. He does confesse he feeles himselfe distracted,
But from what cause he will by no meanes speake.

Guil. Nor do we finde him forward to be sounded,
But with a crafty Madnesse keepes aloofe :
When we would bring him on to some Confession
Of his true state.

Qu. Did he receiue you well ?

Rosin. Most like a Gentleman.

Guild. But with much forcing of his disposition.

Rosin. Niggard of question, but of our demands
Most free in his reply.

Qu. Did you assay him to any pastime ?

Rosin. Madam, it so fell out, that certaine Players
We ore-wrought on the way : of these we told him,
And there did seeme in him a kinde of ioy
To heare of it : They are about the Court,
And (as I thinke) they haue already order
This night to play before him.

Pol. 'Tis most true :
And he beseech'd me to intreate your Maiesties
To heare, and see the matter.

King. With all my heart, and it doth much content me
To heare him so inclin'd. Good Gentlemen,
Giue him a further edge, and driue his purpose on
To these delights.

Rosin. We shall my Lord.   *Exeunt.*

King. Sweet *Gertrude* leaue vs too,
For we haue closely sent for *Hamlet* hither,
That he, as 'twere by accident, may there
Affront *Ophelia.* Her Father, and my selfe (lawful espials)
Will so bestow our selues, that seeing vnseene
We may of their encounter frankely iudge,
And gather by him, as he is behaued,
If't be th'affliction of his loue, or no.
That thus he suffers for.

Qu. I shall obey you,
And for your part *Ophelia*, I do wish
That your good Beauties be the happy cause
Of *Hamlets* wildenesse : so shall I hope your Vertues
Will bring him to his wonted way againe,
To both your Honors.

Ophe. Madam, I wish it may.

Pol. *Ophelia*, walke you heere. Gracious so please ye
We will bestow our selues : Reade on this booke,
That shew of such an exercise may colour
Your lonelinesse. We are oft too blame in this,
'Tis too much prou'd, that with Deuotions visage,
And pious Action, we do surge o're
The diuell himselfe.

King. Oh 'tis true :
How smart a lash that speech doth giue my Conscience ?
The Harlots Cheeke beautied with plaist'ring Art
Is not more vgly to the thing that helpes it,
Then is my deede, to my most painted word.
Oh heauie burthen !

Pol. I heare him comming, let's withdraw my Lord.
                                    Exeunt.

Enter Hamlet.

Ham. To be, or not to be, that is the Question :
Whether 'tis Nobler in the minde to suffer
The Slings and Arrowes of outragious Fortune,
Or to take Armes against a Sea of troubles,
And by opposing end them : to dye, to sleepe
No more ; and by a sleepe, to say we end
The Heart-ake, and the thousand Naturall shockes

That Flesh is heyre too ? 'Tis a consummation
Deuoutly to be wish'd. To dye to sleepe,
To sleepe, perchance to Dreame ; I, there's the rub,
For in that sleepe of death, what dreames may come,
When we haue shuffiel'd off this mortall coile,
Must giue vs pawse. There's the respect
That makes Calamity of so long life :
For who would beare the Whips and Scornes of time,
The Oppressors wrong, the poore mans Contumely,
The pangs of dispriz'd Loue, the Lawes delay,
The insolence of Office, and the Spurnes
That patient merit of the vnworthy takes,
When he himselfe might his *Quietus* make
With a bare Bodkin ? Who would these Fardles beare
To grunt and sweat vnder a weary life,
But that the dread of something after death,
The vndiscouered Countrey, from whose Borne
No Traueller returnes, Puzels the will,
And makes vs rather beare those illes we haue,
Then flye to others that we know not of.
Thus Conscience does make Cowards of vs all,
And thus the Natiue hew of Resolution
Is sicklied o're, with the pale cast of Thought,
And enterprizes of great pith and moment,
With this regard their Currants turne away,
And loose the name of Action. Soft you now,
The faire *Ophelia?* Nimph, in thy Orizons
Be all my sinnes remembred.

Ophe. Good my Lord,
How does your Honor for this many a day ?

Ham. I humbly thanke you ; well, well, well.

Ophe. My Lord, I haue Remembrances of yours,
That I haue longed long to re-deliuer.
I pray you now, receiue them.

Ham. No, no, I neuer gaue you ought.

Ophe. My honor'd Lord, I know right well you did,
And with them words of so sweet breath compos'd,
As made the things more rich, then perfume left :
Take these againe, for to the Noble minde
Rich gifts wax poore, when giuers proue vnkinde.
There my Lord.

Ham. Ha, ha : Are you honest ?

Ophe. My Lord.

Ham. Are you faire ?

Ophe. What meanes your Lordship ?

Ham. That if you be honest and faire, your Honesty
should admit no discourse to your Beautie.

Ophe. Could Beautie my Lord, haue better Comerce
then your Honestie ?

Ham. I trulie : for the power of Beautie, will sooner
transforme Honestie from what it is, to a Bawd, then the
force of Honestie can translate Beautie into his likenesse.
This was sometime a Paradox, but now the time giues it
proofe. I did loue you once.

Ophe. Indeed my Lord, you made me beleeue so.

Ham. You should not haue beleeued me. For vertue
cannot so innocculate our old stocke, but we shall rellish
of it. I loued you not.

Ophe. I was the more deceiued.

Ham. Get thee to a Nunnerie. Why would'st thou
be a breeder of Sinners ? I am my selfe indifferent honest,
but yet I could accuse me of such things, that it were better my Mother had not borne me. I am very prowd, re-
uengefull, Ambitious, with more offences at my becke,
then I haue thoughts to put them in imagination, to giue
them shape, or time to acte them in. What should such
                                                    Fel-

Figure 26 *Page 265 of* The Tragedie of Hamlet, *from* Mr William Shakespeare's
Comedies, Histories and Tragedies *[First Folio], 1623. British Library G.11631.*

Performance texts

It is not only editors who 'play around with' the text of a Shakespeare play. Directors and actors often feel free to create their own texts. The 'editing' of the texts for performance may involve cutting, conflation or amalgamation of several versions, or even rewriting.

If the play is *Hamlet*, those involved with performance almost always begin by shortening the printed text from which they are working. The earliest text we have is Q1. It is very short, and this fact is probably not unrelated to the printers' boast that the King's Men acted the play not only in the City of London, but also 'in the two Vniversities of Cambridge and Oxford, and elsewhere' (Hibbard, 1987, p.88). The so-called 'Players Quarto' of 1676 prints the longest text we have, Q2, but it also indicates the cuts that the Duke of York's Company had employed in performance since 1661. On the whole, the history of cutting in *Hamlet* has been designed to affect our view of the central character, either ennobling Hamlet's character or else concentrating attention on his psychological, emotional or spiritual condition. Brook's cuts in his 1962 stage production and his 1970 film version of *King Lear* seem to have been motivated by a more general philosophical view of the play's vision, eradicating as he did some of the play's hopefulness.

In other cases, either out of a desire to be 'scholarly' or out of a reverence for the genius of the author, actors, actor-managers and directors have fought for more text rather than less. David Garrick (1717–79), John Philip Kemble (1757–1823) and William Macready (1793–1873) each tried to perform more of Shakespeare's lines than their immediate predecessors had, and Frank Benson in 1899, Peter Hall in 1975 and 1994, and Kenneth Branagh in 1996 have aimed to present the 'complete text' of Hamlet, in other words, an amalgam of Q2 and the Folio.

Nor has it been merely a matter of reducing or retaining the text. Some directors have been prepared to alter and create text, usually to suit the tastes of their age. In the interests of supplying his audience not only with sentimental reassurance but also with an intelligible moral message, Nahum Tate famously gave his 1681 *King Lear* a happy ending. Garrick likewise softened the catastrophe of his 1772 *Hamlet* by rewriting the fifth act.

The printed text of a Shakespeare play is not, of course, the only form in which the play exists. Each performance is itself a text – distinct from the printed version – and we need to attend to its unique qualities. Whatever the words delivered, it matters what kind of actor plays Hamlet, and how he is played – the very act of casting initiates a distinctive interpretation. The age and physical appearance of the actor inevitably constrains the kind of Hamlet communicated to an audience. In 1709, Thomas Betterton acted Hamlet at the age of 74 and there have been many female Hamlets, beginning with Sarah Siddons in 1777. Whoever plays the part, the characterization and style of delivery will create the play anew. In 1969, Nicol Williamson growled and gabbled lines that, in a series of productions between 1930 and 1944, John Gielgud had intoned poetically. Some actors have invented 'stage business', some of which has been retained for a while. A piece of business that Betterton made his own was the action of knocking over a chair as Hamlet jumped at the appearance of his father's ghost. A century later, in 1814, Edmund Kean crawled across the stage during the play scene (3. 2). Many Hamlets copied him, and the crawl is recorded for posterity in Sven Gade's film of 1920 (Figure 27).

Figure 27 *Asta Nielsen as Hamlet (crawling) with Eduard von Winterstem as Claudius and Mathilde Brandt as Gertrude during the play-within-the-play scene of the German film* Hamlet *directed by Sven Gade, 1920, Art Film. Reproduced by courtesy of Det Danske Filminstitut.*

Such business is an element in what we might call the visual text of the play. In constructing this text, as well as deciding how and when to move the actors around the stage, a director must choose the historical period in which to set the play – if s/he does not reject altogether the idea of setting it in an historical period. In the case of *Hamlet*, the idea of using scenery and costume to suggest the correct historical period in which the story was meant to take place was largely an invention of the nineteenth century, which loved things Gothic, as well as stage spectacle and lavish visual detail. In the twentieth century, film directors such as Grigori Kozintsev (in his 1964 Russian version) and Branagh have continued this pictorial tradition, but their choice of historical period is very different. Of course, one option (probably the one with the longest history) is to set the play in the present day. Sir Barry Jackson claimed he was only 'getting back to Garrick', or reverting to Shakespeare's own practices, when he mounted *Hamlet* in modern dress at the Kingsway Theatre, London in August 1925.

Every performance of a play by Shakespeare is unique. Even if the same words are delivered in the same order, the play experience is bound to be subtly different each night. The actors will inevitably deliver their lines with slightly different emphases or at a different pace at each performance. Within the run of a particular production, the production always changes, if only a little, as actors relax into their parts, learn how the audience is likely to react to their jokes and gestures, receive new instructions from the director, or begin to improvise.

References

Edwards, P. (ed.) (1985) *Hamlet*, Cambridge: Cambridge University Press.

Hibbard, G.R. (ed.) (1987) *Hamlet*, Oxford: Oxford University Press.

The Norton Shakespeare (1997) ed. S. Greenblatt, W. Cohen, J.E. Howard and K.E. Maus, New York and London: W.W. Norton.

HAMLET

Ann Thompson and Neil Taylor

Aims

The first aim of this chapter is to introduce the different versions of *Hamlet*: the First Quarto, the Second Quarto and the Folio. The balance of the chapter is taken up with a close reading of the play, at the end of which you should be in a position to identify and discuss the issues and dilemmas facing the character Hamlet.

Introduction: key issues

What does **Hamlet** *mean?*

If you were to show a picture of a man in black holding a skull (see Figure 28) to anyone familiar with western culture and ask them what it meant, most people would say that the picture 'means' *Hamlet*. But what does *Hamlet* mean? And what does it mean to us, at the beginning of the twenty-first century, to study *Hamlet*? In *Meaning by Shakespeare* (1992), Terence Hawkes takes a stab at answering this question:

> At one time [*Hamlet*] must obviously have been an interesting play written by a promising Elizabethan playwright. However, equally obviously, that is no longer the case. Over the years, *Hamlet* has taken on a huge and complex symbolizing function and, as a part of the institution called 'English literature', it has become far more than a mere play by a mere playwright. Issuing from one of the key components of that institution, not Shakespeare, but the creature 'Shakespeare', it has been transformed into the utterance of an oracle, the lucubration of a sage, the masterpiece of a poet-philosopher replete with transcendent wisdom about the way things are, always have been, and presumably always will be.
>
> (p.4)

We shall attempt in this chapter to address principally the 'Elizabethan *Hamlet*' that survives (somewhat problematically, as we have shown in Interval 2) in the three texts of 1603, 1604/5 and 1623, although we also refer to the 'universal *Hamlet*', the cultural phenomenon that has accumulated over 400 years. We suggest that you read (or re-read) the play before proceeding further with the discussion.

It is perhaps startling to find Hawkes describing Shakespeare as a 'promising' playwright, but this deliberately reminds us that *Hamlet* is a comparatively early play in his repertoire. It is the first of what we have come to think of as the 'major'

Chapter 5

Figure 28   *Jonathan Pryce as Hamlet in the Royal Court Theatre production directed by Richard Eyre, 1980.
Photo: John Haynes.*

tragedies, a group including *Othello*, *Macbeth* and *King Lear*. In an edition of the *Complete Works* arranged in chronological order (like the 1986 Oxford volume), *Hamlet* comes twenty-second out of 38 plays, preceded by only three other tragedies: *Titus Andronicus*, *Romeo and Juliet* and *Julius Caesar*, two of which we now categorize as 'Roman plays'. The other plays are all comedies or histories. But, as Margaret Healy has pointed out in her chapter on *Richard II*, many of Shakespeare's plays are hybrid in form, and do not fit neatly into generic categories.

In the case of *Hamlet*, we find a high degree of self-consciousness about generic distinctions. Consider, for example, Polonius's announcement of the Players as: 'The best actors in the world, either for tragedy, comedy, history, pastoral, pastorical-comical, historical-pastoral, tragical-historical, tragical-comical-historical-pastoral, scene individable, or poem unlimited' (2. 2. 379–82). Whilst this is usually and quite properly seen as a parodic catalogue of all possible options, in his 1982 edition of *Hamlet* Harold Jenkins also notes of the phrase 'tragical-historical' that the first play to be so designated on its title-page was *The Tragicall Historie of Hamlet*, as it is called on the title-pages of both Q1 and Q2 (Jenkins, 1982, p.259). In Q1, but not in Q2 and the Folio, the words 'tragic' and 'tragedy' occur in the very last moments of the play, when Horatio says to the newly arrived Fortinbras, 'If aught of woe or wonder you'd behold, / Then look upon this tragic spectacle' (17. 106–7),[1] and then 'I'll show to all the ground, / The first beginnings of this tragedy' (113–14). Curiously,

---

[1] All quotations from Q1 in this chapter are from Irace, *The First Quarto of Hamlet* (1998).

Q1 also has Hamlet exclaim after 'The Murder of Gonzago', 'And if the king like not the tragedy, / Why then belike he likes it not' (9. 158–9), where Q2 and the Folio have 'For if the King like not the comedy, / Why then, belike he likes it not' (3. 2. 269–70). At this point, both 'tragedy' and 'comedy' seem to be used as synonyms of 'play', but it is in relation to Polonius's announcement of the Players and in Horatio's final lines in Q1 that *Hamlet* seems most conscious of its own genre.

Revenge and madness

'Begin, murderer. Pox, leave thy damnable faces and begin. Come: "the croaking raven doth bellow for revenge"', says Hamlet on the entry of Lucianus in the scene with the play-within-the-play (3. 2. 230–2). 'The Murder of Gonzago' is not in fact concerned with a revenge killing, but the line is appropriate to Hamlet's own situation. As elsewhere, he is alert to the dangers of overacting – he has previously described the Player as one who 'would drown the stage with tears, / And cleave the general ear with horrid speech' (2. 2. 539–40) and advised him not to 'saw the air' or 'tear a passion to tatters' (3. 2. 4, 8–9). This suggests that, for a sophisticated playgoer such as Hamlet, tragedy based on revenge was by 1600 something of a cliché, an opportunity for melodramatic spectacle and bombastic rhetoric. There had been a number of revenge plays influenced by the Roman dramatist Seneca, whose bloodthirsty tragedies had been translated into English by Elizabethan poets; some of them personified Revenge as an agent from hell and most of them included ghosts.

The earliest references to a play on the *Hamlet* story are derogatory ones. The writer Thomas Nashe mocked the whole tradition of 'English Seneca read by candle-light' in 1589, and another writer, Thomas Lodge, referred in 1596 to a 'ghost which cries so miserably at the Theatre, like an oyster-wife, "Hamlet, revenge"'. It is generally thought that these references are to an earlier play which Shakespeare used as a source for his *Hamlet*, which is usually dated 1599–1601 (see Jenkins, 1982, pp.82–3). Shakespeare's own most famous play by 1599 was probably still *Titus Andronicus*, a very Senecan revenge tragedy, which included rape and cannibalism as well as numerous murders. He had also made extensive use of revenge as a motive in the form of the family feud, not only in *Romeo and Juliet* but also in many of his history plays.

In *Hamlet*, revenge also motivates the actions of Fortinbras and the final actions of Laertes, both of whom are engaged, like Hamlet, in revenging the deaths of their fathers. It is possible to see revenge as a peculiarly Elizabethan obsession, but you may also feel that revenge continues to be a powerful motive for action in modern narratives, especially westerns and plots involving crime and detection. Presumably it is less common for individuals to embark on revenge actions in real life today, since we have reasonably efficient police forces and judicial systems to punish wrongdoers more impersonally on our behalf, but the impulse to undertake private revenge can arise again when these systems fail or are themselves corrupt or implicated in the crime – as indeed they are in *Hamlet*.

The association of madness with revenge is very common in Elizabethan plays; 'Hieronimo's gone mad again' was a much-quoted line from Thomas Kyd's *The Spanish Tragedy* (*c.*1587), probably the most famous and successful of revenge tragedies along with Shakespeare's *Titus Andronicus*. In these plays, as in *Hamlet*, madness has a dual function. A pretence of madness is assumed by the protagonists as a form of disguise or protection to reassure their powerful enemies that they are really harmless and should not be seen as serious threats; thus, they can continue to be present at court, waiting for their opportunity to act. At the same time, the intensity of the grief they feel and the frustration of being unable to take adequate action to assuage it may cause them to become genuinely mad. For the audience of *Hamlet*, the question of whether Hamlet is 'only pretending' or not comes up quite often, especially in relation to his dealings with Ophelia and Gertrude. By the end of the play, Hamlet is using his madness to deny responsibility for any wrong he may have done Laertes (5. 2. 163–81): this seems close to the modern judicial definition of 'diminished responsibility'.

Tragedy and death

Tragedies are about death; histories are about politics. Setting aside the more sophisticated definitions of genre, we can usually categorize an Elizabethan play by its ending: a comedy, it is said, ends in the church, whilst a tragedy ends in the churchyard. Most of the characters are present in the final scene of a play from this period, arranged either as couples or as corpses. *Hamlet* certainly includes some stage time in the churchyard, and it has its quota of bodies. Horatio asks that these be displayed on a 'stage' (the word is used twice in the last 26 lines of the play) while he explains the circumstances of their deaths. He promises to speak of

> ... carnal, bloody, and unnatural acts,
> Of accidental judgements, casual slaughters,
> Of deaths put on by cunning and forced cause;
> And, in this upshot, purposes mistook
> Fall'n on th'inventors' heads.

(5. 2. 325–9)

It is possible to find examples of each of these in the play, but it seems to us that, beyond the fact that tragedies end in death (usually, although not always, multiple deaths), *Hamlet* is also, to an unusual extent, a play about death.

It is no coincidence that the man with the skull 'means' *Hamlet*. The context of this image in the play is Hamlet's lengthy discussion in the graveyard with the First Clown about the physical decay of human bodies (5. 1. 70–199). This discussion has been prefaced by Hamlet's assertion that he has 'Compounded [Polonius's body] with dust, whereto 'tis kin' (4. 2. 5) and his insistence on elaborating for Claudius how 'a king may go a progress through the guts of a beggar' (4. 3. 30–1). The deaths of three fathers (old Fortinbras, old Hamlet and Polonius) instigate three trains of action in the play and the deaths of two sons (Hamlet and Laertes) close it. Hamlet, like Macbeth, is required to make the decision to become a murderer.

But is Hamlet also obsessed with the idea of his own death? Re-read his first soliloquy ('O that this too too solid flesh would melt' (1. 2. 129–59)), his final words to Horatio before the duel (5. 2. 157–61) and his most famous soliloquy (3. 1. 58–92). Is he thinking about killing himself in these speeches?

In all three speeches, Hamlet is perhaps as much concerned with the act of taking his own life, and with his own readiness to die, as he is with the act of killing Claudius. The two concerns may be linked, since to take on the role of the revenger is in effect to court one's own death (revengers, in plays of this period, are rarely left alive at the end of the play).

The topic of self-slaughter comes up again in relation to Ophelia, notably in the Clowns' discussion of whether she 'drowned herself in her own defence' (5. 1. 6–7), thus meriting 'Christian burial' (1), and the priest's description of her death as 'doubtful' (209). The attitude to suicide constitutes a marked distinction between Shakespeare's Christian plays and some of his pagan plays: for Christians, suicide is a sin, whilst for non-Christians (notably Shakespeare's Romans) it can be a virtue. Cleopatra turns death by her own hand 'after the high Roman fashion' (*Antony and Cleopatra*, 4. 16. 89) into a triumph, but when Horatio tries to drink poison, crying 'I am more an antique Roman than a Dane' (5. 2. 283), Hamlet prevents him, although admittedly he does this so that Horatio can tell his story rather than to save him from damnation.

History and politics

One of the Clowns comments cynically that 'If [Ophelia] had not been a gentlewoman, she should have been buried out o' Christian burial' (5. 1. 22–4). The principal characters in Shakespeare's tragedies are not just ordinary people but rulers and leading politicians. The families are royal families and what happens to them will affect their countries. Hamlet is the son of a king; this causes Polonius to tell Ophelia that he is 'a prince out of thy star' (2. 2. 141), although it seems later that Gertrude would have countenanced the match (5. 1. 228). Guildenstern and Rosencrantz flatter Claudius with their speeches about his importance as the 'spirit upon whose weal depends and rests / The lives of many' (3. 3. 8–23). This is an ironic eulogy of kingship in the circumstances, but a reminder to us of how much real power monarchs wielded in the Middle Ages and Renaissance. As in *Richard II* and *Macbeth*, the death of a single individual is elevated through metaphorical language into the almost cosmic significance of what it means to kill a king.

The internal politics of Denmark in *Hamlet* are slightly confusing, mainly because of apparent discrepancies in Hamlet's own position. When he complains that he 'lack[s] advancement', Rosencrantz is disbelieving: 'How can that be when you have the voice of the King himself for your succession in Denmark?' (3. 2. 311–13). Claudius has announced this publicly (1. 2. 109) and Polonius clearly regards Hamlet as the heir (1. 3. 20–4). Later, though, Hamlet complains that Claudius 'stole' the kingdom (3. 4. 90) and that he 'Popped in between th'election and my hopes' (5. 2. 66), implying perhaps that he should be king by then, not heir apparent. The procedures of an elective monarchy, in which a brother rather than a son can legitimately succeed, are never made clear in the play, although Norway apparently has the same system: at 1. 2. 28–30, we learn that old Fortinbras has also been succeeded by his brother. No-one apart from Hamlet questions the legality of Claudius's title, nor is it seen to depend on his marriage to Gertrude, although that presumably strengthens his position.

External political relations are equally complicated. Marcellus asks why Denmark is urgently gearing up for war at the beginning of the play (1. 1. 70–8). He is informed by Horatio that the preparations are to meet the threatened attack of young Fortinbras, who aims to retrieve the lands lost at his father's defeat by old Hamlet in a 'sealed compact', by which both kings apparently agreed partially to disinherit their sons (78–106). One would think from this discussion that the loss was recent and the retaliation impulsive, but we learn later (5. 1. 132–3, 149–50) that old Fortinbras died 30 years earlier. Claudius seems to deal easily with this threat by diplomatic means (1. 2. 17–39, 2. 2. 60–85) and grants Fortinbras permission to march his army through Denmark on his way towards his new target, Poland. Later (but only in Q2) Hamlet encounters these troops and is impressed by the 'divine ambition' displayed by their leader in his determination to sacrifice his men for

> ... a plot ...
> Which is not tomb enough and continent
> To hide the slain.

(4. 4. 9.52, 9.54–5)

He prophesies with his dying voice that 'th'election lights / On Fortinbras' (5. 2. 297–8), but the Norwegian prince rests his claim rather on 'some rights of memory in this kingdom' (333).

From at least Thomas Betterton's production in the Restoration period, as recorded in the 1676 Quarto edition of *Hamlet*, to Matthew Warchus's production for the Royal Shakespeare Company in 1997, much of this political material has been cut on stage, presumably because it was regarded as mere 'background' to the individual and family drama that came to dominate the western theatrical and critical tradition. Many generations of English and American theatregoers never saw or heard of Fortinbras and the play ended with Hamlet's death; the rest was literally silence. By contrast, in eastern Europe (especially in the countries of the former Soviet Union), *Hamlet* was regularly seen as primarily a political play, in which an individual hero was struggling not only against a crime within his own family but with a corrupt and sinister state.

Reading Hamlet: *key scenes and questions*

The reading of *Hamlet* that follows concentrates (although not exclusively) on what seem to us key scenes in the play, in the order in which an audience would usually encounter them. We shall be building on the discussion of the texts of the play in Interval 2, and drawing your attention to the existence of the many different versions of *Hamlet*: on stage, in written and printed editions and in interpretation or criticism.

How is an audience to respond to the opening scene?

Imagine a matinee performance at a large open-air theatre. Two actors come on dressed as guards or sentries. Although in the real world it is broad daylight, they are carrying lanterns or torches to indicate that in the play's world it is night. They challenge each other, nervously disputing for authority – 'Who's there? / Nay, answer me' (1–2). They establish the time – ''Tis now struck twelve' (5) – and the temperature – ''Tis bitter cold' (6) – and one reassures the other that he has had 'quiet guard' (7), although he remarks without explanation that he is 'sick at heart' (7). Thus, *Hamlet* begins in an atmosphere of tension and expectation, heightened further when Horatio enters and asks, 'What, has this thing appeared again tonight?' (19).

This question, at line 19, is (according to the standard punctuation of modern editors) the seventh of the play's many questions. Hamlet will soon pun on the word 'question' when he says to the Ghost 'Thou com'st in such a questionable shape / That I will speak to thee' (1. 4. 24–5). Interrogation and doubt pervade this play, just as unresolved questions pervade its critical history; Peter Brook echoed the opening line of *Hamlet* when he called his 1996 adaptation of the play *Qui est la?* (*Who's there?*).

Night-time scenes must have been more of a challenge to an Elizabethan company than to a modern company, who can rely on lighting and other effects, yet Shakespeare seems almost to specialize in them. **How does Shakespeare establish and maintain the mood in the opening scene?**

The scene moves from midnight to dawn in under 200 lines: by 147–8, Horatio is saying, 'But look, the morn in russet mantle clad / Walks o'er the dew of yon high eastern hill'. This effect is repeated in 1. 4–1. 5 when the sequence of Hamlet's visit to the platform, beginning before midnight (see 1. 2. 251–2), again ends with the disappearance of the Ghost at dawn (1. 5. 58, 89–90).

The opening scene also raises another, broader question about the importance of time in *Hamlet*. **How long does the action take until its completion, if we take the opening scene as the first day (or rather night)? How does Shakespeare convey the passage of time?**

Shakespeare handles in three or four hours of stage time a history or narrative that would take several months or years to unfold in real life. He does not (like the Greek dramatists) start very near the end of his story and compress events into a single day, relating rather than showing everything that has happened earlier; nor does he, like a novelist, make statements such as 'Six months later, Hamlet had still not decided to kill Claudius' or 'Ophelia died the next day'. In addition to giving us the immediate setting in time and place, the opening scene of the play provides 'the story so far'.

Some of the scene-setting in 1. 1 has frequently been abbreviated on stage: most of the discussion of Denmark's preparations for war (70–8), the details of the compact between old Hamlet and old Fortinbras (85–8), and the proceedings of the latter's son (94–103) were cut at least as early as 1676. As we have said above, some of these cuts are part of a larger pattern of reshaping the play, whereby its politics are reduced to a bare minimum and Fortinbras is sometimes omitted altogether. It is generally assumed that something always has to be cut from *Hamlet*, given that the longest text (Q2 plus a few passages from F1) takes around four hours to perform.

Would you see these opening lines as expendable or would you argue for their retention?

The issue at stake is whether we need to know the nature of Denmark's preparations for war, the precise details of the agreement between old Hamlet and old Fortinbras, and the supposed threat from young Fortinbras, or whether these things are not essential to the play as a whole. This obviously involves making a judgement about what is essential to *Hamlet*, and whether we are really talking about at least two *Hamlets* – a shortened one for theatregoers and a longer one for readers.

A considerable challenge in the theatre is the appearance of the Ghost in this scene. Again, modern productions can gain assistance from lighting, rising mist, whistling winds or eerie music, although Elizabethan productions would have had the considerable advantage that many members of the audience would have believed in ghosts – certainly they would have believed in the Christian idea of an afterlife and the existence of heaven and hell. Taking this scene together with the subsequent appearances of the Ghost in 1. 4, 1. 5 and 3. 4, you might consider whether Shakespeare has any problems with the representation of the supernatural: is the Ghost a person or a thing? (In some editions, at 1. 1. 108, 1, Q2 has the stage direction '*It spreads his arms*'.)

How would you attempt to overcome the potential disbelief and cynicism of a modern audience?

Would it be better to appeal to the audience's sense of period and emphasize the Elizabethan nature of the Ghost, or to draw on more modern treatments of the supernatural, such as the horror genre in fiction and film? One radical modern solution has been to have Hamlet speak the Ghost's lines as well as his own in 1. 4, 1. 5 and 3. 4, indicating that the Ghost exists only in his imagination.

It is not uncommon in Shakespearean tragedy that the hero does not appear in the opening scene: Macbeth, for example, does not appear until 1. 3, although his martial exploits are described in 1. 2. *Antony and Cleopatra* is relatively unusual in this respect, although even there we get Philo's scene-setting speech before the hero and heroine come on. We do not learn much about Hamlet from the opening scene, apart from the fact that he is 'young Hamlet' (1. 1. 151) and presumably the son of old Hamlet, 'our last king' (79), as 'young Fortinbras' (94) is the son of old Fortinbras (see 5. 1. 132–50 and 159–75 for more precise information about Hamlet's age). The only 'major' character to appear in the opening scene is Horatio, who is introduced as one of the 'rivals [partners] of [Barnardo's] watch' (1. 1. 10), along with Marcellus, and who is able to supply local knowledge at 78–106. In the next scene, however, it becomes apparent that he is also a fellow student of Hamlet's, playing truant from the University of Wittenberg (1. 2. 163 onwards).

How important is Horatio's role as Hamlet's confidant?

If you track Horatio through 3. 2, 4. 6, 5. 1 and 5. 2, you will notice his rather non-committal responses to Hamlet's enthusiasm at the end of 3. 2 and again to Hamlet's account of the aborted trip to England in 5. 2. 2–81. An actor might play him as simply less excited than Hamlet or even as disapproving of him. When Hamlet praises Horatio's character at 3. 2. 49–67, we can either accept his words as the truth about Horatio or assume that he is a biased observer. It would certainly appear that Hamlet praises Horatio for qualities he himself lacks.

Act 2, Scene 2 is a long, episodic scene, but it has a rich, suggestive structure. One element in that structure is Hamlet's transformation, but before we hear about that we have to get through the opening section of the act, in which Polonius laboriously instructs his servant to spy on his son (a section of the play that is often omitted in productions, although the casting of Gérard Depardieu as Reynaldo made it a memorable episode in Kenneth Branagh's 1996 film version). We have witnessed Hamlet's interview with the Ghost in 1. 4 and 1. 5, and its violent effect upon his emotional state (Laurence Olivier swooned in his 1948 film), and the last section of 2. 1 further transforms our attitude to the prince. It is unclear how much time has passed between Hamlet's encounter with the Ghost and his appearance in Ophelia's chamber.

How do we respond to Ophelia's description of Hamlet?

Ophelia describes Hamlet as the stereotypical lover – pale, sighing, dishevelled, fixated – suggesting that his state of mind is unhinged by love. The audience has to weigh Ophelia's view against the possibility that Hamlet is cynically using her innocent love to help him develop a disguise, so that he can advance a plot against Claudius. Hamlet has claimed that he may put on an 'antic disposition' (1. 5. 173) or affected madness, supposedly in response to the overwhelming burden of care thrust upon him.

Another unifying element in 2. 2 is Claudius. The scene begins with him and ends with him. It begins with him in control, as he was on his first appearance in 1. 2. – he is telling two of his subjects 'we much did long to see you' (2. 2. 2). It ends with him as the victim of a plot to expose him – one of his subjects is telling us 'I'll catch the conscience of the King' (2. 2. 582). This shift reflects the moral, political and dramatic movement of the play as a whole: by the time the scene is over, a huge transformation has taken place. What sets out as a presentation of the king holding court, first to ambassadors from abroad and then to subjects who will help him in his surveillance of Hamlet, ends with Hamlet having usurped the king's position and holding court, first to those same subjects, and then to travelling actors who will help him in his surveillance of the king. Act 2, Scene 2 mirrors the structure of 1. 2, beginning with the public face of Claudius and ending with the private face of his nephew.

Act 2, Scene 1 began with Polonius giving orders to his man, Reynaldo. It ended with him giving orders to his daughter, Ophelia. Not just this scene, but the play as a whole explores the twin hierarchies of the family and of the state. In both, there is a polarization of those who command and those who are commanded, those who act and those who are acted upon, those who speak and those who remain silent. We have twice seen Polonius the public man in his private, domestic role, in 2. 1 and, earlier, in 1. 3, where he had warned his children – and they had warned each other – about the potential dangers in the world that lies beyond the control and protection of the family. Polonius the father proves to be as inadequate and lethal as Polonius the chief courtier. Indeed, the play's narrative concerns not just his family but the royal family, and neither can protect itself from a tragic sequence of events that amounts to a project of mutual self-destruction.

The distinction between the old and the young is an important one within the play. We are made conscious of Laertes's 'youth' (2. 1. 24) and of the fact that Hamlet belongs to 'the younger sort' (117). Polonius brackets 'youth' with 'liberty' (24), meaning freedom, then repeats 'liberty' (33) so that its meaning moves on to incorporate licence. He wishes to draw a distinction between the 'slips' (22) of mere youth – the wildness and savagery of 'unreclaimed blood' (35), which everyone experiences in their younger days – and 'incontinency' (31) – which crosses a line and becomes a matter of serious alarm. He regards the young as morally vulnerable, at risk from others and from themselves. But his own behaviour confuses the issue: his care and concern for his children and their honour lead him first into an elaborate (slightly comic, but also slightly sinister) conspiracy to set a kind of private detective on his son's trail, and in 2. 2 to 'loose' (163) his daughter as a decoy or bait for Hamlet (almost as if Polonius were a pimp and Ophelia a prostitute).

The play's action can be read as a matter of the generations locked in struggle; such a conflict constitutes the basic narrative element in any number of Shakespearean plays. In *Hamlet*, the conflict is repeated in three families: those of Polonius, old Fortinbras and old Hamlet. In 2. 1, the opening stage direction refers to Polonius as 'old'; in 2. 2, Claudius alludes to Hamlet's youth (12) and associates Rosencrantz and Guildenstern with it (11). The ambassadors from Norway bring news of a young man taking advantage of his uncle's age (line 60 onwards). Polonius brings news of a young man sent mad by frustrated love – frustrated because an old man fears that a young man might take advantage of his daughter's youth (line 93 onwards). And Hamlet taunts Polonius for his age, commenting behind his back 'These tedious old fools!' (215).

But the chief polarity in the play is that of Hamlet and the rest of the court. It is worth noting that Q1 is out of step with the other two texts in introducing Hamlet's most famous soliloquy in 7, the equivalent of 2. 2, rather than in 3. 1. It is also out of step in its version of the soliloquy: you might compare the two versions reproduced in facsimile in Interval 2 (Figures 25 and 26). For anyone accustomed to the Q2 or F version, the Q1 version seems very strange and, indeed, almost laughable. But is anything more than familiarity with the other texts determining our reaction to it? Actors have found that it works well on stage precisely *because* it is unfamiliar and the audience is not mouthing the speech in unison. It is perhaps surprising that at this stage in the play Hamlet is asking 'to be or not to be' rather than 'to kill or not to kill'.

How is Hamlet's isolation at the court of Denmark presented?

The tone of Hamlet's meeting with Rosencrantz and Guildenstern in 2. 2 is complex. Perhaps he is genuinely pleased at first to see them, but his perception of those whom he has liked to think of with affection and trust – his mother, his girlfriend and his old school friends – has been contaminated and corrupted. Both parties in this section of the scene – Hamlet and his friends – are involved in manoeuvres, each trying to outsmart the other. He wants to know what they are up to, and they are sounding him out to discover for Claudius whether his madness is genuine or a cover for something else.

In Tom Stoppard's play *Rosencrantz and Guildenstern Are Dead* (1967), Hamlet's schoolfriends are put centre stage, while Hamlet and Shakespeare's other main protagonists are pushed to one side, even pushed offstage altogether. We think this is illuminating, in that it calls attention to the fact that Shakespeare has created two kinds of character, demanding two kinds of acting. For many readers and playgoers, Hamlet is endlessly explorable as a character. He seems to them to be so interesting as a mind in action that it is meaningful to speculate upon his motivation at a number of levels – even, since the psychoanalyst Sigmund Freud took an interest in him, at the level of his unconscious. Generations of critics have seen Hamlet as quite different in this respect from the majority of Elizabethan stage characters – as being a fully rounded character in a psychological sense. Indeed, many interpreters have treated him as if he were a real person.

Rosencrantz and Guildenstern, by contrast, have no character really, and certainly no depth. Some directors choose to think that Shakespeare is making this point himself. They interpret the variation between Claudius and Gertrude at 2. 2. 33–4 ('Thanks, Rosencrantz and gentle Guildenstern' and 'Thanks, Guildenstern and gentle Rosencrantz'), not as a piece of polite courtly wordplay (neither of them is given precedence over the other), but as a correction by Gertrude of Claudius's inability to distinguish between two ciphers at court. This should not divert us from recognizing that they are rather typical of a lot, indeed most, of Elizabethan drama and Hamlet is not. They are types rather than individuals and they exist on a conceptual plane that is quite divorced from that of the realist novel. They are more like the indistinguishable lovers in *A Midsummer Night's Dream* – where Shakespeare makes comedy out of the inability of the men to distinguish between the women.

One of the play's most arresting, and simple, phrases occurs in one of Hamlet's speeches to Rosencrantz and Guildenstern: 'Denmark's a prison' (2. 2. 239). Although this phrase occurs in only one of the three texts (F), many directors, particularly those wishing to use the play as an implicit commentary on political oppression in eastern Europe and Russia, have asked their designers to use this phrase as their inspiration and create sets reminiscent of cages. One or two others have staged the play in literal prisons (Broadmoor in 1992 and Brixton in 1995). Grigori Kozintsev's film of 1964 begins with Hamlet riding into the castle of Elsinore and the doors being shut behind him as if he had ridden into prison or into a trap. A director could find support for such a reading by pointing to the fact that Hamlet tries to catch Claudius in his 'Murder of Gonzago', that in Q1 he will only talk to his mother if the doors are locked ('but first we'll make all safe' (11. 6)), and that in all three texts he once again wants the doors locked at the end (5. 2. 254).

Hamlet ends 2. 2 planning his play to catch the conscience of the king and exploring the relationship between acting in the theatre (where reality is simulated by means of a shared act of the imagination on the parts of actors and audience), and acting in the everyday sense of performing deeds in the real world. The Player appears to enter so deeply into the story of the fall of Troy that it has become reality to him; Hamlet exclaims in amazement at his emotion for the Trojan Queen:

> What's Hecuba to him, or he to Hecuba,
> That he should weep for her? What would he do
> Had he the motive and the cue for passion
> That I have?

> (2. 2. 536–9)

Perhaps, in addition to these famous questions, we might ask another: why did Shakespeare have Hamlet ask the Player to recite that particular speech rather than something else? Is it possible, for example, to argue that Hamlet is particularly interested in the death of Priam (a father-figure)? Or that he identifies with Pyrrhus, who seems paralysed in the midst of his violent career (see 2. 2. 460–2)? The fall of Troy was for the Elizabethans a major source of tragic images and references: they subscribed to the medieval myth that Britain had been founded by one Brutus or Brut, who fled from the fall of Troy, and they sometimes referred poetically to London as 'Troynovant' (New Troy).

At the end of Act 2, Hamlet has determined, 'I'll have these players / Play something like the murder of my father' (2. 2. 571–2) and he also predicts that 'The play's the thing / Wherein I'll catch the conscience of the King' (581–2). On one level, this is what is achieved in 3. 2. – 'I'll take the Ghost's word for a thousand pound', Hamlet cries triumphantly (263–4). But, characteristically for this play, his triumph is not a straightforward one, and it is surrounded by a lot of other things that are going on at the same time. The scene can also tell us much about Hamlet's (and Shakespeare's?) views on acting, Hamlet's relations with Horatio, Ophelia and Rosencrantz and Guildenstern, his attitude to his mother, and the state of his own mind.

The play-within-the-play is a device that will be familiar to you from *A Midsummer Night's Dream*, where Act 5 also gives us a court performance interrupted by the on-stage audience's comments, but in *Hamlet* the Players are professional actors (some productions indicate that they are bored or patronized by Hamlet's attempts to teach them their job). Hamlet has asked them to insert a speech written by himself (2. 2. 517–19), and this is presumably what he means by 'the speech' and 'my lines' at the beginning of 3. 2. Shakespeare does not specify which speech this is and critics have not been able to agree on the matter. Hamlet quickly moves away from this crucial issue to more general comments on acting technique, which were presumably of topical interest in London at the time, raising the perennial question of what constitutes a realistic acting style. Each generation seems to find its own style of acting more 'natural' or 'lifelike' than that of the previous generation, which is usually dismissed as 'mannered' or 'stylized'. As we can see from watching films of, say, 30 years ago, what seems natural at one time looks very strange at another, because the conventions of real-life behaviour change.

Hamlet commissions Horatio to help him to 'rivet' (3. 2. 78) his eyes to Claudius's face in the hope that his 'occulted guilt' (73) will 'unkennel' (74). He clearly believes this has happened when Claudius stops the performance at line 247, but some awkward questions remain. If the hitherto self-possessed Claudius is vulnerable to this kind of exposure, why does he not react to the dumb show? (Some productions explain this by having Claudius and Gertrude chat to each other during the dumb show, paying no attention to it.) Why does Claudius rise at this exact moment? Is it because the murderer has been identified as 'nephew to the King' (223) as well as seducer of his victim's wife? Does Claudius fear that his own nephew may be about to kill him there and then? A comparable play-within-the-play in Kyd's *Spanish Tragedy* ends in a blood-bath, with the characters dying in the play when they pretend to die in the play-within-the-play. However, Claudius's response occurs only half-way through *Hamlet* and the off-stage audience would not expect an event such as his murder until the end of the play.

There are other things to watch besides Claudius in this scene. Hamlet insists on sitting with Ophelia, and his brief speeches to her are full of sexual puns and insults (see 3. 2. 101–38, 224–30). Their most recent encounter was the traumatic 'nunnery scene' (3. 1. 91–160) and this is the last time we see Ophelia before she enters 'distraught' at 4. 5. 20. **How would you have the performer playing Ophelia behave here? Is she hoping for a reconciliation with Hamlet or is she showing increasing signs of distress? What does eventually motivate her madness and death?**

It might be argued that it is unnecessary to excuse Ophelia's behaviour as well as Hamlet's, as she too is merely the victim of a repressive society. If you re-read her dialogue and songs in 4. 5, you can find evidence that her madness is caused by the breakdown of her relationship with Hamlet as well as by her father's death. The evidence in the play that she knows her lover killed her father is ambiguous (although some film versions feel the need to motivate her condition more clearly by having her come upon Polonius's body).

Editors and critics have been worried by Hamlet's attitude to Ophelia in this scene (and of course in 3. 1) and have tried to explain it. In his 1934 Cambridge edition of the play, John Dover Wilson introduced a 'lost' stage direction, bringing Hamlet on 8 lines before his usual entry, so that he overhears Claudius and Polonius setting up the plot against him and assumes Ophelia has betrayed him by being a willing accomplice.

As many critics have noted, Hamlet is at least as interested in berating his mother as in trapping his step-father (see, for example, Traub, 1995). The play-within-the-play seems as much directed at Gertrude, with the Player Queen's insistence that 'None wed the second but who killed the first' (3. 2. 162) and Hamlet's aside, 'Wormwood, wormwood' (163). Later, he comments on the Player Queen's vow to be faithful after her husband's death ('If she should break it now' (204)) and pointedly asks his mother how she likes the play. Her notorious reply, 'The lady protests too much, methinks' (210), indicates either that she is thicker-skinned than her husband or that she is genuinely innocent (see the discussion of this below). Is it this needling of Gertrude that finally alerts Claudius to ask if there is any 'offence' in the play (212–13)?

After the play-within-the-play, Hamlet seems elated, almost manic, in his conversations with Horatio and with Rosencrantz and Guildenstern, although he finds time to teach the latter pair a moral lesson about manipulation by using the recorders (316–41) and incidentally picking up his praise of Horatio as one who is 'not a pipe for Fortune's finger / To sound what stop she please' (63–4). At the entry of Claudius and Gertrude, Hamlet has said to Horatio 'I must be idle', apparently indicating that he is about to adopt his 'antic disposition' (3. 2. 83).

How much of Hamlet's behaviour in this scene is mere 'performance'? What do you make of his language at the end of the scene when he is left alone?

By this point in the play, you should be in a position to consider why Hamlet felt the 'antic disposition' was necessary in the first place. If it is a way of seeming harmless and deflecting suspicion that he knows the truth about his father's death, Claudius's words at the opening of 3. 3 would indicate that it has failed. A different motivation, which might apply to Shakespeare rather than to Hamlet, is that to have a character who is mad, or pretending to be mad, is a good way of adding another level to the dialogue: everything such a person says can be interpreted in more than one way.

It does seem, from the frequency with which he uses this device, that Shakespeare liked to complicate his plays in this way. His use of disguise in comedy promotes similar effects, as you will find when you read *Twelfth Night*.

The crucial question we might expect to be answered at this stage in the play is 'How guilty is Gertrude?' Did she embark on an affair with Claudius while old Hamlet was still alive? Did she know about or conspire in his murder? We need to establish what exactly Hamlet thinks Gertrude has done and what she confesses or reveals. This is notoriously difficult to do. In Jenkins's Arden edition of the play, the note on Gertrude's echoing of Hamlet's phrase 'As kill a king?' (3. 4. 29) provides a confident interpretation of her response: 'Her reaction manifests her innocence' (Jenkins, 1982, p.320). However, the New Cambridge editor, Philip Edwards, voices what may be a more widespread frustration when he says of the same line: 'It is extraordinary that neither of them takes up this all-important matter again. Gertrude does not press for an explanation; Hamlet does not question further the Queen's involvement' (Edwards, 1985, p.175). Edwards refers readers to Q1, where

Gertrude offers a firm denial – 'But as I have a soul, I swear by heaven, / I never knew of this most horrid murder' (11. 83–4) – and he assumes that this variant arose because the silence on this matter in the longer texts 'was thought to be a fault in the theatre' (ibid.); hence the actors or reporters of the supposedly pirated text helpfully emended it. In Q1, Gertrude is also much more explicit in her response to Hamlet's request that she assist him in his revenge, promising 'I will conceal, consent, and do my best, / What stratagem soe'er thou shalt devise' (11. 97–8).

In his famous 1919 reading of the play, T.S. Eliot argued that this 'fault' of the lack of clarity about Gertrude's guilt makes Hamlet's attitude to her excessive, producing emotions without what he called an 'objective correlative': underlying facts that would justify them. For him, this made the play enigmatic, 'the "Mona Lisa" of literature', but also 'an artistic failure' (1990 edn, pp.44–5). Act 3, Scene 4 has become central to modern feminist discussions of the play like those of Jacqueline Rose (1985) and Lisa Jardine (1996). It has always, of course, been central to discussions of Hamlet's relationship with his mother – as much for what is not said as for what is. In her dense and quite difficult discussion of both the play and Eliot's reading of it, Rose argues that what is inscrutable or unmanageable in the play for Eliot and other influential male readers (notably the psychoanalyst Ernest Jones in *Hamlet and Oedipus*, 1949) is femininity itself. You might wish to consider at this point whether you would expect male and female readers (or for that matter performers, critics, editors or teachers) to read this play differently and, if so, in what ways. Is it the case, for example, that a male reader would accept Hamlet's judgements of Gertrude and Ophelia as simply true, whereas a female reader might question them? Would a male reader be more irritated by Hamlet's failure to take decisive action? Whilst in 3. 4 Hamlet may seem perfunctory in his murder of Polonius and casual in his attitude to 'the guts', particularly in the light of his recent refusal to kill Claudius when presented with an opportunity, he seems verbose in lecturing his mother – and priggish in telling her she is too old for sexual passion.

Act 3, Scene 4 is usually referred to as 'the closet scene', as it takes place in Gertrude's private chamber or 'closet'. This was the name given in Shakespeare's time to a room whose privacy was, as Jardine writes, 'signified by its location as the final room in a run of chambers serving increasingly "private" functions – the reception room opening into the retiring room, opening into the bedroom, off which is found the closet' (1996, p.150). It should be an intimate domestic space (like Ophelia's chamber, where Hamlet has startled her: see 2. 1. 75 onwards), although in this case the presence of Polonius as spy brings the political situation in Denmark to intervene in the conflict between son and mother. A 'closet' was usually a small room reserved for study and prayer, not a bedroom, although many productions and films of *Hamlet* have featured a bed in this scene, which emphasizes the idea of an invasion of privacy for modern audiences and raises the erotic temperature. (See Figure 29: in this 1989 production the Ghost seems to be embracing Gertrude to protect her from Hamlet.)

In Q1, Gertrude subsequently describes Hamlet's behaviour in this encounter as follows, when Claudius asks her how she found her son:

Alas, my lord, as raging as the sea.
Whenas he came, I first bespake him fair,
But then he throws and tosses me about,
As one forgetting that I was his mother.

(11. 103–6)

Figure 29 *Mark Rylance as Hamlet, Clare Higgins as Gertrude and Russell Enoch as the Ghost in the Royal Shakespeare Company production directed by Ron Daniels, 1989. Joe Cocks Studio Collection, Shakespeare Centre Library.*

It is not clear, even in Q1, whether we are to take this as an accurate account of what 'really' happened. Gertrude may be exaggerating in order to keep her promise not to reveal Hamlet's actual (or at least professed) sanity, but many performers of Hamlet become quite violent in this scene, showing him in danger of breaking his promise at the end of 3. 2 that he would 'speak daggers to her, but use none' (366).

Again, Q1 gives us a unique suggestion about the staging of this scene with its stage direction *'Enter the Ghost in his night-gown'* (11. 56), perhaps a surprising contrast with the full armour of Act 1, but appropriate to the intimate setting. Many editors (including the Norton editors) quote this direction in their main text, rather than the more neutral Q2/F version *'Enter Ghost'*, and it has influenced many productions.

Why does the Ghost appear at 3. 4. 93, 1? And why does Gertrude not see the Ghost?

In some productions, the Ghost's appearance seems intended as an intervention to protect Gertrude from Hamlet's increasingly violent anger. Or does the Ghost appear, as Hamlet says, because he has become diverted from his real purpose (3. 4. 97–9)? In the banquet scene in *Macbeth* (3. 4), only the guilty Macbeth sees the Ghost of Banquo. Following this logic, Gertrude's *inability* to see the Ghost might suggest her innocence.

You might, finally, consider the ending of this scene, and indeed this act, in the light of the comment by the textual scholar W.W. Greg quoted by Jenkins at the opening of the next act, 4. 1: 'It is a disaster that editors have followed a late [1676] quarto in choosing this of all points at which to begin a new act' (1982, p.334).

Is there in fact any justification for a break in the action here?

The action does seem to be continuous: Gertrude remains on stage when Hamlet leaves and is found in a state of distress by Claudius; it is not seriously suggested that significant time has passed – indeed, Gertrude stresses the continuity with 'Ah, my good lord, what have I seen tonight!' (4).

You should bear in mind that act divisions were introduced to Shakespeare's theatre after the first stagings of *Hamlet*. They were needed at the indoor theatre, the Blackfriars, so that the candles could be trimmed and replaced; the open-air Globe, where *Hamlet* was first performed, had no such requirements. Act divisions in modern texts are entirely the invention of editors, who tend to follow conventions set by each other (even in a case like this where they believe it is wrong), simply for ease of reference.

How does Shakespeare compensate for Hamlet's absence from the stage in Act 4?

Much of Act 4 is taken up with the question of what Claudius and Gertrude are thinking. At the beginning they are shaken and in disarray, but Claudius is nevertheless thinking quickly and cleverly of ways in which he will deal with the disastrous situation that has suddenly emerged. His profession of 'so much ... love' (4. 1. 18) for Hamlet suggests a need to keep in with Gertrude, yet he shows no real concern for her distress, merely commenting, 'There's matter in these sighs, these profound heaves; / You must translate. 'Tis fit we understand them' (1–2). At first, he seems trapped within the parameters of fear for his own safety and fears for his political standing, but he then moves swiftly to adopt a course of action – Hamlet's transportation out of Denmark. Meanwhile, the complexity of the play's web of trust and distrust is further developed, for, however ambiguous Gertrude's behaviour has been in the past, she is now engaged in deceiving him.

In 4. 3, Claudius continues to think out the political consequences of Hamlet's actions. He knows that he must calculate how 'the distracted multitude' (4) reads events at court. His hold on power is ultimately subject to the compliance of his subjects, a group he despises for their vulnerability to the seductive forces of appearance. Some interpreters, such as the film director Kozintsev, do attempt to define the relationship between the court and the people – for example, by showing Hamlet striding through a crowd of courtiers as his first soliloquy is given in voice-over. But the play itself provides no real answer, concentrating as it does on the power struggle between individuals at court without exploring their support outside in the streets and fields. Hamlet develops a theory of that relationship, but it is one that moves rapidly into another, the relationship between life and death:

> A certain convocation of politic [parliament of crafty] worms are e'en at him ... We fat all creatures else to fat us, and we fat ourselves for maggots. Your fat king and your lean beggar is but variable service – two dishes, but to one table. That's the end.

> (4. 3. 20–5)

To Claudius, Hamlet is now a political enemy. If Claudius were to hear him saying to Rosencrantz and Guildenstern 'The King is a thing – ... Of nothing' (4. 2. 26, 28), he would regard it as a political threat, a signal of intended insurrection. But

Hamlet's attack on the 'fat king' is an attack on the flesh itself, even the flesh of the lean beggar. It is a contempt not merely for the usurper but for humanity's vainglorious belief in its own status as not just above the worms but free of death.

With the transition from 4. 4 to 4. 5, we move from a scene about shame to a scene about guilt. In F, Horatio plays an active role at first in establishing a picture of, and a sympathetic attitude to, Ophelia in her madness. In Q2, his speeches are attributed to an anonymous Gentleman. The effect of giving them to Horatio is that he represents his absent friend, Hamlet, here. Either Horatio (Q2) or Gertrude (F) fears of Ophelia that 'she may strew / Dangerous conjectures in ill-breeding minds' (4. 5. 14–15). Indeed, Ophelia's mad talk will, when he meets her again, help fuel Laertes's quest for personal revenge against Hamlet.

However, the immediate effect of the mere *news* of Ophelia's ravings is, as Gertrude quickly explains (significantly, in an aside), the intensification of Gertrude's sense of guilt. This is because she is involved in a cover-up, and not just a single cover-up but a multiple cover-up. She may or may not have known that Claudius killed her husband; she may or may not have committed adultery with Claudius before her husband died; she has sworn to Hamlet that she will keep from Claudius the knowledge that Hamlet knows he killed old Hamlet and that Hamlet is only pretending to be mad; she is now also trying to protect both Hamlet and Claudius from the political and personal consequences of people knowing that Hamlet has killed Polonius and Claudius is shipping Hamlet out of the country rather than putting him on trial.

In Q2 and F, Ophelia remarks, 'Lord, we know what we are, but know not what we may be' (4. 5. 42–3), and no doubt everyone present thinks 'How true!' For not only does the play present a series of transformations – the honest into the dishonest, the sane into the mad, the living into the dead – but it is full of unexpected turns of events – 'accidental judgements, ... purposes mistook / Fall'n on th'inventors' heads' (5. 2. 326–9), which educate Hamlet into a resigned fatalism: 'There's a divinity that shapes our ends, / Rough-hew them how we will' (5. 2. 10–11).

Q1 has an unusually detailed and vivid stage direction: '*Enter Ofelia playing on a lute* [a stringed instrument], *and her hair down, singing*' (13. 14). With her hair down and her wits lost, Ophelia has abandoned the restraint and self-consciousness bred into her by her father and the court. What is released is not just personal to her but a collective unconscious, involving folk-lore (ballads, folk-tales, flowers). Some stage or film Ophelias are poignantly but poetically distracted gentlewomen, but Kathryn Pogson in Jonathan Miller's 1982 production was grotesquely disfigured by grief or shock into a state of embarrassing lunacy, and Kate Winslet in Branagh's 1996 film suffers the indignity of being hosed down in a corner of a cell.

What is the theatrical impact of the handing over of a letter or the reading of a letter on stage?

In some instances, a letter may simply be a quick way of conveying information that Shakespeare either cannot or does not choose to dramatize: try to imagine how different this play would be if it contained a scene in which Hamlet directly courted Ophelia in the kinds of terms he uses in the letter Polonius reads at 2. 2. 110–24. A letter or message can be the focus of the action and a letter can change the direction of the action, especially when it goes astray or is opened by the wrong recipient – as when Hamlet intercepts Claudius's letter (5. 2).

The play involves a number of letters – Claudius's letter to Norway, carried by Voltemand and Cornelius; Norway's reply, which they bring back, seeking permission for young Fortinbras to march across Denmark; Hamlet's letters to Ophelia, intercepted by Polonius and read out to Claudius and Gertrude; Hamlet's love-tokens received and then returned to him by Ophelia; Hamlet's additions to the 'Murder of Gonzago' handed to the First Player for 'delivery' to Claudius; Claudius's letter to the King of England, intercepted by Hamlet and altered by him (Olivier felt he must show the contents to the film audience); England's reply, delivered by the English ambassador to Horatio; and Hamlet's message 'to the unsatisfied', which he asks Horatio to deliver for him in his eternal absence.

Act 4, Scene 6 concerns a letter: it is written by Hamlet, addressed to Horatio, transported first by a (Danish?) ambassador, then by a sailor, who delivers it to Horatio and who waits while Horatio reads it out. Furthermore, in Q1, 4. 6 is preceded by another scene (14), between Horatio and the Queen, in which Horatio describes the contents of the letter he has received from Hamlet. Gertrude is put in the know about her husband's plot to have Hamlet killed, and she asks Horatio to carry a message to Hamlet encouraging him in his plot against Claudius's life.

Act 4 ends with more letters, this time from Hamlet to Claudius and Gertrude, saying that he is alive and home. Why does Hamlet not slip back secretly into the country? We can regard this as the conventional confidence of the folk-hero, as the noble honesty of an agent of justice, as the senseless bravado of an incompetent revenger, or as a suicide's deliberate act of self-betrayal.

Even before this puzzle is set us, we are struggling to know how to feel about Claudius, who invokes Laertes's conscience (4. 7. 1), but does so in order to establish his own innocence. Then he justifies his decision not to punish Hamlet for killing Laertes's father by claiming, first, that his love of Gertrude inhibits any move against her son and, secondly, that Hamlet's popularity is such that Claudius would risk a rebellion if he opposed the prince. As the New Cambridge editor remarks, we may well be impressed by Claudius's candour, but he is being less than candid at the same time, for he fears exposure and he is actually trying to ensure that Hamlet *is* punished, in England (Edwards, 1985, p.204).

This degree of complication in the construction of Claudius's part typifies Shakespeare's disturbing ability to spring surprises in his presentation of moral character in the play. Hamlet challenges and shocks us by the perversity of his treatment of Ophelia and his mother, and the coolness with which he rationalizes the deaths of Polonius and Rosencrantz and Guildenstern. At the same time, Claudius the villain is capable of making statements that almost amount to tragic self-revelation or general insights into the nature of things, as when he tells Laertes, 'There lives within the very flame of love / A kind of wick or snuff that will abate it' (4. 7. 95.1–2). We must, he says, act at the right moment because everything, even love, changes, peaks and then declines.

The moral and emotional switchback ride continues. No sooner has Laertes expressed his desire to kill Hamlet, observing that the idea 'warms the very sickness in my heart' (4. 7. 53), than Claudius has drawn him into a 'shuffling' (109) device to effect that end without arousing anyone's suspicion – 'even his mother shall uncharge the practice / And call it accident' (65–6). No sooner has the accident been arranged than Gertrude brings news of another kind of ambiguous accident, Ophelia's death by drowning. For some readers and playgoers, the scene at this point swerves into pathos, sentimentality and melodrama of the most acute kind.

Laertes's 'Drowned? O, where?' (4. 7. 136) and Gertrude's set-piece speech that follows have been criticized as inept writing on Shakespeare's part. (The death of Ophelia has been famously represented in films and, indeed, in paintings, yet ironically it is not something that a stage audience witnesses, except in its imagination.)

How does Shakespeare draw together the many strands of the plot in the final act? Are his dramatic resolutions plausible?

Act 5, Scene 1 has as its setting a graveyard (easily represented on the Elizabethan stage by opening up the trapdoor in the middle of the stage), and in it we witness a prince conversing with the humblest of his subjects. This is an emblematic representation of the truth that we are all equal in death, but it is also the first and only time in the play that we meet the common man. Shakespeare sometimes uses this device to humanize his main protagonists – think of Richard II and his groom or the clown who brings Cleopatra the asps – but social lowering coincides here with the introduction of comic repartee and songs. The shift in tone, indeed the very presence of such material in a tragic drama, was what eighteenth-century readers of Shakespeare found so objectionable: it offended against their ideas of propriety.

At the same time, the Clown, by the topics he introduces, reminds Hamlet and us of the fact that death is our fate. The great leveller not only casts his shadow over Hamlet himself (he has, after all, only just escaped death by a whisker), but allows him to engage in social satire at the expense of those social types – the proud, the rich, the powerful – whose vanity deceives them into thinking themselves non-participants in the dance of death. The idea of death also stimulates a form of freedom in those who confront it honestly in their thoughts, for they thereby gain a perspective on their own mortality which can enable them to relax into a stoic acceptance of whatever fate flings them. This is Hamlet's new state of mind, for paradoxically he turns violent for the first time as he leaps into Ophelia's grave and begins to grapple with her brother, while at the same time he becomes calm and philosophical, resigned to his fate.

The structure of the scene involves a complex of dramatic ironies: Hamlet is not recognized by the Clown; Hamlet does not know Ophelia is dead and that it is her grave he has come across; Claudius and the rest of the funeral party do not know they are being watched by Hamlet as if they were actors in a play and he the audience; and Hamlet's leap into the grave is effectively a leap into his own grave, for he thereby reveals himself to his enemy, loses his advantage over him and seals his own death-warrant. Yorick's skull is a *memento mori*, like the one in Hans Holbein's painting *The Ambassadors*, discussed in Chapters 1 and 2. Yorick is also an indicator of Hamlet's age (30) and the fact that old Hamlet defeated old Fortinbras the day Hamlet was born.

The spontaneous fight between Hamlet and Laertes in Ophelia's grave is frustrated by the intervention of Claudius. It thus sets up expectations for the next and final scene, where the action of the whole play is finally resolved in the formal duel between the two antagonists. Many of Shakespeare's plays – think of *Macbeth* – culminate in the meeting in duels or battles of the 'mighty opposites' who have dominated the action up to that point. One of the respects in which *Hamlet* qualifies this convention is that Hamlet is, at least at first, unaware that Laertes is a significant adversary, an arm of the man whom he *has* regarded as his enemy. This kind of variation is typical of Shakespeare: in *Macbeth*, Macbeth fails to realize that Macduff was not 'of woman born'; in *Antony and Cleopatra*, Antony would dearly like to resolve things by fighting Octavius, but he is not allowed to.

In Act 5, Scene 2, the last scene and dénouement of the play's action, Hamlet both triumphs over and is defeated by, first, Claudius, then Laertes, and finally Fortinbras. In Laertes's case, the duel provides both outcomes: 'They bleed on both sides' (247), as each combatant brings about the death of the other. Among the ironies here is the moral ambiguity of what Hamlet says to Laertes before the duel takes place: he denies responsibility for Polonius's death (and Ophelia's) on the grounds that it was his madness that was acting through him (163–81).

In Claudius's case, the triumph is that he is exposed as a villain and Hamlet publicly kills him; the defeat is the fact that Claudius finally manages to have Hamlet killed. The irony here is surely the hollowness of Hamlet's triumph: in other words, the ultimate tragic irony that the protagonist who is obliged to solve and punish a crime finds himself drawn into a sequence of events that tarnishes his own moral and legal status to the extent that, by the end, he is himself a criminal who must, by the very standards he has been trying to uphold, be punished by death. In Fortinbras's case, the triumph is that by naming him as the next King of Denmark Hamlet secures the succession; the defeat is that Fortinbras takes over Hamlet's country and reverses the outcome of their fathers' wager.

Gertrude dies because she drinks from the poisoned cup designed by Claudius (and Laertes) to kill Hamlet. In some productions, she seems to realize that the cup is poisoned and therefore commits suicide. There is a sense in which Hamlet may be said to commit suicide by his actions in the second half of the play; Ophelia's death is probably suicide; and Horatio certainly moves as if to commit suicide once he sees that Hamlet is dying. He wishes to take poison in order to follow his friend to the grave – 'I am more an antique Roman', he says, 'than a Dane' (5. 2. 283), meaning that his philosophy accommodates the Stoic philosophical position, which involves disregard for pain and pleasure in the interests of personal integrity. Death is preferable to compromising one's principles, and human autonomy and control are symbolized and celebrated in the final act of self-determination, suicide.

Hamlet's story has been of a supremely self-conscious being, wishing to understand and control his life but discovering that he is quite unable to do so, and settling for a fatalistic surrender of control to the 'divinity that shapes our ends, / Rough-hew them how we will' (5. 2. 10–11). Horatio is his model of the Stoic, but Hamlet denies him the right to take his own life, commanding him as a subject to absent himself from felicity, to stay alive and tell Hamlet's story to the world. Friendship prevails.

Hamlet's final words are 'The rest is silence' (5. 2. 300). Or at least in Q2 they are. In Q1, they are 'Farewell Horatio. Heaven receive my soul' (17. 104). If Q2 is chosen, there is a striking contrast with the Hamlet we have got to know over four hours, for he has been characterized, in his own phrase , by 'Words, words, words' (2. 2. 192). His articulacy – his eloquence, his verbosity – has been one of his defining characteristics, and when he falls silent, then indeed he does seem to be dead. Yet he begins the play as a silent presence (he has to be urged into public utterance after 64 lines of 1. 2); once he has listened to the ghost of his father, wild and whirling words render him less than articulate; and finally he demands that, once he is dead and silent, Horatio must go on speaking on his behalf.

Ingmar Bergman's 1986 production ended with Fortinbras gunning down the entire court; Branagh's 1996 film ended with his army attacking the palace in SAS style. Alternatively, as we pointed out earlier, many productions have cut Fortinbras entirely. Curiously, in Act 4 Fortinbras leads his army off-stage just before Hamlet enters, whilst in 5. 2 Hamlet is dead before Fortinbras enters. It is a supreme irony, in a play built so unremittingly on ironies, that in 4. 4 Hamlet should contrast himself so powerfully with, and at the end of the play name as his successor, someone whom he has so nearly, but in fact never, met.

From first to last, *Hamlet* provokes our questions and refutes our simplistic answers. We might deduce from the evidence of the three surviving texts that Shakespeare himself, or his acting company, did not have any problems with the idea that it could exist in more than one form. Arguably, it has been staged, read and interpreted in more numerous and varied ways than any other text. What does it mean? We might do better to ask how it can carry the weight of meanings that have been ascribed to it and what it means for our culture that *Hamlet* should remain, after 400 years, one of its key texts.

References

Edwards, P. (ed.) (1985) *Hamlet*, Cambridge: Cambridge University Press.

Eliot, T.S. (1990) 'Hamlet', 1919, in *Major Literary Characters: Hamlet*, ed. H. Bloom, New York: Chelsea House, pp.43–6.

Hawkes, T. (1992) *Meaning by Shakespeare*, London: Routledge.

Irace, K.O. (ed.) (1998) *The First Quarto of Hamlet*, Cambridge: Cambridge University Press.

Jardine, L. (1996) *Reading Shakespeare Historically*, London: Routledge.

Jenkins, H. (ed.) (1982) *Hamlet*, London: Methuen.

Jones, E. (1949) *Hamlet and Oedipus*, New York: W.W. Norton.

Rose, J. (1985) 'Sexuality in the reading of Shakespeare', in *Alternative Shakespeares*, ed. J. Drakakis, London: Methuen, pp.95–118.

Stoppard, T. (1967) *Rosencrantz and Guildenstern Are Dead*, London: Faber.

Traub, V. (1995) 'Jewels, statues and corpses: containment of erotic power in Shakespeare's plays', in *Shakespeare and Gender*, ed. D.E. Barker and I. Kamps, London: Verso, pp.120–41.

Wilson, J.D. (ed.) (1934) *Hamlet*, Cambridge: Cambridge University Press.

TWELFTH NIGHT   *Chapter 6*

Penny Rixon

Aims

Building on the work done in Chapter 1, this chapter will explore how far *Twelfth Night* shares the comic perspective of *A Midsummer Night's Dream*. The main focus will be on the double vision at the heart of the play: its concern with twinship, the ambiguity of gender and the duplicity of language. The play's production history will be explored in order to show how *Twelfth Night* is peculiarly likely to provoke radical changes in performance strategy and critical response.

Introduction

Twelfth Night, Or What You Will was written several years after *A Midsummer Night's Dream*, although no one knows exactly when and where it was first performed. There is a record of a response from a member of one of its first audiences, however, as an entry for February 1602 in the diary of John Manningham gives a short account of a performance at the Middle Temple. Helen Hackett mentioned in Interval 1 that the players were often asked to play at private venues and it is clear that this performance took place at a feast, although its occasion was not the same as that which is associated with the title of *Twelfth Night*, the Feast of the Epiphany, which is celebrated on 6 January.

Before getting to grips with the play, it might be an idea to revisit a notion explored in connection with *A Midsummer Night's Dream* and *Richard II*: the carnivalesque. If you look back at Chapter 1, you'll find that Twelfth Night is mentioned as one of the main festivals associated with carnival in pre-industrial Europe. In fact, some historians regard it as the winter counterpart of Midsummer's Day in the festive cycle, and it is interesting in this context that Manningham absent-mindedly began to write *A Midsummer Night's Dream* as the title of the play he had seen and then crossed it out. Twelfth Night rituals are steeped in the ethic of carnival, which, as you saw in Chapter 1, is thought by some critics to be inherently subversive, or at least a time at which previously repressed social energies could be released. In many parts of Europe, student communities celebrated with a cake containing a dried bean, the person receiving it being crowned 'king' of the feast, a custom which offered plenty of chances for burlesquing the powerful and thus undermining established authority.

Disguise, including cross-dressing, and masquing were also involved in the celebrations. So it *was* a time of excess and of inversion of norms, but it is also important to remember that it marked the end of the twelve-day revels of Christmas: even while the wine was flowing, the revellers were conscious that tomorrow it was back to work with the cold, hungry winter ahead. If the play's title is intended to sum up its spirit, it should be remembered that this feast was balanced between the festivity of the party and the inevitable morning after.

I say 'if', because the full title of the play includes that enigmatic alternative title '*Or What You Will*'. What does it mean? Is Shakespeare signalling that this play is steeped in the ambivalent nature of Twelfth Night revels, or does the subtitle suggest that the play is simply a frothy entertainment and therefore any title will do? Some critics, such as the editors of the Arden text, J.M. Lothian and T.W. Craik (1975), argue that the title *Twelfth Night* has no special significance beyond a general connection with the festive season. One of the things you will need to decide as you study the play is where you stand on this issue.

Another of your goals will be to decide whether the comedy of this play has anything in common with that of *A Midsummer Night's Dream*. One of the main points made in Chapter 1 was the difficulty of reaching a comprehensive definition of terms like 'comedy' and 'comic', and it could be that in this play Shakespeare is exploring different manifestations of this wide-ranging genre.

Generic signals

One of the most striking features of Act 1 is how quickly it gets all the main strands of the action under way. Scene 1 briefly introduces Orsino, the ruler of Illyria, and establishes that he is consumed by unrequited love. This is followed by another short scene in which Viola, left destitute and alone after a shipwreck, devises a strategy for survival, and then we jump to the other main location of the play, Olivia's house. In Scene 4, after three days the disguised Viola has not only established herself as Orsino's favourite, but has fallen in love with him ('Whoe'er I woo, myself would be his wife!' (41)), while by the end of Scene 5 Olivia is in love with Viola–Cesario.

Shakespeare could move so fast because he could rely on the fact that the audience would subconsciously recognize that plays are not transcriptions of real life. The important point is that if you are aware of the generic conventions, the clues in the text will help you to read the play as what most critics call a 'romantic' comedy.

The play's location is just such a clue. Illyria is supposed to refer to an area in the vicinity of the former Yugoslavia, but for many in Shakespeare's audience it would simply have signalled a fantasy location associated with Greek romances. You should notice that Illyria – like Athens in *A Midsummer Night's Dream* – is a very different kind of dramatic location from the Rome and Egypt of *Antony and Cleopatra*, where certain cultural attributes of Rome and Egypt are deeply embedded in the plot and themes of the tragedy. Illyria is typical of the romance genre, which tends to use place as a backdrop for fantastic events.

Another clue is the shipwreck that separates loved ones, carrying with it the implicit promise of eventual reunion. Here, this generic expectation is reinforced by the vivid picture of Sebastian being borne aloft on the waves 'like Arion on the dolphin's back' (1. 2. 14), because, in Greek mythology, Arion is carried across the sea to safety by a dolphin. The audience may reasonably conclude that Sebastian has also survived, and that they can expect to see him on stage at some point in the play.

The genre also conditions our responses to the characters. We will probably feel instinctively that Viola should be rewarded, whereas the monumentally stupid Sir Andrew and the pompous Malvolio deserve comic humiliation.

If you simply summarize the plot, the play could indeed be dismissed as a piece of escapist entertainment, but before coming to such a conclusion it is a good idea to look more closely at the language. **Please re-read Scenes 1 and 2 now, and pay special attention to the dramatic language Shakespeare employs.**

Ideas about love are prominent in the opening scene. Orsino is deep in meditation on the nature of love when we first see him, and most of his lines develop and amplify this preoccupation. Like Theseus in *A Midsummer Night's Dream*, he links love and 'fancy', although unlike the sceptical Athenian, he holds both in high esteem. In the latter part of the scene he moves from the abstract to the particular, focusing on what he thinks are the qualities of his beloved and fantasizing about what she might be like if she fell in love.

Yet although the speech ostensibly concerns itself with enduring love, the language harps on the notion of instability. The first three lines express this quality through an elaborate conceit, which turns on the idea of deliberately over-indulging in delicious food in order to induce nausea, so that delight is constantly generating disgust. In line 7, Orsino moves from revelling in the music to commanding that it stop immediately because it is no longer enjoyable. Lines 11–14 introduce the simile of the sea, a powerful symbol of mutability, and describe the defining characteristic of love as transmuting everything it comes into contact with, and also depreciating things which are normally prized. And when Curio introduces the idea of hunting, Orsino uses it to construct another conceit, one which sees the hunter turn into the hunted and love itself mutate into a destroyer (20–3).

Performance can emphasize the idea of instability, not only through the actor's body language, but also through the auditory shock of the sudden interruption of the music. More subtle effects come through *hearing* the verse, as the listener subconsciously registers the effect of the abrupt pause and the shift in stress pattern in line 7, for example: 'Stéaling and gíving ódour. Enoúgh, no móre'. There is thus quite a disturbing undercurrent in the first scene.

The language also registers some down-to-earth concerns in 1. 2. Did you notice how it begins to establish a notion of social hierarchy? Not only does the Captain call Viola 'Lady' and 'Madam', but he also apologizes for relaying gossip about those above him in the social scale: 'as, you know, / What great ones do the less will prattle of' (28–9). This may seem a trivial point, but this focus on rank and status is important in the play as a whole because of the way it insists on the social gradations that demarcate the different characters.

What is more, a modern sensibility might miss the fact that Viola's disguise involves a dramatic change in status as well as gender. For someone of her rank, going into service is a significant step down, which deprives her of autonomy. Such service was in real life a normal stage in the education of young gentlefolk, as historians have established, but there is a crucial difference between Viola's situation and that institutionalized practice, because Viola has no family to guarantee her safety. She is working to survive in a world where all the normal supports have fallen away; she has lost all the power conferred by her rank and must live on her wits, in competition with others in a similar position.

Olivia is conscious of rank, asking Cesario 'What is your parentage?' (1. 5. 247) at the point where she is clearly becoming fascinated by the messenger. Viola's answer, 'Above my fortunes, yet my state is well. / I am a gentleman' (248–9), reassures Olivia: at least she is attracted to someone of her own class. A little later in the scene, Viola's inborn loathing of dependency provokes a scornful rejection of Olivia's money: 'I am no fee'd post, lady. Keep your purse' (254), and Olivia's reaction to this suggests that she sees it as evidence of gentle upbringing. You might like to compare this with Feste's attitude to gratuities, displayed at several points in the play. The point to note here is that, although the play begins by invoking the fantasy world of romance, it also insists on our recognizing other realities, in which people need money to survive, and in which they do not necessarily marry their ideal partner.

One other concern of the language in Scene 2 that you might have noted is the questioning of the reliability of appearance, a theme that was also a central concern of *A Midsummer Night's Dream*. Deciding to trust the Captain, Viola acknowledges that accepting someone's worth just because he looks like a decent citizen may not be wise:

> There is a fair behaviour in thee, captain,
> And though that nature with a beauteous wall
> Doth oft close in pollution, yet of thee
> I will believe thou hast a mind that suits
> With this thy fair and outward character.

(1. 2. 43–7)

She then devises a plan involving the use of disguise that will mislead anyone who trusts *her* (his?) outward appearance.

There is one other characteristic feature of the language that I would like to explore before moving on to major themes. **Read the following extracts from Act 1, and see if you can identify a prominent feature of the way language is used in both of them.**

    1. 3. 37–67   ('Sir Toby Belch ... I am barren.')
    1. 5. 17–62   ('Many ... gentlemen.')

What I had in mind was the way that both passages involve sustained playing on words, and this device introduces another variation on the theme of duplicity. The stupid Sir Andrew consistently misinterprets what is said to him, first in thinking that 'Accost' is Maria's name and then, in his aside, assuming that Toby's explanation has a bawdy meaning. Maria employs her superior wit to make Sir Toby (and the audience) laugh at Sir Andrew's expense: for example, when Sir Andrew talks metaphorically of jokes being at her fingers' ends, she signals to the audience a more literal interpretation of the phrase, implying that he himself is the biggest joke of all. In 1. 5. 15–25 the participants in the skirmish are more evenly matched, as Maria avoids the trap posed by 'I am resolved on two points', earning the professional entertainer's respect. Feste then gives a demonstration of more advanced skills in order to save his job, deftly combining wordplay with formal logic to prove that Olivia is a fool.

Wordplay is a staple both of the period's culture and of a certain type of comedy, but I think that *Twelfth Night* goes far beyond convention in the way that it puts the fluidity, even the deceptiveness, of language right at the heart of the play. Language is as likely to deceive as appearance: when spoken, the words 'heart' and 'hart' are identical; 'good gifts of nature' can be turned around to signify mental vacuity. In almost every case, the device generates a consciousness of two alternative worlds, so that a sense of double vision pervades the play. For example, Feste's catechism of Olivia in 1. 5 proves her a fool only in terms of otherworldly religion, deliberately ignoring the other dimension of natural human grief.

What is more, at the heart of the play is a *visual* symbol of doubleness, a pair of twins, two distinct people with one outward form. In addition, concern with the way that costume can change a person's identity in Scene 2 extends throughout the play. Although *Twelfth Night* does not contain a play-within-a-play, it shares *A Midsummer Night's Dream*'s self-consciousness. This time, however, the device is used to reinforce the dual perspective of the play, and it does so by continually juxtaposing the fictional world of Illyria with that of the playhouse, where audience and actor collaborate in producing an illusion.

Because the play seems so deeply permeated by a sense of alternative possibilities, this chapter will explore some of the ways in which this double vision operates. I think it's one of the things that transforms some fairly mundane ingredients into a play of great complexity, with a dimension of darkness that can threaten the comic spirit in ways not found in the *Dream*. What we have here is a play that uses conventions of romance and of farcical comedy – disguise, mistaken identity, comic stereotyping, gender confusion, wordplay – but whose language constantly insists on a more complex and more painful world. The recent performance history of *Twelfth Night* reveals an increasing preoccupation with this aspect of the play. From the time of Manningham and Samuel Pepys through to the early twentieth century, productions tended to go for the farcical approach, but since the mid-1970s, film and theatre companies have seemed intent on competing to see who could produce the gloomiest version of *Twelfth Night*. At the time of writing (1999), however, the pendulum seems to be swinging the other way, with the 1997/8 Royal Shakespeare Company (RSC) production decking stage and actors out in jewel-bright colours and playing at a speed that allowed no dwelling on the tragic potential of the play's events.

'Smiling at grief'

At this point it is worth noting that the sources for *Twelfth Night* do not have the complexity or depth of the play itself. It is generally agreed that the main source for the story is *Gl'Ingannati* (*The Deceived*), an Italian play of the 1530s, described by the Arden editors as 'a Plautine comedy of mistaken identity' (Lothian and Craik, 1975, p.xxxvi), which misses no opportunity to exploit bawdy possibilities. Shakespeare may not have drawn directly on the original but on derivatives such as Barnabe Rich's prose narrative *Apolonius and Silla*, which he had definitely read. If you know Shakespeare's earlier work, *The Comedy of Errors,* however, you will probably have noticed that twins figure largely there, in this case, two pairs of identical twin brothers. That play is modelled on a Roman play, the *Menaechmi* of Plautus, in which one pair of twin brothers, separated at birth, are finally reunited after a series of farcical events based on mistaken identity. Crudely speaking, the sources tend to exploit situations for laughter, putting obstacles in the way of love simply to create entertaining ways of demolishing them.

Our reading of the first two scenes suggested that Shakespeare may have had different priorities, and further exploration of the play reinforces this impression. Orsino's language, in his discussions with Cesario in 1. 4 and 2. 4, emphasizes the destructive nature of the intense love felt by all three characters, giving plenty of warrant for a more serious interpretation in performance. Orsino demonstrates how unrequited love can destroy a person's capacity to do anything but brood upon 'the constant image of the creature / That is beloved' (2. 4. 18–19). His love for Olivia is obsessive. In romantic never-never land, this kind of passion may be noble and uplifting, but in the real world it can be both terrifying for its object and ultimately destructive. Despite Olivia's consistent refusals, Orsino is unable to conceive of rejection and, more than once, the words he uses hint at the anti-social potential of his love:

> Be clamorous, and leap all civil bounds,
> Rather than make unprofited return.

> (1. 4. 20–1)

> I cannot be so answered.

> (2. 4. 86)

> My love can give no place, bide no denay.

> (2. 4. 123)

The image of the engulfing sea in 2. 4. 98–9 is ominous in this context. What is more, the audience has no grounds for believing that Olivia might cave in at some point. This is no girl playing hard to get, but a woman who is surprised by her inability to respond to so eligible a suitor:

> Your lord does know my mind, I cannot love him.
> Yet I suppose him virtuous, know him noble,
> Of great estate, of fresh and stainless youth,
> In voices well divulged, free, learned, and valiant,
> And in dimension and the shape of nature
> A gracious person; but yet I cannot love him.
> He might have took his answer long ago.

> (1. 5. 226–32)

It is noteworthy that here Olivia is appealing to criteria – economic, social and temperamental compatibility – characteristic of a realistic rather than a romantic attitude to marriage. But she is, after all, turning Orsino down.

Faced with 'I can't' rather than 'I *won't* love him', an obstacle that cannot be conveniently dispelled by any stock comic device, Orsino's obsession threatens order and stability rather than promising integration and the creation of new life, and our consciousness of his power as a ruler underlines the danger. The climax comes when the Duke, thinking himself balked of his desires, almost turns into a brutal tyrant, ready to punish Olivia in any way he can, when he believes that Cesario has betrayed his trust:

> Come, boy, with me. My thoughts are ripe in mischief.
> I'll sacrifice the lamb that I do love
> To spite a raven's heart within a dove.

> (5. 1. 125–7)

Similar considerations apply to Viola. Although she cannot express her grief openly except in soliloquy, much of the rhetoric she uses to Orsino and Olivia in her role of Cesario powerfully conveys both the pain of a love that may remain unfulfilled and its potential for destruction. In Viola's case, the images are of *self*-destruction:

> She never told her love,
> But let concealment, like a worm i'th' bud,
> Feed on her damask cheek. She pined in thought,
> And with a green and yellow melancholy
> She sat like patience on a monument,
> Smiling at grief.

(2. 4. 109–14)

The image is of death-in-life and perpetual sterility, and the enigmatic response to Orsino's question about whether the imaginary sister died hints at the fate Viola herself might suffer if she fails to win his love.

A variation is played on this theme of dangerous love in the case of Olivia, because her desperate passion for Cesario leads her to flout conventional standards of behaviour for women of her class. Her reiterated demands that the boy return to report Orsino's reaction are transparent, and Viola's speech makes it clear that Olivia's body language is explicit from quite early on:

> She made good view of me, indeed so much
> That straight methought her eyes had lost her tongue,
> For she did speak in starts, distractedly.

(2. 2. 17–19)

Like Helena in *A Midsummer Night's Dream*, Olivia risks social disgrace. As she becomes increasingly infatuated, Olivia pushes the boundaries of acceptable conduct even further back. In confessing to the trick involving the ring and then making an outright appeal to Cesario, she recognizes that she is transgressing the code which forbids women to initiate wooing:

> Have you not set mine honour at the stake
> And baited it with all th'unmuzzled thoughts
> That tyrannous heart can think?

(3. 1. 110–12)

By 3. 4 she is ready to settle for bribery if she cannot have true love:

> I have sent after him, he says he'll come.
> How shall I feast him? What bestow of him?
> For youth is bought more oft than begged or borrowed.

(3. 4. 1–3)

In 3. 4, she acknowledges once again how outrageous her own behaviour is, but is unable to control herself:

> I have said too much unto a heart of stone,
> And laid mine honour too unchary out.
> There's something in me that reproves my fault,
> But such a headstrong potent fault it is
> That it but mocks reproof.

(3. 4. 178–82)

That these obstacles to happiness are ultimately removed does not negate the pain; indeed, the very implausibility of the means of resolution – Orsino and Olivia's ability to switch their love to a convenient object – underlines the fact that in the real world people do not usually get what they want. In this sense, one aspect of the comic vision in *Twelfth Night* could be described as a willingness to confront the misery experienced by most human beings and accept the brief interludes of happiness with gratitude.

Critical comedy

But there are other types of comedy in this complex play. One of the key areas in this context is gender, with the comic conventions of cross-dressing and mistaken identity employed to dramatize conflicts between individual desire and social constraint.

At this point, you might like to think about what expectations of gender behaviour are apparent in the play. Concentrating on the first two acts, note any stereotypical assumptions made about the way men or women ought to behave. Your examples can either be explicit statements or actions that imply these beliefs. You could also cite any instances where these notions are explicitly contested.

It is not difficult to find instances of characters expressing opinions about the behaviour appropriate to both genders. Orsino is convinced of the fundamental difference between men and women, even if he is characteristically inconsistent about what this is. At one point he claims that men are less reliable than women:

> For, boy, however we do praise ourselves,
> Our fancies are more giddy and unfirm,
> More longing, wavering, sooner lost and worn,
> Than women's are.

> (2. 4. 31–4)

A few lines later he is arguing precisely the opposite, claiming that no woman can experience love as intensely as he does because 'they lack retention' and implying that women are physiologically incapable of an enduring passion (91–101). Even Viola seems to endorse the view of women as weak and gullible when she realizes that Olivia has fallen in love with her 'outside':

> How easy is it for the proper false
> In women's waxen hearts to set their forms!
> Alas, our frailty is the cause, not we,
> For such as we are made, such we be.

> (2. 2. 27–30)

Yet in the scene with Orsino, her responses urge the similarity between men and women – 'In faith, they are as true of heart as we' (2. 4. 105). Furthermore, in the story of her invented sister, she reminds the audience of her own fortitude in working to effect Orsino's happiness at the expense of her own. Indeed, she proceeds to the polar opposite of Orsino's position by claiming that women are more likely to be faithful than men:

We men may say more, swear more, but indeed
Our shows are more than will; for still we prove
Much in our vows, but little in our love.

(2. 4. 115–17)

Some of you might have argued that Viola's behaviour in 1. 5 implies an acceptance of the belief that men and women are differently constituted. Cesario's language is assertive in that scene, as s/he wittily insists that s/he has the right to be taken seriously by the lady of the house. This creates a contrast with the way the character had appeared when in female costume in 1. 2 and in her soliloquies and asides to the audience.

In addition, there are insistent references throughout the play to a tradition that focuses on the transience of women's beauty, implying that failure to produce children renders their lives utterly pointless. Derived from classical literature, this idea is a commonplace in Renaissance poetry, and is often used as a way of persuading a woman to yield to her lover's demands for sex. Ironically, it is Viola who introduces the idea in her first attempt to win Olivia for Orsino:

Lady, you are the cruell'st she alive
If you will lead these graces to the grave
And leave the world no copy.

(1. 5. 211–13)

Orsino reiterates it in his moralizings on choosing a suitable wife (2. 4. 35–6), and the theme reappears in Feste's song in 2. 3. We can also see the same concern in the first seventeen of Shakespeare's sonnets, in which the older speaker urges his young male friend to produce an heir – or 'copy' of himself – who will preserve his beauty. As Shakespeare graphically puts it in Sonnet 12, 'nothing 'gainst time's scythe can make defence / Save breed to brave him when he takes thee hence' (lines 13–14).

In Act 3 the whole idea of fighting carries implicit notions of gender stereotyping. Men are supposed to know how to fight, and they are expected to be courageous in doing so at the least slight to their honour. Sir Toby's contempt for both Cesario and Sir Andrew derives from this kind of assumption, although, of course, Viola's remark that 'A little thing would make me tell them how much I lack of a man' (3. 4. 268–9) reminds the audience that, in her case, the scorn is undeserved. Sebastian's readiness to defend himself when insulted and his obvious skill in duelling further reinforce the belief.

You may well have cited other references, but the main point to make here is that the play reminds us of the more rigid codes of gender identity that were characteristic of Shakespeare's England. At the same time, I would argue, the action consistently undercuts stereotypes, showing human beings to be capable of a much greater fluidity than society usually allows them. For example, the play shows us two women who have, as a result of accidents – a shipwreck in Viola's case and the premature death of her father and brother in Olivia's – escaped from the male control that is normal in patriarchal societies. Both characters are able to function without the protection of men. The double vision here exposes the gulf between the restrictive pattern of organization imposed by society and the actual capacity of individual human beings of either gender.

What is more, the theme carries through into the ways in which the play stages sexual attraction. **In this context, I would like you to look again at a brief extract from 1. 4, where Orsino assures Cesario that s/he has a good chance of success with Olivia. Read the extract below carefully and think about how your experience of seeing it in a modern production might differ from the experience of Shakespeare's contemporaries.**

ORSINO   It shall become thee well to act my woes –
                She will attend it better in thy youth
                Than in a nuncio's of more grave aspect.

VIOLA   I think not so, my lord.

ORSINO   Dear lad, believe it;
                For they shall yet belie thy happy years
                That say thou art a man. Diana's lip
                Is not more smooth and rubious; thy small pipe
                Is as the maiden's organ, shrill and sound,
                And all is semblative a woman's part.

(1. 4. 25–33)

The main point I want to make is that the original Orsino spoke these lines to a young male actor, playing the part of a young woman cross-dressed as a young man. Shakespeare's audience would have had a dizzying series of overlapping ambiguities in view as they watched this play. That boy, as pointed out in Interval 1, would have appeared at the beginning of the play as a convincing woman, and the words of the play would have kept reminding the audience that, whatever s/he looked like, s/he was representing a female. In the extract under discussion, the language plays complex games with the situation. This is another example of the dual vision which pervades the play. The hairless face and high voice that seem to be signs of Cesario's boyish immaturity simultaneously (ironically?) betray Viola's fictional gender. Finally, the phrase 'a woman's part', taken in another sense, foregrounds the theatrical convention, bringing us back to the boy actor. Shakespeare plays similar games with the ambiguity of the cross-dressed boy actor disguised as a man in *The Merchant of Venice* and notably *As You Like It*, where the Epilogue flirtatiously teases male and female spectators about the ambiguous perspective they have on this kind of performance.

But a modern performance cannot duplicate this effect. What you will normally see in a modern production is a woman dressed up as a boy, and I have not yet seen a production which leaves the audience in any doubt about Viola's 'real' gender. In this respect, productions of the last 50 years or so are instructive. In the early part of this period, there was a marked tendency to emphasize Cesario's femininity: even though the actor wore male attire, the cut of the clothes, hairstyle and make-up insisted on our recognizing that we were looking at a woman. In the 1970s some actors moved towards a crop-haired, flat-chested, androgynous version of the character but, as I think the photograph of Harriet Walter in Figure 30 proves, the intention even then was not to fool the spectator, particularly in view of the fact that in the real world this look was highly fashionable. In the 1990s there was a tendency to cast authentically boyish actresses in the part, like Helen Schlesinger in Adrian Noble's production for the RSC (1997–8). The latter development perhaps comes

Figure 30 *Harriet Walter as Viola and Donald Sumpter as Orsino in the Royal Shakespeare Company production of* Twelfth Night *directed by Bill Alexander, 1987. Photo: Alena Melichar.*

closer to the effect created on Shakespeare's own stage, although it is to be doubted whether a modern audience could ever truly share the experience of the first production, because both the conditions of playing and attitudes towards gender and sexuality have undergone profound changes.

This point can be illustrated by close analysis of Cesario's first meeting with Olivia in 1. 5. 149–268. Cesario begins with a rhetorical declamation at line 149, possibly accompanied by a histrionic flourish. There then follows a sustained metaphor of playing in lines 153–165, during which Olivia at one point actually asks Cesario if s/he is an actor. As before, this self-referential language serves to remind the audience of the artifice behind the theatrical illusion, especially the fact that 'comedians' are exclusively male. At the same time, a seventeenth-century audience would be seeing two convincing impersonations of women in Maria and Olivia, next to another boy actor who has persuaded them that he represents a woman earlier in the play, though at present he looks like a boy. In 2. 2 that actor will address them in a soliloquy which harps on the character's status as both male and female at once:

> I am the man ...
> Alas, our frailty is the cause, not we,
> For such as we are made of, such we be.
> ... As I am man,
> My state is desperate for my master's love.
> As I am woman, now, alas the day,
> What thriftless sighs shall poor Olivia breathe!

(2. 2. 23, 29–30, 34–7)

There is a related ambiguity in the idea that Viola has a twin brother. Sebastian may resemble Viola in height and build, and he will probably be wearing identical or similar clothes. But since genuine identical twins are unlikely to be playing the role, he will not be perceived as identical, particularly when he speaks. In contrast, a reader has to understand the idea of twins intellectually, but an audience has to assimilate the fact that the visual experience is in one sense at odds with the conceptual one. Of course, audiences have no difficulty disregarding the evidence of their own eyes, as was shown in the chapter on *A Midsummer Night's Dream*, but what happens is that they subconsciously experience a dual perspective. Oberon is invisible, but they can see him; Viola and Sebastian are identical, but they don't look the same; what is more, the two actors on stage look like boys, but one of them is a woman.

In *Twelfth Night* Shakespeare fuses the identical-twin device with the cross-dressing idea, which is present in both his narrative sources and was conventional in his own theatre, to produce twins of different sexes who are so alike that they are regularly taken for each other. By combining the motifs of cross-dressing and separated twins – which in the sources are used as disconnected means of producing farce and bawdy comedy – Shakespeare embeds the idea of gender ambiguity at the heart of the play. Examining the way the other characters interact with the twins further illuminates the play's determination to explore a range of possibilities.

To this end, have another look at 3. 3 and 3. 4. 276–337, and think carefully about how you would describe the relationship between Sebastian and Antonio.

What strikes me is the way that Antonio's language in both scenes indicates a passionate love for the younger man. He begs to become Sebastian's 'servant', a word routinely appropriated in the period by the man in a heterosexual relationship. Alone, he exclaims 'I do adore thee so', and in 3. 3 he confesses that he has thrown caution to the winds because of love: 'My desire, / More sharp than filèd steel, did spur me forth' (4–5). His love drives him to enter enemy territory, even when he knows it is foolish to do so; like Olivia, he is well aware of the risk he is running, but he cannot control himself. When he thinks he has been betrayed by Sebastian, he suffers all the anguish of a jilted lover: 'But O, how vile an idol proves this god!' (3. 4. 330).

It is up to you to decide what you make of all this, but some background on changing fashions in critical thinking on this play might be helpful. In the early 1970s, it was not possible to conceive of this relationship as anything other than a strong male friendship, which, we were taught, was characteristic of Elizabethan culture. Mainstream performance practice took the lead from academic criticism, downplaying the erotic element in Antonio's feeling for Sebastian. The idea that the relationship might involve sexual desire was just not available, and schoolchildren who sniggered in response to Antonio's language were put firmly in their place by being told they didn't understand the convention. Similarly, earlier critics played down the idea that Shakespeare's sonnets could have any homoerotic content, even though the first 126 of them are unequivocally addressed to a beautiful young man with whom the speaker is in love.

Some critics would explain this attitude as a result of the play being viewed through the lens of the pervasive homophobia of a period that rearranged Shakespeare in its own image. As attitudes to same-sex relationships have become more liberal in many communities, scholars have begun to reassess this whole area of Shakespeare's world. One of the props of previous orthodoxy was that Shakespeare couldn't possibly have meant to deal with a truly homoerotic relationship because his own society regarded such attraction as damnable. Critics like Stephen Orgel (1996) and Jonathan Goldberg (1992) have attempted to prove that this is a gross over-simplification of the situation. While it is true that both religious and legal authority roundly condemned sodomy, evidence is beginning to emerge that there existed a cultural space for homoerotic relationships:

> Despite the anxiety expressed in the antitheatrical literature, despite the institutionalization of marriage and patriarchy, English Renaissance culture, to judge from the surviving evidence, did not display a morbid fear of homoeroticism as such; the love of men for other men was both a fact of life and an essential element of the patronage system.

> (Orgel, 1996, pp.35–6)

If you accept this position, you might feel that Antonio's love functions as yet another basis for a relationship in a play that seems to be exploring different permutations of love and desire. His pursuit of a younger man is thus a kind of counterpart of Olivia's willingness to flout patriarchal attitudes and go after the 'man' she wants instead of meekly obeying authority and waiting to be sought. The device of mistaken identity allows the play to offer a gallery of possibilities as far as relationships are concerned and, indeed, to suggest some that go beyond what was permitted by patriarchal norms. Once again, the carnival spirit allows people to be and do things normally denied them, and there is more than one way of reading the ending of the play. You can see the triumph of traditional marriage as reasserting natural order *or* you can see it as the unnatural imposition of a discipline that suits the established social order.

Authority, both secular and religious, recognized only one channel for sexual expression: heterosexual marriage. At the end of the play, such a model seems to reassert itself, with Olivia's miraculous acquisition of a genuine male indistinguishable from the object of her desire, and Orsino's sudden recognition of Viola's love for him. Yet Viola, unlike Rosalind in *As You Like It*, does not reappear in female dress at the end of the play. Whatever is implied in Orsino's final couplet: 'when in other habits you are seen, / Orsino's mistress, and his fancy's queen' (5. 1. 374–5), what an Elizabethan audience would have seen is a man taking the hand of the boy he loves. And if Sebastian really is so similar to Viola that he will do just as well for Olivia as the 'boy' she knows, is there really any radical difference between men and women? A modern production could signal its questioning of traditional values by drawing attention to the apparent neatness of the play's dénouement; you might take some time to think about how you might do this if you were directing the final scene.

'If this were played upon a stage, now'

It is the experience of theatre that has produced these revelations and, as you may have noticed, the play is full of scenes in which characters consciously mount performances for others for a variety of motives. You might like to go back through the play and make yourself a list of examples. It is in this context that I would like to discuss the most enigmatic figure in the play: Feste, the professional jester. One of the few characters who is not personally involved with anyone else, he is almost an embodiment of that dual vision I have identified as the dominant characteristic of this play. The beginning of Act 3 illustrates the point by the way that he constantly undercuts the language fed to him by Viola, constructing an alternative reality for everything she says. He is well aware of what he is doing:

> To see this age! – A sentence is but a cheverel glove to a good wit, how quickly the wrong side may be turned outward.

> (3. 1. 10–12)

Here he seems to locate the instability of language in the culture of the period, a point which he reiterates a few lines later: 'words are grown so false I am loath to prove reason with them' (21–2). In 4. 2, he provides the most sustained example of the metatheatrical nature of the play, putting on a costume to play Sir Topas and at one point conducting a dialogue with himself to torment Malvolio, after which he exits with a song referring to theatrical conventions in the old morality plays. And in the closing verse of his final song he acts in a manner similar to Puck in his epilogue, calling attention to the imminent transition from the fictional world to the everyday one: 'But that's all one, our play is done, / And we'll strive to please you every day' (5. 1. 394–5).

Some critics see Feste as personifying clear-sightedness in a play that is full of deluded characters. He certainly shows a striking insight into Orsino's nature:

> Now the melancholy god protect thee, and the tailor make thy doublet of changeable taffeta, for thy mind is a very opal. I would have men of such constancy put to sea.

> (2. 4. 72–4)

Yet his characteristic language suggests that clear sight is not a matter of perceiving the truth behind illusion, as has been argued by some, because the play stops short of endorsing any one perspective; instead, there are only alternative illusions. We could also add that while Feste's perception may be clear, his speeches are rarely easy to understand. In this speech, for example, a sentence like 'thy mind is a very opal' is metaphorical and allusive: an audience might reasonably ask how Orsino's mind can be an 'opal'. We may sense that Feste is teasing Orsino, but the precise operation of his humour is always enigmatic. The complexity of Feste's speeches anticipates the Fool in *King Lear*, who exhibits a similar delight in a dense and allusive verbal style. The performance of Feste is the key to the performance of the whole play: make him a jolly professional entertainer and the play becomes a romp; go for a darker interpretation and a shadow falls over the comedy. Anton Lesser, playing him for the Renaissance Theatre Company (1988) as a haunted drunk, suggested nameless horrors lurking somewhere just out of sight, and his desperation pervaded the whole play (see *Royal Shakespeare Company: Great Performances*, 1996). A good exercise to consolidate your knowledge of the play is to try out different strategies for casting and directing this part, and you might like to begin by considering how you would handle the songs.

Although he is not the only musician in the play, Feste's three full-length songs, 'O mistress mine' in 2. 3, 'Come away, come away, death' in 2. 4, and 'When that I was' at the end of the play, make quite an impact in performance. Take another look at them, and try to decide how they function in the play as a whole as well as how you might want to handle them if you were the director.

It is as well to realize at the outset that records of Shakespeare's own practice are too shaky to be of much assistance: 'O mistress mine' is the only one of the three songs for which a contemporary setting (by Thomas Morley) exists, and there is no proof that Morley's version was the one used in Shakespeare's theatre.

One thing that many of you may have noticed is the melancholy element in his songs. 'O mistress mine' is a witty recapitulation of the *carpe diem* (Latin, 'seize the day') tradition, in which the singer's 'mistress' is urged to 'kiss' the singer because 'Youth's a stuff will not endure' (2. 3. 35–48). As Stephen Greenblatt observes, 'There is in this wonderful song, as in all of his jests, a current of sadness' (*The Norton Shakespeare*, p.1767). 'Come away, death' is the prolonged lament of a lover doomed by the cruelty of his beloved. On the other hand, certain factors mitigate the gloom of these songs, because both are manifestations of a highly artificial literary tradition, which gives the actor playing Feste a warrant to sing them with conscious irony. In Noble's production (Figure 31), Stephen Boxer gave a wonderfully camp rendition of 'Come away, death' while dancing the tango with a death's head. On the other hand, if a director wants to accentuate the darker elements in the play, choosing mournful tunes and having the songs sung without accompaniment rather than performed as professional entertainments is another option.

Figure 31 *Scott Handy as Orsino and Stephen Boxer as Feste in the Royal Shakespeare Company production of* Twelfth Night *directed by Adrian Noble, 1997–8. Photo: Zuleika Henry.*

Power and hierarchy

In taking so long to get to the subplot, I am conscious that my response differs markedly from that of many earlier writers on *Twelfth Night*, including John Manningham. It was the scenes involving Malvolio that he thought worthy of comment, and he clearly found them very funny. However, it is possible to see the subplot as also concerned with serious issues, only this time in the realm of class rather than gender.

To begin this topic, I would like you to look back at the first act and focus on the question of social organization. Re-read Act 1 carefully, concentrating on the differences between the households of Orsino and Olivia.

The first point to make is that there are at least two separate domains within the play: there is the household of Orsino and the household of Olivia, and the first act establishes that the chief action of the play will oscillate between them. Orsino's is clearly the grander establishment, as befits the ruler, but apart from that, the organization is quite similar in both places.

Both are based on a hierarchical model, but there is quite a complex network of relationships within that hierarchy, with some subtle social distinctions being suggested by the language. If a production wants to minimize the fantastic in the play, it can exploit the tensions and pettiness of a claustrophobic household. In his first appearance, Duke Orsino is shown as surrounded by people who are there to do his bidding. Valentine and Curio are named, but the mention of 'other Lords' allows as many retainers as the company's budget will stretch to, nor should we forget the musicians who are providing the 'strain' he listens to as the play opens. Subtle use of body language and gesture can create the sense of a real household with all its petty jealousies, backbiting and jockeying for favour.

By 1. 4 a new servant, the page Cesario, has been taken on and is 'like to be much advanced' (2), enjoying the Duke's absolute confidence and being employed on his most personal business. Indeed, the reward offered for a successful mission would be handsome if Viola had really been of the servant class:

> Prosper well in this
> And thou shalt live as freely as thy lord,
> To call his fortunes thine.

> (1. 4. 37–9)

In performance, the company will have to decide how Valentine and the other staff behave towards this new favourite. Are they going to show magnanimity, or convey by covert expression and body language how much they detest the upstart? Or would it be better to combine the two attitudes, with some retainers clearly resentful, but others deciding to butter up the new arrival? The relationship between servants in a house is actually quite important in the play as a whole.

Olivia's household is somewhat more complex, although similar in its basic structure. Maria's status is clarified soon after she appears: 'My niece's chamber-maid' (1. 3. 43). 'Chambermaid' for Shakespeare did not have the connotations of underpaid drudgery that it does in modern usage, and in fact it is made clear later that Maria is a gentlewoman. Nevertheless, it is important to realize that, although her language seems to imply equality with Sir Toby, his birth still sets him above her. His dependence is very different from hers, because he holds his position by virtue of his kinship with Olivia. Modern spectators sometimes miss this point, particularly when Toby is played as a slobbish alcoholic, as is common now – they may wonder how marriage with him could be a desirable reward – but in the society of the play, such a marriage would be a significant step up for Maria. This is implicit in Feste's remark that she deserves the match:

Well, go thy way. If Sir Toby would leave drinking thou wert as witty a
piece of Eve's flesh as any in Illyria.

(1. 5. 23–5)

Feste himself demonstrates the precariousness of the servant's life, reinforcing the
anxiety latent in Viola's question to Valentine about Orsino's constancy. As a fool
who clearly has been associated with the household for some time ('my lord, a fool
that the lady Olivia's father took much delight in' (2. 4. 11–12)), he is still vulnerable
to instant dismissal for being absent without leave. Even if Maria delivers the line
'or to be turned away – is not that as good as a hanging to you?' (1. 5. 15–16) as a
joke, she speaks no more than the truth, because a discharged servant faced bleak
economic consequences.

What is more, the competitive, backstabbing nature of a life in service is very
evident in the scenes involving Olivia's household in Act 1. Malvolio, clearly piqued
that Feste has wormed his way back into favour, tries to publicly humiliate his rival
in the hope of reversing Olivia's decision and, although he fails at this point, his
eminence in the household makes him a dangerous enemy. It is worth looking in
detail at the reasons for the hatching of the plot that ends in his humiliation. **Re-read
2. 3. 78–155 and establish in your own mind the reasons for the hostility of Maria,
Feste, Sir Toby and Sir Andrew towards Malvolio.**

On the surface, the other characters are furious at Malvolio's sanctimonious
interruption of their impromptu party, but the language subtly suggests quite a
complex set of motives. In Maria's case the direct provocation is a threat:

Mistress Mary, if you prized my lady's favour at anything more than
contempt you would not give means for this uncivil rule. She shall
know of it, by this hand.

(2. 3. 109–11)

Her subsequent tirade to her friends reveals a history of mutual loathing between
these two servants of similar rank, though long observation of his behaviour has
alerted her to the fact that he has bold social aspirations. He is a 'time-pleaser' (132),
which in our terms is a sycophant, someone who will say what his master wants to
hear in the hope of gaining promotion by it. This type repeatedly appears in both
comedy and tragedy of the period – Oswald in *King Lear* is a striking example of
such a figure – and is always the target of social criticism. According to Maria,
Malvolio has been preparing for his anticipated rise in the social scale by learning
things that are useful to a courtier ('an affectioned ass that cons state without book
and utters it by great swathes' (132–3)), and it is precisely this knowledge of him
that suggests to her the way to bring him down.

Sir Toby's desire for revenge is even more firmly grounded in class hostility.
Malvolio's rebuke turns the world upside down in that the steward is permitted to
lay down the law to a member of the hereditary aristocracy:

Sir Toby, I must be round with you. My lady bade me tell you
that though she harbours you as her kinsman she's nothing
allied to your disorders. If you can separate yourself and
your misdemeanours you are welcome to the house. If not,
an it would please you to take leave of her she is very
willing to bid you farewell.

(2. 3. 85–90)

Sir Toby, drunk as he is, is fully aware of the implications of what has just been said: 'Art any more than a steward?' (102–3). Feste says little in this scene, but the actor may indicate his approval of these sentiments by his body language: Malvolio's earlier public humiliation of him is more than enough motivation for such an interpretation.

It is important to understand why the conspirators do as they do, because for many modern spectators the plot against Malvolio is the most problematic episode in the play. Late-twentieth-century production history is for the most part at odds with Manningham's perception of the sub-plot as a splendid practical joke, and, in a number of recent productions, its climax has been an uncomfortable experience, undercutting any sense of the restoration of harmony at the end of the play. We need to examine the possible causes of this trend. First, we need to explore the implications of what Malvolio actually does.

Re-read 2. 5 and 3. 4, paying particular attention to performance issues, and consider how far you would accept the notion that Malvolio's behaviour in these two scenes establishes a justification for the fate he suffers later in the play.

I think this question is one where it would be wise to begin by replying 'It very much depends on how the scenes are played'. Malvolio represents the desire to rise dramatically in the social scale by making an advantageous marriage. The motif is a staple of folk and fairy tale as well as of sixteenth-century romance. It is also no different from what Maria is doing, so at first sight it does not seem to warrant such vicious retribution. As I have shown, however, this play mingles romance with elements of something closer to the harshness of real human experience, and one way of seeing Malvolio's fate might be as an expression of collective anxieties about social instability in the early seventeenth century. Maria's plot succeeds because she knows Malvolio so well and, once the bait is taken, the character pours out what are clearly deep-rooted fantasies of self-aggrandizement. Sir Toby is incensed even before Malvolio starts constructing scenarios of humiliation for him, because he instinctively rejects the validity of a servant's elevation to the ruling class. That this kind of rise threatens long-established privilege is made clear once Malvolio starts to think about the delicious possibilities consequent on his marriage:

MALVOLIO	Seven of my people with an obedient start make out for him. I frown the while, and perchance wind up my watch, or play with my – [*touching his chain*] some rich jewel. Toby approaches; curtsies there to me.
SIR TOBY	Shall this fellow live? ...
MALVOLIO	I extend my hand to him thus, quenching my familiar smile with an austere regard of control –
SIR TOBY	And does not Toby take you a blow o' the lips, then?
MALVOLIO	Saying 'Cousin Toby, my fortunes, having cast me on your niece, give me this prerogative of speech' –
SIR TOBY	What, what!
MALVOLIO	'You must amend your drunkenness.'

(2. 5. 52–6, 59–65)

This is funny, but only because Malvolio stands little chance of becoming Olivia's husband. Authority has shifted, the servant corrects the master, the world has turned upside down indeed. In this context, it is worth looking more closely at the implications of the word 'puritan', used three times in 2. 3. 125–31, as well as Feste's comment about how Malvolio 'brought me out o' favour with my lady about a bear-baiting here' at 2. 5. 6–7.

Although Maria initiates the discussion in 2. 3 by claiming that her enemy is 'sometimes ... a kind of puritan' (125), she uses the term rather loosely, as she contradicts her first remark almost immediately with 'The dev'l a puritan that he is, or anything constantly' (131). Certainly Malvolio himself displays none of the religious traits of a caricatured puritan like Ben Jonson's Ananias and Tribulation in *The Alchemist* (1610) or Mistress Underman and the Gossips in Thomas Middleton's *A Chaste Maid in Cheapside* (1613). But in the first years of the seventeenth century the word did not mean the same thing as it would after the 1640s. For Shakespeare and his contemporaries the term had a number of different associations, as Margot Heinemann has shown (1980), and it is not only the puritan as religious separatist or opponent of 'popish' practices that is targeted here. Heinemann quotes a speech made by James I in 1604 in support of the notion that the term 'puritan' could be used 'to define a political as well as a religious alignment' (p.22); looked at from this perspective, Malvolio might be seen as reflecting the rise of a powerful group, which threatened the power of the hereditary ruling class at the same time as attacking its values. The word 'group' can give a misleading sense that puritans shared a coherent agenda; in fact there was a very diverse collection of people who shared this tendency at the beginning of the 1600s, and as yet they had no organized political programme.

Nevertheless, in his dislike of popular entertainment and drinking, Malvolio exhibits the kind of hostility towards the theatre that was characteristic of puritans like the writer Philip Stubbes, whose *Anatomy of Abuses* (1583) is a sustained attack on the immorality he saw in the theatre. Indeed, a significant strand of Shakespeare criticism has identified Malvolio as an anti-festive scapegoat. As Stephen Greenblatt puts it: 'comedy ... depend[s] on a collaborative spirit from which Malvolio conspicuously excludes himself. He is a man without friends' (*The Norton Shakespeare*, p.1764). The point is that a modern audience may see a pathos in Malvolio's incarceration which would not have been apparent to Elizabethan theatregoers like Manningham. For them, Malvolio (whose name means 'ill will') may have richly deserved his humiliation.

So a modern audience can laugh at the incarceration scene only if it refuses to take any of the action in the play seriously, *or* if it sees Malvolio as embodying destructive forces that need to be exorcised. He then becomes a personification of negative elements in society and the audience can laugh at him because they do not perceive him as a fellow human being deserving of their sympathy (Figure 32). From this standpoint, relishing the humiliation of Malvolio serves to exorcise deep-rooted fears about social mobility and anti-festive forces within society.

This observation leads back to a point made about different types of comedy in Chapter 1. I mentioned there the kind of comedy theorized about by Sir Philip Sidney and practised by Ben Jonson, among others. You will remember that both Sidney and Jonson claim that comedy should identify contemporary abuses and, by making people laugh at them, expose them to ridicule. This kind of comedy *needs* the audience to switch off its sympathy with the targets of ridicule and reject what

Figure 32 *Baliol Holloway as Malvolio in the Regents Park, London production of* Twelfth Night, *1934. Photo: Mander and Mitchinson Collection.*

they stand for. At the end of Jonson's *Volpone,* for example, one central character is condemned to rot in prison and the other to end his life in the galleys, but the audience feels little pity for their fate, because the play has consistently excluded the possibility of that kind of emotional response. Was Shakespeare using this comic mode in his subplot in *Twelfth Night*? And was he working in this mode because Malvolio embodied precisely those forces within early modern English society that feared and disliked the theatre as an immoral influence on public behaviour?

Productions in the earlier part of the twentieth century tended to play this plot for laughs, setting the character up as a comic villain at whose fate audiences could jeer in the same way as they would rejoice when Captain Hook gets eaten by the crocodile in J.M. Barrie's *Peter Pan*. Some time around the mid-century this angle began to seem less appropriate, so that by 1969 even Donald Sinden, an actor with a taste for broad comedy, found he had to revise his earlier interpretation of the play after accepting the part in John Barton's production:

> When I reread *Twelfth Night*, however, I soon realised that this was not the play I thought I knew. Troubled, I telephoned John Barton: 'I am afraid you may have to recast Malvolio – I find him tragic.' 'Thank God for that', he replied, 'I thought I would have to talk you round to it.'

(Brockbank, 1985, p.43)

So something seems to have happened to effect a radical change in the way that many people perceive the subplot, something that removes it from what modern sensibilities find comic.

Ian Judge (RSC, 1994–5), for example, was chiefly struck by the vulnerability of the character, so he broke with the tradition that had tended to cast thin men in the role. He used Desmond Barrit, self-dubbed the fattest Malvolio on record, who modelled his interpretation on a Welsh Baptist minister (Figure 33). This Malvolio established a real rapport with the audience in 2. 5, sharing his rapture and his fears with them, and consequently their laughter was affectionate rather than savage. In 3. 4 he was embarrassingly unaware of his grotesque appearance in what resembled a black-and-yellow pavilion, and again the audience saw him as all too human.

Now re-read 4. 2 and think about performing the scene. How far is it possible to play this scene for laughs in a modern production, and what kind of strategies would you employ to maximize its comic potential?

There are two main barriers to the belly-laugh version: the point about the cruelty of the scene, which has already been mentioned, and the fact that, once again, there is a great deal of language that has lost its point for a modern audience. For example, even the humbler members of Shakespeare's audience might have grasped the

Figure 33 *Desmond Barrit as Malvolio in the Royal Shakespeare Company production of* Twelfth Night *directed by Ian Judge, 1994. Photo: Clive Barda/ Performing Arts Library.*

Pythagoras joke at 44–53 in which 'Sir Topas' sets Malvolio a question designed to test whether he is mad or sane. Malvolio seizes on it with relief, giving the answer that ought to have proved his sanity to any orthodox cleric, only to be devastated to find that this priest is a renegade. A modern audience, on the other hand, may miss the point. And how many modern spectators grasp the fact that much of Sir Topas's dialogue is based on the common sixteenth-century belief that a person with symptoms of lunacy is possessed by evil spirits? Because the verbal humour is no longer accessible, a production that wants to be funny will have to work much harder with visual gags, perhaps having Feste make grotesque faces or rude gestures.

Yet if he does this, he exacerbates the element of cruelty and this is the main threat to comedy at this point in the play. And however unpleasant Malvolio has been earlier, it is still difficult not to shudder at the experience conveyed in lines like 'They have laid me here in hideous darkness' (26–7), not to mention the anguish that can be conveyed when the torture is visible in performance.

Of course, it *is* possible for a director to defuse all this tension and play both the sub-plot and the main plot simply for farcical humour in a world where no serious consequences occur, and this is the kind of production I remember from my earliest encounters with the play. Intriguingly, the most recent production I have seen, Noble's for the RSC (1997–8), seems to have reverted to this mode. Yet Malvolio, unlike Egeus in *A Midsummer Night's Dream,* is allowed to express his refusal to be absorbed into the comic closure of the play, stalking off stage with a vow of revenge. As Ralph Berry has argued, it may well have been Shakespeare's intention to end the play with this demolition of the festive spirit:

> The Illyrian world of fulfilled romance, genial comics, and harmless
> pranks metamorphoses into an image of the real world, with its grainy
> texture, social frictions, and real pain inflicted upon real people.

> (Berry, 1981, p.118)

What Malvolio represents may have been temporarily defeated, but his pain promises trouble for the future. What is more, although Shakespeare died long before the extraordinary events of 1642 mentioned in the chapter on *Richard II,* perhaps Malvolio's refusal to be appeased reflects a sense that social frictions in the real world of the early seventeenth century threaten stability to an unprecedented degree.

I hope that this exploration of *Twelfth Night* has extended your thoughts about comedy. I have suggested that this play has strong elements of the romance genre that produce one kind of comedy, but it also uses different comic strategies to target perceived abuses or dangers in a community. To range more widely, you might like to think now about whether it is possible to define certain material as inherently comic or whether pretty well anything is susceptible to comic treatment. One other topic for consideration is whether comedy is more tied to a specific culture than tragedy: you saw, for example, a marked difference in the way that people have responded through the ages to the practical joke plot, and you will no doubt have noticed how quickly verbal humour becomes unintelligible. Finally, you might like at this point to see if you are any closer to formulating a comprehensive definition of the term 'comedy'.

References

Berry, R. (1981) *'Twelfth Night:* the experience of the audience', *Shakespeare Survey,* vol.34, pp.111–19.

Brockbank, P. (ed.) (1985) *Players of Shakespeare: Essays in Shakespearean Performance by Twelve Players with the Royal Shakespeare Company,* Cambridge: Cambridge University Press.

Goldberg, J. (1992) *Sodometries: Renaissance Texts and Modern Sexualities,* Stanford, CA: Stanford University Press.

Heinemann, M. (1980) *Puritanism and Theatre: Thomas Middleton and Opposition Drama under the Early Stuarts,* Cambridge: Cambridge University Press.

Lothian, J.M. and Craik, T.W. (eds) (1975) *Twelfth Night,* The Arden Shakespeare, London and New York: Routledge.

Orgel, S. (1996) *Impersonations: The Performance of Gender in Shakespeare's England,* Cambridge: Cambridge University Press.

Royal Shakespeare Company: Great Performances (1996) vol.1, Edenwood Productions Ltd (video).

MEASURE FOR MEASURE

Chapter 7

Dennis Walder

Aims

The aim of this chapter is to suggest the continuing relevance of *Measure for Measure* by introducing you to some of the main themes and issues of the play, and the sometimes surprising ways they are handled in detail. The pivotal link between power and sexuality is examined as a way of understanding what is usually thought of as the play's enigmatic, yet compelling nature: its disturbing, and sometimes contradictory, qualities. To understand this play is to understand what kind of play it is – neither strictly comedy nor strictly tragedy, but inhabiting the space between.

Introduction

One of the best-known poems of the nineteenth century begins like this:

> With blackest moss the flower-pots
> Were thinly crusted, one and all:
> The rusted nails fell from the knots
> That held the pear to the gable wall.
> The broken sheds look'd sad and strange:
> Unlifted was the clinking latch;
> Weeded and worn the ancient thatch
> Upon the lonely moated grange.
> She only said, 'My life is dreary,
> He cometh not,' she said;
> She said, 'I am aweary, aweary,
> I would that I were dead!'

This is Alfred, Lord Tennyson's 'Mariana' (1830). It offers us a poignant portrait of a lonely, rejected woman, effectively imprisoned in surroundings of neglected rottenness, which serve to emphasize her unfortunate state.

Who was she? That same Mariana who, in Shakespeare's play, *Measure for Measure*, was betrothed to the Duke's deputy, Angelo, subsequently cast off by him as a result of the loss of her dowry upon the high seas, and left to live on, dejectedly, at the 'moated grange' (3. 1. 210–56). In the course of the play, by means of various contrivances initiated by the Duke (who gives us her story), she is eventually brought to a happy end – marriage to Angelo. Whether or not this is really a happy end is a question to take up later. In any case, Tennyson's poem does not enter into it. Instead, what it does is to create, out of a minor character in what was then a relatively unpopular and even unfamiliar Shakespeare play, a strangely compelling image of yearning and despair.

This suggests an attitude which it was typical of the general approach to Shakespeare of the time to encourage: that of treating his plays as if they were about real people. It is as if Mariana were a real woman who happened to be mentioned briefly in *Measure for Measure,* but whom it seems possible to depict more fully if she is taken out of it. This attitude is perhaps not altogether surprising in an age dominated by a conception of realism most evident in the major literary form of the time: the novel. One thing most nineteenth-century novels seemed to do was invite their readers to identify with the characters to an extent which led to them being talked about as if they were real. As anyone who has studied the novels of Charles Dickens, for example, will realize, this involves some difficulties, not least that it tends to make works which are not strictly realistic, but which partake of romance or fantasy, seem aberrant.

But Shakespearean drama is typically a mixed form, a form which often involves highly improbable romance elements, mingled with a deep interest in recognizable, sympathetic emotions and challenging moral issues. This is particularly evident in *Measure for Measure.* The play was apparently written within the basic convention of a Renaissance comedy (its plot is in fact derived from a story in the *Hecatommithi (One Hundred Tales),* a collection of tales by Giraldi Cinthio, 1504–73), that is, within a comic convention of conscious artifice, involving coincidence, unlikely behaviour and a 'happy ending', which usually takes the form of marriage. And it was classed as a comedy in the First Folio. But although it contains wonderfully comic moments, and does end in a batch of marriages, it is also a seriously disturbing work, which explores matters of profound moral concern. We do sympathize with some of the characters, but *intermittently.* This is quite disconcerting. As Arnold Kettle once put it to me:

> In plays like *Twelfth Night* or *As You Like It* the audience isn't bothered by this mixture of conventions nearly as much because the comedies clearly *are* comedies and though you sometimes get an undercurrent of more 'serious' emotion, this is absorbed quite easily into the play. Whereas the marrying off of the couples at the end of *Measure for Measure* is difficult to bring off without a sense of considerable incongruity, for during the play depths have been sounded that continue to reverberate and jar on the comic convention in which the play is written.

(Personal correspondence, 1983)

This may oversimplify *Twelfth Night* and *As You Like It* a little, but it suggests why attempts to categorize the play floundered, until a critic (F.S. Boas in *Shakespeare and his Predecessors,* 1896) came up with the idea of classifying it as a 'problem play' – a name which has stuck.

The term 'problem' was derived from the new, socially aware drama of the 1890s, the drama of Henrik Ibsen and George Bernard Shaw, and at least involved a recognition of *Measure for Measure's* serious, demanding feel. For some, the problem was Shakespeare's own, reflecting a supposed crisis in the author's life; for others, it reflected the supposed cynicism of the Jacobeans. More persuasive nowadays, I think, is the view that the play is a 'problem' in the modern sense of posing powerful and conflicting arguments about moral issues. This is the sense in which most readers, audiences and theatre directors find the play a problem, although (in my view rightly) the term itself is not as popular as it was, say, in the 1950s, when E.M.W. Tillyard's *Shakespeare's Problem Plays* (first published at the beginning of that decade) held sway. According to Tillyard, who himself urged caution about using the term, plays such as *Troilus and Cressida, All's Well That Ends Well* and *Measure for Measure* were 'powerfully united by a serious tone amounting at times to sombreness; they show a strong awareness of evil, without being predominantly pessimistic' (1965, p.13). On *Measure for Measure* in particular, Tillyard attacked earlier critics for judging the main characters 'by the standards of actual life', but then went on to defend his interpretation of the chaste Isabella in terms of a character in a Walter Scott novel (ibid., pp. 118–20).

Recognition of the play's serious moral concern had already produced a number of major studies of *Measure for Measure* by critics such as L.C. Knights (1906–97) and F.R. Leavis (1895–1978) which helped reinstate it as a work to read and perform. At the same time, in reaction to the view that it was darkly problematic, an influential group of scholar–critics began to promote its Christian, even emblematic qualities, stressing Shakespeare's roots in the medieval morality play tradition, and explaining the improbabilities in the Duke's behaviour, for example, as consistent with a notion of him as a God-like figure who is testing his people. G. Wilson Knight provided the most striking example of this approach in *The Wheel of Fire* (1930). Nobody can deny the religious, indeed specifically Christian, elements in the play –including its title, which is derived from Matthew 7:1–2: 'Judge not, that ye be not judged. For with what judgement ye judge, ye shall be judged: and with what measure ye mete, it shall be measured to you again.' But most critics today, myself included, would argue that a complete interpretation of the play in these terms simply leaves too much out.

My own feeling is that what is most important to grasp about *Measure for Measure* is that it is a play liable to upset and disturb in a radical way, because it is about things which still matter deeply to us in our everyday lives nearly four centuries later. This is not to deny its comic elements, much less the overall comic convention, according to which 'All's Well That Ends Well'. But, like *that* play, *Measure for Measure* has too much that is deeply troubling and incongruous for us to leave it at that. The play is a very special mixture of convention and realism in the broad sense that obliges us to ask questions about private and public morality, and the link between them, going way beyond what seems appropriate to the comedy genre. We have to admit that this is a play that ultimately cannot be categorized in the terms with which we are familiar.

What then can we do? I want to argue in what follows that we can at least establish with a fair degree of certainty what the play is about, and how it expresses what it is about. It seems to me to be a play about sexuality, power and justice, and the relations between them. These matters are central and, I believe, their very centrality largely accounts for the sharp oppositions of view, the difficulties, the 'problem', which *Measure for Measure* seems to have generated – and indeed continues to generate, because these are matters about which it is hard to agree. Furthermore, since the play takes these matters to *extremes* (a woman who seems to prefer her chastity to her brother's life; a man sentenced to death for fornication; and so on), these disagreements are likely to be strong.

What I shall do here, then, is deal with each of these topics or themes in turn, leaving it to you to expand on, or differ from, what I have said. You will see that, although I have drawn a little upon the relevance of the play to Shakespeare's time, my main aim is to show that it is important and relevant for modern audiences. For this reason, my discussion is organized in such a way as to move from the issues which seem to me most obviously and broadly present – the issues of power and authority and justice – towards an issue which may seem less obvious at first, but which is undoubtedly the subject of intense topical debate today: the position of women. These themes are connected, but it may be helpful to separate them to some extent. They are also connected by the interest they held for Shakespeare's contemporaries, as recent scholars and critics have ably demonstrated. But before you read them, you should feel sure that you have a grip on the main themes.

Before going any further, read the play through quickly at least once, if you have not already done so, to get the gist of it. The plot is easy enough to follow; it is the *meaning* of what is going on that is not so straightforward. How do we respond to the strange, complex tone of particular words, lines, passages and scenes? This question is implicit throughout, and will be taken up from time to time during my discussion of its themes. But, as you will see, I have kept in mind the performance aspect of the play throughout my discussion.

Measure for Measure *and 'government'*

Consider the opening speech of the play (1. 1. 3–22): what does it tell us immediately about the subject of *Measure for Measure?* What direction does it suggest the play is going to take?

As you would expect, the speech has an expository function: setting in motion the story or plot at the same time as it reveals some preliminary information about the character or characters who are to be involved in that plot. So here we have the Duke of Vienna announcing his intention to leave the city and appoint a deputy, Angelo, to govern it in his place. One of his deputies, Escalus, has long experience of the necessary skills, but the Duke has 'with special soul / Elected' Angelo 'our absence to supply' – a man with a reputation for virtue, it seems. Appropriately for a ruler making a public speech before his court or retinue, the Duke talks in formal, even grand tones, the roundabout syntax of his rhetoric enabling him to begin with the key phrase, 'Of *government* the properties to unfold / Would seem in me t'affect speech and discourse' (emphasis added).

But why should it seem 'affected' in him to 'discourse' about such a subject, about the 'properties' or qualities required to govern or control a state?

It might appear affected because, if anybody ought to know about how to govern, it is the Duke. And yet, at the same time, he is suggesting that his deputy Escalus has a level of 'science' or knowledge of the question of government that exceeds his own. Surely, therefore, if he intends to leave his court, he should commission Escalus to replace him? He does not. Indeed, his opening speech hints at a somewhat stilted, actorish ruler. All in all, his opening speech does not inspire confidence in his authority. And, as we soon learn, the younger and less experienced deputy himself asks that 'there be some more test made of my metal' (48) before the exalted stamp of the Duke's position and authority be put upon him. Nevertheless, the Duke departs with alacrity.

The 'properties' of 'government' are placed under question from the start. Who controls the state, and how and how well he does so, are what we are to consider, and what make us want to know where the play is going to take us from here. Identifying with the character of the Duke hardly comes into it. Or does it? In any case, when, at the end of the play, the Duke resumes authority, and the attributes of his rule, the 'terror' and 'love' with which he has 'dressed' Angelo, revert to his keeping, it is only after the widest range of responses to 'government' on the part of governors and governed have been tested and explored – including even those ungovernable low-life characters we meet in Act 4.

The real starting point in a performance is not necessarily given by the first words uttered on stage. The cast has to appear, and the nature of that appearance – their movements, dress, gestures – all constitute the opening. Here, as with most of Shakespeare's plays, we have hardly any stage direction to go by, simply: *'Enter DUKE, ESCALUS, [and other] lords'*, which we could have assumed ourselves from the dialogue. We have to interpret the dialogue to imagine how a performance would look in practice. This is less difficult than it seems, because Shakespeare provides guidance to flesh out at least the bare essentials of the scene. It does not take much imagination to realize that *Measure for Measure* begins with a display of power and authority: a ruler enters with members of his court. The Duke we would expect to be distinguished from the rest by a crown (a standard prop), and a garment signifying his superior position in the government of the state; but also, since he is about to depart and hand over to Angelo, we expect him to be wearing, say, a travelling cloak, or something indicating what he intends.

If it seems excessive to try to imagine in such detail how the play begins on stage, you might recall that the next time we see the Duke, he asks *to be disguised* as a friar (1. 3). To appear as a friar is to adopt the garb of another authority: that of the church. In fact it is to do much more than that, because for contemporary Protestants it was the garb of a questionable, Popish authority – it was a commonplace to represent hypocrites and 'fornicators' as Catholic clerics, and most frequently friars, upon the stage. The disguised Duke goes on to exercise that suspect authority when he attends at the prison during Act 3, although what he does there goes beyond the simple exercise of a religious role. But to begin with, the adoption of this disguise suggests an abdication of authority – hence the *real* Friar's presumption, implicit in the Duke's first words of 1. 3, that he (the Duke) will adopt a disguise to further some love-errand. Traditionally, men disguised themselves as friars for clandestine purposes, using the holy garb as a useful means of getting about where they might otherwise arouse suspicion, although by the late sixteenth century the implications had become more than a little dubious. Nevertheless, love will be a matter of some importance to the Duke, if not at this stage of the action.

What, then, is most important when the Duke reappears? What does his exchange with Friar Peter in 1. 3 reveal?

Briefly, it reveals a motive for the Duke's otherwise inexplicable behaviour at the beginning of the play, summed up by his concluding remark: 'Hence shall we see / If power change purpose, what our seemers be' (1.3. 53–4). The rhyming 'see' and 'be' seem to clinch it: the Duke has relinquished his authority to test what effect power has on those to whom it is delegated. The new deputy's behaviour is by no means a foregone conclusion; on the contrary, the Duke's words imply that the appearance of virtue which has been ascribed to Angelo may be found to be just that – an appearance, not a reality. But for this to emerge, Angelo has to be given the chance to govern.

What else does the Duke's conversation reveal? It seems that he himself has been an indifferent governor; indeed, he has delegated authority to Angelo in order to reinforce the 'strict statutes' and 'most biting laws' which he has for these fourteen years 'let slip', so that Vienna is now approaching a condition of moral anarchy ('liberty' means 'licence', 'licentiousness'):

> And Liberty plucks Justice by the nose,
> The baby beats the nurse, and quite athwart
> Goes all decorum.

> (1. 3. 29–31)

The impudence of 'plucking by the nose', and the baby beating the nurse, while fitting for the idea of a ruler as father, has a quite serious dimension, suggested by the Duke's use of the word 'decorum'. It is a word of much resonance in Shakespeare's works. Perhaps the most profound expression of the consequences of the disruption of 'decorum' is to be found in *King Lear*.

Hence the time has come to enforce the laws and restore order. But rather than do so himself, the Duke argues that such a sudden change of policy in him might appear arbitrary, and so, he says,

> I have on Angelo imposed the office,
> Who may in th'ambush of my name strike home,
> And yet my nature never in the fight
> T'allow in slander.

> (1. 3. 40–3)

These lines may not seem easy to understand at first sight. At least it should be clear that the Duke is justifying his action, on the grounds that remaining out of sight while Angelo does the dirty work will preserve him from discredit. **Is this justification convincing?**

I would say yes and no. In the first place, it is significant that the Duke implicitly separates the *source* of his authority – his 'office', his 'name' or status – from his *nature* or person. He can 'impose' his role upon another precisely because he sees it as detachable from himself and his personal, moral nature. This raises the question of what 'nature' is required in a ruler; and it raises the further question of whether the Duke could be said to exhibit such a nature. Moreover, there is the question of whether the man upon whom the Duke has devolved his authority, Angelo, has this nature too.

Now if the Duke, as he says, wishes to protect his reputation by allowing Angelo to 'strike home' against corruption in the state, and so take all the consequent 'slander' upon himself, leaving the Duke free, his 'name' untarnished, this is surely rather a devious way to set about it. Is he, too, a 'seemer'? The appropriate word for it might be 'practice' – a loaded word, used in the Duke's opening speech to Escalus (1.1.12) and again in 3. 1. 494, to refer to Angelo, but applicable also to his own behaviour.

For contemporary audiences it would have suggested political cunning, and would probably have reminded them of that master of the craft of politics, Niccolo Machiavelli (1469–1527), whose treatise *The Prince,* which taught that the effective use of power might necessitate unethical methods, had been selectively translated into French and was well known to the Elizabethans and Jacobeans.

But does the Duke's 'practice' work? The answer takes us to the heart of *Measure for Measure,* and the pivot of its action: the testing of Angelo's authority, and his moral right to govern Vienna, by means of Isabella's appeal to him on behalf of Claudio, her condemned brother. We cannot, strictly speaking, assume that condemnation itself is an abuse of his position because, as the Duke's remarks have made clear, the law was there, but had not been enforced – especially in relation to sexual behaviour. (If it seems an absurd law, remember that we are dealing with an unrealistic plot – although there are fundamentalists who might disagree.) Angelo may simply be seen as a 'strict deputy' compared with, say, Escalus who, as their exchange at the beginning of 2. 1 reveals, is of a more forgiving nature ('Let us be keen, and rather cut a little / Than fall and bruise to death'). The crucial element is suggested by Angelo's remark alluding to the title of the play, a remark which will be repeated (although not in the same words) later: 'Let mine own judgement pattern out my death, / And nothing come in partial' (2. 1. 30–1). His own behaviour, he says, should be subject to the same strictness: it should be measured by the same measure.

As we know from the rest of the play, Angelo fails this test, offering to ransom the life he has condemned in exchange for Isabella's chastity. And he subsequently makes things even worse for himself, morally, by ordering that Claudio be speedily executed even after, as he believes, Isabella has submitted to him. But, at the first sign that Angelo's ability to govern is compromised, the Duke begins to reassert his power in secret, starting with the 'bed-trick' by which Angelo's rejected Mariana replaces Isabella, and culminating in his carefully arranged reappearance in Act 5.

What I am suggesting is that the nature of authority, and the proper exercise of the power that goes with it, is central to *Measure for Measure.* This is made quite clear during the confrontation between Angelo and Isabella in 2. 2. Of course there are other issues at stake, which we will come to later, such as the nature of justice and the impact of personal desire, and sexuality, upon the situation.

But let us first consider the play's concern with the question of what makes the good governor – a term with special resonance in Shakespeare's time, as a result of such hugely influential works on the subject as Sir Thomas Elyot's *The Book Named the Governor* (1531) and Sir Thomas Hoby's translation of Castiglione's *The Book of the Courtier,* first published in 1561. It is important to remember that texts such as Shakespeare's communicate with other texts and with the whole complex of culture at the time. In understanding a play in the present, we need also to consider what it seems to have signified at the time – in so far as we can reach an understanding of that, through the documents available to us.

Where exactly, in the key scene between Angelo and Isabella in Act 2, Scene 2, lines 26 onward, does the question of the nature of the 'governor' become overt? And what does the scene reveal about power and its use?

Figure 34 *John Gielgud as Angelo and Barbara Jefford as Isabella in the Shakespeare Memorial Theatre, Stratford production of* Measure for Measure *directed by Peter Brook, 1950. Photo: Angus McBean/ Harvard Theatre Collection.*

Figure 35 *Gillian Barge as Isabella and Julian Curry as Angelo in the National Theatre production of* Measure for Measure *directed by Jonathan Miller, 1974. Photo: Sophie Baker.*

Isabella arrives to face Angelo as someone who has given up – or rather, is about to give up – the world for a life dedicated to God. She faces the representative of earthly power, and attempts to persuade him to alter his judgement. It is a rich and complex moment, interpreted in production in many different yet often equally persuasive ways (compare, for example, Figures 34 and 35). But the importance of the issue of 'government', or the moral right to exercise power, is surely unquestionable. 'I would to heaven I had your potency', exclaims Isabella, challenging Angelo's 'potency' as a ruler even as she does so (and, perhaps, on a less conscious level, as we may later think, his 'potency' as a man). Angelo argues that his 'were the very cipher of a function' (an empty, powerless position) if he agreed to condemn Claudio's fault, but release the man himself from the charge, as she asks. But Isabella goes on to suggest that the exercise of authority is not the same as wielding power:

> O, it is excellent
> To have a giant's strength, but it is tyrannous
> To use it like a giant.

> (2. 2. 109–11)

True authority, she contends, involves the *proper* use of power. The distinction between proper and improper uses of power is crucial, and Isabella drives her point home, taking the initiative from Angelo as she does so:

> Could great men thunder
> As Jove himself does, Jove would never be quiet,
> For every pelting petty officer

> (2. 2. 113–15)

would go thundering away all the time. It is for the supreme authority to exercise supreme power, not 'man, proud man', who,

> Dressed in a little brief authority,
> Most ignorant of what he's most assured,
> His glassy essence, like an angry ape
> Plays such fantastic tricks before high heaven
> As makes the angels weep.

> (2. 2. 121–5)

Not surprisingly, Angelo is silenced. Lucio, the Provost and Isabella herself all speak before he is able to reply. How should he look as they do so? His response becomes noticeably defensive: 'Why do you put these sayings upon me?' he eventually asks. 'Because', Isabella replies, 'authority' – by which she evidently means *real* or justifiable authority, as opposed to his false authority –

> ... though it err like others,
> Hath yet a kind of medicine in itself
> That skins the vice o'th'top.

> (2. 2. 137–9)

And this 'medicine' involves self-examination:

> Go to your bosom;
> Knock there, and ask your heart what it doth know
> That's like my brother's fault.

(2. 2. 139–41)

Only by knowing his own nature, and facing up to what is there, can Angelo justify his own exercise of power. Self-government is a part of government. Angelo cannot know how to run the state if he does not know how to run himself. Excessive strictness in one is mirrored by excessive strictness in the other; and both are revealed in this play as a futile attempt to control what seems 'naturally' uncontrollable – in Lucio's memorable phrase, 'the rebellion of a codpiece' (3. 1. 358–9).

The Duke, of course, is said by the apparently reliable Escalus to have been one who, 'above all other strifes, contended especially to know himself (3. 1. 456–7); and Angelo is obliged by his sudden attraction to the pleading Isabella to realize that he has not known himself: 'what art thou, Angelo?' (2. 2. 177). But knowing yourself is not enough; it is how you act upon that knowledge that matters, and instead of relinquishing his authority when he realizes that he has become totally unfit to rule ('Thieves for their robbery have authority, / When judges steal themselves' (180–1)), he goes on to blackmail Isabella into giving herself up to him. The misuse of power becomes absolute, when Angelo not only proceeds (*as he believes*) to 'seduce' Isabella, but also decides to have her brother executed anyway to hide his tracks. Ironically, the Duke has placed Angelo in his own position only to witness things becoming more seriously corrupt than they had ever been. If, like an indulgent parent (as he referred to himself in his exchange with Friar Peter in 1. 3), the Duke has allowed things to slip, he has remained above the corruption evident in the state – or so it seems.

When the Duke stands before the assembled crowd at the opening of Act 5, still dressed as a friar and so, on one level, speaking with moral and religious if not secular authority, while on another opening that authority to all kinds of questions, he simply reiterates his earlier charge:

> My business in this state
> Made me a looker-on here in Vienna,
> Where I have seen corruption boil and bubble
> Till it o'errun the stew; laws for all faults,
> But faults so countenanced that the strong statutes
> Stand like the forfeits in a barber's shop,
> As much in mock as mark.

(5. 1. 310–16)

It seems that the severest penalties that the law might impose have become as familiar and unthreatening as 'forfeits'. But the fact that the Duke has said all this before and, moreover, that he does not mention Angelo and Isabella at this point, somewhat undermines his attack, as does his highly suspect choice of a friar's garb. Perhaps we should take his remarks as a formal announcement, prior to his crafty attempt to bring things round satisfactorily as he emerges in his 'true' figure as the ruler, that it is insufficient simply to have laws, since the question remains: who is willing and able to enforce them, and how?

During Act 4, the Duke has been exerting his power against Angelo's machinations (you might look at Scenes 2–4 to see exactly where this is revealed). Then, when he is finally unveiled, he stands revealed as, after all, the rightful authority come to restore order and justice to the state – in terms which suggest a religious or at least transcendent dimension ('like power divine' remarks Angelo at 5. 1. 361). The stunning impact on stage of this change in the ruler should not be forgotten; equally, it should not be forgotten that this happens only after the Duke's authority has been seriously questioned: indeed, so seriously that we must feel his position is compromised, despite the apparent restoration at the end.

Earlier, more religiously inclined critics, such as G. Wilson Knight, see the Duke's implausibility or arbitrariness as consistent with, or at least explicable in terms of, his allegorical or Christian role. Countering this (very influential) view, A.D. Nuttall (1968) found the Duke irresponsible and inept, having ruled Vienna badly, then placing a dubious deputy in charge to repair the damage, to carry on himself like an unctuous fraud in disguise. **The editor of the Penguin text, J.M. Nosworthy, goes so far as to suggest that 'in the purely political context, the Duke is no less reprehensible than Angelo' (1969, p.21). Would you agree?**

If so, we have reached a remarkable position. The Duke seemed (and may still seem to some) to represent goodness, Angelo the forces of evil – to put it at its starkest. So how can he be 'no less reprehensible' than his deputy? Of course, it depends what we understand by 'purely political'. To my mind, it is impossible to draw a line between the 'purely political' and everything else – either in life or in *Measure for Measure*. 'Government' involves matters of personal as well as communal morality. There is nothing 'pure' about it, certainly not in this play. Nor was the separation of these spheres of life something that Shakespeare's audiences would have accepted; on the contrary, it was precisely the point of intense interest.

Very early on in *Measure for Measure* the association of private and public is firmly established. Can you identify *where*, exactly?

I would say we realize with some force the impossibility of separating the most intimate, private concerns from public life when we learn in 1. 2 that a man called Claudio has been arrested and is to be executed, no less, for getting Juliet 'with child'. As Mistress Overdone says, 'Why here's a change indeed in the commonwealth' (1. 2. 85–6), since the immediately preceding scene concluded merely with the two deputies, Escalus and Angelo, agreeing to discuss further the 'strength and nature' of the authority delegated to them (1. 1. 79–80).

Most striking is Claudio's reaction to his sudden condemnation:

> Thus can the demigod Authority
> Make us pay down for our offence, by weight,
> The bonds of heaven. On whom it will, it will;
> On whom it will not, so; yet still 'tis just.

> (1. 2. 100–3)

The last lines are difficult, partly because they hide an allusion familiar to an audience better versed in the Bible than we are: an allusion to Romans 9:15 and 18, concerning the authority of God. The point seems to be that Claudio accepts his condemnation, even though (as he goes on to explain) he and Juliet were betrothed 'upon a true contract': he cannot argue against 'authority', which has behind it the sanction of heaven.

But we are not left there – any more than we are in the history plays, in which even the anointed king may be shown as unfit to rule and liable to be deposed. The phrase 'the demi-god, authority' may be uttered so as to sound rather belittling; it is not *quite* the term likely to be used by someone overawed by the justice of the power that has just sentenced him to death for getting his fiancee pregnant. Claudio goes on to explain to the lecherous Lucio that his plight proceeds from 'too much liberty', which seems once again to confirm his self-condemnation, as well as the looseness of the city's morals in general. **Or does it? Re-read 1. 2. 104–10, and consider the effect of these lines in the light of my discussion. Do they confirm the judgement of authority, and so by implication the Duke's action in handing over the reins to Angelo? Or do they undermine it?**

Something of both, I would suggest. The tensions of this speech sharpen tensions we have experienced throughout the play between 'liberty' and 'restraint'. The repellent impression of human behaviour implied by the image of rats devouring poison is modified by the contradictory notion that it is, after all, in our nature to be thirsty and so to drink.

To follow our appetites beyond the limits of the 'natural' law may lead to destruction; and syphilis, as the external manifestation of this 'excess' at the time, provides a pervasive current of imagery for the play, touching even the Duke, who is accused by Lucio of being a 'bald-pated lying rascal', not showing his 'visage', with 'a pox' to it (5.1. 345–6). But at the same time, following appetite is a tendency 'proper' to humanity, an urge that craves free satisfaction and which we cannot, even if we should so desire, hope to suppress. Hence the revelation to Angelo of his own desires; hence, too, the revelation (to us, if not to her) of Isabella's desires. But these revelations do not leave us with a clear idea of how 'natural' desires may be safely and fruitfully controlled, expressed or 'governed'.

Rather, what does emerge is a clear sense that 'government' has deeply personal as well as political overtones. Hence Claudio's further speculations about the reasons for Angelo's resuscitation of the 'enrolled penalties', which have so long remained unused:

> Whether the tyranny be in his place,
> Or in his eminence that fills it up –
> I stagger in.

> (1. 2. 140–3)

Yet he goes on to conclude that it must be 'for a name', that is, for his reputation as a ruler. Poor Claudio! Power for him is not something abstract or metaphysical, unfortunately. It is here and now, a confluence of particular personal, social and historical factors. His situation – especially as it emerges in the prison scenes in Act 3 – makes us feel this acutely. That he should be ambivalent about authority is so understandable, so human: on the one hand, guiltily aware that he has broken the moral law and so, according to the new dispensation, the civil law as well, and yet also feeling that it must be wrong to be so condemned, 'to die, and go we know not where' (3. 1. 118 onwards). He does not wish to question the government by which he is ruled, yet he cannot help doing so. If we identify with anyone in *Measure for Measure*, it is surely Claudio, above all when he is given these justly famous lines sharply and movingly expressing the fear of death, overwhelming his sister's pleas.

This takes me to the root of the politics of the play, and the reason why the Duke's behaviour is at times questionable, although it is obviously Angelo's which is the more reprehensible, since his becomes tyrannical. *Measure for Measure* expresses a profound anxiety about the nature of the ruler, a feeling which, I would argue, cannot altogether be erased by the *apparently* satisfactory resolution at the end. The instability of the seat of authority is visible right up to the last moments of the play, when we watch the Duke, disguised, place Angelo there to 'be ... judge / Of your own cause' (5. 1. 165–6), and the deputy does indeed 'find this practice out' (236), that is, the machinations of the hidden power behind it all, the Duke. Stress is laid upon the *justice* of the *results,* as we shall see in the next section; but 'practice', in the sense of dubious behind-the-scenes manipulation, has been involved.

Why should this play leave us in such a state of uncertainty? It is sometimes forgotten that the production of a play involves not only questions of cast, costume, dialogue, setting and so on, but that it is also an event, in a particular place at a particular time. This is important. We do not know exactly when and where most of Shakespeare's plays were performed, but the evidence includes the information that, according to the authoritative Revels Accounts, 'Mesur for Mesur' by 'Shaxberd' was performed in the Banqueting Hall of Whitehall on 26 December 1604 by 'his Majesties plaiers'. In other words, the play was performed at Court before the king, James I, whose reign had begun the preceding year, on the death of Elizabeth. Some supposed topical allusions in the play – the Duke's aversion to the popular gaze (1.1. 67–72) or Mistress Overdone's 'what with the war, what with the sweat ... I am custom-shrunk' (1. 2. 72–4) – have been taken to suggest that it was written and performed during the summer season of 1604, when the theatres re-opened after the plague. It is improbable that James did not like the popular gaze, since his first act on succeeding Elizabeth was to proceed in leisurely fashion through his kingdom from Edinburgh to the capital. But he arrived in London in July 1603 to find he had to bar the public from his crowning ceremony and cancel the customary royal procession because of the spread of the plague. The performance, if not the writing, of Shakespeare's play may be said to have been rather well-timed in dealing with a ruler hidden from his people, who works unseen by them, before finally making a triumphant reappearance. Furthermore, this was a ruler whose Chief Justice was then coming down very hard on the brothels of London.

We may suppose James was aware of the play and interested in its concerns, both as the ruler of a people who did not yet know him, and as a man whose interest in government was obvious. Several years earlier (in 1598) he had written a study of the subject, entitled *Basilikon Down* ('The King's Gift'). He was, moreover, a follower of drama, who quickly took Shakespeare's company, previously known as the Chamberlain's Men, under his direct patronage as the King's Men, or Players. James brought with him a conception of government which he soon made known: 'The state of monarchy', he informed his parliament, 'is the supremest thing upon earth. For kings are not only God's lieutenants upon earth and sit upon God's throne, but even by God himself they are called gods' (Hurstfield, 1971, p. 176). He was reinstating the old concept of the divine right of kings to assert his prerogative over the House of Commons and extend his powers. (It was a short-lived prerogative: a generation later his son, Charles I, was to be tried and executed.) What can be sensed in the writings at this time of everyone, from dramatists such as Shakespeare to political and legal theorists such as Lord Chief Justice Coke, is a rise in tension, an awareness of extremes whose reconciliation seemed less and less likely. Moderation or 'measure' (another word for it) in relations between ruler and ruled may have been strongly desired; but the likelihood of its appearance was doubtful, especially in the light of the uncertainties which were felt about King James's own moral nature.

In Shakespeare's play the Duke's departure leads to a disorder which seems to be resolved when he resumes his rightful place as head of state; but there are overtones to his actions which suggest that all is not quite as simple as that, overtones which create a hovering uncertainty about the play's conclusion. We do not, indeed cannot, know how far these uncertainties arose out of contemporary circumstances and assumptions, but they probably did. Shakespeare was evidently a dramatist acutely interested in the live issues of his day; the enduring appeal of his work lies in the fact that these issues continue to trouble and disturb us. This should become more apparent in what follows, when I take up another theme of the play – justice.

Measure for Measure *and justice*

When the Duke defines the properties required to govern in his opening speech, he explains that Escalus is 'as pregnant in' their 'art and practice' as any; the older deputy knows

> The nature of our people,
> Our city's institutions and the terms
> For common justice.

(1. 1.9–11)

Justice is the link between private and public morality, the cement which holds government and people together. Its significance as a theme in *Measure for Measure* has already been suggested, for instance in considering Claudio's position and his plea. But let us look at it a little more closely. **What kind of justice does the play in the end seem to advocate? What is its relationship with mercy? It has been said (by a modern lawyer, John Mortimer) that 'Man's justice and natural justice, and the eternal conflict between them, is what Shakespeare's *Measure for Measure* is all about' (1982, p.74). Do you agree?**

First of all, it is worth stating a fundamental point: that *Measure for Measure* is the *kind* of play which seems to give rise to such apparently abstract questions. But they are only *apparently* abstract; as we have seen, there is nothing abstract about the punishment of death for fornication, and the play makes us feel this very sharply in the scenes concerning Claudio. Nevertheless, as should be obvious, this does not mean that Claudio's case is simply an instance of rampant misjudgement. If he questions the nature of the authority which has judged him, he does not, indeed cannot, question the strict justice of the judgement, since that is the law (which is not so absurd, if we recall the position of some fundamentalists and puritans then and now). He does not deny his guilt: as the Duke reports, after talking to Claudio in prison, 'He professes to have received no sinister measure from his judge, but most willingly humbles himself to the determination of justice ... and now is he resolved to die' (3. 1. 465–70).

Nor does Isabella deny his guilt, although she clarifies exactly how far that guilt extends, in almost the last words she utters in the play: 'My brother had but justice, / In that he did the thing for which he died' (5. 1. 440–1). And she began that scene by crying out for 'justice, justice, justice, justice!' (25) against Angelo, who has been the judge. She wants him to be judged or measured by the same standards of justice as her brother.

Again, as the role or function of a ruler has been distinguished from his nature, so the role of judge is to be distinguished from his nature. Otherwise how could Angelo become subject to justice, after having justly condemned Claudio? Angelo has enforced the law, because it is the law. Should a judge do more? Clearly, yes, if the judge's personal qualities necessarily come into it.

Let us give Angelo his due: if we consider the opening of Act 2, we will see him arguing with Escalus about the condemnation of Claudio in terms that are fairly persuasive. **Can you summarize his argument, and that put against it by Escalus? Re-read in particular lines 1–31.**

'We must not make a scarecrow of the law', Angelo begins, and it is a formidable argument, given what we have already heard about the corruption of the city, dramatically established by Lucio and his friends' talk about erasing the commandment which does not suit you, or Mistress Overdone and Pompey's enthusiasm for their brothels in the suburbs. Justice must be seen to be done, and Claudio is to be made an example of the reinforcement of the laws that had been allowed to slip by the Duke. Moreover,

> I do not deny
> The jury passing on the prisoner's life
> May in the sworn twelve have a thief or two
> Guiltier than him they try. What knows the law
> That thieves do pass on thieves? What's open made to justice,
> That justice seizes.

> (2. 1. 18–23)

Escalus, on the other hand, argues on general humanitarian grounds: let us 'cut a little', not so much; after all, Claudio had 'a most noble father'; and, more persuasively – and ironically, in retrospect – had 'time cohered with place, or place with wishing', who knows whether Angelo himself might not have fallen to temptation in the same situation (2. 1. 5, 7 and 11). Anyone may sin; so no man should be condemned. Angelo's response seems to be that of a man of integrity: 'Let mine own judgement pattern out my death, / And nothing come in partial. Sir, he must die' (30–1). As we see at the end of the play, he is consistent: when the full depth of his depravities is revealed, he pleads not for mercy, but for death.

Yet this is refused him. There is a higher value, and that is mercy (which is where a Christian reading of the play begins to become persuasive). For us to feel the full strength of this, however, it is necessary to feel the full strength of Angelo's own viewpoint. Hence, even when he is confronted by Isabella, arguing on behalf of Claudio, he is made to put his case persuasively. It is notable that Shakespeare's play does not take us straight into the famous exchange between them, after the anticipatory remarks made at the beginning of 2. 1; instead, a brilliantly comic scene-within-a-scene is offered. **Can you see why? What purpose is served by what happens from line 41 to the end of 2. 1?**

Measure for Measure is a great play of duets, as producers of it (in the theatre and for television) have long recognized: between Isabella and Angelo, Claudio and Isabella, the Duke and Claudio, and so on. We have just experienced another, between Escalus and Angelo; but here the drama opens out momentarily to embrace a wider range of characters and moods, before closing in again to concentrate with increasing intensity upon the two major protagonists, Angelo and Isabella.

What we see is a whole state apparatus, treated comically (and perhaps subversively), in contrast to the main plot. Angelo and Escalus turn their attention to another case: one brought by Elbow the constable and concerning yet another sexual misdemeanour. It seems that Pompey, Mistress Overdone's 'parcel-bawd', now running a 'hot-house' (the Jacobean equivalent of a 'massage-parlour') since the brothels have been closed down by Angelo's proclamation, has attempted to procure Elbow's wife for one Master Froth, 'a foolish gentleman' as his name would suggest. Pompey, one of Shakespeare's great comic creations, represents the pragmatic fact that sexual activity will go on, even if regulation of it is desirable (it is worth looking at his several later appearances to evaluate this point). He is also given a memorable line to defend the right of underdogs like himself and his associates to survive, whatever their rulers of any moral stripe wish or say: 'Truly, sir, I am a poor fellow that would live', he responds to Escalus's interrogation (2. 1. 199). The scene as a whole dissolves into a farrago of stewed prunes and malapropisms, until Angelo leaves in impatience, hoping Escalus will find 'good cause to whip them all'. But Escalus is unable to disentangle everything, and lets them off with a conditional discharge.

As always in this play, there is a solemn matter here, too: society clearly must have laws, but how are they to be administered? Is Escalus too lax, while Angelo is too severe? Are both of them threatened by the subversive potential of the welter of tavern and bawdy-house life represented here? Angelo's peremptory exit, as if unable to take any decisive action – which he leaves to *his* deputy, Escalus – may strike us as an implied admission of weakness. What Pompey has to say for himself is highly significant: when Escalus interrogates him about his trade – 'Is it a lawful trade?' – his reply is 'If the law would allow it, sir' (201–2). If Angelo makes the law an absolute, implying that it is above human frailty, Pompey implies that it is no more than an arbitrary human invention, which could be changed at will. Again, we look for a mean between these extremes, but where is it to be found? Not, apparently, in Angelo or Isabella. The two of them, like the Duke, and perhaps even Claudio, tend to dominate discussion of the play; but this voice, these voices, should be listened to as well. They represent a humorous and humane view, which runs like a thread through *Measure for Measure*, even appearing in the concluding scene when Lucio, irrepressible and (I believe this is how he should be played) irresistible, keeps interrupting the Duke's portentous utterances, as if he is never to be persuaded of the justice of the system or its inviolability. Like Pompey, he is a voice that can be imprisoned, but not silenced. The dignity of the Duke (which we may have come to question by now) wishes whipping and hanging upon him for his slanders, but this is commuted, we are relieved to learn in the closing minutes of the play, to having to marry 'a punk' he made pregnant (5. 1. 501–16).

Significantly, it is Lucio who urges Isabella on when she comes to plead for her brother's life in Act 2, Scene 2:

> ... To him again; entreat him.
> Kneel down before him, hang upon his gown.
> You are too cold.

(2. 2. 43–5)

But it is not only a matter of her being too cold: Isabella's plea begins with an endorsement in principle of Angelo's proceedings, since her brother's 'vice' is likewise the one she most abhors, and 'most desire[s] should meet the blow of justice' (30). She asks that the fault should be condemned, and not her brother. When Angelo responds, surely correctly, that his would be 'the very cipher of a function' to condemn only faults, and not those who commit them, Isabella has to agree: 'O just, but severe law!' (39–42). Lucio's urging, however, leads to a more impassioned appeal from her, and the introduction of a key word: 'mercy' (51). Calling on Angelo (whom we would expect to start responding to this, although we are to learn of his darker motives towards the end of the scene) to participate in her own 'remorse', she suggests that, had Claudio and he changed situations, he might have 'slipped' too. It is a repetition in stronger terms of Escalus's earlier argument for universal tolerance. Where the other deputy could only rather weakly call out 'heaven forgive him, and forgive us all' (2. 1. 37), Isabella now marshals all her considerable powers of argument against Angelo, picking up his 'too late' and almost throwing it back at him, as she points out that mercy is a 'ceremony' more fitting for the great then any other symbol of power. Although this is rejected, too, Angelo soon begins to take on a defensive posture. Encouraged by Lucio's 'Ay, touch him; there's the vein' (2. 2. 73), Isabella drives on to enlarge her theme so as to include the ultimate power – that of God. She reminds him of their common religion, based on the forgiveness and remission of sin:

> Why, all the souls that were were forfeit once,
> And He that might the vantage best have took
> Found out the remedy. How would you be
> If He which is the top of judgement should
> But judge you as you are? O think on that,
> And mercy then will breathe within your lips,
> Like man new made.

(2. 2. 75–81)

Faced, in effect, with the Sermon on the Mount, it is not surprising that Angelo can do no more than weakly mutter, 'It is the law, not I, condemn your brother' (82), an evasive reply indeed. (Some would disagree, arguing that Angelo doesn't become defensive until line 136: 'Why do you put these sayings upon me?'; whereas here he is still confident, stern, cold.) As we have seen, the tension between these two increases still further, as Isabella denounces Angelo's arrogant identification of himself with divine authority, reducing man in office to a grotesque caricature, an angry ape who makes the angels weep. Angelo appears to feel the force of what she says, and asks her to return the next day.

But what else has been going on during their exchange? There is surely an ironic undercurrent here, which performers in particular have to be aware of through-out, even if it is only fully revealed by Angelo when he is left alone at the end of the scene. What is this undercurrent, and how is it expressed?

Evidently, Isabella's energetic virtue has aroused Angelo, much to his surprise and distress. Ironically, in appealing to the man beneath the robes, she has released precisely those sexual impulses they both claim to abhor and wish to punish. For Angelo, Isabella has succeeded where less virtuous women have failed: the 'strumpet' could not stir him; 'this virtuous maid / Subdues me quite' (189–90). Claudio earlier described Isabella as someone with a 'prone and speechless dialect' (1. 2. 160) – hardly 'speechless', we may say, but certainly she has moved this man, using the most effective means to trap him, although she could hardly have known it: 'O cunning enemy, that, to catch a saint, / With saints dost bait thy hook' (2. 2. 184–5).

Angelo recognizes for the first time the power of sexuality (Isabella's as well as his own), which he has so easily dismissed up to now. It is deeply comic that, just when an appeal is being made to his highest motives, his lowest should be responding. Her apparent innocence makes him desire her with a feverish longing expressed in painfully ironic imagery, recalling the conclusion of Shakespeare's Sonnet 94, that: 'sweetest things turn sourest by their deeds / Lilies that fester smell far worse than weeds'. But first there is one of those strange, abrupt, Shakespearean noises, which demands a long pause (some editors give 'ha' a line to itself, to bring this out):

> The tempter or the tempted, who sins most, ha?
> Not she; nor doth she tempt; but it is I
> That, lying by the violet in the sun,
> Do, as the carrion does, not as the flower,
> Corrupt with virtuous season.

(2. 2. 168–72)

We understand, even if we cannot share, Angelo's horror at the absurdity of his own emotions here. Unfortunately for him, and for Isabella and her brother, he cannot resist what he recognizes. Even God becomes merely a 'name' in his mouth for him to 'chew', as we learn the next time we see him. Meanwhile, in his heart there grows 'the strong and swelling evil / Of my conception', an erotic image that suggests how overwhelmed he is by his own imaginings (2. 4. 6–7).

It is important to recognize these moments in which Angelo soliloquizes as moments in which the play demands a certain understanding, if not sympathy, for him. This is despite what he goes on to do, driven by his lust. Otherwise it is difficult, if not impossible, to respond to the climactic moment in the play, when the demands of strict justice are overcome by clemency, and he is himself released from condemnation to death by the Duke. The final question put by the play in this context is: is anyone fit to judge another?

This is why we should also understand that Isabella is not simply a figure to be approved of. How could she be, when she goes to her brother ostensibly expecting him to die to protect her chastity? There is more to it than that, as I suggest in the next section. To be sure, the audience is encouraged to take her side when, in 2. 4, Angelo openly reveals that he wishes to seduce her by offering her brother's life as ransom, and thus shows up the falseness of that kind of mercy. But we also react with a certain distaste when, at the height of her anguish, Isabella accuses Claudio of proving that mercy would to him be a 'bawd' (3.1.152). If we have any sympathy for Claudio (and I have argued that we do) then this seems to be going too far.

Human judges are all imperfect, so justice must be tempered with mercy; but we need to see and feel what mercy is to understand this fully. If Angelo's strict notion of justice is shown up to be inadequate, so too is Isabella's. In 2. 4, Angelo begins by arguing that Claudio has sinned mortally, and so must pay the penalty; when Isabella tries to argue in reply that some sins are worse than others, he immediately turns this against her: 'Might there not be a charity in sin / To save this brother's life?' (63–4). She agrees, only to find that the sin he has in mind is the surrender of her chastity, fornication, not bending the law to free her brother. Once Isabella abandons what we might call the consistency of her extremism, she becomes vulnerable. But remember that it is not so much Angelo's reasoning that defeats her, rather it is the contradictions in her own position, which are revealed under pressure from him. Moreover, Angelo ultimately holds all the *power*, as his closing words indicate: 'Say what you can, my false o'erweighs your true' (170).

Audiences are shocked by the soliloquized lines: 'Then Isabel live chaste, and brother die: / More than our brother is our chastity' (184–5). But Isabella is in a dilemma. She is not a woman of cold chastity, any more than Angelo is ultimately a man of strict control over his passions; but she has been trapped. I will look at this in more detail in a moment. What should be said here is that after the outburst against her brother we hear no more of her self-righteousness, and she colludes with the Duke in attempting to re-establish justice in the state in order to save Claudio. The Duke, however, leads her to believe that Claudio is dead, presumably as a necessary stage in preparation for her great moment in Act 5 when, contrary to what happens in Shakespeare's source, she pardons the corrupt deputy *before* she learns that her brother is, after all, alive.

The balance between justice and mercy provides the essence of Act 5, although it is difficult at times to follow every twist and turn in the plot. But, if we focus on what happens to Angelo and Isabella, things soon become clear: after repeatedly testing Angelo's conscience, by making him the judge in his own cause, the Duke finally allows his disguise to be pulled away to face the obdurate man with his own guilt. Angelo asks for immediate execution: he is taken out to marry Mariana, to whom he was contracted and with whom he has unwittingly slept; and, on his return, he hears what seems to be his just sentence:

'An Angelo for Claudio, death for death'.
Haste still pays haste, and leisure answers leisure;
Like doth quit like, and measure still for measure.

(5. 1. 401–3)

The echo of the title of the play might well lead the audience into thinking that he is going to be executed; but there is a dramatic surprise in wait for us, which clinches the point about mercy. The dramatic power of the moment that follows may be gathered from this account of Peter Brook's historic 1950 Stratford production:

> Mariana has passionately implored Isabella to kneel to the Duke for Angelo's pardon; the Duke has warned her that to do so would be 'against all sense' – 'He dies for Claudio'. The pause that followed must have been among the longest in theatre history. Then hesitantly, still silent, Isabella moved across the stage and knelt before the Duke. Her words came quiet and level, and as their full import of mercy reached Angelo, a sob broke from him. It was perfectly calculated and perfectly timed; and the whole perilous manoeuvre had been triumphantly brought off.

> (Muir and Wells, 1982, p.143)

Women and Measure for Measure

The relationship between sexuality, power and justice is seen at its most acute in debates about the position of women in society. The importance of the subject nowadays is obvious. What is less well known is that it was also widely debated in Shakespeare's time – as Juliet Dusinberre's book *Shakespeare and the Nature of Women* (1975) has shown.[1] It is often suggested that Puritanism is an important historical factor in *Measure for Measure*, because of the characterization of Angelo as 'precise' (1. 3. 50) – the word 'precise' being glossed by most editors including the Norton (p.2023) as 'strict' or 'puritanical'. But this is over-simple; Puritanism was not, as is commonly believed nowadays, merely a movement to suppress sexual (and other) feelings, although it was certainly involved in a serious attempt to modify the conditions and standards of behaviour of contemporary society, including attitudes towards chastity, marriage and sexuality.

As Dusinberre has shown, Puritan debate about freedom of conscience and individual rights included one very important subject: the position of women. Everyone from James I downwards had a view on this subject – as one may gather from the king's writings on *Demonologie* (1597), an attack on witches, not to mention the fact that England had just come to the end of 50 years of rule by women (Mary and Elizabeth). The dramatists of the time were no exception. The tension between individual freedom and submitting to the male world's view of women is palpable in the characters of women as disparate as Viola in *Twelfth Night* and Goneril in *King Lear* – not to mention Isabella in *Measure for Measure*. Isabella's role in the play, despite Tennyson's poem, is what is most interesting from this point of view, not least because she is, after all, the leading female character – indeed, we may call her the heroine.

But is 'heroine' the right word? Think for a moment of some other Shakespearean heroines – Cleopatra, Ophelia, Desdemona, Viola, Miranda, Cordelia, for example –who seem, on the whole, to be more deserving of that label. Why? One answer is suggested by what has been a very common response to Isabella: 'What', asked L.C. Knights some years ago, 'are we to think of Isabella? Is she the embodiment

---

[1] An introductory account of contemporary attitudes to women may also be found in Briggs, 1997, pp.47–78.

of a chaste serenity, or is she, like Angelo, an illustration of the frosty lack of sympathy of a self-regarding puritanism?' (1942, in Stead, 1971, p.138). We have already seen that Angelo's case is not so simple. Neither is Isabella's. But, even if these alternatives are rejected, her behaviour has commonly been found rather unsympathetic, lacking in ordinary human qualities – despite the fact that in Act 5 not only does she forgive Angelo, but she also, apparently, goes on to marry the Duke.

What, then, is the reason for the disapproval? The answer is not hard to find: it lies in her reaction to her brother's plea to save his life by serving the corrupt deputy's lust. How could she, we are supposed to ask ourselves, come out with 'More than our brother is our chastity'? Why doesn't she show some ordinary human feeling and agree to lay down her chastity on his behalf? Perhaps her worst moment, from this point of view, occurs when she realizes (she has not, it seems, expected this) that Claudio is not so keen to die in order to preserve her virginity. But what kind of character is it that could have expected otherwise? **Does Isabella's speech to Claudio reveal a character that is unfeeling and unsympathetic? Re-read 3. 1, especially lines 138–48, and compare your answer with mine.**

To begin with, even on the assumption that she is like a 'real' young woman, we would surely find her rather an obtuse young woman, if she could go to the prison assuming her brother would simply accept the proposition that, as she finally utters it, 'If I would yield him my virginity, / Thou might'st be freed' (96–7). Claudio's immediate response to Angelo's proposal, to give him credit, is shock: 'O heavens, it cannot be!' (97). But, as their conversation develops, it hits him: 'Death is a fearful thing' (116). The Duke has already attempted to prepare him to die well; although, given his disguise, it is remarkable that the traditional Christian hope of immortality was not a part of the consolation offered. The Duke defines death rather as a welcome absence of the pain and uncertainty of living. As in Hamlet's famous soliloquy, however, it is the awful physical presence of death, and the uncertainty of what comes afterwards – 'Ay, but to die, and go we know not where' (118) – that press in upon Claudio. So, when he exclaims:

> Sweet sister, let me live.
> What sin you do to save a brother's life,
> Nature dispenses with the deed so far
> That it becomes a virtue

> (3. 1. 134–7)

we quite agree, in all sympathy, although he has gone a little further than perhaps he should, in claiming that it would actually be a *virtuous* act to sleep with Angelo. In any case, Isabella's response is immediate, horrified, and extreme:

> O, you beast!
> O faithless coward, O dishonest wretch,
> Wilt thou be made a man out of my vice?

> (3. 1. 137–9)

And so on. These are hardly the words of a 'serene' or 'frosty' woman. From the harsh exclamation 'beast!' to the concluding short, monosyllabic line 'No word to save thee' (148), heavily tolling his death knell, her speech is a speech of rage, almost frenzy.

Isabella's refusal to corrupt herself on Claudio's behalf becomes a litany of vituperation, an attack upon him which takes some fairly surprising and nasty paths: 'Is't not a kind of incest to take life / From thine own sister's shame?' (140–1). She even questions the legitimacy of his birth, thereby questioning also their tie, as well as the sexual behaviour of their parents. Her hysterical exaggeration surely has something pitiful about it. It is as if all her repressed sexuality has suddenly found an outlet, its massive but distorted energy bursting through and destroying all ordinary human considerations. The irony is that this (literally) unbending figure ('Might but my bending down / Reprieve thee from thy fate, it should proceed' (145–6)) comes in the end to kneel. A strange reversal indeed for someone allegedly 'frosty' and unsympathetic. Or does her apparently unsympathetic behaviour here represent the unthinking response – shocking and unexpected, indeed – of a woman of great potential forced into a position in which she is unable to do anything else, if she is to maintain any self-respect, or even, on a more fundamental level, her very identity?

What I am suggesting is that to understand Isabella's behaviour, it is important to understand her *position.* For it then becomes less easy to condemn her, or to find her simply 'serenely chaste' or 'frosty'. That there are unresolved ambiguities about her position seems to me unquestionable. If we turn to the very end of the play – that part of it when, with the traditional expectations of comedy in mind (compare *Twelfth Night)* we might assume all confusions, distractions and uncertainties to be cleared up – what actually happens? When the Duke asks Isabella: 'Give me your hand and say you will be mine' (5. 1. 486), how many of us in the audience are *positive* that we know what her response will be?

Of course, it is not only Isabella's position that is ambiguous: this is a puzzling and surprising offer from a man who earlier told Friar Peter that 'the dribbling dart of love' (an unpleasant, demeaning image) could not pierce or affect his 'complete bosom' (1. 3. 2–3); or who could remark of himself later, to Lucio, that unlike that lusty fellow, he was not 'inclined' towards the love of women (3. 1. 365). But more surprising, and confounding, is Isabella's response to him. The woman who could place her brother's life at less value than her own chastity, now accepts conjugal love.

Or does she? Shakespeare does not provide a clear answer, since Isabella's response is silence. What *are* her last words then, and do they provide any clue to how we may expect her to behave?

Her last words are: 'Thoughts are no subjects, / Intents but merely thoughts' (5.1. 445–6). What do they mean? I do not find it easy to say. On one level, it is a part of her unexpected and rather staggering plea on behalf of Angelo's life, which leads the Duke to pardon the man (see Figure 36). Just as no one can control a person's thoughts, so are our intentions beyond control and, the implication is, not subject to the law either. Since Angelo's evil intentions did not in the end result in her loss of chastity, he should not be condemned. Moreover, as we have seen, she accepts that her brother's life was legally taken (he has not yet reappeared). But how will she behave during the rest of the scene, in the light of this reasoning? Will she come forward and join hands with the Duke, in gratitude for his crafty manipulations, and so leave the stage with him, her 'intent' to live chastely being merely a 'thought'? Or will she decide to stay behind with Claudio, whom we would expect her to rush toward and embrace when she recognizes him, alive after all? Or might she reveal some uncertainty about the Duke, perhaps even an aversion to him?

Figure 36 *Shakespeare Memorial Theatre, Stratford production of* Measure for Measure *directed by Anthony Quayle, 1956. Photo: Holte Photos.*

All these possibilities (and more) have been adopted in performance. Since Shakespeare has not, in the Duke's last words, considered it 'meet' to inform us 'what's yet behind' Isabella's behaviour, we are left to decide for ourselves. How we do so depends on how we understand her role in the play; that, in turn, depends to an important extent upon what we feel about the position of women in general. As N.W. Bawcutt puts it: 'No other Shakespearian heroine has a situation resembling Isabella's, and our reaction to her will inevitably be conditioned by our personal convictions about sexuality and female behaviour' (1994, p.56). This is easily shown. It has often been suggested that the 'extremism' I have talked about, Isabella's determination that 'More than our brother is our chastity', represents an exalted expression of female virtue.

One version of this view argues that, as a novice of the strict Order of Saint Clare, Isabella is bound to refuse to commit a mortal sin. It is worth adding that this view stems not only from the orthodox Catholic position which we may suppose Isabella would have held, but also from the historical perspective adopted by critics such as J.M. Nosworthy, who claims that to understand Isabella's behaviour 'in its proper perspective' we must remind ourselves of the uncomplaining submission of hundreds of Tudor martyrs, who preferred to burn for a short time on earth than forever in hell (Nosworthy, 1969, pp.30–1). **For Isabella, eternal damnation is hardly preferable to the merely temporal suffering of her brother's execution. How far does this strike you as a reasonable approach to her behaviour?**

Like these Christian martyrs, Isabella is faced with a proposal to commit what she considers a deadly sin, and so of course she would 'rather give my body than my soul' (2. 4. 56) – except that to allow Angelo to have his way means both. If 'any doubt' remains in our minds about her choice of chastity over fornication and her brother's life, we should, continues Nosworthy, 'further remind ourselves of the uncompromising doctrine of the Roman Catholic Church to which she belongs' (ibid.). This line of argument is clinched by citing the moment of her first appearance in the play: she enters in conversation with one of the nuns of the order she is on the point of entering, and speaks 'not as desiring' privileges, but rather wishing 'a more strict restraint' even than that imposed by the order (1. 4. 1–5).

Do you find this convincing? How does your reading of her speech at 3. 1. 137–48 affect it? Does it bear out what is proposed as a way of understanding her? Consider again her response to Angelo, after he finally reveals he wants her to 'lay down the treasures of your body' (2. 4. 96) as ransom for Claudio (2. 4. 100–9).

'Is this the kind of language we might expect of a sincere "votarist" of the Order of Saint Clare?' is what one may ask, whatever Nosworthy says of the Tudor martyrs. Images of passionate sexuality, torture and death – bloody welts like 'rubies' on the skin, stripping oneself for death – may be acceptable reflections of a yearning for martyrdom (and historically familiar, for example, from representations of female martyrdom), but I am not so sure.

To my mind, a more convincing response than Nosworthy's is that reported by A.C. Hamilton, who, when teaching a class of students which included a Mother Superior, naturally asked her what she thought of Isabella, and was somewhat stunned to hear her firm reply: 'I know the type, and I would never have her in my convent' (1977).

Of course, in any historically informed consideration, Isabella would not be thought of as a nun in any conventional modern sense; nuns were extremely suspect to the Protestants of late-sixteenth-century London, making the sado-masochistic overtones of Isabella's speech less than surprising. In addition, the sexually charged overtones of Isabella's utterance – impossible to ignore in a play riddled with *double entendres* – may make it likely that even the Duke should desire her by the end of the play; more importantly, they suggest that chastity for her involves the incomplete suppression of some very powerful urges. These urges, unconsciously echoed, as her words are echoed, by Angelo (I have begun, / And now I give my sensual race the rein' (2. 4. 159–60)), work away beneath the surface to produce her strained and exorbitant reaction to Claudio.

Moreover, her *position* is not the same as Angelo's. Consider this: it has been said that there were only two ways in which women displayed their independence of men and the law in the sixteenth and early seventeenth centuries: by leading food riots, and by 'adhering to dissident religious opinions, whether puritan or Catholic' (Stone, 1979, p.141). Could it be that the reason Isabella's chastity means so much to her is because it represents her identity as an independent being? It *is* a matter of life and death: not only because to give up her virginity is a mortal sin, but because, on another level, it means giving up her *self*. Hence her determination not to sacrifice her chastity can nowadays be seen as a desperate, doomed attempt to express her self-determination as a woman, harried by the different and competing demands of male society, represented by Claudio and Angelo, and even by the Duke, for all that he is supposed to mean well.

That the whole issue was important to Shakespeare's purpose is suggested by the fact that he altered the story as he received it from his sources in order to highlight Isabella's determination. In Cinthio's tale in the *Hecatommithi*, the woman propositioned by the wicked judge is finally persuaded to yield by her brother's appeal. And the attitudes of the men in the play are interestingly revealed: **'Be that you are; / That is, a woman. If you be more, you're none', exclaims Angelo (2. 4. 134–5). What does he mean? It might help if you re-read the whole of Scene 4.**

What he means is clear enough: since to be a woman is to be weak and frail, and hence submissive to male desires, to resist those desires, on whatever grounds, is not to be a woman at all. To reject Angelo is to reject the woman's role – as defined by men. It is a familiar argument. Femininity is assumed to be a negative quality, something which makes women inherently inferior, saddled with the burden of their bodies which, since Eve was expelled from the Garden, they have to carry around in quiet resignation. Put on the 'destined livery' of a woman, Angelo continues (138); by exhibiting 'frailty', Isabella exhibits what is traditionally expected of her, and so she becomes trapped. 'I have no tongue but one' (139), that is, no voice or argument but the one she has been using. And so she is driven into a corner, the only position she feels is left to her.

When Angelo accuses her of making the law a 'tyrant' herself, by resisting the pressure on her chastity when she had earlier tried to excuse Claudio's 'merriment' as not a vice, she is caught in a contradiction: why should her chastity be worth more than her brother's? The reason is not one she can adequately express, beyond saying 'I something do excuse the thing I hate / For his advantage that I dearly love' (2. 4. 120–1). But it should be clear that what Angelo is doing is, in effect, using the 'double standard' of male sexual morality to enforce his will. *He* is the tyrant here. Without being able to show this, there is nothing left for Isabella except to submit, or hang on to her chastity. The reason she cannot call the 'double standard' into question is because she herself holds the traditional view, unaware of where it leads her, as we see from what she says before Angelo asks her to 'Be that you are', that is, 'soft', 'credulous', vain – she accepts women's 'frailty', and of course Angelo enjoys 'this testimony of your own sex' (122–31).

For further confirmation of the view of women's role expressed in the play, we have only to look at the Duke's reprimand to Juliet for her 'sin' in willingly having become pregnant by Claudio: given that 'your most offenceful act / Was mutually committed', the Duke concludes, 'Then was your sin of heavier kind than his' (2. 3. 28–30).

Why 'heavier'? If the Duke goes on to reinstate the rejected Mariana (who commits the same sin as Juliet, but apparently without incurring the same blame), and helps ensure that Isabella keeps her chastity as well as her brother, does this mean he should be rewarded with her hand in marriage? Perhaps, since Isabella's last words return to the theme of women being at fault for men's misdoings: she excuses Angelo because

> I partly think
> A due sincerity governed his deeds,
> Till he did look on me.

(5. 1. 437–9)

'Women? Help, heaven!' as she earlier exclaims (2. 4. 127). But there is no heaven, only the Duke, and his views may be gathered from the interrogation of Mariana:

MARIANA	Pardon, my lord, I will not show my face Until my husband bid me.
DUKE	What, are you married?
MARIANA	No, my lord.
DUKE	Are you a maid?
MARIANA	No, my lord.
DUKE	A widow then?
MARIANA	Neither, my lord.
DUKE	Why, you are nothing then.

(5. 1. 168–76)

The 'nothing' she is reduced to by this questioning is itself a common euphemism for 'vagina' in contemporary usage: the audience is meant to be amused, we take it. 'All witchcraft comes from carnal lust, which in women is insatiable', observed the authors of the standard book on the subject, the *Malleus Maleficarum* (1486).

It would be pleasant to suppose that, in an age when women were burnt alive as witches for expressing their sexuality (among other things, including talking too much), a playwright was able to suggest the contradictions inherent in a view which defined them totally in male terms. If so, we might suggest that Isabella's likely response at the end of the play would have been a silent, but firm, shake of the head; but it is more likely that she was expected to signal by her expression her silent agreement, and join the head of the ceremonial train, led out by the Duke. Nevertheless the greatness of *Measure for Measure* is that it is open to either possibility. The 'problem' of the play may well be the problem inherent in a society dominated by men.

Conclusion

I have concentrated on those parts of the play in which the Duke, Angelo, Isabella and Claudio are most concerned, and on what strike me as the three major themes, 'government', 'justice' and 'women'. There are a number of other characters, just as there are other themes, or different ways of defining these; but what I have most wanted to suggest is that whatever you make of it, *Measure for Measure* is an intriguing work, frustrating our attempts to read or watch it as close to 'real life', yet close enough to the concerns which matter to us today. The Romantic critic William Hazlitt (1778–1830) tried to capture the contrary spirit of the play when he noted that 'there may be said to be a general system of cross-purposes between the feelings of the different characters and the sympathy of the reader or the audience' (1817, in Stead, 1971, p.48). I don't know which production Hazlitt may have seen, but it is notable that many performances during the eighteenth and early nineteenth century were revised 'performance' versions – from which, for example, the juicier imagery had been surgically removed, and in which the Duke's concluding speech had been rewritten so as to render his courtship of Isabella rather warmer and more convincing (see, for example, Osborne, 1996, pp. 180–1). Not only does this suggest the importance of keeping in mind the variety of ways in which scenes from the play may be performed; it also reminds us that a character even as minor in terms of text as Mariana may loom much larger as a physical presence on stage, and indeed, as for Tennyson, signal a set of meanings for different historical moments and contexts which it is not always easy to reach. Nowadays, I think, we are less interested in Mariana than in the potentially subversive, unruly presence of Lucio, whose irreverent gossip, directed at the disguised Duke in particular, offers much scope for further enjoyment and study of this puzzling, contradictory, but rewarding play.

References

Bawcutt, N.W. (ed.) (1994) *Measure for Measure*, World's Classics, Oxford: Oxford University Press.

Briggs, J. (1977) *This Stage–Play World: Texts and Contexts, 1580–1625*, Oxford: Opus.

Dusinberre, J. (1975) *Shakespeare and the Nature of Women*, London: Macmillan.

Hamilton, A.C. (1977) 'On teaching the Shakespeare canon: the case of *Measure for Measure*', in *Teaching Shakespeare*, ed. W. Edens *et al.*, Princeton: Princeton University Press, pp.95–113.

Hazlitt, W. (1971) 'Characters of Shakespeare's plays', 1817, in *Shakespeare, 'Measure for Measure': A Casebook*, ed. C.K. Stead, London: Macmillan, pp.47–9.

Hurstfield, J. (1971) 'The historical and social background', in *A New Companion to Shakespeare Studies*, ed. K. Muir and S. Schoenbaum, Cambridge: Cambridge University Press, pp.168–79.

Knights, L.C. (1971) 'The ambiguity of *Measure for Measure*', 1942, in *Shakespeare, 'Measure for Measure': A Casebook*, ed. C.K. Stead, London: Macmillan, pp.138–51.

Mortimer, J. (1982) '*Measure for Measure*', in *Shakespeare in Perspective*, ed. R. Sales London: Ariel Books, BBC.

Muir, K. and Wells, S. (eds) (1982) *Aspects of Shakespeare's 'Problem Plays'*, Cambridge: Cambridge University Press.

Nosworthy, J.M. (ed.) (1969) *Measure for Measure*, Harmondsworth: Penguin.

Nuttall, A.D. (1968) '*Measure for Measure*: quid pro quo?', *Shakespeare Studies*, vol.4, pp.231–51.

Osborne, L. E. (1996) 'Rethinking the performance editions', in *Shakespeare, Theory, and Performance*, ed. J.C. Bulman, London and New York: Routledge, pp.168–86.

Stone, L. (1979) *The Family, Sex and Marriage in England 1500–1800,* Harmondsworth: Penguin.

Tillyard, E.M.W. (1965) *Shakespeare's Problem Plays,* Harmondsworth: Peregrine.

KING LEAR

Chapter 8

Graham Martin and Stephen Regan

Aims

This chapter seeks to understand the tragic power of *King Lear* in relation to the social and political conflicts of its own time, but it also raises questions about the continuing impact of the play on modern audiences and readers. The chapter is in two parts. Part 1 investigates some of the major sites of critical enquiry, including Cordelia's response to her father, the role of the Fool and Lear's madness. Part 2 considers a range of critical perspectives and concentrates on a number of topics that continue to provoke debate: religion, nature, history, power and morality, gender and performance. By the end of the chapter, you should have a detailed knowledge of the text, a strong awareness of the play's moment in history and a confident grasp of the main critical issues relevant to analysis and interpretation.

Introduction

It was common in Shakespeare's day for plays to be performed at court during the Christmas holidays, and the first performance of *King Lear* is reputed to have taken place before King James I on St Stephen's Day, 1606. The occasion was loaded with a political significance that continues to reverberate across the centuries. Since his accession in 1603, James I had dreamed of uniting England and Scotland, but his desire for a United Kingdom was continually frustrated by the disapproval of the English Parliament. The spectacle of an ageing monarch dividing up his kingdom must have had a powerful impact on an audience keenly aware of parliamentary debates about the projected 'union'. At one level, *King Lear* dramatizes the dangers of political division and might be seen to endorse the views of James I. At another level, the play delivers a stern rebuke to the absolutist, patriarchal power wielded by kings, and this opens out into a wide-ranging critique of the social and economic injustices of Jacobean England. The play stands as a paradigm of royal authority disputed and arraigned, in which a concern with territorial possession gives way to the monarch's chastening realization that he has taken too little care of his subjects.

St Stephen's Day, now popularly known as Boxing Day (26 December), has long been associated with goodwill and hospitality, especially in the form of charity to the poor and the homeless. It was therefore a suitable occasion for an audience to meditate upon the significance of a king cast out in a storm and forced to seek comfort from the lowliest of his subjects. The thought of *King Lear* being played for the court on St Stephen's Night in 1606 ought to encourage us to dwell on the possible social relevance of the play in its first moment of reception, but it should not dissuade us from seeking to realize the potential significance of the play in our own time, especially when the future of the United Kingdom is once again a topic of intense debate. That early production of *King Lear* ought to remind us, as well, that the meanings of dramatic works are not confined to the words on the page, but are generated and inflected by particular performances in particular social and institutional settings.

King Lear as it was played on St Stephen's Night in 1606 raises a further topic of debate and one that has profound implications for current discussions about 'text' and 'performance'. The version of the play that was used on that remarkable evening was not the version that most of us read when we study *King Lear.* There were two basic texts of *King Lear* in circulation during the seventeenth century. One was printed in the popular Quarto format in 1608 and the other appeared in the First Folio, the earliest edition of Shakespeare's plays, published in 1623. The version used in the 1606 performance was the Quarto, which would have been in a written rather than printed format, prior to its publication two years later. Each version contains substantial passages missing from the other: the Folio contains over 100 lines of text that are not in the Quarto, but it omits nearly 300 lines that *are* in the earlier version. In addition, there are significant variants in speeches that appear in both the Quarto and Folio texts. In the Folio, for instance, the second speech of the play contains a reference to the division of the 'kingdome', which in the Quarto appears in the plural, 'kingdomes'. The Quarto seems to stress Lear's intention to divide the unified kingdom of Britain into three autonomous territories (which might plausibly be construed as England, Scotland and Wales).

The Lear story had been popular since the Middle Ages, appearing in many different versions, from which we can deduce that it would have been known to Shakespeare's audience. There had been a previous stage version, *The True Chronicle History of King Lear*, belonging to the 1590s, but republished and perhaps acted again in 1605. Shakespeare took details from other versions of the story in circulation during this time, but in none of these sources was there any basis for the story of the Earl of Gloucester and his sons, Edgar and Edmund. Here Shakespeare drew upon another source altogether, Sir Philip Sidney's romantic prose narrative *Arcadia* (1590).

Recent studies of *King Lear* in relation to its social history, its textual history and its performance history have ensured that a lively critical debate surrounds the play. For much of the twentieth century, however, *King Lear* has been attended by a more conservative and patently unhistorical criticism, preoccupied with the timeless wisdom of Shakespeare's tragic vision. As we have seen in Chapter 3, many of the conventional assumptions about Shakespearean tragedy that persisted until at least the 1960s derived from A.C. Bradley's highly influential book *Shakespearean Tragedy*, first published in 1904. Undeterred by the pagan setting and frequent pagan allusions in *King Lear*, Bradley presents the play as a Christian parable of sacrifice and salvation: 'There is nothing more noble and beautiful in literature than Shakespeare's exposition of the effect of suffering in reviving the greatness and eliciting the sweetness of Lear's nature' (1967 edn, p.284). A more fitting title, he thinks, would have been *The Redemption of King Lear.* Similarly, G. Wilson Knight, in *The Wheel of Fire* (1930), insists that *King Lear* is essentially a 'purgatorial' play.

Other critics, including William Empson in *The Structure of Complex Words* (1951), have seen the play as entirely un-Christian in its conception of 'the gods'. The Christian affirmation of Lear's suffering was sharply questioned by William Elton's book, *'King Lear' and the Gods* (1966). While accepting that the play establishes important parallels between the Christian world of the Renaissance and the pre-Christian world of Lear's ancient Britain, Elton argues effectively that the world-view of *King Lear* is one of pagan agnosticism. Christian readings of the play began to give way to secular humanist interpretations, which discovered a strong sense of affirmation, not in Lear's spiritual renewal, but in his heroic endurance on earth. An extreme version of the humanist perspective was offered by the critic Jan Kott, whose *Shakespeare Our Contemporary* (1965) detected in *King Lear* a bleak, existentialist vision of humanity's absurd and alienated condition. Both Christian and humanist critics have traditionally rested their case on a view of tragedy that accepts the inevitability and universality of suffering, and elevates that suffering into something beautiful and enigmatic. Since, for such critics, tragedy is an inescapable part of the human condition, their purpose is not to enquire into the possible causes of tragedy, but to marvel at its awesome power, succumbing to what Bradley calls 'the mystery we cannot fathom' (1967 edn, p.279).

The interpretation of *King Lear* proposed in this chapter is based on a materialist and historicist view of tragedy: it suggests that tragedy is neither inescapable nor incomprehensible, but the consequence of specific social conflicts and pressures. In this respect, the chapter follows the example of Arnold Kettle, formerly Professor of Literature at the Open University, whose ground-breaking essay 'From *Hamlet* to *Lear*' (1964) helped to dispel some of the mystification in theories of tragedy and sought to understand *King Lear* in terms of the political upheavals of its own time. This is not to consign the play to the past, but to see how its creative engagement with the human dilemmas and injustices of its day might illuminate those of our own time. This chapter shares Kettle's conviction that 'the experience and meaning of the play cannot be confined within the limits of seventeenth-century social thinking' (Kettle, 1988 edn, p.82). *King Lear*, from this perspective, does not preach submission to the unalterable laws of destiny, but gestures beyond itself to a more humane and tolerable way of being.

Before proceeding with this chapter, you should read *King Lear* at least once. The chapter is in two parts. Part 1 concentrates on some frequently posed questions about issues arising out of the play, including Cordelia's response to her father in the opening scene (Figure 37); the sub-plot involving Gloucester and his sons; the role of the Fool; and Lear's madness. These preliminary issues have been chosen because they are principal sites of critical enquiry, as well as sources of disagreement among readers and audiences of the play. The aim of Part 1 is to make you reasonably familiar with the text and confident about the issues it raises, so that you can then embark on Part 2. This discusses some prominent interpretations of the play from a range of critical perspectives, concentrating on: religion, nature, history, power and morality, gender and performance. (Act, scene and line references throughout the chapter are based on the conflated text of *King Lear* in *The Norton Shakespeare*.)

Part 1 Preliminary issues

Cordelia

Let us look first at Cordelia's abrupt and unyielding answers to her father in 1. 1. 86–107. What reasons do you think there might be for the way in which Cordelia speaks to Lear at this point in the play?

The following are three possible explanations of Cordelia's behaviour that might have occurred to you.

1   All plots require an initial act of disruption to create the momentum necessary to engage our interest. In the Lear plot, this stems from Cordelia's refusal to say what is expected of her. Shakespeare simply chooses to begin the story in this way, and no further explanation is required.

2   Cordelia is a 'chip off the old block': stubborn, with a touch of her father's self-righteousness. Shakespeare wants to underline this family trait as the seed of the whole painful story.

3   Shakespeare wants to set up a contrast between public, political relationships and private, personal relationships. The request Lear makes of his daughters confuses this key distinction. Cordelia's refusal to comply points to the moral superiority of loyalty to the personal realm ('So young, my lord, and true'(107)).

You will see that these are different sorts of explanation, relating respectively to *plot*, *character* and *theme*, so none necessarily excludes another. See what evidence you can find for them before we look more closely at each in turn.

Plot

A general statement about plots ('All plots require an initial act of disruption') cannot be defended on the basis of only one plot, but if you glance back over the other plays you have read in this book, you will see that it works quite well. For example, in *Hamlet*, the appearance of the Ghost to Hamlet disrupts the political state of affairs set up by the succession of Claudius and his marriage to Gertrude. In *Twelfth Night*, the Duke's scheme to woo Olivia receives a check, and the shipwrecked Viola resolves to start her new life in Illyria disguised as a young man. If this kind of analysis interests you, follow the idea through for the other plays in the book.

You may, however, feel that such an approach is too formalist, a mere exercise in making abstract comparisons. It is, nevertheless, one way to bring home the fact that plays involve the construction of stories. Any story must have a beginning, which then leads somewhere, otherwise why should we stay to listen, or watch or read? To sketch in a general state of affairs, and then disturb it, is an excellent way to set up this forward-pressing narrative movement.

What is the state of affairs disrupted by Cordelia's blunt 'Nothing'? It is the 'darker purpose' (34) announced by Lear in his first speech – his decision to divide the kingdom into three parts to be ruled by his daughters and sons-in-law – a political event that is the first thing the audience hears about in the opening exchange between Gloucester and the Earl of Kent. Cordelia's refusal to answer her father in the manner of Goneril and Regan frustrates the unfolding of his scheme, and sets

Figure 37 *Love test of the three daughters: G. Volchek as Regan, E. Radzins as Goneril and V. Shendrikova as Cordelia in Act 1, Scene 1 of* King Lear *directed by Grigori Kozintsev, 1970, USSR from a translation by Boris Pasternak. Courtesy of National Film Archive/Stills Library, British Film Institute.*

going the chain of events that is the play. To some extent this sets a limit to our curiosity about Cordelia's behaviour. This initial situation is Shakespeare's donnée, his narrative premise. The way Shakespeare sets up this story shows that he does not want us to worry unduly about the whys and wherefores of the opening, but rather to listen to and watch what follows.

Is it a stable state of affairs that Cordelia disrupts? Hardly. What Cordelia checks is Lear's intentions for the future, rather than a previous condition. Is it only in Lear's mind that these plans have an existence? Or did other people know about them? We do have the opening exchange between Kent and Gloucester, which makes it clear that Lear's general plan was no secret. In that sense, Cordelia's refusal to play the part Lear wants her to play challenges an initial set of assumptions. We do not know, though, whether the court knew about Lear's plan for a public exchange of political power based on declarations of love by his daughters. How should we interpret the phrase 'darker purpose'? It does suggest that Lear is springing a surprise on the court. But is he also springing a surprise on his three daughters? If you were producing the play, would you suggest that he is, so that their speeches come across as spontaneous? Or would you make it clear that they had been forewarned and knew what their father expected of them, so that the whole exchange becomes a public charade played by the Lear family (who are all in on the secret) for the benefit and to the astonishment of the court? We could then say that the state of affairs Cordelia disrupts might be a family ritual – in which Lear demands love from his daughters in a fashion all too familiar to them.

One other possibility should be canvassed: that Cordelia's refusal to speak brings into question Lear's wisdom in dividing his kingdom in the first place. In this case, *that* decision, taken at some earlier point, becomes the truly disruptive event. Kent responds to Lear's rejection of Cordelia by advising him to 'Reverse thy doom' (149), that is, 'Hold on to your power'. In the next scene, Gloucester expresses alarmed amazement at what has happened (1. 2. 24), whilst in later scenes the Fool gibes at Lear for giving up his personal power. No one, however, seems to express any major political objections. Indeed, Regan thinks her father took too long to make up his mind (2. 4. 245).

Yet here, as scholars of the Elizabethan period remind us, we need to exercise our historical imagination. Think back to *Richard II*. We can see clearly Elizabethan worries about the smooth succession from one royal authority to the next being explicitly addressed in that play. The stability of the Elizabethan state had depended, so it seemed to contemporaries, on the life of its monarch, and then on the uncontested succession of James VI of Scotland. Consider the impact of the opening scene of *King Lear* against such a history: a strong, ageing monarch proposing to divide his kingdom among three sets of rulers, one of whom might be the King of France. How could this not strike a contemporary audience as a recipe for political disaster – civil war, or foreign invasion, or both? If we remember the play's later events – rumours that the Dukes of Albany and Cornwall are manoeuvring against each other, that the King of France is about to invade the kingdom and does eventually send an army – we can see that Shakespeare kept this political dimension in place, a frame within which the fates of the characters are played out. In sum, from a political angle, there was a stable state of affairs that Lear himself disrupted. Why? We do not know. Old age, he says. But why abdicate in this most politically dangerous of ways? We do not know. Here, we run up against another donnée of the play, one guaranteed to engage the real political hopes and fears of Jacobean audiences, for whom James I had only recently come to power, after a period of intense political anxiety about what might happen when Elizabeth I died.

Character

We suggested above that the three different explanations of Cordelia's answers did not rule each other out, but you may now feel like concluding that if the scene is, in the end, Shakespeare's way of getting the play going, the question of Cordelia's motives disappears. Nevertheless, what do you think of the second possible explanation, which has been adopted by several producers of the play: that Cordelia has a self-righteous streak, which must attract some blame for what follows? How would you direct the actress playing the part? Should we see her as an aspect of the obdurate and steely will of which Lear boasts (his behaviour in the storm scenes bears him out) and which both Goneril and Regan display in their treatment of their father? **Does Shakespeare offer producers some latitude in their interpretation of Cordelia's behaviour, or does he make it clear what attitudes and feelings govern her behaviour and speech in this scene?**

It seems that Shakespeare has been remarkably explicit about the sources of Cordelia's behaviour. Had her first words been 'Nothing ... Nothing ... I love your majesty / According to my bond; nor more nor less' (1. 1. 86–92), it would have been open to a producer to read into them a kind of legalistic, self-approving temper, a stubborn, Lear-like, personal determination to obstruct her father's emotional claims. But in fact Cordelia's first speeches are 'asides' to the audience, by means of that non-realistic convention Shakespeare uses so often to explain what a character is up to. Cordelia has two such 'asides', following her sisters' declarations of love:

What shall Cordelia speak? Love, and be silent.

(1. 1. 60)

Then poor Cordelia!
And yet not so; since, I am sure, my love's
More ponderous than my tongue.

(1. 1. 75–7)

We might still want to cling to the 'chip-off-the-old-block' explanation at the level of settled will-power. The pressures on Cordelia to shift her ground are evident enough and her resistance is impressive. But the idea of self-approving virtue could only be supported by interpreting these 'asides' as hypocritical, although in a profounder way than Goneril and Regan. We would have to conclude that Cordelia was entirely self-deceived about loving her father better, more genuinely, than her sisters. Do subsequent events support that? Surely not. Remember Cordelia's actions in Acts 4 and 5. It seems that these 'asides' are Shakespeare's way of preparing us to accept Cordelia's behaviour as simply the point we start from, to stop us probing into motives. He invites us to 'suppose' such a person as Cordelia, and leaves it at that.

Indeed, if we stand back a little from this particular episode, is it not also true that, in comparison with characters like Antony, Cleopatra, Macbeth, Lady Macbeth or Hamlet, the characters in *King Lear* are delineated simply and straightforwardly, without adequate explanations of their motives? Why is Kent loyal to the point of self-destruction? No answer is given except that of the Fool, that Kent is 'a fool'. Why is Gloucester so easily persuaded that Edgar is a villain? Why does Edgar not make a point of seeing his father to clear things up? Again, no real answer is forthcoming. *King Lear* is a play in which, against Shakespeare's common practice, the characters are not probed for their deeper, more elusive motivations and impulses. It is not a play interested in depicting its characters with psychological realism, the kind of play that makes it easy to mistake Shakespeare for a nineteenth-century novelist. This is not, of course, to imply that it does not have something to say about human reality. Characterization of this kind makes difficulties for modern productions. Actors, producers, audiences – we are all accustomed to expecting answers to questions of the kind 'Why does so-and-so behave in that way?', 'What complex undertow of relationships accounts for this surface action?' If these questions go unanswered, we are apt to retort that the dramatist has not conceived his characters in sufficient depth and with proper consistency. In thinking like this, we touch upon a common cultural and moral assumption of our times. So, is *King Lear* a play in which we meet a challenge to this assumption?

Theme

What evidence can we find for the view that Shakespeare wants to set up a contrast between public and political relationships, over and against personal and private relationships? Cordelia seems to be identified with the latter sphere, in contrast to her sisters, who seem to be wedded to the former. The Duke of Burgundy, likewise, with his worldly insistence that no dowry means no marriage, is aligned with the realm of public and political priorities, unlike the King of France, who admirably regards Cordelia as a dowry in herself. In addition, there is Kent, the honest counsellor who stands up for personal truth – 'be Kent unmannerly, / When Lear is mad' (145–6) – against the prudent counsels of pragmatism in politics, and suffers the consequences. There seems to be a pattern here.

Did you notice anything about the way the characters speak that might support this? How would you describe the style of speech of Lear, Goneril and Regan, compared with that of Cordelia and Kent?

Would you agree that the first three make speeches, a performance the other two either refuse, or take on with reluctance? Cordelia implicitly protests against the kind of speaking demanded of her.

LEAR   Nothing will come of nothing, speak again.

CORDELIA   Unhappy that I am, I cannot heave
                        My heart into my mouth.

                                                            (1. 1. 89–91)

What she has to say cannot be uttered in public discourse. Kent, on the other hand, although he adopts a plain manner, makes a rather powerful speech of his own. Experienced in court affairs, he commands a public idiom well enough to debate effectively with the king, who is reduced to the threat of speechless violence to shut him up (139–67). However, Kent shares with Cordelia a deep distaste for what we might call 'courtly speech'. Here words bear no relation to intended deeds, and the speaker (Lear, Goneril, Regan) divorces language from feeling, or uses language to fence and parry with the listener, hiding his or her true meanings behind it. (Compare Regan and Goneril's prose exchange, which closes the first scene, with their flowery public speeches.)

However, there is a problem about seeing this as an opposition between public falsity and private truth. The two realms of discourse are set in contrast, yet the fact that Kent can speak in both underlines a significant complication. This opening scene about 'the division of the kingdom' is pre-eminently a public affair. We may reasonably speculate about earlier behind-doors political negotiations between Lear, Albany, Cornwall, France and Burgundy (who actually refers to prior negotiations about Cordelia's proposed dowry), where the real decisions were made. Following this line, critics and producers often represent the public ceremony of Lear's abdication speeches as a routine formality, not unlike today's Queen's Speech at the opening of a new Parliament, which is personally delivered by the queen but written by the Prime Minister as an outline of the plans of the government. Such an approach is tainted by anachronistic modern assumptions. Lear's royal public existence is not a shell, a decorative uniform for some inner private reality to which, after his abdication, he can securely retreat. Having surrendered royal power, and finding his authority contested, he responds as to a radical challenge to his personal identity: 'Who is it that can tell me who I am?' (1. 4. 205). When Lear denounces Kent, it is in the courtly style. When he curses Goneril and Regan, again the speech is elaborate, formal and deliberate.

There is no question here, though, of smooth-tongued eloquence aiming to deceive. Lear's ferocious threats of punishment for those who oppose his will cannot be thought to lack *sincerity*. He means every word of them. Then again, if we glance back at Cordelia's 'rejection' speech, it includes the words 'I love your majesty / According to my bond; nor more nor less' (1. 1. 91–2), and she goes on to explain what this 'bond' is: a set of duties that she owes Lear, as king and father. Cordelia, that is, defends her refusal to say more than 'Nothing' on the grounds of these feudal, public relationships: Lear has been a good father and king, and she a good daughter and subject. Here, perhaps, we perceive a touch of Lear's argumentative spirit, when she adds that if she married she would owe half her love to her husband, so that her sisters are in error in offering all their love to Lear. Kent's personal bluntness, too, is justified in terms of 'duty' (147). It is the public duty of a good counsellor to warn his ruler, at whatever personal risk, against a rash or unwise decision. We might even think of the whole scene in implicitly allegorical terms: the king, seduced by Flattery (Goneril and Regan) despite the virtue and sound advice of Good Counsel (Kent and Cordelia).

Yet we also sense, of course, a more complex handling of the crisis than that. Evidently Cordelia is the favourite daughter, with whom, as he says, the ageing Lear expected to spend his remaining years (123–4). Indeed, it is Lear who introduces the personal note into the public declarations of gratitude and love. Faced with Cordelia's reasonable point about loving according to her bond, Lear barks back: 'But goes thy heart with this?' (104). He is demanding more than formal recognition and public tributes. The savage character of his rejection of Cordelia (108–19), couched though it is in the terms of legitimate responsibility ('paternal care, / Propinquity and property of blood' (113–14)), bespeaks feelings of a different order and source than the courtly public debate can account for.

It may be that Shakespeare is presenting us not so much with a contrast between deceitful public protestation and private candour, as with an insight into the political sphere, in which relationships, however personal they must seem within a royal family, are really governed by political considerations. At one point, we hear Goneril and Regan making their loving avowals; a few minutes later, they are speculating on the political threat concealed in Lear's decision to reside with them, bringing with him the considerable force of 'a hundred knights' (133). They do not think of Lear as an ageing father who requires care and attention, but as a continuing danger to their political authority. And with reason. When Lear storms out of Goneril's castle, what does he say?

> Thou shalt find
> That I'll resume the shape which thou dost think
> I have cast off for ever.

> (1. 4. 285–7)

Lear injects into this political predicament a degree of personal animus that has no place in it. While it is clear that Cordelia and Kent are morally preferable to Goneril and Regan, in the sense of being trustworthy and undeceiving, what is illustrated is that the 'political' has no place for the 'moral': the issues, the language, the relationships are entirely different, perhaps irreconcilable. Those who speak up for the 'moral' are forced into silence (Cordelia) and banishment (Kent). Lear uses a language of morality, but it is a false use. He is entirely preoccupied with power, and (this is the most striking example of the slender knowledge of himself that Regan mentions in lines 291–2) he has no understanding that, far from wanting to be rid of power, he passionately wants to hang on to it. Could it be that this knot of inner contradiction is the real source of his fearsome yet ludicrous rages? It is here, perhaps, that our analysis of *King Lear* as a tragedy might begin.

The double plot

We can now turn to consider the question of the play's parallel plots. **Why do you think there are two distinct 'stories' – the story of Lear and the story of Gloucester?**

The following are some possible answers.

1   The Lear story in itself did not employ all the available talent in Shakespeare's company (the King's Men), so the Gloucester story provided useful extra parts.

2   The Lear plot was in itself too thin, and Shakespeare's audiences were accustomed to the variety of theatrical interest provided by double plots.

3   Shakespeare wanted to generalize some of the issues raised by Lear's experience, which would otherwise have rested on too slight a fictional basis.

3   Shakespeare wanted to introduce a different, but complementary, set of issues, by means of the Gloucester subplot.

Let us consider the first two answers together. You may have thought these possible reasons for the introduction of the Gloucester story trivial, merely circumstantial matters. But are they? We know almost nothing about Shakespeare's creative practice. Nevertheless, a process of close collaboration with his fellow actors in the King's Men seems highly probable. We should not think of Shakespeare as a brooding genius turning out his plays in lonely seclusion. Rather, he worked in a sort of actors' and writers' co-operative, a group that owned its own theatre, theatrical properties and acting scripts. A key to its remarkable record of artistic and financial success over nearly 30 years lay in a shared and sustained commitment to a joint venture. It is therefore reasonable to suppose that Shakespeare would have needed to take into account the number of actors' parts that any new play he was working on would make available. By introducing the Gloucester subplot, three excellent parts (Gloucester, Edmund and Edgar) and a small one (the Old Man in 4. 1) would be added. In the case of Edgar, this would provide a demanding and varied role. Of course, this can only be speculation, but it is worth floating none the less, if only to remind us that Shakespeare's plays were the product of a particular theatrical situation, as well as a product of their author's mind.

The second possible reason, that the audience expected the variety of incident made possible by double plots, has positive evidence in its favour. Double plots are a very common feature of Elizabethan and Jacobean plays, and audience expectation may properly be considered as one factor in the way Shakespeare planned his plays. In *King Lear*, we can see that Shakespeare adapted the double-plot convention or practice to his aims for the whole play. Moreover, compared with the sources from which Shakespeare took the Lear story, his version *is* less varied in interest. Of the several relationships and characters that might have been developed, Lear alone receives full characterization, and his tale (compare the variety in *Antony and Cleopatra*) is reduced to a single strand: the results of the opening scene. This could have been a reason for introducing the additional story of Gloucester and his sons.

What did you think about the third and fourth possible reasons for the introduction of the Gloucester story? Granted that we notice elements shared by both stories, as well as some that are not, how explicit has Shakespeare made the connections and how seriously does he intend them? **Can you point to scenes or speeches that act as clues to the audience to see the stories in relation to each other?**

Gloucester surely draws an obvious parallel between his and Lear's situation in his superstitious speech to Edmund:

> These late eclipses in the sun and moon portend no good to us ...
> This villain of mine [that is, Edgar] comes under the prediction; there's son against father. The king falls from bias of nature; there's father against child ... And the noble and true-hearted Kent banished!

> (1. 2. 96, 101–3, 107–8)

But Gloucester at this point does not see the significance of the comparison. For him it is just a sign of bad times, so the speech is clearly intended as a clue to the audience to notice connections. Then, in 3. 4, with the entry of Edgar disguised as Poor Tom, the parallel becomes very close, articulating thereby a central theme of the play. Lear is expelled into the storm by his hard-hearted daughters as much against the 'bias of nature' as Lear's treatment of Cordelia, and Edgar is expelled from family and society by Edmund's false accusation and his father's credulity. It is Tom's behaviour that finally pushes Lear into madness, and it is Tom who then comes to symbolize, in Lear's mind, the essential condition of humanity: 'unaccommodated man is no more but such a poor, bare, forked animal as thou art' (3. 4. 98–100). Here, then, the two stories are welded together. Shakespeare clearly wants us to think about their interconnection as a key to what the play as a whole is about. A third example of an unmistakably explicit connection appears in 4. 6, when the mad Lear meets the blinded Gloucester (an exchange to which we will return).

Bearing these points in mind, we can now see more clearly that, although Lear's story dominates throughout, the Gloucester story is interwoven with it from the play's first moments, when Gloucester and Edmund appear before the abdication scene. We can see, too, why Shakespeare brings a number of principal characters together in 2. 2 at Gloucester's castle, so that Regan, and Cornwall as well, are implicated in Lear's rejection. We can see why, in the next scene, we learn of Edgar's plight, which places him in the vicinity of Lear's wanderings in the storm. By the time we reach Act 3, the alternations between the 'mad' outdoors scenes involving Lear, the Fool, Poor Tom and Kent, and the events in Gloucester's castle that lead to his being blinded, begin to resemble a set of variations on the same basic theme. **In what ways do you think the two stories raise different (if complementary) issues?**

There seem to be at least two points of contrast. First, neither Gloucester nor Edgar appears to deserve his fate, as we surely feel Lear does. 'Deserve' perhaps puts the point too strongly; rather, we can see that Lear is in a large measure responsible for what happens to him. His story unfolds straightforwardly from the two major blunders he makes in 1. 1: the division of the kingdom and the banishment of Cordelia. In the most literal sense, Lear chooses his fate: rather than make an accommodation with his daughter, he walks out into the storm (which is also an internal, mental storm). Lear is not a victim, he is not at all 'More sinned against than sinning' (3. 2. 58), and his heroic stature derives directly from that fact. Gloucester, by contrast, may bear some responsibility for events, but is more of a victim of forces beyond his control. As Edgar says to his dying brother, 'The dark and vicious place where thee he [that is, Gloucester] got / Cost him his eyes' (5. 3. 171–2). This is true enough, as far as it goes, as the cause of Gloucester's blindness. (Edmund's bastardy was the motive behind the treachery that put Gloucester in Cornwall's power.) Yet the punishment seems disproportionate, to say the least, setting aside the fact that it is Gloucester's loyalty to Lear that prompts Albany's vicious treatment. Then again, Edgar's fate is surely the direct responsibility of Edmund, not the result of any foolish or wicked act of his own, unless we are to assume that Edgar's trust in his brother was so stupid as to merit such a severe penalty. The other main difference between the Gloucester and Lear stories is raised by Gloucester's suicide attempt. This brings in issues not directly touched upon in Lear's experience.

What do you think is the structural and thematic purpose of the 'Dover cliff' scene (3. 6)?

This scene has a critically important role in the play, because it is here that the two stories – that of Lear and his daughters and that of Gloucester and his sons – converge and complement each other most emphatically. The different responses of Lear's daughters to their father find a parallel in the divergent responses of Edmund and Edgar to their father, but we also discover a strong correlation between the tragic circumstances in which Lear and Gloucester find themselves.

From 4. 1 onwards, when Edgar as Poor Tom encounters his blinded father and leads him to Dover, we are offered a moving example of a child's caring companionship for a parent. Edgar's love for his father in 4. 6 anticipates the fond reunion between Cordelia and Lear in the scene that immediately follows (4. 7). Gloucester's suicide attempt is occasioned by the despair and misery that accompany his blindness, but through Edgar's intervention he comes to know the value of patience. The dialogue between Lear and Gloucester in 4. 6 turns on ideas of sight and on the subtle distinctions between physical vision and moral vision. Lear comments, 'Your eyes are in a heavy case, your purse in a light. Yet you see how this world goes', to which Gloucester replies, 'I see it feelingly' (143–5). Both Lear and Gloucester understand that 'A man may see how this world goes with no eyes' (146–7). Lear instructs Gloucester, 'Thou must be patient' (172), a line that is echoed later in Edgar's comforting words to his father in 5. 2:

> Men must endure
> Their going hence, even as their coming hither;
> Ripeness is all.

(5. 2. 9–11)

The Fool

Why do you think the Fool has such a prominent role in the early acts?

Here are some suggestions which you may have considered.

1   Shakespeare often uses minor or anonymous characters to say important things.

2   The Fool provides an implicit commentary on the action as a whole, and not just temporary relief for Lear.

3   Shakespeare's presentation of the Fool in *King Lear* draws upon historical actualities.

Before reading further, look back over scenes that include the Fool, especially in Acts 1 and 3, and see how far the text supports or confutes such arguments. We will then consider each of these suggestions in detail.

The use of minor characters

In 3. 1, a conversation between Kent and a Gentleman tells us that Lear, having left Gloucester's castle, is now wandering about in the storm, his only companion 'the fool, who labors to out-jest / His heart-struck injuries' (16–17). (You will find another case in 4. 3, where an anonymous Gentleman (perhaps the same one) informs Kent about Cordelia's reaction to the news of Lear's ill-treatment.) What the Gentleman says about the Fool must, therefore, be taken seriously. Shakespeare clearly did not assume that his more complex scenes had a self-evident meaning, and he therefore indicated by hints and intimations that he wanted his audience to attend to these scenes in a particular way, to engage in an active process of interpretation. Act 3, Scene 2 broadly supports what the Gentleman has said in 3. 1. It opens with a long speech by Lear invoking the elements in support of his feelings about Goneril and Regan, interspersed with remarks and a song from the Fool attempting to mitigate Lear's rage. Is this the Fool's principal function: to distract Lear from his obsession with his daughter's ingratitude? You will find other instances of this in 3. 4. Yet is that the only effect of the Fool's remarks? Following the first part of Lear's speech ('Blow, winds, and crack your cheeks! rage! blow!' (3. 2. 1)), the Fool says:

> O nuncle, court holy-water in a dry house is better than this rain-water out o' door. Good nuncle, in, ask thy daughters' blessing! Here's a night pities neither wise men nor fool.

> (3. 2. 10–12)

Lear pays no attention, and continues with his invocation ('Rumble thy bellyful! Spit, fire! spout, rain!' (13)). The Fool's next intervention is a song, whose first three lines (26–8) the editor of *The Norton Shakespeare* glosses as: 'Whoever finds his penis a lodging before providing shelter for his head will end up in lice-infested poverty.' This is jokey enough in its sardonic style, but is the song intended to distract Lear? Is Lear listening? In a moment, Kent enters and addresses him, but Lear is utterly absorbed in his inner debate, calling on the gods to seek out the wicked, imagining himself both as a sort of judicial investigator of hypocrites, and as 'a man / More sinned against than sinning' (57–8). Only at the end of this speech does he show any sign that he knows the Fool is there (70–1), while to Kent he gives no spoken recognition.

So, while the Fool may be trying to distract Lear from 'his heart-struck injuries', he is certainly not succeeding. If we look again at his actual words, do they not have clear implications for the audience? What does his first remark mean? Broadly, we can interpret the Fool's remark as 'better to flatter the powerful [that is, Regan and Goneril] and do what they ask, than stay out in the storm'. 'Here's a night pities neither wise men nor fool' implies that, however eloquently and impressively Lear rages against the elements, they will pay him no attention whatsoever. The Fool's comments, that is, offer the audience a different perspective on Lear's situation: realistic, unillusioned, commonsensical.

What of the song? It is certainly a down-to-earth, sensible piece of popular wisdom (do not raise a family if you have no house or money), but it is also of only indirect application to Lear's situation: Lear has been the opposite of realistic, hence his present position. The Fool's two further contributions to this scene are also songs, one delivered after Lear has left the stage. Must we not then conclude that the Fool has an important role vis-à-vis the audience, as well as his role vis-à-vis Lear?

If you now glance back over the Fool's contribution to earlier scenes, you will find this borne out. See, for example, 1. 4 and 2. 4, and ask yourself what, as audience, we learn about Lear's situation from the Fool's jokes, witticisms and snatches of song.

Commentary on the action

George Orwell, contesting the view of the Russian writer and intellectual Leo Tolstoy (1828–1910) that the Fool was a 'tedious nuisance', proposed that

> his jokes, riddles and scraps of rhyme, and his endless digs at Lear's high-minded folly, ranging from mere derision to a sort of melancholy poetry ... are like a trickle of sanity running through the play, a reminder that somewhere or other in spite of the injustices, cruelties, intrigues, deceptions and misunderstandings that are being enacted here, life is going on much as usual.
>
> (Orwell, 1966, p.423)

What do you think of this idea? We have seen that the Fool's comments in 3. 2 express a down-to-earth realism, which brings an ironic perspective to bear on Lear's behaviour. In your review of earlier scenes, did you find this effect? In 1. 4, for example, the whole burden of the Fool's jokes is that Lear simply has not grasped the truth of his situation. When Goneril enters, and Lear asks why she looks so cross, the Fool cuts in with:

> Thou wast a pretty fellow when thou hadst no need to care for her frowning; now thou art an O without a figure. I am better than thou art now; I am a fool, thou art nothing.
>
> (1. 4. 167–9)

When Goneril makes her speech about the riotous behaviour of Lear's followers (75–88), and Lear responds with his partly sarcastic, partly bewildered 'Who is it that can tell me who I am?' (205), the Fool tells him: 'Lear's shadow' (206). A third instance, from 2. 4, is the Fool's exchange with Kent, sitting in the stocks:

KENT	How chance the king comes with so small a train?
FOOL	An thou hadst been set i' the stocks for that question, thou hadst well deserved it.

> (2. 4. 59–61)

Kent, that is, should have foreseen that Lear, having yielded power to his daughters, would soon find his train of knights being cut down. It is noticeable, too, in such scenes that many of the Fool's remarks are directed as much at the audience as at Lear himself, who often gives vague or no replies. To underline for the audience that what the Fool says is important, Shakespeare has Kent remark after one of the Fool's quips about Lear having given his power away, 'This is not altogether fool, my lord' (1. 4. 132). Kent, you might recall, has been dismissed by Lear in the opening scene of the play – 'Hence, and avoid my sight!' (1. 1. 124) – and at this point he is disguised as a servant called Caius.

Orwell is surely right, therefore, in conceiving the Fool's role as that of commentator on the play's action, certainly in so far as it involves Lear. But do you agree with

Orwell that the Fool's general effect is to remind us that, despite the intrigue and the cruelty enacted in the play, life is going on much as usual? Or is it that the Fool's comments add up to a more precise and less comforting message: that politically Lear's action was a disaster? Might there not also be an element of malice in many of the Fool's remarks? As the king retorts after one of the Fool's jokes about the link between lands and rent and power, 'A bitter fool!' (1. 4. 117). The Fool's situation is, after all, precarious. Lear is his only protector. Lear's mistakes have direct and painful consequences for the Fool, as well as for Lear. He is also in Lear's power: Lear more than once threatens him with whipping. Being the dependant of so irascible and self-absorbed a person as Lear must have meant hourly uncertainty about how one might be treated. Some, at least, of the fool's 'bitter' jokes can reasonably be seen as a way of getting his own back for the plight that Lear's folly has brought about. We should beware, in other words, of sentimentalizing the Fool.

Historical actualities

Lear's Fool is quite close to the real Fools who were a feature of Renaissance courts. He is 'all-licensed' (1. 4. 175), that is, privileged – like Henry VIII's Fool, Will Somers – to joke at the expense of the powerful. (That is doubtless why Goneril particularly dislikes him: we can suppose that she has heard some of his remarks to Lear about the results of his abdication.) He is intelligent, bawdy, knows popular sayings and songs, plays with words, and enjoys doing so. Indeed, this is a trait of all Shakespeare's Fools. However, as suggested above, while the Fool has a certain privilege and freedom, he is finally dependent on the king's favour, as a real Fool would have been.

One further point may be added. The Fool in *King Lear* is identified with a sensibility and voice that we must call 'popular', and which the staging practice of the Elizabethan productions provides with a particular theatrical location: downstage, in direct relation to the audience. As we have seen, we derive from the Fool's comments an ironic perspective on Lear's situation. The Fool's remarks are as much for the audience as for on-stage consumption. While Shakespeare drew upon real social conditions, he also used his material in a new way, adapting theatrical practice to the expression of a more complex view of Lear's situation than could be derived from any other character in the play. Kent can tell Lear that he is rash, but he is then banished. Only the Fool can tell Lear that he has become a 'shadow' (1. 4. 206), and get away with it.

Lear's madness

Why is Lear's madness central to the play?

Here are two possible responses to this question.

1   Lear's madness gives Shakespeare the chance to explore the condition of mental breakdown at length and in detail. (Earlier chapters in this book have shown that Shakespeare seems to be interested in various forms of madness (Hamlet, Ophelia, Malvolio), and more generally in the phenomenon of extreme mental disturbance (Lady Macbeth).)

2   Lear's madness is no more than a theatrical device by means of which Shakespeare expresses his own critical political opinions in oblique form.

Check through the text, noting the points when madness first threatens Lear, when it overcomes him, whether it goes through distinct stages, and when he recovers.

In the numbered paragraphs that follow, there is a suggested chronology for the transformation of Lear's state of mind.

(i) After his quarrel with Goneril, and just before setting out for Gloucester's house, where he expects to find Regan, Lear is partly mulling over what has happened, partly attending to the gibes of the Fool. He then says: 'O, let me not be mad, not mad, sweet heaven! / Keep me in temper; I would not be mad!' (1. 5. 38–9). ('Temper', here, means not our modern 'good temper' but 'balance', 'under control', as in our modern 'temperate'.)

(ii) At Gloucester's house, faced with Regan's cold reception, madness begins to threaten Lear, although he does not at first call it that. When he asks Gloucester for a second time to announce him to Regan and Cornwall, he mutters more or less to himself: 'O me, my heart, my rising heart! but, down!' (2. 4. 115). The next provocation is Regan's suggestion that he should return to Goneril: 'I prithee, daughter, do not make me mad' (213). Then, after the discussion about how many followers Lear really needs (concluded in Regan's final thrust 'What need one?' (253)), Lear bursts out with 'O, reason not the need!' (254), denounces both sisters, pleads to the gods for patience, and then prophesies: 'O fool, I shall go mad!' (281). These words are followed by the stage direction '*Storm and tempest*'.

(iii) In the storm scene, Kent finds Lear raging at the elements and suggests he come out of the wind and rain into the hovel. Lear replies: 'My wits begin to turn' (3. 2. 65). But he then speaks to the Fool in an unexpectedly thoughtful way, which certainly does not suggest that he is demented:

> Come on, my boy. How dost, my boy? Art cold?
> I am cold myself. Where is this straw, my fellow?
> The art of our necessities is strange,
> That can make vile things precious. Come, your hovel.
> Poor fool and knave, I have one part in my heart
> That's sorry yet for thee.

> (3. 2. 66–71)

(iv) Two scenes on, Lear is still being persuaded by Kent to enter the hovel, is still brooding angrily on his daughters' behaviour, and says:

> Your old kind father, whose frank heart gave all –
> O, that way madness lies; let me shun that;
> No more of that.

> (3. 4. 21–3)

(v) Lear's madness begins later in this scene when, disturbed by the Fool's entry into the hovel, Edgar emerges '*disguised as a madman*' (45, 1) and utters scraps of nonsense, to which Lear responds: 'Hast thou given all to thy two daughters? And art thou come to this?' (49–50). Of course, this might be sarcasm, in the vein of Lear's satirical denunciations, and so it could be played. Indeed, later Kent says no more than 'His wits begin to unsettle' (149). But by this point Lear is calling Poor Tom a 'philosopher' (142) and 'learned Theban' (145), genuinely supposing he is a wise man. If by 'madness', we mean such delusion, then clearly at this stage Lear is mad (the satirical point is being made by Shakespeare that Tom is wise in having plumbed the corruptions of social life and seen them as they are).

(vi) Two scenes later, now inside the hovel, we are presented with the 'mad' trial when Lear, as judge, supported by Edgar and the Fool, tries Goneril and Regan for their crimes. At the end of this scene, Kent says that had Lear been able to sleep soundly there and then, instead of being taken to Dover at Gloucester's urgent request, he might have recovered his senses (3. 6. 90–3).

(vii) Cordelia gives an account of Lear as 'mad as the vexed sea' (4. 4. 2), wandering about in the fields near Dover; she sends out soldiers to find him (6–8); and discusses with the Doctor how he might be cured.

(viii) Following Gloucester's attempted suicide, Lear meets him and Edgar. Lear is *'fantastically dressed with wild flowers'* (4. 6. 80, 1) and still in the grip of the delusions of the trial scene. Yet, in his exchange with Gloucester, Lear talks very intelligently (see, for example, his speech about 'the great image of authority' (152–67), which Edgar calls 'Reason in madness' (69)), and he evidently recognizes Gloucester (171). Here, then, is a mixture of delusion and sanity.

(ix) Rescued by Cordelia's soldiers, Lear is given rest and sleep, and on waking is evidently in his right mind once again (4. 7. 45 onwards).

(x) In the play's final scene, Lear may be again on the verge of madness. When he appears bearing the dead Cordelia in his arms, he seems very uncertain of Kent's identity (5. 3. 277–93), but the better explanation is surely that he can attend to nothing but Cordelia's death.

Lear's state of mind is thus a prominent aspect of four of the play's acts. The Lear story is, for all practical purposes, the story of his loss and recovery of sanity. We could distinguish five stages. The first is Lear's fear of going mad, marked by furious denunciations of Goneril and Regan, and a notable self-absorption. He sees himself as a pure victim of his daughters' ingratitude, having in no way contributed to the catastrophe. The second stage, still infused with revengeful anger against his daughters, broaches more general themes. We hear not just of the injustice he suffered, but of injustice as such, not only of his sufferings in the storm, but of the Fool's, and of those of outcasts generally (the 'Poor naked wretches' he speaks about in 3. 4. 29–37). The third stage is the condition of complete delusion, the trial scene. The fourth stage is the scene with Gloucester, where Lear is calmer, with glimpses of sanity, although still in the main deluded. The fifth stage is his recovered state after the reconciliation with Cordelia.

The inner coherence of these changes in Lear's state of mind is strong evidence that Shakespeare had developed a distinct view of madness. Lear's characterization is in a different mould, in this respect, from Hamlet's. Lear's madness becomes, in fact, his route to sanity, if by that we mean a better understanding of the self and its relations with others. Looking back on the Lear of the opening scene from the vantage point of Act 4, we might even suggest that Lear begins the play in a state of mind so unbalanced as itself to deserve the term 'mad', and that the subsequent evolution of his madness is a way of coming to terms with his own overbearing, emotionally greedy, self-dramatizing personality.

In summary, the detailed exploration of Lear's state of mind, and the severe curtailment of other possibilities offered by the story, together suggest that

Shakespeare was particularly interested in the theme of madness, with the result that he built the play around this issue.

Let us look at the second possible reason suggested above for Lear's madness being central to the play. Is there any evidence for the idea that Lear's madness provided Shakespeare with a vehicle for the expression of politically subversive thoughts and feelings? It should be said immediately that this is a tricky line of approach. The history of Shakespearean criticism is strewn with the remains of hypotheses of this kind. Deducing what Shakespeare may or may not have thought is entirely dependent on evidence drawn from the plays. Since Shakespeare left no separate account of his beliefs – whether religious, political, social or moral – we have no external guide as to which plays embodied his personal conclusions about the issues of his time. To take a case in point, the critic E.M.W. Tillyard (1944) argued persuasively for Shakespeare's belief in an 'Elizabethan World Picture', a vision of a stable social and political hierarchy, headed by a divinely appointed monarch, which found its most sympathetic endorsement in Shakespeare's history plays. Although such views are uttered by characters in many of the plays, there is no certainty that Shakespeare believed in them, and ample evidence to suggest that he might not have done so. We must always keep in mind that Shakespeare's plays are not discursive essays in political and social theory, but fictions, in which certain human possibilities are tried out in imaginary form. That is the chief reason why we should be sceptical about any discussion of Shakespeare's plays that tries to allot their author a fixed set of beliefs about the world.

Given these general caveats, what of *King Lear*? Is it entirely fantastic to suppose that Lear's character offered Shakespeare the chance to air ideas that could be conceived as challenging the status quo? Consider, for a moment, the fact that *King Lear* was performed at the court of James I on 26 December 1606. **How do you think James might have reacted to this latest production by the acting company that bore the name of the king, in view of the fact that he held more than usually emphatic views about the divine source of royal authority?**

We can reasonably imagine James shaking his head at Lear's proposal to divide the kingdom, sharing Gloucester's alarm over the abdication, responding favourably to Lear's appeals to the gods to back him up, and seeing the Fool's jokes about Lear's folly in surrendering power as plain political good sense. But, as we look through the play, it is clear that Shakespeare is careful to present Lear, even *in extremis*, as an impressive figure. During the storm scenes, Kent always addresses him very respectfully; Gloucester, at great personal risk, takes Lear's side early on (3. 3. 1–13); and, after Lear has set off for Dover, Edgar's speech rounds off the scene with 'What will hap more tonight, safe 'scape the king!' (3. 6. 107). Despite his abdication, all the good characters go on calling Lear 'King', and, even at his most unbalanced, in the meeting with Gloucester near Dover, his kingliness is insisted on. The blind Gloucester falls to his knees when he hears Lear's voice, asking 'Is 't not the king?' (4. 6. 105), to which Lear, *'fantastically dressed with wild flowers'* though he may be, replies 'Aye, every inch a king!' When Cordelia's soldiers find him, and Lear thinks he has been captured, we find:

LEAR	Come, come; I am king My masters, know you that?
GENTLEMAN	You are a royal one, and we obey you.

(4. 6. 193–5)

These references have a more complex effect, according to their context, than that of mere obeisance to royalty. However, Shakespeare does seem to have gone out of his way to ensure that nobody could accuse him of presenting in the figure of Lear a disrespectful slighting of royalty. In so far as Lear's tribulations are his own fault, the lesson is that a king with his wits about him would not act as Lear does in the opening scene of the play. In so far as they are caused by others, they amount to a clear denunciation of self-seeking and hard-hearted subjects, who deserve (and in the end come to) a variety of sticky ends. All of this, we may presume, would have met with the approval of James I.

But is that the whole story? Glance back over the Lear scenes in Acts 3 and 4. **Do you notice any speeches in which Lear expresses ideas that, closely considered, might have given James I pause for thought?**

We have touched briefly on one example already: Lear's unexpected concern for the Fool (3. 4. 27–8). This is his first explicit gesture of recognition that others may suffer as well as himself. (Compare his reaction to the sight of Kent in the stocks (2. 4. 106–9): Lear takes it only as an insult to his own dignity.) This humane impulse of Lear precedes his powerful speech beginning 'Poor naked wretches, whereso'er you are, / That bide the pelting of this pitiless storm' (3. 4. 29–30), where we suddenly have a glimpse, as if in a flash of lightning, of a world outside Lear's court, in which his present physical state – shelterless, cold, hungry and soaked to the skin – is an everyday occurrence. The key sentence in this speech is, surely, the self-critical 'O, I have ta'en / Too little care of this!' (33–34). Lest we miss the logic of this fellow-feeling for the 'wretched of the earth', the speech ends in a diatribe against the greed of the rich and powerful, among whom almost all the characters in the play have to be numbered. And perhaps also that court audience of the play on 26 December 1606?

The other example is surely Lear's later denunciation of legal authority, as in the speech that Edgar calls 'Reason in madness' (4. 6. 169), an indication to the audience that Shakespeare does not want all Lear's speeches to be written off as nonsensical raving:

> Through tattered clothes small vices do appear;
> Robes and furred gowns hide all. Plate sin with gold,
> And the strong lance of justice hurtless breaks;
> Arm it in rags, a pygmy's straw does pierce it.

> (4. 6. 158–61)

The idea that the legal institutions and practices of society, as a system of punitive enforcement, work merely against the poor clearly has profound implications.

We have no way of knowing how such speeches affected contemporary audiences, but so much of what Lear says in his madness turns on the psychological sources and operations of political and legal authority that we must suppose the theme to have been deliberate on Shakespeare's part. The mad Lear becomes the voice of distinctly critical views about the world, formulated in speeches of notable cogency and penetration. In other words, whilst Shakespeare does seem to have conceived Lear as a study in mental breakdown, he handles the development of his derangement in such a way as to make room for something other than a merely personal dimension. The psychological analysis is accompanied at several points by social and political analysis, or, if that puts the case too strongly, let us say by social and political questioning, evidently planned and sustained.

There was an old tradition, strongly represented in medieval poetry, of moral criticism of the corruption of the legal process by the rich and the privileged, and their cruel indifference to the poor. As you will remember from *Hamlet* and *Measure for Measure*, Shakespeare had already provided such critical sentiments with a sympathetic theatrical presentation. Their occurrence in *King Lear* clearly is not a sudden outbreak of subversive thinking on Shakespeare's part. What we may legitimately point to is the unprecedented depth and penetration of his handling of the matter. The Russian author Anton Chekhov (1860–1904), pressed for his solutions to the social problems reflected in his plays, replied that the artist's business was not to produce solutions but to ask questions. In *King Lear*, it seems apt to think of Shakespeare asking questions about legality, privilege, power, poverty and cruelty, both personal and institutionalized, in just such a Chekhovian spirit.

Part 2 Interpretations: religion, nature, history, power and morality, gender and performance

Is King Lear *a 'religious' play?*

Look back at the play's first scene and see whether you can find any suggestions that Shakespeare wanted the audience to think of it as set in a pre-Christian society.

There appear to be at least two pieces of evidence for this. When Lear utters his rejection of Cordelia (1. 1. 108–19), he swears by pagan deities: the sun, 'The mysteries of Hecate, and the night' (Hecate was the goddess of the moon and of witchcraft) and the stars. When he and Kent argue, both invoke Apollo (159, 160).

But is this just for the sake of a first impression? Is the rest of the play consistent with this pre-Christian emphasis? In 4. 2. 47, Albany speaks of 'the heavens' and of 'visible spirits', whereas the analogous Christian ideas would be 'Heaven' and perhaps 'angels' or 'messengers from God'. Albany's words might be thought of as vague pagan prefigurations of Christian ideas, but not more. Elsewhere, the term used is 'the gods'. While specific references to 'God' in stage plays was officially frowned upon, these 'gods' can hardly be thought of as a censored version of 'God'. Their relation to human life is far too unclear. Is Gloucester in 3. 7. 35 right about them ('By the kind gods, 'tis most ignobly done'), or Edgar in 5. 3. 32–3 ('thou art a traitor; / false to thy gods')? Does the stage direction that follows Albany's 'The gods defend her!' (5. 3. 255) imply that they are incapable of protecting Cordelia (*'dead in his arms'*), or just unwilling to do so? Elsewhere, Gloucester speaks of 'You ever-gentle gods' (4. 6. 212) and Cordelia prays to 'you kind gods' (4. 7. 14) to cure her father's madness. The only thing certain about 'the gods' in *King Lear* is that, invoked on all hands, and characterized in several different ways – just, indifferent, kind, malign, helpless, or merely refusing to help – they remain enigmatic. The general impression that emerges from these examples suggests that Shakespeare had in mind a pre-Christian society, with a conception of powerful deities whom prayer might or might not persuade to intervene in human affairs. To this we may add the deliberate juxtaposition of Gloucester's superstitious belief that human events are influenced by solar and lunar eclipses (1. 2. 96–7) with Edmund's scornful rejection of such ideas (109–25). Astrology was widely believed in Shakespeare's times, and Edmund's vigorous contempt could be that of a contemporary intellectual sceptic. (Edmund, as we shall see, invokes 'nature', not any god; he could be called the play's materialist.)

The contrast with the monotheistic Christian conception of God, with his elaborate and puzzling plan for humankind, is evident enough. Yet there are references to Christian thinking. For example, it is said of Cordelia that she 'redeems nature from the general curse' that the behaviour of Goneril and Regan has brought down (4. 6. 200). There are two levels of meaning here. The text implies that Goneril and Regan have brought down a 'curse' on Britain by contributing to its political divisions. But the lines also refer to the biblical Fall of Man, brought about by Adam and Eve's disobedience, a 'general curse' from which mankind is delivered only by a Christ-like redeeming figure. This Christian allusion is reinforced by later words from Lear. Waking from curative sleep and supposing himself to have died and gone to hell, he greets Cordelia as a 'soul in bliss' (4. 7. 46). Then, in the last scene, we find allusions to St Mark's gospel when Kent, Edgar and Albany compare the sight of Lear with the dead Cordelia in his arms (5. 3. 262–3) with the end of the world as described by Christ to his disciples. In this respect, the three noblemen would seem to speak, not as members of a pre-Christian society, but as Shakespeare's contemporaries, who possess a good knowledge of the Bible.

Whatever is to be made of these passing allusions to Christian thought, and some commentators think them crucial, they do little to counter the general impression of a world with only vague religious ideas. There is a notable *absence*, in this respect, of any clerical personages, of the Christian Church as an institution, or of references to Christian religious practice. (Compare Ophelia's burial in *Hamlet*, or the religious order Isabella plans to join in *Measure for Measure*.) If we are looking for a straightforward lesson that the first-night audience of *King Lear* might have drawn from the play, it would be more along the lines of 'just what you might expect from a society lacking the benefit of the Christian revelation'.

However, the gods in *King Lear* can be viewed from a different and, with consideration, perhaps more positive perspective. Characters in *King Lear* do believe in gods, and repeatedly invoke their help. What is also evident is that direct help is unavailable. In the storm scenes, Lear invites the gods to take his part. Do they? Lear is helped, if helped at all, by Kent and Gloucester. Cordelia prays that the gods may cure him. What the play shows are human remedies – herbal cures, sleep, kindness, and above all Lear's discovery that Cordelia harbours no accusations or blame. Gloucester's view of the gods, as is consistent with his superstitious nature, alters as a result of Edgar's help in the 'suicide' scene. Before his suicide attempt, Gloucester thinks the gods are cruelly detached spectators who 'kill us for their sport' (4. 1. 38); afterwards, he finds them 'ever-gentle' (4. 6. 212). Albany's request that the gods 'defend' Cordelia (5. 3. 255) is answered by the entry of Lear carrying her dead body. We may say, then, that people in this play appeal to the gods as a way of articulating their feelings about an insoluble crisis, an imminent catastrophe or some awful recognition about the reality of their lives. In *King Lear* the gods solve nothing. However vividly they exist in the minds of the characters, as effective agents in the play supernatural values are strikingly absent. Values are constructed, challenged, destroyed, recovered and transformed by human actors through recognizably human deeds.

Lear's world is not pre-Christian in such a way that its audience would think it entirely alien. The scattering of allusions to Christian ideas lends that world a reassuring aura of familiarity. A further instance of this ambiguity is powerfully theatrical: the use of thunder. The onset of Lear's mental crisis is announced by the stage direction '*Storm and tempest*' (2. 4. 281, 2), and Lear's defiance of the elements described in 3. 1, and shown in 3. 2, is accompanied by the stage direction '*Storm still*', which prefaces each of these scenes. The stage convention of the period was that thunder represented divine displeasure; the actual noise emanated from the canopy that stretched over the stage and was known as 'the heavens'. The thunder that Lear both appeals to and defies as 'elements' (3. 2. 15) can be read in two ways. It can be seen as a merely natural phenomenon, in which case Lear's imprecations belong to the superstitious practices of a pre-Christian society, both pitiful and ludicrous. Yet it can also be read as the sign of a Christian God's wrath at Lear's disastrous mistakes. This double-edged effect leaves an imaginative space for the further implication that the storm is an objectification of Lear's mental turmoil.

Nature in King Lear

The second interpretation of the play we now want to consider makes extensive use of contemporary Elizabethan and Jacobean thinking about 'nature', a concept that appears frequently in the text.

Locate in the text Edmund's soliloquy (1. 2. 1–22), Gloucester's speech to Edmund (1. 2. 96–108), and Lear's speech to Regan (2. 4. 164–74). Each speech makes use of the term 'nature', but the word does not always mean the same thing in these speeches. What are the three different meanings given to the term?

(i) Edmund's speech appeals to an idea of nature prior to the social world in which legal concepts like 'base' and 'legitimate' have purchase. Defined as a 'bastard', born beyond the legitimacy of wedlock, Edmund asks this 'nature' to take his part, and a phrase such as 'the lusty stealth of nature' (1. 2. 11) suggests an animal-like, predatory quality.

(ii) Gloucester's speech to Edmund invokes different ideas altogether. In 'the wisdom of nature can reason it thus and thus, yet nature find itself scourged by the sequent effects' (97–9), the first usage means something like 'reason' (explanations for the eclipses that are worrying Gloucester), and the second refers to the world of human and social obligations. The second usage also appears in 'The king falls from bias of nature; there's father against child' (102–3), where 'nature' again refers to human loyalties and values.

(iii) Lear's speech to Regan invokes again the idea of nature as a norm for human values: 'The offices of nature' (2. 4. 172) include, for Lear, 'bond of childhood, / Effects of courtesy, dues of gratitude' (172–3).

In sum, the three senses in which 'nature' is used are: (i) the pre-social appetite for survival and dominance; (ii) reason, or scientific knowledge; and (iii) a nexus of social and personal values that enables us correctly to judge human actions.

In *Shakespeare's Doctrine of Nature: A Study of 'King Lear'* (1949), John F. Danby proposes that the whole play is constructed in terms of conflicting contemporary conceptions of nature. Danby conceives the play as a 'thinking-through' of the clash between two main competing usages: Lear's ((iii), above), which is also Gloucester's, Kent's, Edgar's and Albany's; and Edmund's ((i), above), which is shared by Goneril and Regan.

Nature to Lear, as to those who side with him, signifies an interwoven structure of moral, social and political loyalties that defines what it is to be a normal human being, a structure sanctioned by the gods. Goneril and Regan are 'unnatural hags' (2. 4. 273), because they do not behave 'naturally' to their father – with obedience, solicitude, kindness – just as they no longer grant him the privileges and deference due to a king. Lear's denunciation of both Cordelia and Goneril (1. 1. 108–19; 1. 4. 273–87) strikes a quasi-religious note. He invokes, as might a priest, the curse of the goddess who is the fount of the 'natural' values outraged apparently by Cordelia but actually by Goneril. Lear asks the Fool, 'Who is it that can tell me who I am?' (1. 4. 205) because his conception of himself as father and absolute ruler has been challenged at the root by the behaviour of the 'unnatural daughters'. Outside the political and social network of relationships that he calls 'nature', Lear has no identity – not, at least, until he constructs a different one. That is what his 'madness' means.

His departure from the kind of habitation represented by the castles of Goneril or Gloucester, where he had an acknowledged place, is a topographical version of his banishment from the structure of 'nature'. Wind, storm and rain, an empty heath, represent his state of mind exactly. So, too, when he strives to strip off his clothes, we should recognize that these are not just material coverings: they signify his place within the 'natural' scheme of things. Robes have hierarchical and political meaning ('Thou art a lady', he says to Regan, noting her fine clothes (2. 4. 262)), and those without them are the poor and vagrant. In Lear's conception of nature, the poor have their place, and he has duties of charity towards them. When he says 'O, I have ta'en / Too little care of this' (3. 4. 33–4), he recognizes that he has not discharged this 'natural' obligation. We should remember that, in cutting off Cordelia, he has directly violated the 'natural' order that fathers and daughters should preserve in relation to each other, just as Goneril and Regan have violated it. The chain of events that makes Lear impotently invoke nature in his defence against his daughters' treatment was thus set in motion by his own act. His greeting of Poor Tom – 'Thou art the thing itself' (3. 4. 98) – represents his attempt to develop a new idea of human nature outside the traditional structure. Instead of clothes, nakedness; instead of social obligations and relationships, solitude; instead of houses, heathland and storm; instead of humanity, a 'bare, forked animal' (99–100).

Edmund is the principal voice of a different idea of nature. Edmund's 'nature' is the term that validates a thrusting, competitive, amoral individualism before which all shared values must give way. In his *Leviathan* (1651), the political philosopher Thomas Hobbes (1588–1679) offers the most explicit account of this different view of nature, which had been gaining ground during the sixteenth century, and would certainly have been familiar to Shakespeare's audiences. Hobbes argued that

> in the nature of man, we find three principal causes of quarrel. First, competition; secondly diffidence [that is, suspicion, mistrust]; thirdly, glory. The first maketh man invade for gain; the second for safety; and the third for reputation ... Hereby it is manifest that during the time men live without a common power to keep them all in awe, they are in that condition which is called war; and such a war, as is of every man, against every man ... continual fear and danger of violent death; and the life of man, solitary, poor, nasty, brutish, and short.

(Quoted in Danby, 1968 edn, p.39)

Nature in this usage is not an encompassing structure within which human life achieves mutually beneficent satisfactions, but resembles rather Darwin's account of the natural world as made up of a myriad living species competing against each other in a fierce struggle for survival. It is interesting that in both the Quarto and the Folio texts of *King Lear* the usual name used for Edmund is 'Bastard', and this is how he introduces himself in his soliloquy. He rejects the social and moral structure of the nature to which Gloucester later appeals when he calls Edmund a 'Loyal and natural boy' (2. 1. 85). Notice the irony of the word 'natural', which means to Gloucester loyalty but which offers to Edmund a perfect justification for treachery. From the angle provided by Edmund's idea of nature, Gloucester's nature is a system of self-delusion, by which any tolerably clever and talented individual can profit. We see Edmund profiting, first by using Gloucester's idea of nature as a way of getting rid of Edgar, and then, when Gloucester confides in him about the letter concerning Cordelia's army (3. 3. 7–17), immediately betraying his 'natural' loyalty to a father by telling Cornwall. Whereas for Gloucester reality is the framework of moral and social obligations that imposes duty and responsibility, for Edmund reality is self-advancement, the appetite for power and place, the ruthless assertion of individual will and, wherever necessary, the manipulation of others who may help or hinder this fundamental drive.

Here is a thematic link with Goneril and Regan. Formally, in their speeches of love for Lear, they seem committed to the Lear idea of nature. But it is the brief prose exchange that closes the opening scene that reveals their true commitments. They feel no love for their father, but view him with a cold and keen-eyed shrewdness as they calculate the best way to turn the situation to their advantage. As we have already noticed, the two sisters, and Goneril especially, see Lear's insistence on still calling himself king, and keeping his troop of 100 knights, as a directly political threat. That is their only world. It appears to be the main concern of their husbands, too, as when we hear of the 'snuffs and packings of the Dukes' (3. 1. 26), the manoeuvring for position in their rivalry for complete command of the kingdom. Regan later remarks that it was a mistake to let the blinded Gloucester wander away on his own, because he would arouse political feelings against their rule. That is her only thought about him. Goneril, confronted with Albany's horrified response to the news of her treatment of Lear, calls him a 'moral fool' (4. 2. 59), preaching about 'humanity' when he ought to be facing the political threat to his position that Cordelia's army poses. Regan's attitude to the system of nature as a structure of values is entirely self-serving. When Cornwall's servant attacks his master for putting out Gloucester's eye, he does so in the name of 'service' to his lord (3. 7. 75), implicitly invoking a natural order that justifies his act. For his pains, Regan calls him 'dog' (77), and kills him with the contemptuous dismissal 'A peasant stand up thus!' (83). Similarly, we may contrast the loyalty of Kent to Lear against his own self-interest (as the Fool points out in 2. 4. 72–9), with the loyalty of Oswald to Regan in hoping to kill the blind and helpless Gloucester as a means to self-advancement (4. 5. 40–1).

In addition to the two main conceptions of nature in the play already discussed, another perspective on nature is provided by Cordelia. Lear's conception of nature is self-contradictory. Edmund's view of nature is, in one respect, right. Lear's 'nature' is, to use a modern term, a mystifying ideology that obscures a system of legal oppression, this being one of Lear's central discoveries in his 'madness'. Edmund works this ideology to his own advantage because, in the end, it functions to legitimate power. The farcical bargaining of the opening scene, whereby land and revenues are calculated against love, is shown for what it is: an assertion of political and familial power. But once Lear has abandoned his real power, he can no longer make his system of nature serve his needs. Nature will no longer heed him, however eloquent his appeals. What he proceeds to discover is the mutuality of human need in the face of a natural world that owes humanity nothing. He finds that – far from supporting the feudal hierarchy and its attendant values – nature is neutral, indifferent, and powerful in its capacity both to distress (rain, wind, barrenness) and to heal and support (the herbal medicines provided by the Doctor), according to the use that humankind makes of it.

Cordelia is associated with this latter sense of the natural world as nurturing, and also with a quality of relationship in which the mutuality of open need is the key expression. Cordelia's is the idea of a nature in which the struggle for power has no place. By 'love', Cordelia means the opposite of 'power'. She opposes love to Lear's exercise of power, and only when he has abandoned every claim to power is he able to see what Cordelia has represented. The life he envisages with her in prison is explicitly contrasted with the continuing world of power, in which 'packs and sects of great ones ... ebb and flow by the moon' (5. 3. 18–19). Lear's may be no more than a utopian vision, immediately snuffed out by political realities, yet the fragile possibility of goodness and justice is juxtaposed with the power of the corrupt world, which condemns him and Cordelia to 'a walled prison' (5. 3. 18), and to death. What Lear's sufferings teach us is an ideal conception of relationships to be held up against the real world. We are confronted with an opposition of absolutes. Cordelia may indeed represent all these ideal values, but in the end what the audience sees is: 'LEAR, *with* CORDELIA *dead in his arms*' (255, 2).

King Lear *and history*

Let us now pursue the issue of history in closer relation to the dramatic structure of the play. The conceptions of nature associated with Lear, Edmund and Cordelia in the play had their roots in actual historical developments. Lear's 'nature' corresponded to feudal conceptions in which society was ordered by a hierarchy of estates bound to each other by reciprocal duties and responsibilities, culminating in the king, who was in his turn responsible to God. Edmund's 'nature' looked forward to the secular Hobbesian view of naturally warring individuals, whom only the arbitrary imposition of superior power could bring into cohesive social relationships. Cordelia's 'nature', the utopian possibility of egalitarian, mutually supportive social relationships, had its roots in Christian–communist thinking, which was to emerge in earnest on the political scene during the English Civil War. A link can be made here with a tradition of Christian communion, according to which, in Gloucester's words, 'distribution should undo excess, / And each man have enough' (4. 1. 70–1). This tradition was represented by groups such as the medieval Lollards, the fifteenth-century Anabaptists and the seventeenth-century Levellers and Diggers, all of them radical, egalitarian communities. In these ways *King Lear* engaged with historical processes at work in the society of Shakespeare's time.

To contrast the orthodox Elizabethan idea of a benign nature with the Hobbesian idea of a competitive force is not to make an anachronistic connection between Shakespeare and a seventeenth-century political philosopher, but to use the latter's ideas as an instance of new historical movements in Shakespeare's time, of which Hobbes's thought was a later and developed expression. We can think of Edmund as one of the Elizabethan 'new men', of the kind that worked gladly and profitably for Thomas Cromwell, who was authorized by Henry VIII to dispossess the church of its lands and revenues after his quarrel with the Pope. The traditional position, reflected in the Lear view of nature, was under challenge in Shakespeare's day. Thus, James I's preoccupation with the divine right of kings reflects an insistence upon a conception of political legitimacy – the king's authority as sanctioned by God, and at the same time involving reciprocal Christian responsibilities towards his subjects – because the idea of divine right was coming under pressure. A change in the balance of political forces was taking place: the expansionist, entrepreneurial thrust of the Jacobean period and the beginnings of the conflict between king and Parliament over the issue of monopolies (a major source of political patronage, whereby the king granted his supporters the right to the profitable management of certain kinds of trade) are also prominent features of the early seventeenth century. *King Lear*, in this sense, engages with significant political and economic tensions of the time, the more effectively for their being disguised in a legend about pre-Christian Britain.

As we saw in Chapter 3, Marxist thinking about tragedy insists upon the relationship of a particular form of tragedy (Greek, Renaissance, and so on) to its historical context. Marx argued that Hegel's analysis of historical process as a conflict of ideas, or spiritual forces, should be turned on its head. In Marx's estimation, it is not our consciousness that determines our social being, but rather our social being that determines our consciousness. Tragedies thus reflect conflicts not of abstract ideas and values, but of specific social and historical forces. Raymond Williams summarizes this view as follows:

> The [Hegelian] conflict of ethical forces, and their resolution by a higher force, were seen in social and historical terms. Social development was seen as necessarily contradictory in character, and tragedy occurs at those points where the conflicting forces must, by their inner nature, take action, and carry the conflict through to a transformation.

> Renaissance tragedy has been seen as the embodiment of the conflict between a dying feudalism and the new individualism. It is not eternal justice, in Hegel's sense, that is affirmed in the tragic issue, but rather the general movement of history, in a series of decisive transformations of society. Not all conflicts of this kind lead to tragedy. There is only tragedy when each side finds it necessary to act, and refuses to give way.

> (Williams, 1966, p.35)

Does *King Lear* provide an effective illustration of Williams's description of the Marxist view of tragedy as resulting from historical conflict, or does it differ in some way?

Williams's description could be applied to *King Lear*, but we would surely need to add that the play hardly presents 'the general movement of history'. If Lear and his court, and Lear's ideas about society, are (broadly speaking) feudal, and in that sense, speak for dying social forms, we do not gain any impression of the new social forms that (historically speaking) replaced them. Edmund's individualism, although contemptuously dismissive of the structure of 'natural' (that is, feudal) obligations, is nevertheless not linked with any alternative social embodiment. If Edmund had defeated Edgar, married one of the sisters, disposed of Albany, and himself become king, we could imagine him quite easily, even if cynically, defending his claim to obedience in traditional terms. His thinking about nature may indeed point to later ideas which had direct social relevance, but the play itself provides no direct reflection of that relevance.

If we wish to locate the irreconcilable conflicts in the play, these exist rather at the level of ideology. Thus, on the one hand, there is Lear's ideal conception of natural duties and responsibilities, the system that sanctions his royal authority. On the other, there is the discovery of how little this conception corresponds to the real world: the helplessness and misery of the poor, the corruption of justice by the rich, the identification of law with power (as in Goneril's 'the laws are mine' (5. 3. 157)), the powerlessness of the ideas associated with Cordelia to realize themselves, save in the most vulnerable personal terms. Setting these conflicts before us, the play simply leaves them unresolved. This method seems characteristic of its treatment of social issues. The specific historical dimension is touched on, but hardly, in the Marxist sense, fully explored.

Power and morality

Shakespeare drew upon popular Elizabethan dramatic practice. His own comedies – *A Midsummer Night's Dream*, *Twelfth Night* and others – embody the festive, anarchic spirit of popular Elizabethan holidays and the games and entertainments that celebrated them. His use of the 'upper' and 'lower' acting areas of the public-theatre stages, it has been argued, provided the theatrical means for incorporating the perspectives of two distinct social strata: the rulers and gentry involved in the romantic or heroic action, and the ordinary people with their different point of view on that action. Drawing on such traditions in *Measure for Measure*, Shakespeare presented not a unified overview of the main story, but unresolved conflicts – the play's power lying precisely in their not being resolved. Shakespeare's tragedies often involve a comic mixture of social strata: the Porter in *Macbeth*, Hamlet's adoption of a Fool's role, the Clown admitted into Cleopatra's final scene. The question is: why? Why does Shakespeare exploit in his tragedies methods and effects characteristic of his comedies? Might it be that it provides him with a theatrical means of presenting seemingly unresolvable conflicts?

We have seen already that in *King Lear* the Fool has a key part in the early acts. The Fool is one of Shakespeare's vehicles for bringing to bear on Lear's predicament a point of view entirely alien to the world of Lear's court. The Fool is, formally, a sort of member of that court, but his style of speech, gnomic riddling and satiric quips, sprinkled with popular jokes and songs, draws upon experiences of life from which the court is protected. The Fool is 'oppositional' – but not boldly so like Kent, or silently like Cordelia. His is the opposition of the powerless. This opposition is sly, indirect, wrapped in ambiguity and doubleness.

FOOL	That sir which serves and seeks for gain,
	And follows but for form,
	Will pack when it begins to rain,
	And leave thee in the storm.
	But I will tarry; the fool will stay,
	And let the wise man fly.
	The knave turns fool that runs away;
	The fool no knave, perdy.
KENT	Where learned you this, Fool?
FOOL	Not i' the stocks, fool.

(2. 4. 72–9)

The Fool has learned in Lear's court what Lear himself only recognizes when, taken captive with Cordelia, he says:

> ... we'll wear out,
> In a walled prison, packs and sects of great ones,
> That ebb and flow by the moon.

(5. 3. 17–19)

He has learned the key to the situation Lear finds himself in when he no longer wields political power. The Fool has also learned that, if you challenge the powerful, you end up where Kent is at that point: in the stocks, or worse. The exchange with Kent quoted above, located in the downstage acting position, in semi-direct address to the audience, would be quickly understood by the latter. But it conceals a further cryptic meaning. 'Wisdom' is prudent; it lies in self-preservation, keeping in with the powerful. 'Folly' is not to realize this, or to choose differently. The last two lines of the Fool's first speech in the exchange gloss this shrewd sense of political reality with a covert judgement. The fool who stays loyal is not a knave, whereas the prudent man who flies from trouble is. Moreover, in a different sense, he is a self-deceiving fool locked into a system of endless treachery, double-dealing and struggle for gain, which by its nature can hold no promise of stability. Such utterances both recognize the truth about power politics – a truth that Lear at this stage cannot grasp, because the ingrained pattern of his thinking makes the power structure he has headed 'natural' to him – and yet also undercut it. Who is the fool? The prudent man says, 'Somebody like Kent who cannot read the political situation rightly, defies the king to no purpose, and is banished for his pains.' The Fool gives a different answer: 'The prudent man is the fool, because he fails to see the self-destructive character of the system he upholds.' Oswald is that kind of fool.

When we remember that the Fool's style and presence belong to the popular end of the social spectrum, that it is through him that Lear begins to see the world from the point of view of the 'Poor naked wretches ... That bide the pelting of this pitiless storm' (3. 4. 29–30), and to break loose from the thinking that has governed his royal existence, we can see that such conflicts amount to more than profound word-play. Put briefly, the Fool is the means whereby Shakespeare juxtaposes two irreconcilable political experiences: that of being inside the world of power and privilege, and that of being outside it, and so at its mercy. This is an experience that the 'good' characters (Lear, Gloucester, Edgar, Cordelia and Kent) all undergo in various degrees of intensity, and with various effects. We confront here a central engagement of *King Lear* with the history of its time, which is nevertheless not confined to that time, and which bears crucially upon its being a tragedy. In its exploration of power and morality, the play confirms what Kiernan Ryan has referred to as 'the urgent bearing of *King Lear* on our own predicament' (1993, p.98).

If we say that the play opens up a conflict between the category of the political and the category of the moral, this is a more general way of stating the issue raised by means of the Fool. There is a sense in which *King Lear* presents a moral conflict between good and evil. The characterization of both parties is defined largely in terms of black and white oppositions, rather than complexly defined personalities. The story, too, has its straightforward moral aspect. The good are first defeated with cruel thoroughness, and the evil hold sway, but then the good revive and, in the persons of Edgar and Albany, triumph over the evil. Edgar's emblematic duel with Edmund epitomizes this pattern, without which we would not have a tragedy, only a violent political melodrama. This derives from the system of power, from the ambition for it, its political necessity, and its amoral logic. Edmund is its chief spokesman, with the curiously attractive character of those explicit villains we find in Shakespeare's plays. Considered from his brother's or his father's angle, both of whom he treats atrociously, Edmund appears to be evil. But considered from his own standpoint: 'Well then, / Legitimate Edgar, I must have your land' (1. 2. 15–16)? It is not just that there is something to be said for Edmund, that he has some positive qualities, and that, remembering his illegitimate birth, we sympathize in some degree with his ambitions – although Shakespeare presents him in such a way as to attract such feelings. It is rather that the system of legitimacy, the social set-up Edmund finds himself struggling with, is presented as a truth about the world, which carries its own implications. We have called Edmund the play's materialist, meaning that he sees through the mystifications that mask the system of legitimacy with seeming virtue. An outsider, he exposes the reality of the world of the 'legitimate' insiders.

We might also take some time to consider Cordelia. Her flat rejection of the terms offered by her father is impressive, but as many critics have pointed out, such morally absolute commitment prompts searching questions. Shakespeare asks us to see all around Cordelia's position. Certainly, it is admirable, but it is so presented as to invite our awareness of what it excludes: tact, prudence (not in its pejorative sense of narrow self-seeking, but implying a sound judgement of consequences), perhaps imaginative insight into her father's nature – an insight not denied to her coldly shrewd sisters. Critics who descry in Cordelia's 'Nothing' an attitude tainted by immature self-righteousness or by Lear-like stubbornness surely miss the point as completely as those who wish only to praise her goodness. What the play actually shows is the collision of goodness with differently impelled commitments, such as Edmund's.

The point can be made on a larger scale by considering the interrelationship of power and morality that the play repeatedly puts before us. We see the awful misuse of power in individual cases (Goneril and Regan mistreating their father, Edmund betraying his), and the mad Lear generalizes the case to suggest that the very structure of political power is intrinsically evil, subverting law and morality for cruel and oppressive purposes. But how do we read Lear's speech to Cordelia expressing a rejection of secular power of any kind (5. 3. 7–18)? Is this an ultimately moral position against which all other statements and positions can be tested and found wanting? Some critics read it that way. Yet what are its consequences? One is Cordelia's death. From elsewhere in the play, we know that the powerless do not enjoy the happy condition that Lear imagines might be his and his daughter's in prison (Figures 38 and 39). The task of the survivors is the restoration of the shattered political order. 'Friends of my soul,' says Albany to Edgar and Kent, 'you twain, / Rule in this realm, and the gored state sustain' (5. 3. 318–19). This is considerably more than saying that life must go on. What must go on is politics, the assertion of power by means of the institutions necessary to a state. We are back in the world of Edmund's 'legitimacy'. In sum, what makes *King Lear* a tragedy, as distinct from a tale of the conflict of good with evil, is that it represents this irreconcilability of the political and the moral, each of which is realized as a specific social sphere of action.

We can perhaps link this theme to Shakespeare's time, and again to our own. Historical periods in which the basic political structures are undergoing serious

Figure 38 *Reconciliation of Lear (Yuri Yarvet) and Cordelia (V. Shendrikova) in Act 4, Scene 7 of* King Lear *directed by Grigori Kozintsev, 1970, USSR, from a translation by Boris Pasternak. Courtesy of National Film Archive/Stills Library, British Film Institute.*

change, or at least are felt to be under challenge, will sharpen the contradiction between the political and the moral, whereas in periods when the political structures are stable the contradiction tends to remain hidden. When the system of legitimacy is generally felt to be legitimate, or when those who might question its legitimacy have no voice, then its relation with morality is not experienced as problematic. The modern revaluation of Shakespeare's *King Lear*, and the high esteem in which it is now held, turn out to be signs of our own history, of our own modern sense of the clash between the political and the moral.

The question of gender

It might seem obvious to some readers that discussions of nature, power and morality in *King Lear* should entail a consideration of gender and its significance in the play. For many years, however, gender was not regarded as a very important issue in Shakespeare studies, despite an overt concern with sexual morality in the comedies and an intense preoccupation with male–female power struggles in *Macbeth* and *Antony and Cleopatra*. As we have seen, the conventional view of tragedy that persisted until fairly recently assumed that tragic 'flaws' were inherent in human nature, unavoidably and universally present as part of 'the single state of man' (*Macbeth*, 1. 3. 139). It was also commonly assumed that audiences responded to the tragic spectacle of a play like *King Lear* with the same emotional fervour, regardless of their gender.

Figure 39 *Lear (Yuri Yarvet) and Cordelia (V. Shendrikova) are led off as prisoners in Act 5, Scene 2 of* King Lear *directed by Grigori Kozintsev, 1970, USSR, from a translation by Boris Pasternak. Kobal Collection.*

As part of the revolution in critical responses to *King Lear* since the 1960s, feminist scholars have challenged and revised some of the familiar assumptions about 'man's destiny' in a tragic universe. *King Lear* has been the focus of intense debate, with Lear's daughters frequently being invoked in discussions about the various ways in which feminist critics might respond to Shakespeare. In 1981, Marianne Novy called for a radical reappraisal of the plays, claiming that feminist critics had until then responded to Shakespeare 'with the loyalty that a dutiful daughter might have for a parent' (Barker and Kamps, 1995, p.2). In 1995, however, Deborah Barker and Ivo Kamps were able to give a more stirring account of feminist criticism:

> Feminist critics ... have certainly not responded to the Shakespeare establishment as Cordelia does to Lear's demand for filial devotion. Instead of saying nothing, they have criticized the question, challenged Lear's position as patriarch, reconsidered the position of women in Renaissance society, and so on. If feminists have not thrown Lear out of doors, they have certainly made him share the Kingdom.

(Ibid.)

As other chapters of this book confirm, there is no single, uniform, feminist interpretation of any of Shakespeare's plays. Some feminist critics have continued to argue that the plays are generally sympathetic to women's concerns, whilst others have claimed that Shakespeare's representation of women varies according to genre, with the comedies being noticeably more positive than the tragedies.

Where might a feminist critique of *King Lear* begin? Many feminist critics have chosen to concentrate on what they regard as a misogynistic representation of women in *King Lear*. Several critics have pointed out that the female characters in the play are either demonic or saintly types: Goneril and Regan on the one hand, Cordelia on the other. From this perspective, *King Lear* is a play about the perpetuation of patriarchal power and sexual inequality. Feminist critics have disagreed, however, about the extent to which *King Lear* either tacitly endorses or exposes that patriarchal regime. To what extent is Shakespeare as author complicit in legitimating the existing sexual order?

For Kathleen McLuskie, *King Lear* is a play that dramatizes a connection between sexual insubordination and political anarchy (Ryan, 1993, p.48). The order of the state is seen to depend upon a careful regulation of sexual and family relations, and when Lear rages against the collapse of order, it is women's lust that is blamed as the cause of chaos and corruption (3. 4). From this point of view, Cordelia's enduring love is not a virtue that 'redeems nature' (4. 6. 200) but a response that restores patriarchal authority. How, then, should the play be read or viewed in performance? McLuskie recommends resistance to the emotional power of the play to compel us to sympathize with Lear, and urges us to exchange the pleasure of identification for the pleasure of critical insight and understanding. Her aim is to interrogate, rather than accept, the views of gender and sexuality that inform *King Lear*.

What objections might be raised to this reading of *King Lear*? Is Shakespeare unarguably 'the patriarchal Bard'? Some feminist readings of *King Lear* have presented positive accounts of the play and its sexual politics. Coppélia Kahn, for instance, has developed a psychoanalytical reading of the play, which explores the idea of the 'absent mother' in *King Lear*. Whilst in no way excusing the wrongs of patriarchy, this approach views *King Lear* as a tragedy of masculinity. For Kahn, Lear's progress is not towards the spiritual redemption observed in conservative readings of the play, but towards a recognition and acceptance of 'the woman in himself' (Ryan, 1993, p.105). The tragic power of the play issues from its awareness of the terrible human price paid by a society that represses female instincts and feelings. The approaches adopted by McLuskie and Kahn are strikingly different, but it is worth noting that both critics concentrate largely on Lear and Cordelia. A more comprehensive study of gender relations in the play needs to include some account of how other characters, including Edmund, Goneril and Regan, behave towards each other. A critical reading based on the identification of 'female' instincts and feelings runs the risk of establishing an essentialist view of 'man' and 'woman'. Kahn argues that Regan and Goneril 'betray and disappoint Lear by not being mothers to him' (ibid., p.104), but are we to assume that this behaviour issues from their 'masculine' instincts? What feelings and instincts promote their sexual interest in Edmund?

Both McLuskie and Kahn point to the importance of grounding arguments about gender in careful historical research, including studies of the Elizabethan family and its social structures. Recent feminist criticism, in keeping with this tendency, has

Figure 40 *Adjoa Andoh as Regan, Sandra Yaw as Goneril and Polly Irvin as Cordelia in a BBC/OU audio recording of* Lear's Daughters *directed by Jenny Bardwell, 1997.*

drawn extensively on historical research as a way of reaching a more exact understanding of the sexual, as well as socio-economic, relations that prevailed in the early seventeenth century. The pursuit of sexual equality can then be acknowledged as part of the struggle for personal fulfilment and social justice in the face of those divisive and dominating institutional structures that so often determine what we know as tragedy.

For a further critical perspective on issues of gender in *King Lear*, you might read 'Reason and madness: male and female' in Terence Hawkes's study of the play (1995).

King Lear *in performance*

Whether we are talking about the early performance of *King Lear* on St Stephen's Night in 1606, or late-twentieth-century experimental versions of the play, there can be no neutral or definitive performance. In the light of the preceding section on gender issues, we might begin by asking what kind of performance would be most responsive to the concerns of feminist criticism. McLuskie envisages a production of the text that would highlight a feminist critique by 'removing the privilege both from the character of Lear and from the ideological positions which he dramatises' (Ryan, 1993, p.56). It is not entirely clear whether she is calling for stronger directorial control or extensive rewriting of the play. One conceivable production, although a rather obvious one, would involve the casting of a female actor as Lear and perhaps the displacement of King Lear by 'Queen Lear'. Another possibility is the creation of a supplementary play or counter-text, in which the woman's role is privileged. The function of a play like *Lear's Daughters* (Women's Theatre Group, 1987–8) is to interrogate the spoken and unspoken assumptions about gender that inform the Shakespearean text (Figure 40). It is certainly the case that one very potent feminist response to *King Lear* has been to rewrite the play and even change its genre. Jane Smiley's novel, *A Thousand Acres* (1991), set in modern-day Iowa, is a remarkably imaginative transformation of Shakespeare's tragic drama. However, a production of the text that is sensitive to its sexual politics does not necessarily require special pleading on behalf of its female characters or a complete rewriting of the text. It might function by drawing attention to the material conditions and social structures that serve to perpetuate inequalities of power, including those that exist between women and men.

In discussing questions of performance, we need always to make a careful distinction between live theatre and film recordings, even if what we are watching is a video recording of a play performed on stage. One of the immediate advantages that film productions of Shakespeare's plays have over live theatre productions is that they can manipulate the viewing area so as to convey a more extensive and detailed impression of the social and historical context of the plays. Films that are shot on location rather than made in the theatre can range broadly across a vividly recreated series of settings. The great appeal of the 1970 *King Lear* directed by Grigori Kozintsev is that it shows overwhelmingly the social repercussions of the tragedy. Adopting a modern Russian translation of the play by Boris Pasternak and a sombre orchestral score by Dmitri Shostakovich, Kozintsev presents the action through a roving, wide-angled lens. The purpose of this cinemascope effect is not only to give the play an epic sweep and spaciousness, but also to show Lear's kingdom as a densely peopled landscape. In the opening frames, the peasants who scratch out a living on the seemingly barren landscape are seen moving towards the castle walls to wait for Lear's announcement. A mother tends to a sleeping child carried in a wheelbarrow by its father, a touching instance of human kindness and shared responsibility that prefigures the negation of such values in the scenes that follow. Cordelia and her sisters are presented not as isolated incarnations of goodness and evil, but as women who move in a world of feudal power relations and military operations, and whose lives are caught up in the hierarchical structure of that world.

The emphasis in Kozintsev's film is on shared human endeavour and suffering rather than on the unique and individual suffering of the king. When, in the storm scene, Lear addresses the 'Poor naked wretches', we see him taking refuge in a gloomy hovel already crammed with the poor of his kingdom. With Kozintsev, the sympathetic identification of the king with the lowliest of his subjects is given physical realization. Similarly, Edgar in the guise of Poor Tom is seen to join a long procession of beggars. Kozintsev, whose own account of the film's production recalls the wartime horrors of Auschwitz and Hiroshima, gives unflinching attention to man-made violence and destruction. The desolate landscape across which the beggars move was filmed near Narva, where pollution has killed vast tracts of forest and vegetation (Figure 41). Whilst the film is essentially realist in style, it also employs symbolic devices, including images of fire and water. Through the arch where Cordelia has been hanged, we see water moving in a tranquil moment of reprieve from the fire of battle. These images coincide with the pattern of Christian redemption, but the final gesture in the film is towards the possibility of social renewal. The peasants who gathered for Lear's announcement now sift through the charred ruins and prepare to build their homes again. Kozintsev shows the appalling human cost of tragedy, but also a changing social process in which men and women have the potential to transform the conditions under which they live.

Figure 41 *The Fool playing his pipe at the end of Act 5, Scene 3 of* King Lear *directed by Grigori Kozintsev, 1970, USSR, from a translation by Boris Pasternak. Kobal Collection.*

References

Barker, D.E. and Kamps, I. (eds) (1995) *Shakespeare and Gender: A History*, London and New York: Verso.

Bradley, A.C. (1967) *Shakespearean Tragedy*, London: Macmillan (first published 1904).

Danby, J.F. (1968) *Shakespeare's Doctrine of Nature: A Study of 'King Lear'*, London: Faber (first published 1949).

Elton, W.R. (1966) *'King Lear' and the Gods*, San Marino, CA: Huntington Library.

Empson, W. (1951) *The Structure of Complex Words*, London: Chatto & Windus.

Hawkes, T. (1995) 'Reason and madness: male and female', in *William Shakespeare: King Lear*, Plymouth: Northcote House, chapter 6.

Hobbes, T. (1996) *Leviathan*, 1651, ed. R. Tuck, Cambridge: Cambridge University Press.

Kettle, A. (1988) 'From *Hamlet* to *Lear*', 1964, in *Literature and Liberation: Selected Essays*, ed. G. Martin and W.R. Owens, Manchester: Manchester University Press.

Knight, G.W. (1949) *The Wheel of Fire*, London: Methuen (first published 1930).

Kott, J. (1965) *Shakespeare Our Contemporary*, London: Methuen.

Orwell, G. (1966) *Collected Essays*, London: Heinemann.

Ryan, K. (ed.) (1993) *King Lear: Contemporary Critical Essays*, London: Macmillan.

Smiley, J. (1991) *A Thousand Acres*, New York: Random House.

Tillyard, E.M.W. (1944) *Shakespeare's History Plays*, London: Chatto & Windus.

Williams, R. (1966) *Modern Tragedy*, London: Chatto & Windus.

THE TEMPEST

Chapter 9

Pat Scorer

Aims

This chapter is in two parts. The first part aims to provide a close reading of key passages in *The Tempest* and to locate the play in its historical context. The second part focuses on recent debates about the play, and reflects upon post-colonial reinterpretations in particular. By the end of the chapter, you should have a good grasp of the dramatic structure of *The Tempest*, a knowledge of its historical sources, an awareness of the complex issues of genre that it raises, and a familiarity with recent critical perspectives on the play.

Part 1 *Reading* **The Tempest**

As you reach this final chapter, you will be well aware of the changes time has wrought on performances and interpretations of Shakespeare's plays. As we have seen, even the texts of the plays cannot be said to offer a definitive account of what Shakespeare wrote or intended. Interpretations of *The Tempest* have been complicated by critical debates about the dates and places of its earliest performances, about its possible source materials, about the circumstances of its publication, and about the nature of its genre.

The first recorded performance of *The Tempest* took place at the court of King James I on 'Hollomas nyght' (the evening of 1 November), a suitable time for a play in which spirits appear. There is a further record of *The Tempest* as one of fourteen plays performed in the season preceding the marriage of the king's daughter, Princess Elizabeth, in 1613. These two documented performances have led some critics to stress the idea of *The Tempest* as a Jacobean court play, whilst others have suggested that the play might have been revised for the marriage festivities. It is likely, however, that the play was also performed publicly at the Blackfriars and Globe playhouses.

Even though *The Tempest* was probably written before *Henry VIII*, it has assumed a reputation as Shakespeare's valediction to the stage and the epitome of his dramatic art. *The Norton Shakespeare* (p.3047) points out that Shakespeare collaborated on at least two plays after *The Tempest*. The earliest text of the play appears in the 1623 Folio, where it is placed first and grouped as a comedy, creating further speculation about its place in Shakespeare's *oeuvre*. The very title of the play may give us pause and reason to suspect that the humour of this alleged comedy may not be unalloyed.

How are the key concerns of the play introduced in Acts 1 and 2?

The play opens with a short scene that has given directors ample opportunity to exercise their theatrical ingenuity, demonstrate the technical resources of their theatres and encourage actors in their capacity for mime. A raging storm at sea threatens the lives of a ship's high-born passengers and its mariners:

> Mercy on us!
> We split, we split! Farewell, my wife and children!
> Farewell, brother! We split, we split, we split!

(1. 1. 54–6)

Of course, the ship also carries a number of other passengers, including a court jester called Trinculo and a drunken butler called Stefano, whose presence contributes significantly to the social mix and social interaction of the play.

Before all can turn to disaster, the next scene rapidly ensues. Its setting is simply given as 'Prospero's island', and the dialogue reveals that the tempest is not a natural phenomenon but has been conjured up by the magic of one man, Prospero, who lives with his young daughter on this remote territory. We are in a world where 'art', that is to say, magic and occult knowledge, as well as skill and experience, holds sway.

The second scene of Act 1 consists largely of a lengthy reminiscence, in which Prospero explains to Miranda the reasons for their presence on this desert island: twelve years before, they were exiled from Prospero's dukedom of Milan and, taking to the sea, by chance landed here. Time has passed, Miranda is now fifteen years of age and those responsible for Prospero's banishment and the usurpation of his dukedom find themselves shipwrecked upon this island thanks to his magician's skill and plotting.

You will notice several things in this preliminary account. The island is given no name. Prospero is helped in the furtherance of his magic plot by a spirit, Ariel, whom he found in captivity, freed and set to work for him when he first came to these shores. There is one other indigenous inhabitant, Caliban, who seems to be a monster rather than a spirit, and to whom the island originally belonged because it was the possession of his mother, the witch Sycorax. So Prospero's domain is peopled by four beings, two of whom, Ariel and Caliban, in very different ways serve and do the bidding of the former Duke of Milan, their present master.

The characters in the play are thus divided from the beginning into two groups: those who have newly arrived, shipwrecked by the tempest, and Prospero's tiny company, who inhabit another part of the island. Ariel moves between them at Prospero's bidding and fulfils his commands. He is invisible to others and his presence is often signified by music and songs:

> Where the bee sucks, there suck I:
> In a cowslip's bell I lie;
> There I couch when owls do cry.
> On the bat's back I do fly
> After summer merrily.

(5. 1. 88–92)

These lines suggest a fairy-like dimension in which all is harmony and oneness with nature. Perhaps they also suggest the freedom that Ariel seeks – freedom to live according to his inner impulses as a spirit – and this freedom has been promised to him by his master. His task in bringing together the two factions on the island is to be his last before Prospero sets him at liberty to follow his own inclination.

The link between the long-standing exiles, Prospero and Miranda, and those who have just been driven there by the storm is one of origins: the newcomers include the usurper who currently rules the duchy of Milan, Prospero's brother Antonio, and those who helped him to this unlawful seizure, Alonso, King of Naples, and his brother Sebastian. The link is thus territorial and political, and Milan (and later Naples) is the geographical centre of a territorial dispute. This past history is unfolded for the benefit of Miranda – and, incidentally, of the audience – in the second scene of the first act. We shall need to return to this history and probe it carefully in later sections of this chapter when diverse interpretations of this 'comedy' come under discussion. For the moment, let us simply note that these former enemies of Prospero are the very people he has caused to be washed ashore on his island. It is not clear whether he has revenge in mind or possible reconciliation.

Another important narrative strand introduced is that of the love affair of Ferdinand and Miranda. Alonso, King of Naples, believes that he has lost his son, Ferdinand, in the storm, and is grief-stricken; however, the audience is soon aware that Ferdinand has escaped danger, and he is led by Ariel to Prospero's dwelling. The meeting of Miranda and Ferdinand (1. 2. 412–507) introduces a note of pastoral romance into the play. Ferdinand is the first young man Miranda has ever seen and Prospero appears to disbelieve her spontaneous rush of feeling for him:

> Thou think'st there is no more such shapes as he,
> Having seen but him and Caliban. Foolish wench!
> To th' most of men this is a Caliban,
> And they to him are angels.

> (1. 2. 482–4)

Why does Prospero appear to denigrate and distrust Miranda's and Ferdinand's attraction for each other?

Since it is clear that Prospero himself engineered this meeting of his daughter and the son of the King of Naples and wishes to reward Ariel for bringing it about ('Delicate Ariel, / I'll set thee free for this' (1. 2. 445–6)), there can be little doubt that his show of disparagement and distrust is a form of play-acting. Indeed, Miranda says:

> Why speaks my father so ungently? This
> Is the third man that e'er I saw, the first
> That e'er I sighed for. Pity move my father
> To be inclined my way.

> (1. 2. 448–51)

She is clearly puzzled by his responses to the situation, and does not have the advantage enjoyed by the audience of hearing Prospero declare:

> ... this swift business
> I must uneasy make, lest too light winning
> Make the prize light.

> (1. 2. 454–6)

But as the scene develops – and Prospero returns again and again to the idea of Ferdinand as a 'traitor' or 'impostor' – one cannot help but feel that much more hangs on this moment than the recognition of awakening love between two young people. It is of deep concern to Prospero that the rules of decorum and propriety should be followed by the lovers and that Ferdinand should not have a 'conscience ... possessed with guilt' (474–5). In fact, he accuses the young prince of just such treachery, but does not specify its nature. A possible explanation of Prospero's seeming hostility to their potential union – which thoroughly bewilders his daughter – is that sexual probity is of great importance to him; it may well stand for human integrity and virtue in his entire scheme of things. Or it might well be that Prospero is displaying anxieties about sexuality, of which he himself is only dimly aware. So Miranda and Ferdinand must be challenged and needled, for only thus will they show the mettle of which they are made and their powers of self-control and obedience to a higher authority.

How are tensions between the different groups on the island developed?

Schisms now emerge between the newly arrived nobles. Antonio and Sebastian will soon hatch a plot against Alonso's life, with the aim of securing the kingdom of Naples for Sebastian. Meanwhile, they improve the idle hour by mocking and baiting the faithful, if somewhat talkative, old counsellor Gonzalo, who is attempting to reconcile them all to their present fate. There is cruelty in Antonio's and Sebastian's witticisms at Gonzalo's expense, for their minds are rapier-sharp and their concern is for none but themselves. In comparison with their cold cynicism and satire, Gonzalo's dream of a 'commonwealth', which will unite all men equally in contentment, has a utopian ring.

Actors vary in their interpretations of Gonzalo, much as they do in their portrayals of Polonius in *Hamlet*. The character can be shown as a hilarious buffoon or as a pragmatic and worthy old man. **How might the way in which Gonzalo is played affect the audience's perception of this exchange?**

If Gonzalo is played as an unworldly old fool, the political and social impact of the scene is lessened and his vision is to some extent diminished. Whereas, if he is played straight and with moving sincerity, the egalitarian concept of a common-wealth stays in the mind as an ideal. The topic is one of the early indications in this play that Shakespeare is interested in the form and constitution of political systems:

> All things in common nature should produce
> Without sweat or endeavour. Treason, felony,
> Sword, pike, knife, gun, or need of any engine,
> Would I not have; but nature should bring forth
> Of it own kind all foison, all abundance,
> To feed my innocent people.

> (2. 1. 159–64)

Thanks to Ariel's intervention, Alonso survives the plot to kill him and is able to instigate a search for his missing son. While this is happening, Trinculo and Stefano stray from their masters. They come upon Caliban, whose monstrous form fascinates them, and they share their bottles of wine with him. Caliban, for his part, vows allegiance to Stefano, the provider of this 'unearthly' liquor: 'I'll swear upon that bottle to be thy true subject, for the liquor is not earthly' (2. 2. 116–17).

This is the first of several truly comic scenes that create complicity between the island's original inhabitant and the two drunken servants of the Italian court. They do, in fact, form a third group or faction, which in due course hatches a plan to murder Prospero so that Caliban may regain the island that is his birthright. Thus, by the end of the second act, the intermingling of the two initial factions, first Miranda with Ferdinand, then Caliban with Stefano and Trinculo, hints at the pattern that is taking shape. The central act of the play reinforces these new groupings and paves the way for what is to come.

What is the function of Act 3 in the context of the play as a whole? Writing a guide to *The Tempest* some 20 years ago, the Open University teacher and Shakespeare scholar Brian Stone took Act 3 as the pivot of the play, and developed his interpretation accordingly. Stone, like a number of other commentators, refers to the first two scenes of the play (the storm at sea and Prospero's recapitulation of his own and Miranda's misfortunes) as 'a kind of double prologue before the engaged action of the play begins'. He writes:

> each of the three scenes [that comprise this third act] is self-contained and deals with a main thread of the play: respectively, the development of the love between Ferdinand and Miranda, the plot of Caliban against Prospero's life, and the move towards grace of the sinning nobles after the further activation of Antonio's plot against the life of Alonso. The events in each of these scenes are known to, and in the end purposefully engineered by, Prospero, to whose own development those events therefore specially relate.

> (1984, p.15)

He notes in the play as a whole an 'extended debate between depraved nobility on the one side, and hesitant optimism and solid virtue on the other', and concentrates on Act 3 because he feels that, as compared with other acts, the events in it yield 'broader insights into [*The Tempest*]' and yield them 'more economically' (ibid.).

Read Act 3, Scene 2, focusing in particular on Caliban's speeches, and identify the contradictions in Shakespeare's representation of Caliban.

Let us follow Stone's reflections on the text.

> In this scene, Shakespeare gives us, in his action picture of Caliban, most of the possible evidence for detesting or admiring him, and all within the conspectus of Caliban's single purpose, which he reveals as soon as he is able to, that is, according to my reading of the scene, when he has come out of what appears to be a drunken stupor and speaks for the first time.

> First, Caliban's two major speeches in this scene – ... in verse and not the prose of Stefano and Trinculo – are on subjects so superficially disparate that it is hard to believe that they come from the same mouth. [In lines 83–98] he recommends clumsy but effective ways of killing Prospero, which include ... paunching with a stake. He then urgently advocates the burning of Prospero's source of power, his magic books, and dwells lickerishly on the delights which will accrue to the gang from the possession of Miranda. Caliban's other speech [in lines 130–8] must be put in strict context if it is to be understood: ... you may know that it is often quoted – I would say sentimentally – out of context, as if

it simply expressed a great positive essence of [Caliban's] extraordinary and indeed unique character, which went some way towards redeeming him for his ugly and base qualities. The context I refer to is his joy at the acceptance, by Stefano and Trinculo, of his plan to destroy Prospero in half an hour's time: his first reaction is one of such pleasure that it can be expressed only in terms of a happy song, which, he has learnt, his new confederates can provide at any time. When they get the tune wrong, and the invisible Ariel gets it right for him, his delight expands into a rapturous appreciation of what the music of the island can do for him when it accords with the harmony of his spirit. What he describes, in both the music and its effect upon him [is a strange contradiction], because the harmony of his spirit at that moment is expressed in a fixed murderous intent, as his next words [141] confirm. [Both of Caliban's speeches] are crucial to the final focus of the play, because they insist on [a] kind of ambiguity.

(1984, pp.18–19)

What is the function of the masque in Act 4?

This display, which Prospero sets up for the pleasure of Miranda and Ferdinand, whose betrothal he accepted in the earlier part of the scene, is his gift to them: 'Then, as my gift and thine own acquisition / Worthily purchased, take my daughter' (4. 1. 13–14). It should indeed mark the beginning of celebration and harmony. Ferdinand certainly welcomes the apparitions in that sense, saying:

This is a most majestic vision, and
Harmonious charmingly. May I be bold
To think these spirits?

(4. 1. 118–20)

In reply, Prospero gives one of the clearest indications of his magic powers and the purpose to which he wishes to put them:

Spirits, which by mine art
I have from their confines called to enact
My present fancies.

(4. 1. 120–22)

The masque resumes, and reapers and nymphs join in a 'graceful dance', which Prospero interrupts and causes to end by suddenly remembering:

... that foul conspiracy
Of the beast Caliban and his confederates
Against my life. The minute of their plot
Is almost come. [*To the spirits*] Well done! Avoid; no more!

(4. 1. 139–42)

This moment will be considered later; suffice it for the present that Miranda and Ferdinand recognize Prospero's sudden 'passion' (Ferdinand's word (143)), his distemper (Miranda's term (145)) and his vexation (Prospero's own admission

(158)). He leaves the lovers and summons Ariel, who reports on the mishaps and inescapable traps into which he has led the three drunken traitors. He earns Prospero's praise – and further instructions:

> This was well done, my bird.
> Thy shape invisible retain thou still.
> The trumpery in my house, go bring it hither
> For stale to catch these thieves.

(4. 1. 184–7)

Once Ariel has left to do his bidding, Prospero dwells briefly but poignantly on the thought of Caliban:

> A devil, a born devil, on whose nature
> Nurture can never stick; on whom my pains,
> Humanely taken, all, all lost, quite lost,
> And, as with age his body uglier grows,
> So his mind cankers. I will plague them all,
> Even to roaring.

(4. 1. 188–93)

The final trick he practises against his three would-be assassins is to get Ariel to hang 'glistening apparel' on a lime tree (193), which Stefano and Trinculo soon see, covet and quarrel over. To Caliban's fury, they lose precious time in this distraction – which offers the audience great amusement – and finally *'divers spirits in shape of dogs and hounds'* (251, 2–3) hunt the three and drive them out. Prospero is now ready for what is his and the play's final act:

> At this hour
> Lies at my mercy all mine enemies.
> Shortly shall all my labours end, and thou
> Shalt have the air at freedom. For a little,
> Follow, and do me service.

(4. 1. 258–62)

How are we to interpret Prospero's magic powers?

At the theatrical level of performance, magic opens up all manner of scenic possibilities. From the storm-scene of Act 1 to the betrothal masque of Act 4, the audience is treated to a series of apparitions and rationally inconceivable events. Magic constitutes a mode – the mode of fantasy – which might well suggest light-heartedness and the willing suspension of disbelief. It sits well with the concept of comedy and its implicit suggestion of entertaining muddle and improbability that are ultimately resolved in a happy ending.

An alert spectator – or reader – would probably have picked up Prospero's own admission, in his long exposition to Miranda in Act 1, Scene 2, that his dedication to his studies in the earlier years of his dukedom was not without serious adverse effects (74–7). For it could be perceived as a neglect of his ducal obligations, and the opportunity such neglect afforded those near to him who coveted his power might be said to have led to his defeat and banishment.

We should perhaps ask ourselves whether abstruse studies of an arcane or occult nature are being shown as incompatible with the exercise of good government and aristocratic concern for one's people and dependants. As has been noted in earlier chapters, James I had a particular interest in magic and demonology. Might he have perceived a coded criticism in the play?

If Prospero lost his dukedom and authority at least partly through his dedication to what we loosely term the study of magic, what is the status of his art during his occupation of the island and what is implied by the use he makes of it? We will return to consider this in more detail later.

How are the tensions and conflicts resolved in the final act?

There is a single scene in Act 5 – as there was in Act 4 – and again it takes place before Prospero's cell. Prospero and his dwelling place become the centre of the action, and now Prospero is accoutred in his magic robes and Ariel is with him. He is in control and wishes to be seen in that guise: 'Now does my project gather to a head' (5. 1. 1). Ariel has led the 'King and's followers' (7) to a nearby grove and there they are imprisoned by Prospero's magic until he decides to release them. Ariel feels pity for them and causes Prospero to speak of his own feelings:

> Though with their high wrongs I am struck to th' quick,
> Yet with my nobler reason 'gainst my fury
> Do I take part. The rarer action is
> In virtue than in vengeance. They being penitent,
> The sole drift of my purpose doth extend
> Not a frown further.

> (5. 1. 25–30)

He now sends Ariel to bring the nobles to him. In a soliloquy he meditates on the magic and 'so potent Art' (50) that he has employed to reach his ends. This is the moment when he will renounce his magic practices:

> But this rough magic
> I here abjure. And when I have required
> Some heavenly music – which even now I do –
> To work mine end upon their senses that
> This airy charm is for, I'll break my staff,
> Bury it certain fathoms in the earth,
> And deeper than did ever plummet sound
> I'll drown my book.

> (5. 1. 50–6)

Two questions are perhaps uppermost in our minds. Will he really visit no punishment on those who engineered his usurpation and exile from his dukedom of Milan? Will he keep his promise to Ariel and set the spirit free? He addresses each of the nobles in turn, although only the audience hears him, and reveals his intention for each. For Gonzalo, he has nothing but affection and gratitude, but Alonso, Sebastian and his own brother Antonio require an effort of will. Of Antonio he says: 'I do forgive thee, / Unnatural though thou art' (78–9).

As the prisoners begin to cast off the charm, Prospero sends Ariel for his 'hat and rapier' (84) and proceeds to deck himself in the robes of his former ducal state. He bids Ariel bring the mariners from the wrecked ship and promises the obedient spirit his subsequent freedom. One by one the nobles return to their senses and are greeted with 'Welcome, my friends all' (127). Only to Sebastian and Antonio is his welcome modified, for he indicates that he knows the extent of their treachery both to himself in the past and now to the king of Naples.

With his dukedom restored to him, Prospero listens to Alonso's lament for his lost son, Ferdinand, and responds by saying that he, too, lost a daughter 'In this last tempest' (155). As recompense for their restitution of his rank and status he offers to 'bring forth a wonder' (172) and reveals to the assembled company the figures of Miranda and Ferdinand playing chess in the entrance to his cell. Miranda's words, as she looks about her at the assembled nobles, perhaps best convey the mood of this moment of revelation in the play:

> O, wonder!
> How many goodly creatures are there here!
> How beauteous mankind is! O brave new world
> That has such people in't!

> (5. 1. 184–7)

The charm and naïvety of this pronouncement is brusquely tempered by Prospero's terse reply: ''Tis new to thee' (187).

Alonso accepts Miranda as his son's future wife, and Gonzalo notes that thus the noble houses of Milan and Naples are harmoniously united. However, the play is not quite over at this point, for the crew of the storm-tossed ship have to be brought by Ariel to join their masters, and Caliban, Stefano and Trinculo must also be accounted for. Ariel 'drives' the three drunken miscreants in to face their masters and Prospero explains their identity thus:

> These three have robbed me, and this demi-devil,
> For he's a bastard one, had plotted with them
> To take my life. Two of these fellows you
> Must know and own. This thing of darkness I
> Acknowledge mine.

> (5. 1. 275–9)

Does this reference to a 'thing of darkness' run somewhat counter to the sense of joy we associate with the resolution of comedy? Is the shadow that these words cast over the scene at all diminished by Caliban's vow?

> I'll be wise hereafter,
> And seek for grace. What a thrice-double ass
> Was I to take this drunkard for a god,
> And worship this dull fool!

> (5. 1. 298–301)

The messages coming from the closing scene of the play seem mixed. The pastoral romance of Miranda and Ferdinand reaches its hoped-for conclusion – the blessing of the two fathers on this royal marriage. The return of both the long-term exile, Prospero, and the recently marooned nobles to their own country and the restoration of the former as rightful ruler of Milan suggest a resurgence of justice.

And Ariel achieves his long-promised liberty. But Caliban – and this is where one senses that the joy is tempered by sadness and even distress – is to be left alone on the island, abandoned, although acknowledged by Prospero as 'his own', and yet undoubtedly his one signal failure.

There is an Epilogue, spoken directly to the audience by Prospero. It consists of 20 lines in which the erstwhile magician confesses that his art has now departed, and begs to be released by the spectators from his confinement on the island. These lines have sometimes been seen as Shakespeare's farewell to the theatre, and his plea for understanding from the audience. Equally, they have been interpreted as an apology to his king, James I, for 'dabbling in magic', and possibly for the implied criticism of those that do so, given that this was a subject that fascinated James himself.

The meaning of magic in **The Tempest**

Many productions of the play have placed the major emphasis on Prospero's supernatural powers and on the various manifestations that he conjures up to achieve his ends. You may well be aware of screen versions of the play, not least Peter Greenaway's film, *Prospero's Books* (1991), which delve into the concepts of magic and the occult. A number of Shakespearean academics have been at pains to establish that this is – in common parlance – 'white magic'; that is, it is ultimately beneficent and may rightly be regarded as 'art'. Demonologists in Shakespeare's time, however, were less sure that 'white magic' was better than 'black magic'.

Frank Kermode argued in the 1950s that *The Tempest* was above all a pastoral play and that it centred on the theme of nature and art (Kermode, 1954, pp.li–lix). He was no doubt influenced by the fact that pastoral literature usually celebrated an idealized age of rustic innocence and idleness. Kermode's argument focuses on art as the sum of man's attempts to improve on nature by exercising a civilizing influence over it. He defines Prospero as a 'theurgist' (one who performs magic by the aid of good spirits or miraculous divine action) and says explicitly that his 'Art is to achieve supremacy over the natural world by holy magic. The Neoplatonic mage studies the harmonic relationship of the elementary, celestial, and intellectual worlds' (ibid., p.xl). In this account, the virtues of a civilized society are achieved by art, which enables humankind to transform the natural by means of learning and good breeding. So we must see Prospero's magic powers as the improvement of nature, and his control over spirits of earth, air and water as the result of his lifelong studies and experiments. It is perhaps as well to remember that the study of science excited men's minds in this period and Prospero's commitment to his books echoes the devotion given to early scientific research.

In his delineation of the theme of nature versus art, Kermode notes how the two opposing realms are reflected in the characters themselves. He describes Caliban as 'an inverted pastoral hero, against whom civility and the Art which improves Nature may be measured' (ibid., p.xliii). He invokes the concept of the pastoral with regard to Gonzalo and his 'half-serious talk about his commonwealth' (ibid., p.xxxvii), which for Kermode is 'more appropriate to pastoral poetry which takes a "soft" view of Nature' (ibid., p.xxxviii). This refines his concept of *The Tempest* as a pastoral piece, and it allows him to contrast Miranda and Ferdinand with Caliban. The two young people are both of royal blood and this gives them an innate nobility; Caliban is the offspring of a witch and a demon, and his appearance and many of his actions seem monstrous. Prospero describes Caliban as 'a born devil, on whose nature / Nurture can never stick' (4. 1. 188–9). This creature is Prospero's failure: 'on whom my pains, / Humanely taken, all, all lost, quite lost' (189–90). So there are limits to Prospero's art, to his power and control, and he fails with Caliban. The latter is ineducable by Prospero's standards, but perhaps the sins of those who defy their breeding and education are the greater; Antonio and Sebastian are traitors of a different ilk, and they flout the civilized conventions in which they were reared.

Thus, the magic events produced by Prospero are not, according to such an interpretation, fortuitous or random. They are directed towards a purpose. One might almost see them as a form of atonement on Prospero's part for his earlier neglect of his subjects' needs and rights, for all Prospero's fantastic machinations which we witness on the island are directed towards the betterment and reconciliation of those about him. His insistence on legitimacy, propriety and decorum in Miranda and Ferdinand's relationship is just one aspect of the civilized conduct of life to which Prospero dedicates his art. He deems it necessary to control nature in order to reach the highest form of human achievement and social well-being.

In his introduction to the Oxford World's Classics edition of *The Tempest* (1994), Stephen Orgel remarks that 'From one aspect Prospero's art is Baconian science and Neoplatonic philosophy, the empirical study of nature leading to the understanding and control of its forces' (p.20). It may be difficult for us today to discern such a profound intention behind the illusionism and high jinks of the play's magic moments. Originally, as Orgel states, magic was not a means of empowerment for Prospero but 'a dereliction of duty', a 'retreat from power' (ibid.). He lost all that he possessed except his daughter. So he has a great deal to retrieve, to re-establish and to resituate in the realm of human and divine principles. He must act for the good of all, he must concentrate all his powers on virtue.

Orgel reminds us that the opposing figure here is that of Sycorax, a 'ghostly memory so intensely present in the play, the perverse, irrational, violent, malicious, vindictive principle in nature, progenitor of monsters, lover and agent of the devil on earth' (ibid., pp.20–1). However, a parallel has been drawn between Prospero and Sycorax, in spite of the fact that, in his own account of the past, Prospero sees Sycorax as a virtual emblem of evil. Commentators stress the similarities between their two histories: both were victims of banishment, both found a new life on the island and both reared a child there, for Sycorax was pregnant with Caliban when she arrived. She was the first to make Ariel her servant, as Prospero did later, and thus she controlled the natural spirits of the island. All that Prospero knows of her he has learned from Ariel, for Sycorax died some while before his and Miranda's arrival. What is perhaps most telling is that both Prospero and Sycorax were sorcerers, and Prospero ascribes to Sycorax, whom he never met, such qualities as 'unmitigable rage'. Ariel's imprisonment had been due to Sycorax, whose desire for total servitude is echoed in Prospero's increasing demands and in the unstable moods and flashing tempers on which Miranda comments with bewilderment. The difference between the two would appear to be that Prospero promises Ariel his freedom and, although the latter has to labour long and hard for it, in the end Prospero abides by his pledge.

The sources of The Tempest

What would be the textual justification for thinking that Shakespeare had a source – or sources – for this play, perhaps a known plot or story-line? What traces of contemporary history, even contemporary events, can we find in this seemingly 'magical' comedy?

Although there is not one chief source for *The Tempest*, as there is for several Shakespearean plays, most scholars agree that the action and development of the plot were triggered by three texts. Let us look first of all at the question of storm and shipwreck.

In June 1609, two years before the date of the first known performance of this play, a ship bound for Virginia was separated from the rest of the fleet by a storm and finally foundered on rocks off the coast of the Bermudas. The crew built a new boat and set sail for Virginia in May 1610. This experience was recorded by William Strachey in his *True Reportory of the Wracke* (1610). As Philip Brockbank points out: 'the material offers itself most invitingly to a playwright whose interest in the ways of Providence, and in the conversion and salvation of man, had matured through long practice in allegoric, romantic comedy' (1973 edn, p.185).

The name given to the Bermudas at that time was 'The Devil's Islands', but Sylvester Jourdain's account of their discovery makes it clear that in his view they did not live up to their fearful name. He says: 'But our delivery was not more strange in falling so opportunely and happily upon the land, as our feeding and preservation, was beyond our hopes, and all mens expectations most admirable' (ibid., p.189). This wonderment is much more in accordance with Gonzalo's response to their safe arrival on the island than with Alonso's, Antonio's or Sebastian's frame of mind. For the latter pair, what the island offers is an opportunity to kill Alonso and usurp his throne; for Alonso himself this is, he thinks, the part of the world that has deprived him of his son, whom he believes to have been destroyed in the wild storm. It is the source of grief and despair.

Many commentators have insisted on the importance of the influence of literature about travel in the early 1600s, and undoubtedly the discovery of the Americas opened up new ideas and new narratives on which literary exponents gladly seized. Brockbank thinks of both Prospero and Caliban as 'doubly fashioned from the travel literature' (ibid., p.192). Caliban is 'the epitome of the primitive and uncivilized condition of the native American' and he is also 'a theatrical epitome of the animal, anarchic qualities of the colonizers' (ibid.).

Brockbank is here leaning heavily on the contemporary view that native American Indians were a savage and uncultivated race and therefore represented the opposite of the civilized Europeans who made discovery of their territories in the Renaissance period. Julia Briggs (*This Stage-Play World: Texts and Contexts, 1580–1625*, 1997) is helpful on this topic, which will be taken up again in the second part of this chapter, when the questions of colonialism and post-colonialism come under scrutiny.

The second text of which Shakespeare was surely aware while writing *The Tempest* is Michel de Montaigne's essay, translated into English by John Florio as 'Of the Cannibals' (1603). Montaigne was pondering travellers' tales about savages in the New World, and his central theme was the superiority of uncivilized man. It has been suggested that there are borrowings from this essay in Gonzalo's speech about the ideal commonwealth, but Montaigne's influence goes much further than this. Many have spotted the similarity between the name Caliban and the word 'cannibal', and any grace given to Caliban, by comparison with the corrupt nobles and the drunken servants Stefano and Trinculo, probably derives from Montaigne's thesis (Montaigne, 1991 edn, pp.228–41). However, Caliban, who is both crude and cunning, cannot be said to be an idealized version of the savage. Orgel argues that 'Caliban has almost nothing in common with the prelapsarian savages described in Montaigne's essay "Of the Cannibals"', and that 'He owes more to concepts of the natural depravity of New-World populations, such as are found in explorers' accounts' (1998, p.35).

The third textual source for *The Tempest* is Ovid's *Metamorphoses* (completed in CE 8), which is also referred to in connection with Gonzalo's dream of a commonwealth. In addition, the figure of the witch Sycorax, mother of Caliban, is said to derive from Ovid's account of Medea in Book 7 of the *Metamorphoses* (see Martin, 1998).

Part 2   Alternative critical perspectives

We will now consider some of the major current critical debates about *The Tempest*, focusing on the play in terms of colonialism, genre, gender and language.

The Tempest *and colonialism*

Let us look again at that moment in Act 4 when Prospero brings the masque to an abrupt close because he has suddenly recalled the conspiracy of Caliban, Stefano and Trinculo against his life. If this conspiracy is thought of as a sub-plot, then it must seem to the attentive audience or reader that it disrupts the flow of the main plot at a tender and romantic moment. Even though they have been delineated in a predominantly comic fashion, the perpetrators of the conspiracy now claim Prospero's attention as a potential threat to his personal safety and to his rapidly maturing plans. Is this just a hiccup in the smooth running of things, or does it represent something more important when it comes to our overall perception of *The Tempest*?

This moment in the play is a key factor in a radically different view of *The Tempest* which was mooted in the 1960s and gained ground in subsequent decades. It centres on the concept of colonialism, or rather post-colonialism, and it seeks to re-evaluate the attitude of the central character, Prospero, and the nature of his authority. The post-colonialist perspective does not refute the element of magic (or art) in the play, nor does it deny the presence of pastoral romance and scenes in the comic mode, but it holds a new light up to the character of Prospero and asks whether he merits our unblinking acceptance of his statements and the constructions that he places on events.

The exposition that Prospero delivers to Miranda in the second scene of the play is sometimes referred to as 'Prospero's story', for it recounts a distant past that stands as justification for his present attitude to those he left behind when forced into exile. There is no-one to ratify this story, but subsequent happenings in the play work to support the idea of Prospero's usurpation – and the political treachery of those then surrounding him – as the truth about his past. If we view the action of the play from the point of view of its main spokesman and puppet-master, it centres on himself, his determination to regain his former ducal status and his manipulation of others to achieve this end. It is thus a play that deals with usurpation, legitimacy and rightful authority. Some critics have called this 'Prospero's play', but we need to look outside Prospero's version of events to become aware of the other perspectives from which the story may be seen and which together produce a different and more complex play.

Critics such as Francis Barker and Peter Hulme have proposed an alternative approach to the one we have considered so far. They take issue with Kermode's picture of Prospero as 'a self-disciplined, reconciliatory, white magician' and invite us to study the 'discourse of colonialism' that they see in the play. Discourse, they point out, 'refers to the *field* in and through which texts are produced' (Barker and Hulme, 1985, p.202). Concentration on explicit themes or overt statements in the work (the sort of task on which we have been engaged in our preceding exploration of the play) is replaced by a thorough con-textualizing of *The Tempest*, reading it 'alongside congruent texts' (ibid.), including early literature on travel and documents pertaining to colonization.

Numerous critics have pointed, with differing degrees of emphasis and angles of approach, to the ways in which *The Tempest* relates to the discovery of the Americas and the colonization of the New World (see, for instance, Cartelli, 1986; Greenblatt, 1988 and 1990). Jonathan Bate gives a far too simple and misleading account of post-colonial readings of *The Tempest* when he claims in *The Genius of Shakespeare* that according to 'the new critical radicalism' *The Tempest* 'must bear the blame for the Atlantic slave trade' (1997, p.240). It is worth pointing out that the relevance of exploration and colonization has been a topic of debate in Shakespeare criticism since at least 1808, when Edmond Malone drew attention to the possible influence of the documents of the Virginia Company, which had founded a colony at Jamestown. A spirited intervention by E.E. Stoll suggests that the debate was certainly alive in 1927:

> There is not a word in *The Tempest* about America or Virginia, colonies
> or colonizing, Indians or tomahawks, maize, mocking-birds, or tobacco.
> Nothing but the Bermudas, once barely mentioned as faraway places
> like Tokio or Mandalay.

> (Quoted in Orgel, 1998, pp.32–3)

Later critics have not been as sure as Stoll and most have been prepared to grant some significance to the shaping influence of New World travel writing. Some critics, including Paul Brown, have argued that the colonialist discourse of *The Tempest* had sources much nearer to home than either Virginia or Bermuda in the political conquest of Ireland (Figure 42). Brown argues that Ireland was both 'an opportunity for the expansion of civility' and a site 'for the possible undoing of civilized man' (1985, p.57).

Not all critics with an interest in the play's historical circumstances have seen it as being complicit with colonialism. Some have regarded it as an anti-colonial play, whilst others, such as Brown, have argued that the play is profoundly ambivalent in its attitude to colonialism.

The first requirement is to distance ourselves from unquestioning belief in the accuracy of the ways in which Prospero presents the 'facts' about his residence on the island. Or rather to note the lack of information given: 'Here in this island we

Figure 42 *Irish kneeling in homage to the king, from John Derricke,* The Image of Ireland, *1581, Edinburgh University Library De.3.76.*

arrived' (1. 2. 172). Post-colonial criticism holds that earlier traditional insistence on identifying Prospero's voice with 'direct and reliable authorial statement' (Barker and Hulme, 1985, p.199) must be questioned, put under a microscope. Indeed, scepticism about the validity of assertions made by literary characters – including those of narrators in fiction and speakers in poetry – has been current in one form or another since the development of critical theory in the post-war period, particularly since the 1960s. If the spectator identifies uniquely with Prospero's viewpoint, then what s/he is watching is 'Prospero's play'; for the magician has the 'effective power to impose his construction of events on others' (ibid.). We are now being invited to note the gaps and silences in Prospero's own version of things, and to work out the implications of those omissions.

The first thing that we might note is the silence surrounding Caliban's reduction to slavery and Prospero's assumption that, as a European exile landing by chance on these shores, he has a right to appropriate them and to subject any native occupant to his will. Caliban's protestations are largely ignored and the text 'is systematically silent about Prospero's own act of usurpation' (ibid., p.200).

Prospero is held to be as guilty of usurpation as Antonio was when he seized the dukedom of Milan from its rightful ruler. There is only one creature on the island when Prospero and Miranda arrive – apart from the spirit Ariel imprisoned in a pine tree – and that occupant and owner, as he sees himself, is Caliban. It is, as he firmly states, *his* island, inherited from Sycorax, his mother. It is worth noting that although the information we are given about Sycorax is vague, we do know that she has been banished from 'Argier' (or Algiers) 'For mischiefs manifold and sorceries terrible / To enter human hearing' (1. 2. 266–7). The implication is that Sycorax and Caliban are North African. This has led some critics, including Jerry Brotton (1998), to argue that *The Tempest* is a play set not in the New World but in the African Mediterranean.

The cast list teaches us to think of Caliban as a 'savage and deformed native of the island, Prospero's slave'. He is never seen with other than European eyes and the image given of him is that of an uncouth and distorted being. He is, for Prospero, someone whom he must reduce to submission and slavery. From beginning to end, Caliban is seen as a slave. Hence the sub-plot of his conspiracy against the magician, his master, which is intended to recover for him what is legitimately his. Hand in hand with the idea of usurpation goes, of course, the concept of dispossession. Just as Prospero had been dispossessed, so he dispossesses Caliban. In his exposition to his daughter (Act 1, Scene 2), the ruler of the island does not linger over that earlier act of self-installation (as master), nor does he find it necessary to justify it. He is a civilized white man, and as such it follows that he will take precedence over any other who does not enjoy that advantage of race and culture; and he will use that 'other' to ensure his own comfort and survival.

Many commentators, not necessarily concerned with post-colonial criticism of *The Tempest*, have pointed out that the tasks given to Caliban, most particularly that of cutting and carrying logs, are indicative of his lowly status and his lack of freedom. You may recall that Ferdinand is given the same back-breaking, menial job when Prospero appears to be testing his character and his feelings for Miranda. Ferdinand is well aware of his own noble status and he is in no doubt about the ignominious nature of his enforced occupation:

> This my mean task
> Would be as heavy to me as odious, but
> The mistress which I serve quickens what's dead,
> And makes my labours pleasures.

> (3. 1. 4–7)

The immediate basis for Prospero's easily acquired supremacy over others lies in his magic art, and we certainly see it exercised repeatedly in his hold over Ariel. He exacts the spirit's constant obedience. He is less successful in his manipulations of Caliban; yet the latter's knowledge of the island ensures that over the years there has been enough to eat and drink, and his brute strength has provided wood – and therefore warmth – and the means of survival. It is important to remember Caliban's claim that he loved Prospero in the beginning and 'showed' it in this way:

> [I] showed thee all the qualities o'th' isle,
> The fresh springs, brine-pits, barren place and fertile –
> Cursed be I that did so!

> (1. 2. 340–2)

There is an echo of these words in Caliban's promise to Stefano and Trinculo, when he tells them in Act 2: 'I'll show thee every fertile inch o'th' island' (2. 2. 140). If one looks carefully at this later scene, certain repetitions stand out:

> I'll show thee the best springs; I'll pluck thee berries;
> I'll fish for thee, and get thee wood enough.
> A plague upon the tyrant that I serve!

> (2. 2. 152–4)

It would seem that Caliban has imbibed and inwardly digested ('internalized' might be a better word) the subservient attitude of a subject to his master. He endows Stefano with the qualities of a ruler – indeed, in his drunken loquaciousness, with the quality of a deity – and proposes himself as his servant in a manner that displays the mentality of a creature who now does not see or think beyond his colonized role: 'And I will kiss thy foot. I prithee, be my god' (2. 2. 141). This is repeated three lines later: 'I'll kiss thy foot. I'll swear myself thy subject' (144).

Even if we recognize the effect of unaccustomed liquor on Caliban, his mind-set is unmistakable. He turns away from one 'tyrant' and immediately is in danger of putting himself in the grip of another. He actively creates a new master, who will rule him once he has dispensed with his present slave-owner.

For Barker and Hulme, Prospero 'reduces Caliban to a role in the supporting sub-plot, as instigator of a mutiny that is programmed to fail, thereby forging an equivalence between Antonio's initial *putsch* and Caliban's revolt' (1985, p.206). Caliban is thus relegated to the side of the felons, the illegitimate pretenders to power and authority. The desire to colonize and oppress others, which recurs in different forms in *The Tempest*, reaches its conclusion in the aborted mutiny. Caliban stands as the 'traitor', guilty of what has been called 'the natural treachery of savages' (ibid., p.201). I wrote earlier of the way in which this sub-plot erupted into the main plot at an untimely moment in the celebratory masque:

> I had forgot that foul conspiracy
> Of the beast Caliban and his confederates
> Against my life. The minute of their plot
> Is almost come.

> (4. 1. 139–42)

You may agree with those who insist that this is the only truly dramatic moment in the play. Certainly the abruptness of Prospero's dismissal of the spirits engaged in the masque, the silencing of their music, the unexpectedness of his outcry, the bewilderment of Miranda and Ferdinand, all contribute to this moment of drama. Barker and Hulme argue that the text is very 'emphatic' in its stress on this 'moment of disturbance' (1985, p.202). The stage direction is peculiar in itself – there is a *'strange, hollow, and confused noise'* (142, 1), which does nothing to allay the audience's apprehension.

If it is correct that this is a 'textual excess', a 'disproportion between cause and effect' (ibid.), then it raises questions at a key point in the would-be resolution of an avowed comedy. What does this sudden recollection of potential mutiny awaken in Prospero's mind? He should be sure in his reliance on his magic powers to avert the danger. To put the matter in the crudest terms: does Caliban get under Prospero's skin? Is he a reminder to Prospero of his own failure to civilize this creature and his own role in the master/slave relationship? Might such an anxiety be a reflection of something felt, or half-felt, by the dramatist himself? Is Prospero suddenly given an inkling of the illegitimacy of his own position in assuming the right to govern the island and to manipulate Caliban according to his own needs? Post-colonial criticism would see a fracture, a break in the smooth development of the comic mode at this point, and would declare that the difficulty went unresolved.

As Hulme and other critics readily acknowledge, much of the impetus behind post-colonial readings of *The Tempest* came from debates that were being conducted in the

1950s and 1960s among displaced and exiled intellectuals, including Caribbean writers such as the novelist George Lamming and the poet Edward Kamau Brathwaite. One of the seminal early texts to which these writers responded was Octave Mannoni's *Psychologie de la colonisation* (*The Psychology of Colonization*), published in Paris in 1950. Mannoni, a French colonial official and ethnographer working in Madagascar, based his analysis of colonialism on what he regarded as opposing complexes or neuroses, which he termed the 'Prospero complex' and the 'Caliban complex'. He saw in the colonial unrest in Madagascar not so much an indication of revolt against an oppressive master–servant relationship as an intense reciprocal dependency. The African races, Mannoni believed, were psychologically predisposed to subservience. Caliban, in this respect, functions as an image or type of resentful dependence. Prospero, on the other hand, is seen as a type of failed ruler, who projects his fears and anxieties on to the colonized subject. Prospero's claim that Caliban has tried to rape Miranda is readily understood by Mannoni as an instance of Prospero's attempt to conceal his own incestuous desires:

> Prospero could have removed Caliban to a safe distance or he could have continued to civilize and correct him. But the argument: you tried to violate Miranda, *therefore* you shall chop wood, belongs to a non-rational mode of thinking. In spite of the various forms this attitude may take ... it is primarily a justification of hatred on grounds of sexual guilt, and it is at the root of colonial racialism.
>
> (1990 edn, p.107)

While Mannoni's argument usefully recommended that Prospero, and not just Caliban, be subjected to scrutiny in relation to the history of colonialism, his suggestion that colonized nations were complicit in their own subjection not surprisingly met with a hostile reception. Frantz Fanon, a psychiatrist and revolutionary thinker from Martinique (like Madagascar, another French colony), took issue with Mannoni's ideas about the inherent subservience of colonized peoples, while broadly accepting his analysis of colonial power. In *Black Skin, White Masks*, published in 1952, Fanon, like Mannoni, suggested that Prospero projects on to Caliban his own perverse and dominative desires. Many of the subsequent responses to *The Tempest* by African and Caribbean authors were prompted by Mannoni and Fanon as well as by Shakespeare. Lamming, in his autobiographical work, *The Pleasures of Exile* (1960), wrote movingly of how *The Tempest* enabled him to present 'a certain state of feeling which is the heritage of the exiled and colonial writer from the British Caribbean' (1984 edn, p.9). He was, in his own estimation, 'a colonial and exiled descendant of Caliban in the twentieth century' (ibid., p.13). Shakespeare's play was for Lamming and his Caribbean contemporaries 'prophetic of a political future which is our present' (ibid.).

One of the most impressive reworkings of *The Tempest*, and a powerful piece of post-colonial criticism in its own right, is Aimé Césaire's *Une Tempête* (*A Tempest*), first performed in Paris in 1969. Césaire (born in Martinique in 1913) is one of the best-known poets in the French Caribbean and a highly respected politician. A fierce critic of colonialism, he coined the term 'négritude' as a self-conscious declaration of blackness, a way of insisting that racial difference be treated with dignity and respect. Written in French, Césaire's play is not so much a translation as a determined rewriting of *The Tempest*. The setting of *Une Tempête* is an unnamed Caribbean island, and there are strong evocations of Africa in Caliban's summoning of deities such as Shango and Eshu. At the same time, Césaire makes the play more broadly representative of black experience by drawing on images and ideas that were central to the black civil rights movement in the United States in the 1960s.

Césaire's Prospero is presented explicitly as a European colonizer, whose interest in magic betrays his lust for absolute power. Caliban and Ariel are his two slaves, one a black rebel and the other a mulatto, who espouses a more moderate political stance. Caliban's position is equated with that of militant Afro-American leaders such as Malcolm X ('Call me X', he says at one point in the play), whilst Ariel has more in common with the peaceful protest of Martin Luther King. In a brilliantly innovative scene (one of the notable departures from Shakespeare's text), Césaire has Caliban and Ariel debate the most effective way of achieving freedom. Césaire also departs from *The Tempest* by having Prospero remain indefinitely on the island, locked in a tense and unresolved power struggle with Caliban. If the play seems to end in political deadlock, it nevertheless shows Caliban forcefully rejecting the role that Prospero has created for him and striving for liberty. It is noticeable, however, that as Caliban's role becomes strengthened and affirmed, the role of Miranda becomes diminished and curtailed. Whilst Césaire's text is eloquent about the repressions of race and social class, it has relatively little to say about the inequalities of gender.

The première of *Une Tempête* in the United Kingdom took place in September 1998, some 30 years after Césaire's conception of the play, with a new translation from the French by Philip Crispin. Although surprisingly late in reaching the United Kingdom, the première happened significantly in the year of Empire Windrush,[1] marking the fiftieth anniversary of the post-war arrival of West Indian and other immigrant groups in Britain, and it was staged at the Gate Theatre in Notting Hill, close to one of London's biggest West Indian communities (Figure 43). The production was widely applauded and admired by London's theatre critics. The *Times Literary Supplement* acknowledged 'a remarkable theatrical event' and referred to Césaire's *Tempest* as 'not simply a new reading of Shakespeare but an original play of astonishing power' (*TLS*, 9 October 1998, p.22). Michael Billington, in the *Guardian*, suggested that 'far from being reductively didactic', the play 'lends Shakespeare's myth all kinds of extra resonance' (*Guardian*, 28 September 1998, p.13).

The question that remains is whether Césaire's play effectively subverts Shakespeare's *Tempest*, exposing its collusion with colonial politics, or whether it realizes the radical potential of *The Tempest* by bringing to the surface an implicit critique of colonial power. Is *The Tempest* fundamentally a colonial or an anti-colonial play?

A plausible explanation for some of the pervasive ambiguities in the play was offered by Anne Barton in a pathbreaking introduction to the New Penguin edition of *The Tempest* in 1968 (the year in which Césaire's *Une Tempête* was first published). According to Barton, '*The Tempest* is an extraordinarily secretive work of art. Constantly, it offers the reader or audience half-knowledge where in earlier plays Shakespeare had been delighted to clarify and explain. It invites conjecture' (1968, p.13). Barton goes on to suggest the extent to which the language of *The Tempest* induces a particularly intense and creative response in readers and listeners:

---

[1] *Empire Windrush* was the name of the ship that carried the first major wave of Caribbean immigrants to Britain after World War II.

(a) *Caliban (Andrew Dennis) and Ariel (Michael Wildman).*

(b) *Prospero (Michael Hadley) and Miranda (Kelly Marcel).*

(c) *Caliban (Andrew Dennis) and Prospero (Michael Hadley).*

Figure 43 *Stills from the Gate Theatre production of* The Tempest, *television recording directed by Robert Philip, 1998.*

Spare, intense, concentrated to the point of being riddling, *The Tempest* provokes imaginative activity on the part of its audience or readers. Its very compression, the fact that it seems to hide as much as it reveals, compels a peculiarly creative response. A need to invent links between words, to expand events and characters in order to understand them, to formulate phrases which can somehow fix the significance of purely visual or musical elements is part of the ordinary experience of reading or watching this play. Sometimes the process results in a new creation. Certainly it is not by accident that *The Tempest* has generated, or lies at the heart of, so many other works of art.

(Ibid., p.19)

While she sees *The Tempest* as 'an extraordinarily obliging work of art', however, Barton is inclined to distrust the flexibility of interpretation that it encourages and looks for 'certain definite and objective things which can be said about *The Tempest*' on which to base her own reading of the play (ibid., p.22). More recent criticism, including Orgel's authoritative introduction to the Oxford World's Classics edition of the play, has tended to welcome and celebrate the multiple possibilities of meaning that *The Tempest* makes available. Whereas Barton regards *The Tempest* as a 'secretive' play, Orgel acknowledges its 'characteristic openness' (Orgel, 1994, p.12).

In his wide-ranging commentary on *The Tempest*, Orgel draws attention not just to the multiplicity of interpretations that the play has attracted, but also to the way in which these interpretations have depended, to some extent, on the context of the play's reception. He stresses how we need to be aware of the critical history of the play, including our own moment of reception:

> *The Tempest* is a text that looks different in different contexts, and it has been used to support radically differing claims about Shakespeare's allegiances. In recent years we have seen Prospero as a noble ruler and mage, a tyrant and megalomaniac, a necromancer, a Neoplatonic scientist, a colonial imperialist, a civilizer. Similarly, Caliban has been an ineducable brute, a sensitive savage, a European wild man, a New-World native, ugly, attractive, tragic, pathetic, comic, frightening, the rightful owner of the island, a natural slave. The question of correctness is not the issue in these readings; the play will provide at least some evidence for all of them, and its critical history is a good index to the ambivalences and ambiguities of the text. Historical arguments claiming to demonstrate that Shakespeare could not have intended Prospero to be seen as unattractive or Caliban as sympathetic are denying to the Renaissance's greatest playwright precisely that complexity of sensibility which is what we have come to value most in Shakespearian drama, and in Renaissance culture as a whole.

> (Ibid., p.11)

For Orgel, reading *The Tempest* sometimes involves a process of filling in the blanks, and he is not surprised that many of the interpretations to which it has given rise are mutually contradictory. He reminds us that the play's possibilities of meaning derive in part from its initial status as a play script written to be realized in performance: 'In its own time its only life was in performance, and one way to think of it is as an anthology of performances ... As a printed text, it is designed to provide in addition the basis for an infinitude of future performances, real and imagined' (ibid., p.12). Orgel, like other recent critics, is also fascinated by the play's indeterminate genre.

The Tempest *and genre*

The Tempest was grouped in the Folio as a comedy, and indeed there is much in the structure of the play that might support this classification. The final two acts, set outside Prospero's cell, contain a single geographical focus and thus physically suggest the coming together of the characters, their differences and disputes, in a single locus, which permits resolution and harmonization. However, as Orgel points out, the question of genre in *The Tempest* is complicated:

> The play is, in fact, as much concerned with tragic as with comic themes: the nature of authority and power; the conflicting claims of vengeance and forgiveness, of justice and mercy; the realities of reconciliation and the possibility of regeneration. It opens with a storm scene that recalls *King Lear* both in its natural violence and in the larger issues it raises about the relation of nature to human authority – issues that are succinctly expressed in the Boatswain's question, 'What cares

these roarers for the name of king?' [1. 1. 15–16]. In its concern with political legitimacy and the effects of usurpation, the play reconsiders issues that had occupied Shakespeare's mind from the earliest plays to *Hamlet* and *Macbeth*. The fact that it centres as well on a happy betrothal has tended to obscure for us its insistent concern with the dangerous potential of sexuality and the uncertain future that marriage represents – themes that recall the examples of Romeo and Juliet, ... Angelo and Isabella, the worlds of *Antony and Cleopatra* and *Cymbeline*.

(Ibid., p.5)

Samuel Taylor Coleridge referred to *The Tempest* as 'a romance' and this term has been in use as a description of Shakespeare's 'late plays' since the end of the nineteenth century. Orgel thinks that 'We have invented the category of romance because we believe that certain kinds of seriousness are inappropriate to comedy and because we are made uncomfortable by the late plays' commitment to non-realistic modes' (ibid.).

The question of genre is further complicated by the play's close relationship with the masque, an extravagant spectacle usually performed indoors and combining poetry, music, dance and song with lavish costumes and stage effects. The court masque was popular with European royalty in the sixteenth and early seventeenth centuries and often involved members of the court entering in disguise and acting out an allegorical plot. The masque provided both entertainment and education: it pointed the court the way to ideal conduct through a combination of satire and flattery. As we have seen, *The Tempest* contains a masque that Prospero constructs for Miranda's betrothal, and the play as a whole has much in common with the court masque in its depiction of contrary states (such as ignorance and learning, love and lust) and its recognition of noble ideals. In the early years of James I's rule, there were numerous court masques, including eight by Ben Jonson. It seems likely that Shakespeare was present when these were performed. However, the appeal of the court masque does not in itself explain the generic and thematic complexity of *The Tempest*.

In *Shakespeare and the Spectacles of Strangeness* (1998), John G. Demaray draws attention to the 'unique masque-like qualities' of *The Tempest* and to the importance of the court background to the form and meaning of the play. However, his overriding argument is that the play is essentially a new kind of experimental drama distinguished by its strange and symbolic magical spectacles, including the visionary dreams and reveries that various characters experience (p.5). Demaray argues that 'A profound and continuing wonder stirred in characters by visionary dreams, reveries and magical spectacles is at the deepest core of *The Tempest*' (ibid., p.110). This emphasis on strange visions has a thematic relevance in that a deep experience of wonder inspires virtuous characters and transforms the corrupt. Whilst not wishing to dismiss the colonial dimension of the play, Demaray is inclined to play down its significance and see the New World allusions in *The Tempest* as typical of a court-masquing tradition that featured strange or unusual characters in exotic settings. At the same time as borrowing from the court masque, the play serves as a corrective to the dreams of a Golden Age or new world that were prevalent in court spectacles and also in utopian literature; such dreams are broken by a dawning recognition of the world of actuality:

> As symbolically represented by unique characters and action on a magical Mediterranean island, this awakening to earthly realities – to deceit and moral ambiguity in political and social life and, in the case of Prospero, to the fact of human mortality – has been observed to contain oblique reflections of the 'brave' new, but troubled, colonial world. Yet the drama's varied political, social and religious motifs are absorbed within a sweeping symbolism suggesting that all imagined ideal societies – whether those that might exist in some 'brave new world' of total innocence, or those seriously or mockingly envisaged in the dreamlike fantasy of utopian literature ... all are uniformly subject to the coils of an imperfect, mortal social life.

> (Ibid., p.112)

What Demaray articulates here is a response to *The Tempest* that sees the play as conveying moral truths of abiding universal relevance; he both perceives and accepts an idea of life as fundamentally impaired by our very mortality and therefore simply to be endured as it is. The confusion inherent in this kind of thinking is rendered in the phrase 'imperfect, mortal social life', where no distinction is made between the nature of our mortality and the nature of our social existence. Demaray's reading of *The Tempest* is apt to flatten out the play's engagement with specific political and historical issues into a generalized narrative of human limitations. Nevertheless, his book constitutes a valuable reassessment of Shakespeare's appropriation of diverse theatrical forms and structures, and it shows how *The Tempest* might be understood and appreciated as 'a brilliantly evocative transitional drama' (ibid., p.138).

I would like in conclusion to explore further two aspects of *The Tempest*, which rightly affect its interpretation. The first concerns Prospero's emphasis on, perhaps even his obsession with, the question of chastity and sexuality. The second has to do with language.

The Tempest *and gender*

You will not need reminding of Prospero's rigorous attitude to the potential coupling of Miranda and Ferdinand. And you probably noted right at the beginning of the play the accusation Prospero directed against Caliban – perhaps by way of excuse for his subsequent harsh treatment of him:

> ... I have used thee,
> Filth as thou art, with human care, and lodged thee
> In mine own cell, till thou didst seek to violate
> The honour of my child.

> (1. 2. 348–51)

Kermode points out (1954, p.154) that 'unchastity was a conventional attribute of salvage man', and just as good breeding implies a tendency to virtue (a predisposition to it, Kermode would say), so savageness includes sexual aggression and a tendency to rape ('salvage' is an older version of 'savage', sometimes used to describe Caliban). Caliban, according to Prospero, found it impossible to curb his natural appetites even in the case of those who trusted and befriended him. This lack of (sexual) control assumes particular importance in Prospero's view of the whole human scheme of things. It represents the essence of bestiality, or to phrase it more moderately, of unredeemed nature. It is against these – or comparable – manifestations of 'natural' behaviour that Prospero's civilizing art is pitted. Just as he himself exercises discipline and self-discipline in his studies and personal conduct, so he wishes these qualities upon all who form part of his entourage and therefore part of the human race. Chastity becomes the outward symbol of purity and respect for self and others, which are the keystones of his entire philosophy.

We have already noted the nature of Miranda's gender role, and the interpretation offered is based on the girl's compliance with the will of her father. Prospero might well be said to be Miranda's 'master', as he is the master of Ariel and Caliban, and this element of male supremacy lies deep in the philosophy and lifestyle advocated in the play. Temperance is, for this philosopher/magician, a vital ingredient of civilized conduct. Taking it in its literal, present-day sense of 'moderation in the use of alcoholic liquors', temperance is clearly lacking in the comic scenes with Caliban, Stefano and Trinculo. As drunken fools, they would attract Prospero's censure, even without the much more serious charge of conspiracy. In its wider sense of 'moderation in the indulgence of the natural appetites and passions', temperance is part of Prospero's overall project. Its contrary – intemperance, over-indulgence, lust – is what he would wish to banish from his world of better natures. Is Miranda the victim of such an ideal?

As with post-colonial criticism, feminist criticism of *The Tempest* has been diverse in its approach to the play. Ann Thompson's blunt statement that 'women are notably absent from Shakespeare's *Tempest*' might not offer fertile ground for a feminist reading of the play, but her article '"Miranda, where's your sister?": reading Shakespeare's *The Tempest*' goes on to raise some pertinent questions about 'what feminist criticism can do in the face of a male-authored canonical text which seems to exclude women to this extent' (Thompson, 1995, pp.168, 170). Notwithstanding the absence of women, the article looks closely at the ideology of femininity at work in the play, including its seeming obsession with themes of chastity and fertility. Thompson closes by asking if it is possible for a staging of *The Tempest* to convey anything approaching a feminist reading of the text. Other feminist critics, including Susan Bennett (1996) and Kate Chedgzoy (1995) have replied by suggesting that perhaps the most effective criticism of *The Tempest* is a rewriting of the text. Bennett, writing in support of the Indian critic Ania Loomba, argues that some post-colonial readings of *The Tempest* have been implicitly sexist in ignoring the repression of Miranda: 'In these male-authored challenges to colonial authority, the representation of the female body (Miranda, but also Sycorax) is yet more passive, ever more silent' (Bennett, 1996, p.138).

The Tempest *and language*

The final aspect of *The Tempest* that concerns me is the question of language. Miranda looks back on her kindness to her servant in this way:

I pitied thee,
Took pains to make thee speak, taught thee each hour

One thing or other. When thou didst not, savage,
Know thine own meaning, but wouldst gabble like
A thing most brutish, I endowed thy purposes
With words that made them known.

(1. 2. 356–61)

In his response Caliban shows clearly how language can be used to abuse:

You taught me language, and my profit on't
Is I know how to curse. The red plague rid you
For learning me your language!

(1. 2. 366–8)

The whole function of language and its relationship to human value and virtue are matters raised both explicitly and implicitly in this text and, indeed, in its performance. For theatre and drama it is the prime mode of expression and communication. What can its careful use – and its abuse – tell us about the world of the play?

I am often struck by the virulence of some of Prospero's words addressed to Caliban in this early scene in Act 1. There is a violence in the language here, not least in the original command that Caliban should appear: 'Thou poisonous slave, got by the devil himself / Upon thy wicked dam, come forth!' (1. 2. 322–3). But, within the terms of the play, is this simply a statement of fact – a representation of its (fantastic) actuality?

It could also be said that Prospero uses language as a means of subjecting Ariel to his desires, in his constant evocation of what he requires of the spirit before he will grant his freedom. It might be thought of as linguistic blackmail. There can be concealed violence in the purposes that speech half-reveals and half-conceals.

Whether you agree with these points – or which you agree with – will almost certainly depend on the overall interpretation of the play that you favour. As far as language is concerned, it is good to bear in mind a phrase used by Terry Eagleton in his writing on *The Tempest*: 'Language always threatens to get out of hand and become autonomous.' For Eagleton, Ariel is Prospero's word in action; he 'operates as an extension of Prospero's body' and thus 'takes on a definite material form'. Ariel transforms Prospero's speech into deeds. I particularly like a comparison Eagleton makes between Ariel and Caliban: 'If Ariel needs to be tied down to the life of the body, then creatively Caliban needs to be cranked up to the level of language' (1986, pp.94–5). The body (and *embodiment* is the condition of performed drama) and language intersect significantly when marriage is mooted, and also when Prospero breaks his staff, frees Ariel, his attendant spirit, and gives up his art in order to return to the complementary activity of governing his Italian city. Language has achieved its ends, and its embodiments – Shakespeare's creations – are completed.

References

Barker, F. and Hulme, P. (1985) 'Nymphs and reapers heavily vanish: the discursive con-texts of *The Tempest*', in *Alternative Shakespeares*, ed. J. Drakakis, London: Routledge, pp.191–205.

Barton, A. (ed.) (1968) *The Tempest*, New Penguin Shakespeare, Harmondsworth: Penguin.

Bate, J. (1997) *The Genius of Shakespeare*, London: Picador.

Bennett, S. (1996) *Performing Nostalgia: Shifting Shakespeare and the Contemporary Past*, London: Routledge.

Briggs, J. (1997) *This Stage-Play World: Texts and Contexts, 1580–1625*, Oxford: Opus.

Brockbank, P. (1973) '*The Tempest*: conventions of art and empire', in *Later Shakespeare*, ed. J.R. Brown and B. Harris, Stratford-upon-Avon Studies 8, London: Edward Arnold, pp.183–202 (first published 1966).

Brotton, J. (1998) '"This Tunis, sir, was Carthage": contesting colonialism in *The Tempest*', in *Postcolonial Shakespeares*, ed. A. Loomba and M. Orkin, London and New York: Routledge, pp.23–42.

Brown, P. (1985) '"This thing of darkness I acknowledge mine": *The Tempest* and the discourse of colonialism', in *Political Shakespeare: New Essays in Cultural Materialism*, ed. J. Dollimore and A. Sinfield, Manchester: Manchester University Press, pp.48–69.

Cartelli, T. (1987) 'Prospero in Africa: *The Tempest* as colonialist text and pretext', in *Shakespeare Reproduced: The Text in History and Ideology*, ed. J. Howard and M. O'Connor, New York: Methuen, pp.99–115.

Chedgzoy, K. (1995) *Shakespeare's Queer Children: Sexual Politics and Contemporary Culture*, Manchester: Manchester University Press.

Demaray, J.G. (1998) *Shakespeare and the Spectacles of Strangeness:* The Tempest *and the Transformation of Renaissance Theatrical Forms*, Pittsburgh: Duquesne University Press.

Drakakis, J. (ed.) (1985) *Alternative Shakespeares*, New Accents series, London and New York: Methuen.

Eagleton, T. (1986) *William Shakespeare*, Oxford: Blackwell.

Fanon, F. (1967) *Black Skin, White Masks*, trans. C.L. Markmann, New York: Grove Weidenfeld (first published 1952).

Greenblatt, S. (1988) *Shakespearean Negotiations: The Circulation of Social Energy in Renaissance England*, Oxford: Clarendon Press.

Greenblatt, S. (1990) *Learning to Curse: Essays in Early Modern Culture*, London: Routledge.

Kermode, F. (ed.) (1954) *The Tempest*, Arden edition, London: Methuen.

Lamming, G. (1984) *The Pleasures of Exile*, London: Allison & Busby (first published 1960).

Mannoni, O. (1990) *Prospero and Caliban: The Psychology of Colonization*, trans. P. Powesland, Ann Arbor: University of Michigan (first published as *Psychologie de la colonisation*, Paris: Editions du Seuil, 1950).

Martin, C. (ed.) (1998) *Ovid in English*, Harmondsworth: Penguin.

Montaigne, M. de (1991) *The Complete Essays*, trans. M.A. Screech, Harmondsworth: Penguin.

Orgel, S. (ed.) (1994) *The Tempest*, World's Classics, Oxford: Oxford University Press.

Stone, B. (1984) *The Tempest*, Block VII of the Open University third level course A361, *Shakespeare*, Milton Keynes: Open University Press.

Thompson, A. (1995) '"Miranda, where's your sister?": reading Shakespeare's *The Tempest*', in *Shakespeare and Gender: A History*, ed. D. Barker and I. Kamps, London: Verso, pp.168–77.

THE FUTURE OF SHAKESPEARE

Kiernan Ryan

The final chapter of this book concludes with a fascinating account of how modern African and Caribbean writers, such as Frantz Fanon, George Lamming and Aimé Césaire, appropriated *The Tempest* in order to address the plight of their colonized peoples, because they recognized that Shakespeare's last great play was, in the words of Lamming, 'prophetic of a political future which is our present' (see above, p.294). The idea that Shakespeare's imagination was able to dramatize and explore matters whose full significance would only become apparent centuries after he wrote is an arresting one, which raises important questions about what it means to study Shakespeare now, at the dawn of a new millennium.

All the contributors to this volume have been at pains to place the plays under discussion in their historical contexts, because they share the conviction that our understanding of Shakespeare needs to be anchored in a knowledge of the pressures that originally shaped the language and form of his drama. Without such an historical perspective, the very meaning of much of the texts would remain opaque, their contemporary allusions would be lost to us, and the theatrical conventions upon which their impact depends would be incomprehensible. But what every chapter makes equally clear is that the vision of Shakespeare's drama cannot be confined to Shakespeare's time. To trace the critical reception of a play like *Macbeth*, or to track its performance history on stage and screen, is to become aware of how much its significance has changed, as successive generations have discovered its bearing on their own preoccupations. Thus, as we have seen in Chapter 3, there are now powerful arguments for seeing *Macbeth* as the tragedy of a man fettered to a destructive ideal of masculinity and the ruthless creed of self-promotion summed up in the line: 'For mine own good / All causes shall give way' (3. 4. 134–5). A modern concern with gender, fuelled by the feminist critique of patriarchy, has combined with a modern distrust of the ideology of individualism to turn *Macbeth* into a text for our times and its author into our contemporary.

You may well feel – as many people do – that to place such a construction upon *Macbeth* is to adopt a wilfully unhistorical approach, to foist upon the play an interpretation that is blatantly anachronistic, because it imputes to Shakespeare ideas and attitudes that belong to our world, not to his. In one sense the objection is, of course, entirely justified: terms like 'feminism', 'gender', 'patriarchy', 'ideology' and 'individualism', to say nothing of the politics they presuppose, would have meant nothing to the man who penned *Macbeth* and delighted his public by playing fast and loose with sexual disguise in *Twelfth Night* and *As You Like It*. But in another sense the objection is misguided, because it is based on an insufficiently complex understanding of history and the nature of literature. For one thing, we do not live in a completely different world from the one in which Shakespeare lived and about which he wrote. Most historians now prefer to refer to Shakespeare's time as the 'early modern' era rather than the Renaissance in order to underscore its continuity with the 'late modern' or 'postmodern' epoch to which we are widely assumed to belong. From this point of view, it is not so surprising to find Shakespeare already identifying and tackling issues such as race, gender and social injustice, of which western culture has only recently become acutely conscious.

What the charge of anachronism also fails to grasp is the special nature of imaginative discourse: in this case, the ability of Shakespeare's poetic drama to embody and voice insights into his world – and the worlds that would succeed it – that could not find expression at that time in any other form. For example, we can all probably agree that the analyses and arguments of present-day feminists would have left the Bard, at the very least, baffled and bemused. Yet few critics would now deny that Shakespeare's comedies enact, through their transvestite confusions of sexual identity, the modern feminist distinction between sex and gender: the crucial realization that masculinity and femininity are not simply matters of biology, but culturally created roles that are neither innate nor permanent, but open to question and open to change. Indeed, it might be argued that the comedies convey this recognition more powerfully than its latter-day apologists, precisely because they promote it implicitly, in the concrete, theatrical terms of a dramatized predicament, rather than through explicit, abstract contention. Be that as it may, the point is that Shakespearean comedy displays the same understanding of sex and gender as modern feminism, *but it displays it in a different form*. So when modern critics discuss *As You Like It* or *Twelfth Night* in feminist terms, it would be truer to say that, far from imposing upon the play an illegitimate, retroactive reading, they are actually unlocking implications that it has always possessed, implications historically inscribed in its poetic language and theatrical techniques.

In fact, the accusation of anachronism levelled at modern interpretations, productions and adaptations of Shakespeare could be turned on its head. It might be more accurate to claim that what these new readings of the plays demonstrate – provided that they are grounded in the evidence of the texts – is not the anachronism of their own assumptions, but the anachronism of Shakespeare's imagination, which propelled his plays ahead of their time to speak straight to the heart of our own. To appreciate the capacity of the plays to prefigure the present, however, is also to concede the constraints that our position in the present places on our understanding of them. If a modern concern with colonialism, power, class and sexuality prompts us to find the same subjects foreshadowed in Shakespeare's drama, it inevitably blinds us in the process to all the other interpretive possibilities stored in the texts, waiting to be unpacked by critics, directors and performers of the future, with other matters on their minds. There will always be more to Shakespeare's plays than meets the eye at a particular moment. His drama may presage the obsessions of the modern age, but that does not mean that the most perceptive critics of our day have had the last word. The imaginative reach of Shakespeare's plays exceeds our critical grasp, but by how much, and in what ways, only readers and spectators not yet born will be able to tell.

Another way of putting this might be to say that Shakespeare's drama bears out better than the work of any other writer the truth of Shelley's belief that the poet 'not only beholds intensely the present as it is, and discovers those laws according to which present things ought to be ordered, but he beholds the future in the present' ('A Defence of Poetry'[1]). There is no need, however, to cite Shelley to confirm the importance of the prophetic impulse to a poet and dramatist whose

[1] *Shelley's Poetry and Prose*, ed. D.H. Reiman and S.B. Powers, W.W. Norton, New York, 1977, pp.482–3.

own work constantly proclaims its endeavour to trace in the texture of 'present things' the imprint of what might be. As you will discover if you study the companion volume in this series, *Shakespeare 1609: 'Cymbeline' and the 'Sonnets'*, the sonnets repeatedly project themselves into the future, envisaging some eventual scenario or boldly predicting what shall come to pass, as in the opening lines of Sonnet 55: 'Not marble nor the gilded monuments / Of princes shall outlive this powerful rhyme'. Shakespeare's conviction that his poetry will survive in the mouths of citizens of centuries to come receives its most haunting expression in Sonnet 81:

> Your monument shall be my gentle verse,
> Which eyes not yet created shall o'er-read,
> And tongues to be your being shall rehearse
> When all the breathers of this world are dead.

To read these lines now is to testify to their uncanny prescience, to fulfil Shakespeare's prophecy of their fate by ourselves becoming those 'eyes not yet created', those 'tongues to be' that he foretold. As we read the sonnets, it is hard to escape the eery realization that Shakespeare *knew* that we would be reading them now, in a world and time beyond even his imagination.

The same desire to be transported, like Macbeth, 'beyond / This ignorant present' to grasp 'The future in the instant' (1. 5. 54–6) drives Shakespeare's comedies, histories and tragedies too. *A Midsummer Night's Dream* affords a consummate example of the comedies' commitment to bringing an anticipated state of joyful harmony within the compass of the present, a commitment captured perfectly in Theseus's celebrated lines:

> And as imagination bodies forth
> The forms of things unknown, the poet's pen
> Turns them to shapes, and gives to airy nothing
> A local habitation and a name.
> Such tricks hath strong imagination
> That if it would but apprehend some joy
> It comprehends some bringer of that joy.

> (5. 1. 14–20)

(You might like to consider to what extent *Cymbeline* achieves the same ambition by granting the utopian wish voiced by the Jailer towards the close of the play: 'I would we were all of one mind, and one mind good' (5. 5. 291–2).) The history plays are likewise animated by the spirit of anticipation, as Warwick's remarkable speech about the urge to infer the future from the past attests:

> There is a history in all men's lives
> Figuring the nature of the times deceased;
> The which observed, a man may prophesy,
> With a near aim, of the main chance of things
> As yet not come to life, who in their seeds
> And weak beginnings lie intreasurèd.

> (*2 Henry IV*, 3. 1. 75–80)

And at the turning-point of the mighty tragedy of *King Lear*, the strangely timeless figure of the Fool steps out of the play to predict the fate awaiting 'the realm of Albion' (3. 2. 89), the kingdom of England itself, forcing us to confront the bitter conflict between history and utopia – the way things are and the way they should be – that tears the play apart, before vanishing with the cryptic promise: 'This prophecy Merlin shall make; for I live before his time' (3. 2. 93).

The notion that Shakespeare's imagination might be drawn as much towards a future beyond the horizon of our time as back to its point of departure in the past is worth reflecting upon as your acquaintance with his plays and poetry deepens. It creates a healthy resistance to both the antiquarian attempt to bury Shakespeare's meaning in the museum of the past and the opposite endeavour to erase the centuries that divide him from us and reduce his works to nothing more than mirrors of modernity. Shakespeare's writing is without doubt rooted in the now remote world that cradled it, and it does have the disconcerting knack, nonetheless, of adumbrating our own epoch, 400 years after its author's demise. Yet, however exhaustive our accounts of Shakespeare's work may seem, regardless of whether they are historically slanted or couched in contemporary terms, the texts will continue to replenish their reserves of meaning, as each new generation discovers in them for itself 'the prophetic soul / Of the wide world dreaming on things to come' (Sonnet 107).

FURTHER READING

The books, articles and chapters listed below provide useful critical discussion in relation to the nine plays and two intervals covered in this book. There is also useful critical material in the reference lists at the ends of the chapters and intervals in this book; in the texts in the companion volume, *A Shakespeare Reader: Sources and Criticism* (ed. R.D. Brown and D.W. Johnson, Macmillan, London, 2000); and in the Selected Bibliography sections at the ends of the introductions to the plays in *The Norton Shakespeare*.

Chapter 1 A Midsummer Night's Dream

Barber, C.L. (1959) *Shakespeare's Festive Comedy: A Study of Dramatic Form and its Relation to Social Custom*, Princeton, NJ: Princeton University Press.

Bennett, S. (1990) *Theatre Audiences: A Theory of Production and Reception*, London and New York: Routledge.

Bristol, M. (1985) *Carnival and Theatre: Plebeian Culture and the Structure of Authority in Renaissance England*, London and New York: Methuen.

Dutton, R. (1996) *A Midsummer Night's Dream*, New Casebooks series, London: Macmillan.

Hendricks, M. (1996) '"Obscured by dreams": race, empire, and Shakespeare's *A Midsummer Night's Dream*', *Shakespeare Quarterly*, vol.47, no.1, pp.37–60.

Holland, P. (ed.) (1998) *A Midsummer Night's Dream*, World's Classics, Oxford: Oxford University Press.

Kennedy, D. (1993) *Looking at Shakespeare: A Visual History of Twentieth-Century Performance*, Cambridge: Cambridge University Press.

Laroque, F. (1993) *Shakespeare's Festive World: Elizabethan Seasonal Entertainment and the Professional Stage*, Cambridge: Cambridge University Press.

Levine, L. (1996) 'Rape, repetition and closure in *A Midsummer Night's Dream*', in *Feminist Readings of Early Modern Culture: Emerging Subjects*, ed. V. Traub *et al.*, Cambridge: Cambridge University Press, pp.210–28.

Mangan, M. (1996) *A Preface to Shakespeare's Comedies 1594–1603*, London and New York: Longman.

Miller, J. (1986) *Subsequent Performances*, London: Faber.

Nelson, T.G.A. (1990) *Comedy: The Theory of Comedy in Literature, Drama, and Cinema*, Oxford and New York: Oxford University Press.

Selbourne, D. (1982) *The Making of A Midsummer Night's Dream: An Eye-witness Account of Peter Brook's Production from First Rehearsal to First Night*, London: Methuen.

Waller, G. (ed.) (1991) *Shakespeare's Comedies*, London and New York: Longman.

Williams, G.J. (1997) *Our Moonlight Revels: A Midsummer Night's Dream in the Theatre*, Iowa City: University of Iowa Press.

Interval 1 Shakespeare's Theatre

Barroll, L. (1991) *Politics, Plague, and Shakespeare's Theater: The Stuart Years*, Ithaca, NY: Cornell University Press.

Bruster, D. (1992) *Drama and the Market in the Age of Shakespeare*, Cambridge: Cambridge University Press.

Gurr, A. (1996) *Playgoing in Shakespeare's London*, Cambridge: Cambridge University Press.

Kiernan, P. (1999) *Staging Shakespeare at the New Globe*, London: Macmillan.

Mullaney, S. (1988) *The Place of the Stage: License, Play, and Power in the Renaissance*, Chicago: University of Chicago Press.

Patterson, A. (1988) '"The very age and body of the time, his form and pressure": rehistoricizing Shakespeare's theater', *New Literary History*, vol.20, no.1, pp.83–104.

Chapter 2 Richard II

Barton, A. *et al.* (1990) 'The Royal Shakespeare *Richard II*', in *Staging Shakespeare: Seminars on Production Problems*, ed. G. Loney, New York: Garland, pp.19–56.

Belsey, C. (1991) 'Making histories then and now: Shakespeare from *Richard II* to *Henry V*', in *Uses of History: Marxism, Postmodernism, and the Renaissance*, ed. F. Barker *et al.*, Manchester: Manchester University Press, pp.24–64.

Bergeron, D.M. (1991) '*Richard II* and carnival politics', *Shakespeare Quarterly*, vol.42, no.1, pp.33–43.

Healy, M. (1998) *William Shakespeare: Richard II*, Plymouth: Northcote House.

Heinemann, M. (1990) 'Political drama', in *The Cambridge Companion to English Renaissance Drama*, ed. A.R. Braunmuller and M. Hattaway, Cambridge: Cambridge University Press, pp.161–205.

Holderness, G. (1991) '"A woman's war": a feminist reading of *Richard II*', in *Shakespeare Left and Right*, ed. I. Kamps, New York: Routledge, pp.167–83.

Liebler, N.C. (1992) 'The mockery king of snow: Richard II and the sacrifice of ritual', in *True Rites and Maimed Rites: Ritual and Anti-ritual in Shakespeare and His Age*, ed. L. Woodbridge and E. Barry, Urbana: University of Illinois Press, pp.220–39.

Montrose, L. (1996) 'Shakespeare, the stage, and the state', *SubStance: A Review of Theory and Literary Criticism*, vol.25, no.2, pp.46–67.

Moore, J.G. (1991) 'Queen of sorrow, king of grief: reflections and perspectives in *Richard II*', in *In Another Country: Feminist Perspectives on Renaissance Drama*, ed. D. Kehler and S. Baker, Metuchen, NJ: Scarecrow, pp.19–35.

Norbrook, D. (1996) '"A liberal tongue": language and rebellion in *Richard II*', in *Shakespeare's Universe: Renaissance Ideas and Conventions*, ed. J.M. Mucciolo *et al.*, Hants: Scolar, pp.3–20.

Pilkington, A.G. (1991) *Screening Shakespeare from Richard II to Henry V*, Newark: University of Delaware Press.

Pye, C. (1988) 'The betrayal of the gaze: theatricality and power in Shakespeare's *Richard II*', *English Literary History*, vol.55, no.3, pp.575–98.

Rackin, P. (1990) *Stages of History: Shakespeare's English Chronicles*, Ithaca, NY: Cornell University Press, pp.117–38.

Rutter, C.C. (1997) 'Fiona Shaw's Richard II: the girl as player-king as comic', *Shakespeare Quarterly*, vol.48, no.3, pp.314–24.

Chapter 3 Macbeth

Adelman, J. (1992) *Suffocating Mothers: Fantasies of Maternal Origin in Shakespeare's Plays, Hamlet to The Tempest*, London and New York: Routledge, chapter 6.

Berger, H. (1982) 'Text against performance in Shakespeare: the example of *Macbeth*', in *The Power of Forms in the English Renaissance*, ed. S. Greenblatt, Norman, OK: Pilgrim Books, pp.49–79.

Brooke, N. (ed.) (1990) *The Tragedy of Macbeth*, Oxford: Oxford University Press.

Davies, A. (1988) *Filming Shakespeare's Plays*, Cambridge: Cambridge University Press, chapters 5 and 8.

Greenblatt, S. (1998) 'Shakespeare bewitched', in *Shakespeare's Tragedies: Contemporary Critical Essays*, ed. S. Zimmerman, London: Macmillan, pp.109–39.

Hawkins, M. (1982) 'History, politics and *Macbeth*', in *Focus on Macbeth*, ed. J.R. Brown, London: Routledge & Kegan Paul, pp.155–88.

Helms, L. (1992) 'The weyward sisters: towards a feminist staging of *Macbeth*', *New Theatre Quarterly*, vol.8, no.30, pp.167–77.

Holderness, G. (1989) 'Are Shakespeare's tragic heroes "fatally flawed"? Discuss', *Critical Survey*, vol.1, no.1, pp.53–62.

Jack, J.H. (1955) '*Macbeth*, King James and the Bible', *English Literary History*, vol.22, pp.173–93.

Kiernan, V. (1996) *Eight Tragedies of Shakespeare: A Marxist Study*, London: Verso.

Kinney, A.F. (1991) 'Shakespeare's *Macbeth* and the question of nationalism', in *Literature and Nationalism*, ed. V. Newey and A. Thompson, Liverpool: Liverpool University Press, pp.56–75.

McGrail, M.A. (1992) 'Feminist criticisms and *Macbeth*: a fundamental question', in *Ideological Approaches to Shakespeare: The Practice of Theory*, Lewiston, NY: Mellen, pp.147–53.

Orgel, S. (1988) 'The authentic Shakespeare', *Representations*, vol.21, pp.1–5.

Wills, G. (1995) *Witches and Jesuits: Shakespeare's Macbeth*, New York: Oxford University Press.

Wortham, C. (1996) 'Shakespeare, James I and the Matter of Britain', *English: The Journal of the English Association*, vol.45, no.182, pp.97–122.

Chapter 4 Antony and Cleopatra

Adelman, J. (1973) *The Common Liar: An Essay on Antony and Cleopatra*, New Haven, CT: Yale University Press.

Belsey, C. (1996) 'Cleopatra's seduction', in *Alternative Shakespeares 2*, ed. J. Drakakis, New York and London: Routledge, pp.38–62.

Bevington, D. (ed.) (1990) *Antony and Cleopatra*, Cambridge: Cambridge University Press, pp.13–44.

Callaghan, D., Helms, L. and Singh, J. (1994) *The Weyward Sisters: Shakespeare and Feminist Politics*, Oxford: Blackwell.

Charnes, L. (1992) 'What's love got to do with it? Reading the liberal humanist romance in *Antony and Cleopatra*', *Textual Practice*, vol.6, pp.1–16.

Davies, H.N. (1992) 'In the public eye: *Antony and Cleopatra* now', in *Shakespeare from Text to Stage*, ed. P. Kennan and M. Tempera, Bologna: Cooperativa Libraria Universitaria Editrice Bologna, pp.111–30.

Greene, J.G. (1996) 'Sex, race and empire in Shakespeare's *Antony and Cleopatra*', *Literature and History*, vol.5, no.1, pp.60–77.

Harris, J.G. (1994) '"Narcissus in thy face": Roman desire and the difference it fakes in *Antony and Cleopatra*', *Shakespeare Quarterly*, vol.45, no.4, pp.408–25.

Honigmann, E.A.J. (1976) *Shakespeare, Seven Tragedies: The Dramatist's Manipulation of Response*, London: Macmillan.

Jankowski, T.A. (1992) *Women in Power in the Early Modern Drama*, Urbana and Chicago: University of Illinois Press.

Knights, L.C. (1959) *Some Shakespearean Themes*, Harmondsworth: Penguin.

Lenz, C., Greene, G. and Neely, C.T. (eds) *The Woman's Part: Feminist Criticism of Shakespeare*, Urbana and Chicago: University of Illinois Press.

Singh, J. (1989) 'Renaissance antitheatricality, antifeminism, and Shakespeare's *Antony and Cleopatra*', *Renaissance Drama*, vol.20, pp.99–121.

Sprengnether, M. (1989) 'The boy actor and femininity in *Antony and Cleopatra*', in *Shakespeare's Personality*, ed. N.N. Holland *et al.*, Berkeley: University of California Press, pp.191–205.

Steppat, M. (1980) *The Critical Reception of Shakespeare's Antony and Cleopatra from 1607 to 1905*, Amsterdam: Gruner.

Interval 2 Editing Shakespeare's Plays

Bristol, M.D. (1990) 'Editing the text: the Deuteronomic reconstruction of authority', in *Shakespeare's America, America's Shakespeare*, London and New York: Routledge.

De Grazia, M. (1991) *Shakespeare Verbatim: The Reproduction of Authenticity and the 1790 Apparatus*, Oxford: Clarendon Press.

De Grazia, M. and Stallybass, P. (1993) 'The materiality of the Shakespearean text', *Shakespeare Quarterly*, vol.44, pp.255–83.

Foakes, R.A. (1993) 'Plays and texts', in *Hamlet Versus Lear: Cultural Politics and Shakespeare's Art*, Cambridge: Cambridge University Press, pp.78–111.

Marcus, L.S. (1991) 'Levelling Shakespeare: local customs and local texts', *Shakespeare Quarterly*, vol.42, no.2, pp.168–78.

Marcus, L.S. (1996) *Unediting the Renaissance: Shakespeare, Marlowe, Milton*, London and New York: Routledge, chapter 5.

Osborne, L.E. (1996) 'Rethinking the performance editions: theatrical and textual productions of Shakespeare', in *Shakespeare, Theory, and Performance*, ed. J.C. Bulman, London: Routledge, pp.168–86.

Sherbo, A. (1987) *The Birth of Shakespeare Studies: Commentators from Rowe (1709) to Boswell-Malone (1821)*, East Lansing, MI: Colleagues.

Warren, M.J. (1985) 'Textual problems, editorial assertions in editions of Shakespeare', in *Textual Criticism and Literary Interpretation*, ed. J. McGann, Chicago: University of Chicago Press, pp.23–37.

Chapter 5 Hamlet

Adelman, J. (1992) *Suffocating Mothers: Fantasies of Maternal Origin in Shakespeare's Plays, Hamlet to The Tempest*, New York: Routledge.

Coyle, M. (1992) *Hamlet: Contemporary Critical Essays*, London: Macmillan.

Dawson, A.B. (1995) *Shakespeare in Performance: Hamlet*, Manchester and New York: Manchester University Press.

Empson, W. (1986) '*Hamlet*', in *Essays on Shakespeare*, Cambridge: Cambridge University Press, pp.70–136.

Hapgood, R.H. (ed.) (1999) *Shakespeare in Production: Hamlet*, Cambridge: Cambridge University Press.

Hodgdon, B. (1994) 'The critic, the poor player, Prince Hamlet, and the lady in the dark', in *Shakespeare Reread: The Texts in New Contexts*, ed. R. McDonald, Ithaca, NY: Cornell University Press, pp.259–93.

Jardine, L. (1991) '"No offence i' th' world": *Hamlet* and unlawful marriage', in *Uses of History: Marxism, Postmodernism, and the Renaissance*, ed. F. Barker *et al.*, Manchester: Manchester University Press, pp.123–39.

Levin, H. (1959) *The Question of Hamlet*, Oxford: Oxford University Press.

Loomba, A. (1993) '*Hamlet* in Mizoram', in *Cross-cultural Performances in Women's Re-visions of Shakespeare*, ed. M. Novy, Urbana: University of Illinois Press, pp.227–50.

Marcus, L. (1994) 'Teaching textual variation: *Hamlet* and *King Lear*', in *Teaching with Shakespeare: Critics in the Classroom*, ed. B. McIver and R. Stevenson, Newark: University of Delaware Press, pp.115–51.

Mullaney, S. (1996) 'Mourning and misogyny: *Hamlet, The Revenger's Tragedy*, and the final progress of Elizabeth I, 1600–1607', in *Centuries' Ends, Narrative Means*, ed. R. Newman, Stanford, CA: Stanford University Press, pp.238–60.

Neely, C.T. (1996) '"Documents in madness": reading madness and gender in Shakespeare's tragedies and early modern culture', in *Shakespearean Tragedy and Gender*, ed. S.N. Garner and M. Sprengnether, Bloomington: Indiana University Press, pp.75–104.

Price, J.G. (ed.) (1986) *Hamlet: Critical Essays*, New York: Garland.

Showalter, E. (1985) 'Representing Ophelia: women, madness, and the responsibilities of feminist criticism', in *Shakespeare and the Question of Theory*, ed. P. Parker and G. Hartman, New York: Methuen, pp.77–94.

Taylor, N. (1994) 'The films of *Hamlet*', in *Shakespeare and the Moving Image: The Plays on Film and Television*, ed. A Davies and S. Wells, Cambridge: Cambridge University Press, pp.180–95.

Tennenhouse, L. (1989) 'Violence done to women on the Renaissance stage', in *The Violence of Representation: Literature and the History of Violence*, ed. N. Armstrong and L. Tennenhouse, London: Routledge, pp.77–97.

Weller, P. (1997) 'Freud's footprints in films of *Hamlet*', *Literature/ Film Quarterly*, vol.25, no.2, pp.119–24.

Wells, S. (ed.) (1993) *Shakespeare Survey 45: Hamlet and its Afterlife*, Cambridge: Cambridge University Press.

Wheale, N. (1991) 'Scratching Shakespeare: video-teaching the Bard', in *Shakespeare in a Changing Curriculum*, ed. L. Aers and N. Wheale, London: Routledge, pp.204–21.

Wilson, J.D. (1935) *What Happens in Hamlet*, Cambridge: Cambridge University Press.

Chapter 6 Twelfth Night

Auden, W.H. (1948) 'Music in Shakespeare', in *The Dyer's Hand and Other Essays*, New York: Random House.

Bloom, H. (ed.) (1987) *Modern Critical Interpretations of Twelfth Night*, New York: Chelsea House.

Booth, S. (1985) '*Twelfth Night* 1.1: the audience as Malvolio', in *Shakespeare's 'Rough Magic': Essays in Honor of C.L. Barber*, ed. P. Erickson and C. Kahn, Newark: University of Delaware Press, pp.149–67.

Callaghan, D. (1993) '"And all is semblative a woman's part": body politics and *Twelfth Night*', *Textual Practice*, vol.7, no.3, pp.428–52.

Charles, C. (1997) 'Gender trouble in *Twelfth Night*', *Theatre Journal*, vol.49, no.2, pp.121–41.

Crewe, J. (1995) 'In the field of dreams: transvestitism in *Twelfth Night* and *The Crying Game*', *Representations*, vol.50, pp.101–21.

Gay, P. (1994) '*Twelfth Night*: desire and its discontents', in *As She Likes It: Shakespeare's Unruly Women*, London: Routledge, pp.17–47.

Greenblatt, S. (1988) 'Fiction and friction', in *Shakespearean Negotiations*, Berkeley: University of California Press, pp.66–93.

Hartman, G. (1985) 'Shakespeare's poetical character in *Twelfth Night*', in *Shakespeare and the Question of Theory*, ed. P. Parker and G. Hartman, New York: Methuen, pp.37–53.

Hollander, J. (1959) '*Twelfth Night* and the morality of indulgence', *Sewanee Review*, vol.67, pp.220–38.

Howard, J.E. 'Crossdressing, the theatre, and gender struggle in early modern England', *Shakespeare Quarterly*, vol.39, no.4, pp.418–40.

Jardine, L. (1992) 'Twins and travesties: gender, dependency, and sexual availability in *Twelfth Night*', in *Erotic Politics: Desire on the Renaissance Stage*, ed. S. Zimmerman, New York: Routledge, pp.27–38.

King, W.N. (ed.) (1968) *Twentieth Century Interpretations of Twelfth Night*, Englewood Cliffs, NJ: Prentice-Hall.

Malcolmson, C. (1991) '"What you will": social mobility and gender in *Twelfth Night*', in *The Matter of Difference: Materialist Feminist Criticism of Shakespeare*, ed. V. Wayne, Ithaca NY: Cornell University Press, pp.29–57.

Thomson, P. (1983) '*Twelfth Night* and playhouse practice', in *Shakespeare's Theatre*, Boston: Routledge & Kegan Paul, pp.87–108.

Wells, S. (ed.) (1986) *Twelfth Night: Critical Essays*, New York: Garland.

White, R.S. (ed.) (1996) *Twelfth Night: Contemporary Critical Essays*, London: Macmillan.

Chapter 7 **Measure for Measure**

Adelman, J. (1989) 'Bed tricks: on marriage as the end of comedy in *All's Well That Ends Well* and *Measure for Measure*', in *Shakespeare's Personality*, ed. N. Holland *et al.*, Berkeley: University of California Press, pp.151–74.

Bennett, J.W. (1966) *Measure for Measure as Royal Entertainment*, New York: Columbia University Press.

Bernthal, C.A. (1992) 'Staging justice: James I and the trial scenes of *Measure for Measure*', *Studies in English Literature*, vol.32, no.2, pp.247–69.

Bloom, H. (ed.) (1988) *Modern Critical Interpretations: William Shakespeare's Measure for Measure*, New York: Chelsea House.

DiGangi, M. (1993) 'Pleasure for danger: measuring female sexuality in *Measure for Measure*', *English Literary History*, vol.60, no.3, pp.589–609.

Dodd, W. (1996) 'Power and performance: *Measure for Measure* in the public theater of 1604–1605', *Shakespeare Studies*, vol.24, pp.211–40.

Dollimore, J. (1985) 'Transgression and surveillance in *Measure for Measure*', in *Political Shakespeare: New Essays in Cultural Materialism*, ed. J. Dollimore and A. Sinfield, Manchester: Manchester University Press, pp.72–87.

Goldberg, J. (1996) '*Measure for Measure* as social text', in *New Historicism and Cultural Materialism: A Reader*, ed. K. Ryan, London: Edward Arnold, pp.117–25.

Jankowski, T.A. (1998) 'Pure resistance: queer(y)ing virginity in William Shakespeare's *Measure for Measure* and Margaret Cavendish's *The Convent of Pleasure'*, *Shakespeare Studies*, vol.26, pp.218–55.

Knight, G.W. (1930) '*Measure for Measure* and the gospels', in *The Wheel of Fire: Essays in the Interpretation of Shakespeare's Sombre Tragedies*, London: Oxford University Press, pp.80–106.

Knoppers, L.L. (1993) '(En)gendering shame: *Measure for Measure* and the spectacles of power', *English Literary Renaissance*, vol.23, no.3, pp.450–71.

Levin, J. (1996) 'The measure of law and equity: tolerance in Shakespeare's Vienna', in *Law and Literature Perspectives*, ed. B.L. Rockwood and R. Kevelson, New York: Peter Lang, pp.193–207.

McCandless, D. (1998) '"I'll pray to increase your bondage": power and punishment in *Measure for Measure'*, in *Shakespearean Power and Punishment: A Volume of Essays*, ed. G.M. Kendall, Madison, NJ: Fairleigh Dickinson University Press, pp.89–112.

Neely, J.C. (1989) 'Constructing female sexuality in the Renaissance: Stratford, London, Windsor, Vienna', in *Feminism and Psychoanalysis*, ed. R. Feldstein and J. Roof, Ithaca, NY: Cornell University Press, pp.209–29.

Shell, M. (1988) *The End of Kinship: Measure for Measure, Incest, and the Ideal of Universal Siblinghood*, Stanford, CA: Stanford University Press.

Sohlich, W. (1984) 'Prolegomenon for a theory of drama reception: Peter Brook's *Measure for Measure* and the emergent bourgeoisie', *Comparative Drama*, vol.18, no.1, pp.54–81.

Tennenhouse, L. (1982) 'Representing power: *Measure for Measure* in its time', *Genre: Forms of Discourse and Culture*, vol.15, nos.2–3, pp.139–56.

Tovey, B. (1996) 'Wisdom and the law: thoughts on the political philosophy of *Measure for Measure'*, in *Shakespeare's Political Pageant: Essays in Literature and Politics*, Lanham: Rowman & Littlefield, pp.61–75.

Wilson, R. (1996) 'Prince of Darkness: Foucault's Shakespeare', in *Theory in Practice: Measure for Measure*, ed. N. Wood, Buckingham: Open University Press, pp.133–78.

Chapter 8 King Lear

Armstrong, P. (1994) 'Uncanny spectacles: psychoanalysis and the texts of *King Lear'*, *Textual Practice*, vol.8, no.3, pp.414–34.

Berger, H., Jr (1985) 'Text against performance: the Gloucester family romance', in *Shakespeare's 'Rough Magic': Renaissance Essays in Honor of C.L. Barber*, Newark: University of Delaware Press, pp.210–29.

Bratton, J.S. (ed.) (1987) *Plays in Performance: King Lear*, Bristol: Bristol Classical.

Dutton, R. (1986) '*King Lear*, the triumphs of reunited Britannia, and the Matter of Britain', *Literature and History*, vol.12, no.2, pp.139–51.

Foakes, R.A. (1993) *Hamlet versus Lear: Cultural Politics and Shakespeare's Art*, Cambridge: Cambridge University Press.

Goldberg, J. (1998) 'Perspectives: Dover cliff and the conditions of representation', in *Shakespeare's Tragedies: Contemporary Critical Essays*, ed. S. Zimmerman, London: Macmillan, pp.155–66.

Knight, G.W. (1949) *The Wheel of Fire*, London: Methuen.

McEachern, C. (1988) 'Fathering herself: a source study of Shakespeare's feminism', *Shakespeare Quarterly*, vol.39, no.3, pp.269–90.

Ray, R.H. (ed.) (1986) *Approaches to Teaching Shakespeare's King Lear*, New York: Modern Language Association of America.

Rothwell, K.S. (1997) 'In search of nothing: mapping *King Lear*', in *Shakespeare the Movie*, ed. L.E. Boose and R. Burt, London and New York: Routledge, pp.135–47.

Simpson, D. (1986) 'Great things of us forgot: seeing *Lear* better', *Critical Quarterly*, vol.28, nos.1–2, pp.15–31.

Thompson, A. (1991) 'Are there any women in *King Lear*?', in *The Matter of Difference: Materialist Feminist Criticism of Shakespeare*, ed. V. Wayne, Ithaca, NY: Cornell University Press, pp.117–28.

Zunder, W. (1997) 'Shakespeare and the end of feudalism: *King Lear* as *fin-de-siècle* text', *English Studies: A Journal of English Language and Literature*, vol.78, no.6, pp.513–21.

Chapter 9 **The Tempest**

Baker, D.J. (1997) 'Where is Ireland in *The Tempest*?', in *Shakespeare and Ireland: History, Politics, Culture*, ed. M.T. Burnett and R. Wray, London: Macmillan, pp.68–88.

Belhassen, S. (1972) 'Aimé Césaire's *A Tempest*', in *Radical Perspectives in the Arts*, ed. L. Baxendall, Harmondsworth: Penguin.

Bevington, D. and Holbrook, P. (1998) *The Politics of the Stuart Court Masque*, Cambridge: Cambridge University Press.

Busia, P.A.B. (1990) 'Silencing Sycorax: on African colonial discourse and the unvoiced female', *Cultural Critique*, pp.81–104.

Césaire, A. (forthcoming, 2000) *Une Tempête: A New Translation*, trans. P. Crispin, London: Oberon Books.

Donaldson, P. (1997) 'Shakespeare in the age of post-mechanical reproduction: sexual and electronic magic in *Prospero's Books*', in *Shakespeare the Movie*, ed. L.E. Boose and R. Burt, London and New York: Routledge, pp.169–85.

Dymkowski, C. (ed.) (1999) *Shakespeare in Production: The Tempest*, Cambridge: Cambridge University Press.

Fiedler, L. (1972) *The Stranger in Shakespeare*, New York: Stein & Day.

Gurr, A. (1996) 'Industrious Ariel and idle Caliban', in *Travel and Drama in Shakespeare's Time*, ed. J-P. Maquerlot and M. Willems, Cambridge: Cambridge University Press, pp.193–208.

Hamilton, D.B. (1992) *Shakespeare's Romances and Jacobean Political Discourse*, New York: Modern Language Association of America.

Hirst, D. (1994) *The Tempest: Text and Performance*, London: Macmillan.

Jordan, C. (1997) *Shakespeare's Monarchies: Ruler and Subject in the Romances*, Ithaca, NY: Cornell University Press.

Lanier, D. (1998) 'Drowning the book: *Prospero's Books* and the textual Shakespeare', in *Shakespeare on Film: Contemporary Critical Essays*, ed. R. Shaughnessy, London: Macmillan, pp.173–95.

Loomba, A. (1989) *Gender, Race, Renaissance Drama*, Manchester: Manchester University Press.

Orgel, S (1986) 'Prospero's wife', in *Rewriting the Renaissance: The Discourse of Sexual Difference in Early Modern Europe*, ed. M. Ferguson *et al.*, Chicago: University of Chicago Press, pp.50–64.

Orkin, M. (1997) 'Whose things of darkness? Reading/ representing *The Tempest* in South Africa after April 1994', in *Shakespeare and National Culture*, ed. J. Joughin, New York: Manchester University Press, pp.142–69.

Palmer, D.J. (ed.) (1991) *Shakespeare: The Tempest*, New Casebooks series, London: Macmillan.

Retamar, R.F. (1989) *Caliban and Other Essays*, trans. E. Baker, Minneapolis: University of Minnesota Press.

Ryan, K. (ed.) (1999) *Shakespeare: The Last Plays*, London and New York: Longman.

Vaughan, A.T. and Vaughan, V.M. (1991) *Shakespeare's Caliban: A Cultural History*, Cambridge: Cambridge University Press.

Warren, R. (1990) *Staging Shakespeare's Late Plays*, Oxford: Clarendon.

Wells, S. (1994) 'Problems of stagecraft in *The Tempest*', *New Theatre Quarterly*, vol.10, no.40, pp.348–57.

White, R.S. (ed.) (1999) *The Tempest: Contemporary Critical Essays*, London: Macmillan.

Wilson, R. (1997) 'Voyage to Tunis: new history and the Old World of *The Tempest*', *English Literary History*, vol.64, no.2, pp.333–57.

Wood, N. (ed.) (1995) *Theory in Practice: The Tempest*, Buckingham: Open University Press.

Acknowledgement

Grateful acknowledgement is made to the following source for permission to reproduce material in this book:

Cavafy, C.P. 'On hearing of love', in Keeley, E. and Sherrard, P. (trans.) *C.P. Cavafy: Collected Poems*, ed. Savidis, G. Translation copyright © 1975, 1992 by Edmund Keeley and Philip Sherrard, Princeton University Press. Reprinted by permission of Princeton University Press.

Index

act divisions, 182
acting companies *see* playing companies
actors
    Elizabethan, 37–9
    playing Hamlet, 163, 164
    and shares in playing companies, 43
Admiral's Men, 43
Aeschylus, 81
Alchemist see Jonson, Ben
All's Well That Ends Well, 215
Alleyn, Edward, 39
Ambassadors see Holbein, Hans
Anabaptists, 265
Anatomy of Abuses see Stubbes, Philip
Andoh, Adjoa, 273
Annis, Francesca, 119
Antony and Cleopatra, 26, 125–52
    battle of Actium in, 135
    changing critical perspectives on, 145–52
    comedy in, 149, 150–1, 267
    death of Antony in, 126, 136–8, 141, 151–2
    death of Cleopatra in, 126, 138, 140–1, 142, 143–4, 151
    dramatic irony in, 136
    Egypt in, 129, 130, 141, 142, 146, 147, 149
    fortune in, 129, 139
    gender in, 145, 149, 150–1, 270
    and genre, 145–7
    heroism in, 126, 127, 144
    language and dramatic impact, 127–41
    openness of, 126–7
    productions of, 148–9, 152
    Roman Empire in, 128, 130–1, 141, 142, 147–8, 149
    romantic love in, 142–4
    sexual politics in, 145
    sexuality in, 150–1, 152
    structure of, 141–4
    and tragedy, 83–4, 126, 146, 149, 150–1
Apolonius and Silla see Rich, Barnabe
Arcadia see Sidney, Sir Philip
Aristotle, 84
    on comedy, 20
    and humanism, 26
    Poetics, 81–2
Armin, Robert, 38
As You Like It, 198, 201, 214, 305, 306
Ashton, Robert, 71
astrology, in *King Lear*, 261
audiences
    and the creation of meaning, 30
    at Elizabethan playhouses, 34–5, 37, 39–40, 47
    and *Hamlet*, 172–4
    and *King Lear*, and the Fool, 255

    and *A Midsummer Night's Dream*, 1, 10–11, 25–6, 26–7, 30
    and *Twelfth Night*, 207, 208, 209–10

Baldwin, William, *A Myrroure for Magistrates*, 50, 52, 55
Barge, Gillian, 220
Barker, Francis, 290, 293
Barrie, J.M., *Peter Pan*, 208
Barrit, Desmond, 209
Barton, Anne, on *The Tempest*, 295–6
Barton, John, 208
Basilikon Doron see James I and VI, King
Bate, Jonathan, *The Genius of Shakespeare*, 290
Battle of Alcazar see Peele, George
Bawcutt, N.W., 235
bear-baiting, 35
Beaumont, Francis, 38
    The Knight of the Burning Pestle, 26
Belsey, Catherine, *The Subject of Tragedy*, 86
Benedict, Clare, 5
Benjamin, Walter, 86
Bennett, Susan, 301
Benson, Frank, 163
Bergman, Ingmar, production of *Hamlet*, 186
Berry, Ralph, 210
Betterton, Thomas, 163
    production of *Hamlet*, 172
biblical references, in *King Lear*, 261
Billington, Michael, 295
Black Skin, White Mask see Fanon, Frantz
Blackfriars playhouse, 44–5
    and *The Tempest*, 277
Boal, Augusto, *Theater of the Oppressed*, 86
Boas, F.S., *Shakespeare and his Predecessors*, 214
Bogdanov, Michael, 66
Boleyn, Anne, 72
Book of the Courtier see Castiglione, Count Baldasare
Book Named the Governor see Elyot, Sir Thomas
Bosworth Field, Battle of, 51
Bothwell, Francis Stuart, Earl of, 90
Bouchier, Sir John, 50
Boxer, Stephen, 203
boy actors
    and cross-dressing, in *Twelfth Night*, 198–200
    and female roles, 37–8
Bradley, A.C.
    on *Antony and Cleopatra*, 145, 146
    Shakespearean Tragedy, 84–5, 242, 243
        on *Macbeth*, 94, 113
Branagh, Kenneth, 163, 164
    and *Hamlet*, 174, 183, 186
    and *A Midsummer Night's Dream*, 7
Brandes, Georg, 147
Brandt, Mathilde, 164